Macintosh® Pascal Programming Primer, Volume I

Inside the Toolbox Using THINK Pascal™

Dave Mark   Cartwright Reed

Addison-Wesley Publishing Company, Inc.

*Reading, Massachusetts   Menlo Park, California   New York
Don Mills, Ontario   Wokingham, England   Amsterdam   Bonn
Sydney   Singapore   Tokyo   Madrid   San Juan*

Many of the designations used by manufacturers and sellers to distinguish their products are claimed as trademarks. Where those designations appear in this book, and Addison-Wesley was aware of a trademark claim, the designations have been printed in initial capital letters or all capital letters.

Library of Congress Cataloging-in-Publication Data

Mark, Dave.
   Inside the Toolbox using THINK Pascal / Dave Mark, Cartwright Reed.
      p. cm.—(Macintosh Pascal programming primer; v. 1)
   Includes bibliographical references and index.
   ISBN 0–201–57084–X
   1. Macintosh (Computer)—Programming. 2. Pascal (Computer program language). 3. Macintosh Toolbox (Computer programs). 4. Think Pascal. I. Reed, Cartwright. II. Title. III. Series: Mark, Dave. Macintosh Pascal programming primer; v. 1.
QA76.8.M3M3677   1990   90-20303
005.265—dc20   CIP

ABCDEFGHIJ-MW-91
First printing, December 1990

To Kate and Deneen
and to
Mary and Andy, and Lise and Yoni —
Now you've done it!

Contents

v

8 Using ResEdit   367

9 The Final Chapter   403

Preface

This book shows you how to write Macintosh applications with THINK Pascal. We wrote it to help people to get down to the business of writing code that displays the distinctive Mac "feel."

The *Macintosh Pascal Programming Primer* evolved from an earlier book that used THINK C to demonstrate the art of Mac programming. That book, *Macintosh Programming Primer: Inside the Toolbox Using THINK C*, was and is quite successful, and has received favorable reviews from *MacUser*, *Macworld* and other computer publications. Many readers sent many helpful suggestions on the C book. A common one was that we write a Pascal version, and here it is.

We stress that, although the program designs for these two books are similar, the code has been written from the ground up to take advantage of the THINK Pascal environment. These programs consist of thoroughly tested, debugged, clean Pascal code. We hope that they provide an impetus for you to write your own Pascal Mac applications.

If you have THINK Pascal and don't yet own this book, consider InfoWorld magazine's concluding thoughts in a review of Symantec's Pascal package:

"an excellent software development environment, with authoritative reference material at a reasonable price. All it needs is a tutorial that explains how to use it with the Macintosh Toolbox..."

...We give you the Macintosh Pascal Programming Primer.

Dave Mark　　　　　*Cartwright Reed*
Arlington, VA　　　　*Philadelphia, PA*

Acknowledgments

WE'D LIKE TO express our appreciation to the people who helped make this book possible, or at least coexisted with us harmoniously during its development:

Deneen Melander and **Kate Joyce**, who know us and still smile;

Julie Stillman, **Elizabeth Grose**, **Debbie McKenna** and **Diane Freed**, Addison-Wesley's finest!

Jim Reekes, our big red referee, who kept us from going down for the compatibility count;

Symantec, whose THINK Pascal and THINK C products build the best Mac programs;

Stu Mark, for keeping the studio humming;

Oleh Tretiak, director of Drexel University's Image Processing Center: to **Yoni Nissanov**, **Don McEachron**, **Sanjay Bhasin** and **Phyllis Ebron-Downes**; all curious and amiable workmates;

Andy and **Mary** — Congratulations!

Davood, **Rick** and **Nick** of P&T, and **Andy Richter** -- fellow members of the sacred order of coders;

Charlie Derr — Thanks for all your patience, Carlos. . .

and **Anthony D'Amico**, who provided a reason for *staying* in Philadelphia.

In finishing up, kudos to the down under team in Colorado, the **Outbound** people, who came up with the first practical, inexpensive laptop Mac. If you code in taxis, there's no substitute for an Outbound!

Source Code Disk
for the
Mac Pascal Primer

IF YOU WOULD like the source code presented in the *Macintosh Pascal Programming Primer* on disk, please send in the coupon on the last page (or a copy of the coupon — we're not picky).

We hope you like the *Macintosh Pascal Programming Primer*. If you have any comments or suggestions regarding future editions, you can reach us at this address:

The Mac Pascal Primer – Comments
2534 North Jefferson Street
Arlington, VA 22207

1

Introduction

Macintosh Pascal Programming Primer is a complete course in the art of Macintosh programming. With this book and Symantec's THINK Pascal, you can learn to program the Macintosh.

NO OTHER COMPUTER is like the Macintosh.

The Mac is a new kind of computer. It's fast. It's different.

The Mac plays by a new set of rules. To program it, you need a new rulebook. That's what the *Mac Primer* is.

At the heart of the Macintosh is the Toolbox, a collection of more than 700 procedures and functions that give you access to the Macintosh interface. The *Mac Primer* will teach you how to use the Toolbox, to add the power of pull-down menus, windows, and scroll bars to your programs.

This book serves as a bridge to the Macintosh way of programming.

The Macintosh Vision

Nowadays, the Macintosh line is successful, praised, and emulated. When the Macintosh was introduced in 1984, however, people were perplexed: It was like no computer they had ever seen—a beige box with a little screen and a mouse. People called the Macintosh a toy because it had a graphic interface, and graphics were not the way normal computers operated.

It was no sure thing.

Seven years later, computer hardware and software companies scramble to provide now what the Mac has had for so long. Whether you call the mouse a "pointing device" or refer to a windowed, iconic environment as a GUI (graphical user interface), one thing is clear: the standard is set.

The Mac is different from other systems in three ways:

- The **interface**: A consistent framework of graphic elements simplifies Mac operations for users.

- The **Toolbox**: Comprehensive routines were defined in the Macintosh ROM that drove the interface and allowed software designers to write powerful, easy-to-use applications.

- The use of **resources**: The building blocks for all software on the Macintosh, resources store program information in a series of templates in the program file, simplifying the creation and modification of Macintosh programs.

These three ingredients combined to make the Macintosh the basis for one of the best selling microcomputer lines in history. In the 1990s, the vision holds strong. The Macintosh environment remains unique. The careful planning that went into the original Mac has paid off handsomely, as the Mac line continues to evolve and improve.

To write successful applications for the Macintosh, the would-be Macintosh programmer must understand how those three Macintosh ingredients—interface, Toolbox, and resources—work. First, let's look at the most visible of the three: the Macintosh user interface.

The Macintosh Interface

The Macintosh makes its first impression on users with its graphical user interface. Figure 1.1 shows some of the distinctive elements of the Mac "look." Because new users understand and use the windows and menus of Mac applications intuitively, the Macintosh interface represents an impressive improvement over the command-based interfaces common on other systems. Each element of the interface—windows, menus, dialog boxes, icons—has a specific function associated with it, and extensive guidelines exist for the use of each element.

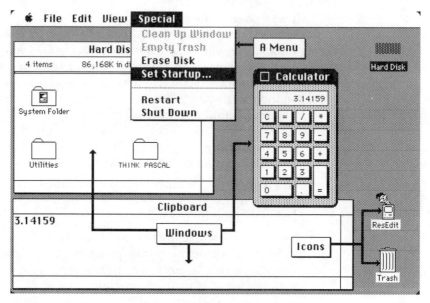

Figure 1.1   Some elements of the Macintosh interface.

The Macintosh interface was appropriated from the Lisa, which lifted it from the Xerox Alto machine. Over time, the interface has become more powerful without sacrificing ease of use. In addition, every new version of the interface on the Mac gets sleeker. To look at the Macintosh running version 1 or 2 of the Finder, or to see the Lisa in operation (while not running under Mac emulation) is rather like examining Microsoft Windows 3.0—quaint, but dated. The new system software reflects Apple's ability to build on the old system without modifying it beyond recognition.

Of course, pretty pictures aren't enough. The beauty of the Macintosh interface lies in how it is created. Each part of the interface is manipulated by a series of routines in the Macintosh ROM. For example, you can create an application's window with one call to the Macintosh ROM.

The routines that underlie the interface—that build windows, control printing, and draw menus—are collectively known as the Macintosh Toolbox.

The Macintosh Toolbox

The Toolbox can be thought of as a series of libraries that make it easy for you to create those features indigenous to Macintosh applications. For example, the Macintosh Toolbox call `GetNewWindow` creates a new window for use in your application.

Using the Toolbox calls to create your applications gives the results a distinctive Macintosh look and feel. Operations common to most applications, such as cutting, copying, and pasting, are always handled in the same way, which makes it easier to learn a new application.

The Toolbox routines are grouped functionally into **Managers**, each of which is responsible for one part of the Macintosh environment (Figure 1.2).

The Macintosh Toolbox undergoes constant updating and modification; each new system revision gives you some shiny new tools as well as the old standbys to work with. As new routines are added to the Toolbox, Apple cleans up problems with older routines.

The Macintosh graphic interface and the Toolbox are two of the features that make the Mac unique. A third is the successfully introduced concept of resources on the Macintosh.

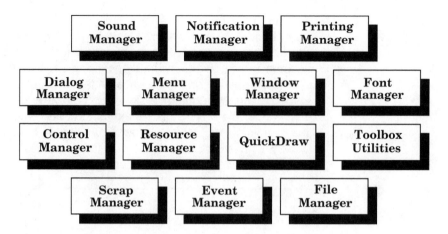

Figure 1.2   Parts of the Toolbox.

Although the Macintosh line has expanded greatly, the basic compatibility of the different Macintosh models has been maintained. Yet, more powerful machines always provide more choices—and more decisions. When the only available Macintosh workstations were the Macintosh and the Macintosh Plus, software developers thought they had a certain flexibility about how they followed the Mac programming guidelines provided by Apple. Now, in the midst of machines that support color, MultiFinder, math coprocessor chips, and new peripherals, the successful developer hews closely to the Macintosh standards.

Resources

If the Toolbox is the library of routines that make up the Macintosh interface, resources are the data that your program uses to execute these library calls. `GetNewWindow`, the Toolbox call that creates a new window, requires you to specify window parameters such as size, location, and window type. To do this, you can supply a resource containing that information, so the new window can be used in your application. Resources come in various types, each serving as a "holder" for a particular kind of data relating to windows, menus, and other parts of the Macintosh interface. For example, a resource of type `WIND` contains information for one specific window in an application.

There may be a number of resources of type WIND, but there is only one WIND type, which is identical for all Mac applications.

Resources are integrated into the design of the Macintosh. Each Macintosh application file may possess dozens of resources. This simplifies many of the tasks of the applications programmer. For example, resources make it easy to localize a program for a different area. If you want to sell your program in, say, France, it is relatively easy to replace resources containing English text with French equivalents.

Resources are also essential in developing the complex code that drives the Macintosh interface and hardware. Because they can be easily copied from one program to another, menus and dialog boxes need not be created more than once. Once you have built up a collection of programs, creating new ones may begin with a cut-and-paste session with your existing programs.

To edit resources, Apple developed a program called **ResEdit**, which allows you to edit any of the resources in *Macintosh Primer* programs. You can also use them to explore other Macintosh applications—even system files! Because these resources exist as part of the completed application, they can be edited without recompilation.

We make extensive use of version 2 of ResEdit throughout the *Mac Primer*. If you've never worked with ResEdit before, Chapter 8 contains a ResEdit tutorial to get you up to speed.

The Macintosh interface, the Toolbox, and resources are the three intertwined subjects that we'll cover using THINK Pascal and ResEdit to create stand-alone Macintosh applications. The next sections discuss our approach to learning about these issues.

About the Book

Most Macintosh reference books, such as *Inside Macintosh* and *Macintosh Revealed*, are excellent texts for those who already understand the Macintosh programming paradigm. They can be frustrating, however, if you're outside the Macintosh programming world, looking in. The *Mac Primer* bridges the gap for those of you who are just learning the basics of Mac programming.

Our aim is to help you write properly structured Mac applications. If you're used to programming on a MS-DOS computer or a UNIX system, the *Mac Primer* is the perfect place to start your Mac programming education. Our formative years were spent programming under UNIX, on machines like the PDP-11 and the VAX-11/780; we've also spent a lot of time with IBM PCs and compatibles. We wrote the *Macintosh Programming Primer* with you in mind.

What You Need to Know

There are only two prerequisites for reading this book. Before starting the *Macintosh Primer*, you should already have basic Mac experience: You should be able to run Macintosh applications and have a good feel for the Mac user interface. In addition, you should have some experience with a programming language like Pascal or BASIC. If you've never used Pascal before, we suggest a companion text, such as *Oh! Pascal,* by Doug Cooper and Michael Clancy, to supplement your instruction.

The *Macintosh Programming Primer* examples are all written in Pascal, using the THINK Pascal development environment. Our general approach, however, emphasizes the techniques involved in programming with the Mac Toolbox. The skills you learn will serve you no matter what programming language you intend to use in the future.

Why We Chose THINK Pascal

Many development environments are available to the Mac programmer. The **Macintosh Programmer's Workshop (MPW)** is a complex and powerful development system written and marketed by Apple. Most of Apple's internal development is done with MPW, and many of the large Macintosh software development houses have made MPW their first choice. MPW uses an "everything but the kitchen sink" approach to software development. The basic system consists of an editor shell that allows you to edit your source code as well as to build and execute complex command scripts. You can do just about anything in MPW, but it is definitely not a system for beginners. In addition to learning the editor and shell, you have to install, configure, and (oh, yes) pay for your choice of compilers. You can buy Pascal and C compilers for MPW, as well as FORTRAN, MacApp, and a few others. MPW is ideal for complex, multilanguage development efforts, but not for learning to program the Macintosh.

THINK Pascal (formerly known as Lightspeed Pascal) is a development environment that is powerful and friendly. It has concise, accurate documentation. For those inevitable bugs, it has the best debugging utilities on the market.

Finally, THINK Pascal is reasonably priced (see Figure 1.3).

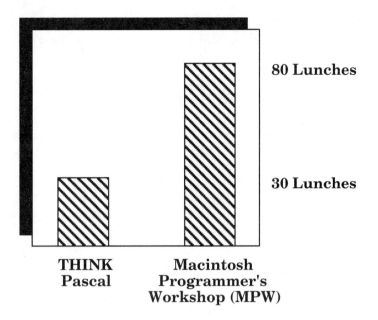

Figure 1.3   Lunch economics.

Using THINK Pascal

THINK Pascal is an integrated development environment. The source code editor follows all the standard Macintosh conventions and is very easy to use. The compiler is smart: It keeps track of the files you're currently working with, noting which have been changed since they were last compiled. THINK Pascal recompiles only what it needs to.

THINK Pascal has a well-thought-out Macintosh interface. For example, to build a stand-alone application, pull down the **Project** menu and select **Build Application**. Installation is simple: Just pull the floppies out of the box, copy the files onto your hard drive,[*] and go!

THINK Pascal's documentation consists of three clearly written manuals. The *User Manual* explains everything you need to know about developing software using THINK Pascal. The other two texts discuss resource editing tools and object programming. THINK Pascal also comes with integrated debugging utilities that allow you

---

[*]For those of you without a hard drive, there are complete instructions for running THINK Pascal on a floppy-based system in the THINK Pascal *User's Manual.*

to test-drive your program while you monitor its progress in other windows. The debugging utilities also work with other Macintosh debugging tools like MacsBug and TMON.

Inside THINK Pascal

The **Project** file is unique to Symantec's Pascal and C development environments. It contains the names of all your source code files, as well as the name you'll eventually give to your application. It also contains compilation information about each source file, such as the size of the compiled code (see Figure 1.4).

THINK Pascal has the capability to do object programming and can work directly with MacApp, Apple's ready-made library of user interface routines. THINK Pascal's debugging facilities are without peer. You can use THINK Pascal to write programs that will run under MultiFinder, take full advantage of the Macintosh II's color capabilities, and use AppleTalk. All of these features are supported in the way Apple intended them to be. THINK Pascal also provides routines to support extensions to Apple's **HyperCard**, or Silicon Beach's **SuperCard**.

THINK Pascal also comes with a full complement of utilities, including ResEdit, the resource editor mentioned earlier, and much useful code on various types of Mac projects, including text editors, cdevs and Desk Accessories. The manual that comes with THINK Pascal explains how to use version 1.2 of ResEdit and is the best discussion on using ResEdit 1.2 available. If you have version 2 of ResEdit, use Chapter 8 of this text to learn how to use it.

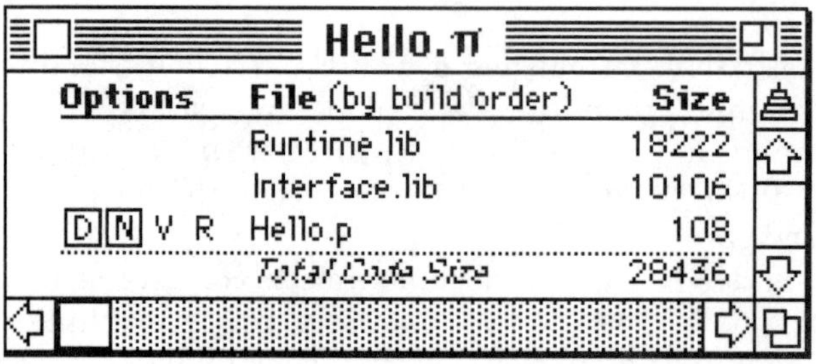

Figure 1.4   THINK Pascal's project window.

Writing Macintosh Applications

Most Macintosh applications share a basic structure (Figure 1.5). They start off by initializing the Toolbox data structures and routines that support the Macintosh user interface. Then the application enters an event loop and patiently waits for the user to do something—hitting keys, moving the mouse, or some other action. Events outside the application are also checked: Desk accessories may be used, or disks may be inserted. No matter how complex the Macintosh program, this simple structure is maintained.

At the heart of the *Macintosh Programming Primer* is a set of fourteen sample applications. Each builds on the basic program structure to provide a successively more sophisticated use of the Macintosh Toolbox. Each new chapter constructs a more powerful implementation of the basic program structure. Chapter 3 programs show how to create windows and draw inside them, Chapter 4 illustrates how to handle events, Chapter 5 implements menus, and Chapter 6 makes use of dialogs. Chapter 7 presents WindowMaker, a complete example of how a Macintosh application should work, from handling the interface and events to taking care of error-checking and memory management.

Each *Mac Primer* example program is presented as completely as possible, and each program listing is discussed extensively. Nothing is left as an "exercise for the reader." Each chapter contains complete instructions and figures for entering, compiling, and running the programs using THINK Pascal.

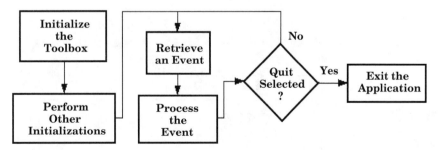

Figure 1.5 How a Macintosh application works.

Chapter Synopsis

The *Macintosh Primer* is made up of nine chapters and seven appendices. This introductory chapter provides an overview and starts you on your way. Chapter 2 starts by going through the installation of THINK Pascal and ResEdit, step by step. Then, THINK Pascal basics are introduced. We present the standard Pascal approach to the classic Hello, World program (Figure 1.6), and discuss drawbacks. We then go on to illustrate the programming conventions that we will use in the *Primer*.

Chapter 3 starts with an introduction to the fundamentals of drawing on the Macintosh using QuickDraw. The Window Manager and windows are discussed. Then, we introduce resources and the Resource Manager.

> QuickDraw, the Window Manager, and resources are very closely related. Windows are drawn using QuickDraw commands from information stored in resource files.

Four programs are introduced in Chapter 3. The Hello2 program introduces some of the QuickDraw drawing routines related to text; the Mondrian program (Figure 1.7) demonstrates QuickDraw shape-drawing routines. ShowPICT (Figure 1.8) illustrates how easy it is to copy a picture from a program like MacDraw or MacPaint into a resource file, then draw the picture in a window of your own. Finally, as a bonus for completing the first three programs, you can try the Flying Line (Figure 1.9), an intriguing program that can be used as a screen saver.

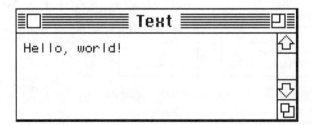

Figure 1.6   Standard Pascal's Hello, World.

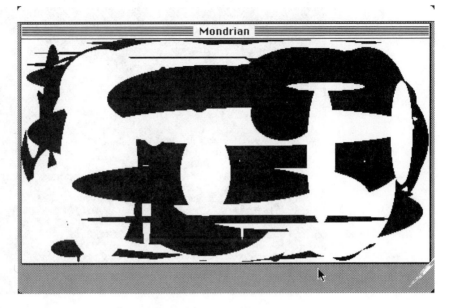

Figure 1.7 Mondrian.

Figure 1.8 ShowPICT.

Figure 1.9   The Flying Line.

Chapter 4 introduces one of the most important concepts in Macintosh programming: events. Events are the Macintosh's mechanism for describing the user's actions to your application. When the mouse button is clicked, a key is pressed, or a disk is inserted in the floppy drive, the operating system lets your program know by queueing an event. The event architecture can be found in almost every Macintosh application written. This chapter presents the architecture of the main event loop and shows how events should be handled. EventTutor, Chapter 4's sole program (Figure 1.10) provides a working model of the event architecture.

The Macintosh popularized pull-down menus (Figure 1.11). Chapter 5 shows you how to add the classic pull-down, hierarchical, and pop-up menus to your own programs. Chapter 5's first program, Timer (Figure 1.12), uses both classic pull-down and hierarchical menus. This chapter also shows you how to create and implement pop-up menus with a little program called Zinger (Figure 1.13).

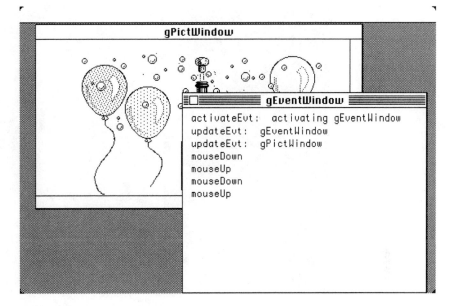

Figure 1.10   EventTutor.

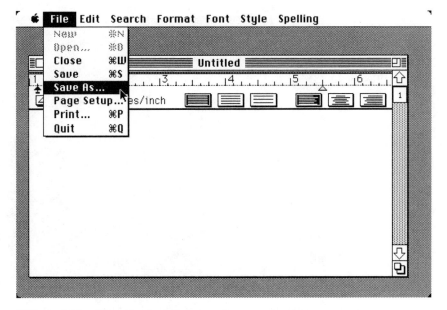

Figure 1.11   The classic pull-down menu.

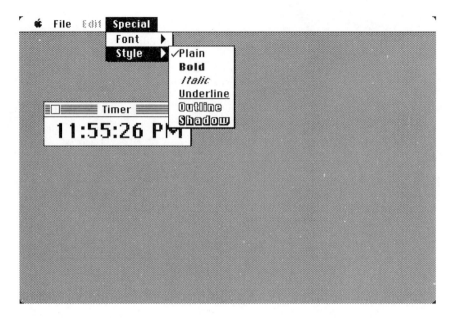

Figure 1.12   Timer with hierarchical menus.

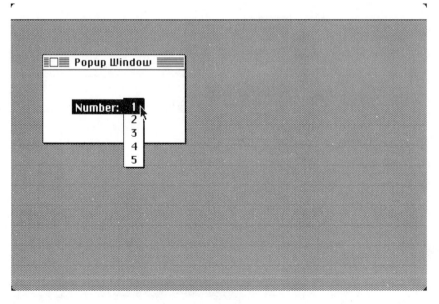

Figure 1.13   Zinger with pop-up menu.

Chapter 6 introduces dialogs and alerts (Figure 1.14). Dialog boxes are another intrinsic part of the Macintosh user interface. They provide a vehicle for customizing your applications as you use them. Alerts are simplified dialogs, used to report errors and give warnings to the user.

The Reminder program in Chapter 6 (Figure 1.15) uses dialogs, alerts, and the Notification Manager to allow you to set an alarm. The application then starts a countdown and notifies you when it goes off—even if you are running another application.

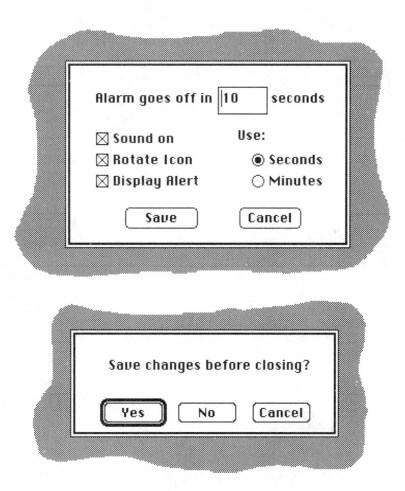

Figure 1.14   Dialog box and alert box.

Chapter 7, the final programming chapter, contains a potpourri of programs illustrating concepts such as error-checking, memory management, printing, generating sound, adding scroll bars to windows, and file management. Each program explores a single topic and provides a working example of reusable code. The WindowMaker program (Figure 1.16) at the beginning of the chapter, which shows

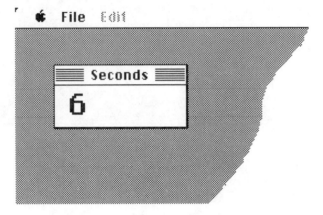

Figure 1.15   Reminder.

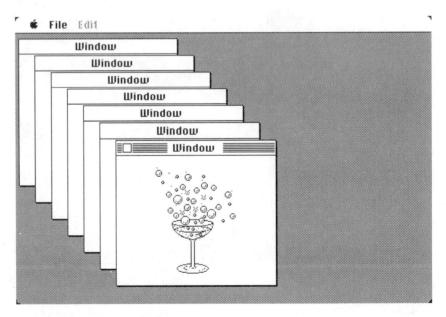

Figure 1.16   WindowMaker.

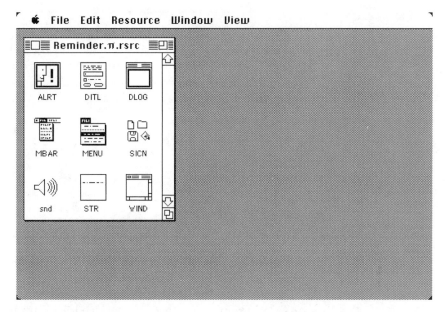

Figure 1.17 ResEdit 2.0.

how to keep track of multiple windows, represents the most mature implementation of the Macintosh interface of all the programs in the book.

Chapter 8 discusses the creation, modification, and use of resources. It starts with a ResEdit tutorial that covers ResEdit 2.0 operation and illustrates the creation of Finder resources (Figure 1.17).

After you've got a handle on the essentials of Macintosh programming, what's next? Chapter 9 talks about some of the tools available to help you with your development efforts. It looks at *Inside Macintosh* and some of the other Mac technical documentation. It also looks at software tools, from compilers to debuggers, as well as Apple's Certified Developer Program and other Macintosh technical resources.

Appendix A is a glossary of the technical terms used in the *Macintosh Primer*.

Appendix B contains a complete listing of each of the *Mac Primer* applications, presented in the same order as they appear in the book.

Appendix C covers some debugging techniques that may be helpful in the THINK Pascal environment.

Appendix D contains a short discussion of HyperCard 2.0 XCMDs, along with an example XCMD written in THINK Pascal.

> For those of you who are not HyperCard aficionados, XCMDs are procedures written in Pascal or C that can be called from within HyperCard. XCMDs allow you to go beyond the limits of HyperCard, performing functions not normally available from within HyperCard.

Appendix E is a bibliography of Macintosh programming references.

How to Use This Book

Each *Macintosh Primer* chapter is made up of the main text and **tech blocks**. The main text is the narrative portion of this text. Read this first. It contains the information you need to input and run the example programs. Because we've placed a premium on getting you going immediately, we have you run the program before discussing how the code works. Impatient programmers are invited to go directly to Appendix B, which contains commented listings of all the programs discussed in the book. If you have questions after typing in the programs, refer to the chapter in which the program is discussed. If you prefer a more sedate pace, read a chapter at a time, type in the programs, and test them as you go. Try the variants to the program if they sound interesting.

At some points, we expand on the narrative with a tech block, indicated by a distinctive gray background. It's OK to ignore them during your first read-through.

> Tech blocks will have this appearance in the main text. If you feel comfortable with the subject discussed in the main text, read the tech blocks for more detail. Otherwise, come back to them later.

Several important terms and conventions are used throughout the *Macintosh Primer*. Whenever you see a notation like this:

(III:256–272)

it refers to a volume of *Inside Macintosh* and a set of pages within that volume. The example here refers to Volume III, pages 256 to 272. References to *Tech Notes,* documentation from Apple's Macintosh Developers Technical Support Group, are annotated like this: (TN:78) (referring to *Tech Note* 78). (See Chapter 9 to find out how to get *Tech Notes.*) These references to *Inside Macintosh* and *Tech Notes* are intended to help readers who are interested in a further discussion of a topic.

All of our source code is presented in a special font. For example:

```
begin
    i := 0;
    DoTheRightThing;
end.
```

Toolbox routines and Pascal functions are also in the code font when they are described in the text. Code should be typed in the same case as presented in the text. C is a case-sensitive language. Please note the similarity between the upper case L and the lower case l, and be careful to type in the correct choice. **Menu titles**, **menu items**, and **dialog items** appear in the book in Chicago font just as they do on the screen.

Finally, **boldface** is used to point out the first occurrence of important new terms.

What You Need to Get Started

First, you need THINK Pascal from Symantec. The examples from the book use version 3.0. You'll also need a Toolbox reference manual. Apple's *Inside Macintosh* series is the authoritative reference on Macintosh software development. We suggest that you purchase Volume I and Volume V of *Inside Mac*. Volume I contains a description of a majority of the Toolbox routines used in this book. Volume V contains color QuickDraw information that also affects the Window and Menu Managers. Volumes II, III, and IV contain helpful, but not indispensable, information about less commonly used routines. Volume VI is due out soon and will contain information about System 7 routines. This text does not use System 7 routines, but all code in the book is compatible with the new functions.

Buy Volumes I and V with your lunch money. Buy Volumes II through IV and VI with somebody else's lunch money.

You'll also need access to a Macintosh Plus, SE, or II-series workstation. You can use this book with anything from a Macintosh Plus with 1 megabyte of RAM and an external drive to a fully loaded Macintosh IIfx. A hard drive is strongly recommended. The screen shots that accompany the text assume that you have a hard disk.

Finally, use the latest system files with *Mac Primer* programs. Don't use any system software older than version 6.02 (earlier versions of System 6 are buggy).

> The compiled, stand-alone programs that are developed in this book may or may not work in the 512K and the 128K Macintosh. In general, if a program uses a ROM call that is not supported by these Macintoshes, we will mention it in a tech block and suggest alternatives (if there are any) for programmers who wish to support the older machines.

Ready, Set . . .

When you finish this book, you'll be able to create your own Macintosh applications.

Get all your equipment together, take the phone off the hook, and fire up your Mac.

Go!

2

Setting Up

This chapter introduces you to the software tools used in this book. It also examines some issues that are specific to the implementation of Pascal on the Macintosh.

THINK PASCAL Is the programming environment we'll use throughout the *Macintosh Primer*. First, we'll show you how to install it; then, we'll look at how to type in and run a sample program. We'll talk about the programming conventions used in this book and some of the rules you need to follow when you use the Mac and THINK Pascal together.

Installing THINK Pascal

Let's start by installing THINK Pascal. These instructions were tested using THINK Pascal 3.0. If you are using a different version, check out the instructions in your THINK Pascal *User Manual*.

Create a folder called THINK Pascal at the top level of your hard disk. Next, insert the floppy disk labeled THINK Pascal 1 into your floppy drive. Drag the following files from the floppy disk into the THINK Pascal folder on your hard drive:

- The THINK Pascal application
- Interface.lib
- Runtime.lib
- The Interfaces folder
- The Libraries folder

Your THINK Pascal folder should look something like Figure 2.1.

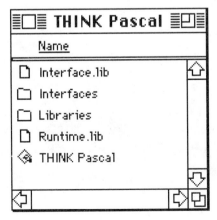

Figure 2.1   The THINK Pascal folder.

THINK Pascal comes with five disks, but only one is used here. Why? Because the rest of the disks contain utilities that aren't necessary for us to deal with now. Most of the disks contain files and utilities that deal with the THINK Pascal ability to do object programming. Working with objects is beyond the scope of this book. After you feel comfortable with the concepts in the *Primer*, examine the object-programming manual that comes with THINK Pascal. (Volume II of the *Primer* also contains a discussion on using class libraries.)

Source Code Files

Set up a place for your source code by creating a folder called Development, or something equally inspiring, also at the top level. We'll create a separate folder inside the Development folder for each *Mac Primer* application (see Figure 2.2).

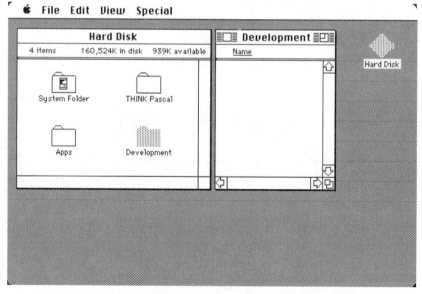

Figure 2.2   The Development folder, ready for some source code.

ResEdit

THINK Pascal comes with a version of ResEdit on one of its disks. Drag it onto the top level of your hard disk. Check the version of ResEdit that you have. It's best to use version 2.0 (or later) for the projects in this book (see Figure 2.3). There is no charge for this utility, which is written and maintained by Apple. It's available on many BBSs, so download it if you wish. If you purchase ResEdit from the Apple Programmer's and Developer's Association (APDA), you also receive additional documentation. See Chapter 9 for more information about APDA. ResEdit versions consistently improve, so use the latest version that you can find.

If you are unfamiliar with ResEdit, read Chapter 8, which discusses ResEdit operations on resources. It illustrates how to install the resources you need to complete a stand-alone program. (This includes the techniques you'll need to add an icon to your own applications.)

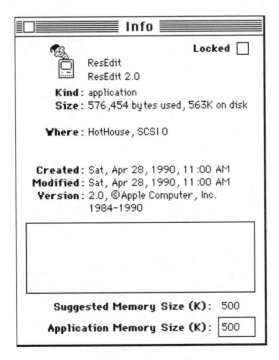

Figure 2.3 Get Info window for ResEdit 2.0. (To see this, select **ResEdit** by clicking on it once. Then select **Get Info** from the Finder's **File** menu.)

Once you have THINK Pascal and ResEdit together on your Macintosh, you're one step away from starting to program. The next section discusses the ground rules for running THINK Pascal code: steps for accessing the Toolbox, naming conventions, and predefined Pascal and Toolbox data types.

Macintosh Programming Issues

Accessing the Toolbox with Pascal

Built into every Macintosh Plus, SE, and Mac II is a set of more than 700 routines, collectively known as the Mac Toolbox. These include routines for drawing windows on the screen, routines for handling menus, even routines for changing the date on the real-time clock built into the Mac. The existence of these routines helps explain the consistency of the Mac user interface. Everyone uses these routines. When MacDraw pulls down a menu, it's calling a Toolbox routine. When MacPaint pulls down a menu, it's calling the same routine. That's why the menus look alike from application to application, which has a rather soothing effect on users. This same principle applies to scroll bars, windows, lists, dialog boxes, alerts, and so on.

If you look at Toolbox calls in the pages of *Inside Macintosh*, you'll notice that the calling sequences and example code presented in each chapter are written in Pascal. For example, the calling sequence for the function GetNewWindow (I:283) is listed as:

```
FUNCTION GetNewWindow (windowID: INTEGER;
wStorage: Ptr; behind: WindowPtr) :  WindowPtr;
```

Each calling sequence starts with either the word FUNCTION or the word PROCEDURE. Just as you'd expect from Pascal, functions return values; procedures don't. In the example, the function GetNewWindow returns a value of type WindowPtr. Here's an example of a call to GetNewWindow from within a program:

```
VAR
    myNewWindow, myOldWindow: WindowPtr;
    myWindowID: INTEGER;
begin
    myWindowID := 400;
```

```
myNewWindow := GetNewWindow( myWindowID,
        nil, myOldWindow );
end;
```

In our code, we receive the value returned by `GetNewWindow` in the variable `myNewWindow`, which is declared as a `WindowPtr`.

Most of the data types found in *Inside Macintosh* are automatically available to you in THINK Pascal. Note that Pascal is not case-sensitive: `Boolean` and `BOOLEAN` both represent the same data type. Although both will compile, the examples presented in the *Mac Primer* will use the case-spelling presented in the *Inside Macintosh* calling sequences. In the previous example, the variable `myWindowID` is declared as an `INTEGER`, not as an `Integer`. Where possible, stick to the standards presented in *Inside Macintosh*.

Naming Conventions

Another standard adopted by the *Mac Primer* concerns the naming of `PROCEDURE`s, `FUNCTION`s, and variables. `PROCEDURE`s and `FUNCTION`s always start with an upper-case letter. Each new word within a name should also start with an upper-case letter. For example, `GetNewWindow` or `SeekSpindle` are fine `FUNCTION` and `PROCEDURE` names; `badPrcName` isn't.

Variables always start with a lower-case letter. Global variables (variables accessible to your entire program) should start with a lower case g. Use variable names like `firstEmployee` and `currentTime`. Use global names like `gCurrentWindow` and `gDone`. The use of variable names such as `glk` and `swpCk7` is discouraged.

(These conventions have been adopted to make the code presented here easy to understand and consistent. If you're feeling ornery, `swpCk7` as often as you want. It's your Mac.)

Predefined Data Types

Although some of the data types you'll encounter in the pages of *Inside Macintosh* will be familiar, many data types are defined specifically for the Macintosh Toolbox. For example, note the calling sequence for the Toolbox `PROCEDURE SetRect`, found in (I:174):

```
PROCEDURE SetRect( VAR r: Rect;
    left, top, right, bottom: INTEGER );
```

The data type `Rect` is used throughout the Toolbox and is defined in *Inside Macintosh* (I:141). A `Rect` holds the upper left and lower right points of a rectangle. You'll see more of these "predefined" Mac data structures later on. As you'll see, access to most of the Toolbox types and constants defined in *Inside Macintosh* is provided automatically by THINK Pascal.

Most of the Toolbox routines are built right into the Macintosh, in read-only memory, or ROM. The original Macintosh came with 64K ROMs; the Mac Plus comes with 128K ROMs; the Mac SE, II, and IIx have 256K ROMs. The Mac IIfx has massive 512K ROMs. Many of the routines built into the newer Macs are not found in the original Mac, Mac Plus, or SE. Likewise, many routines found in the Mac Plus were not found in the original Macintosh. The point is, things change. If you're not careful, the programs you write on one machine might not work on another. In the same vein, if you don't follow Apple's programming guidelines, the program you write on today's machine may break on tomorrow's.

Resources

As was mentioned in Chapter 1, much of a program's descriptive information is stored in resources. Resources may be defined by their `type` and either their **resource ID number** or their **name**.

Each resource has a certain type, and each type has a specific function. For example, the resource type `WIND` contains the descriptive information necessary to create a window; `MENU` resources describe the menus at the top of the screen. Figure 2.4 gives a short list of some of the resource types you'll see in this book.

Each resource type is composed of four characters. Case is not ignored: `WIND` and `wind` are considered different resource types. Occasionally, resource types may include a space—for example, `'snd '`, where the fourth character is a space.

Actually, resource types are just `LONGINT`s (4 bytes) represented in ASCII format. Usually, the types are selected so the ASCII version is readable (like `WIND`, `MENU`, and so on).

Resource ID numbers are unique within their resource type and file. An application can have several resources of type `DLOG`, each of which normally has a unique resource ID within the application file. For example, the program shown in Figure 2.5 has two `DLOG`s with ID = `400` and ID = `401`. The application also has a `WIND` type resource with ID = `400`. Thus, each resource is uniquely identified by ID number and type.

If you prefer, you may also name your resources. All the examples presented in the *Mac Primer* use the resource type and resource ID to specify resources. When you create your resources, however, you might want to specify resource names as well as resource IDs. This will make your resource files easier to read in ResEdit.

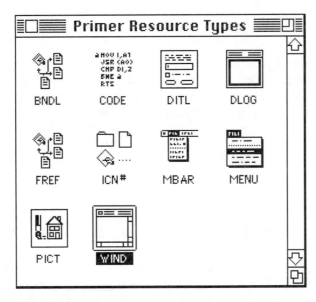

Figure 2.4   Some resource types used in the *Mac Primer*.

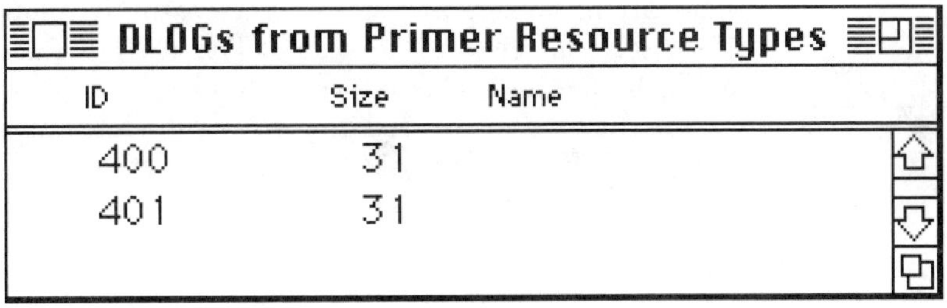

DLOGs from Primer Resource Types		
ID	Size	Name
400	31	
401	31	

Figure 2.5   Two different `DLOG` resources in the same resource file.

ID numbers follow these conventions:

Range	Use
–32,768 to –16,385	Reserved by Apple
–16,384 to 127	Used for system resources
128 to 32,767	Free for use

Certain kinds of resources may have additional restrictions; check *Inside Macintosh* for further information.

In this book, CODE resources will be created in THINK Pascal; most of the other resources will be created using ResEdit.

CODE resources contain the actual code that is to be executed. You may be used to an operating environment that allows you to segment your executable code. The Mac supports segmentation as well. Each segment is stored in a separate CODE resource and is loaded and unloaded as necessary. If you are interested in learning more about code segmentation, an informative discussion begins on page 98 of the THINK Pascal *User's Manual*.

Data Forks and Resource Forks

Macintosh files, unlike files on most other operating systems, each contain two parts: a data fork and a resource fork. The resource fork stores the resources, and the data fork contains everything else. Most word processors store a document's text in the document's data fork and use the resource fork for storing the document's formatting information. HyperCard stacks, interestingly enough, have all their information on the data fork side. The THINK Pascal projects in this book will use the resource fork exclusively.

Now that we've covered these weighty and important topics, let's make THINK Pascal do something, right away!

The Hello, World Program

Now it's time for your first THINK Pascal program. It's the classic program many of you may have encountered before. **Hello, World** draws its name in a window on the screen.

Just to keep things neat, put a new folder inside the Development folder you created earlier. Call the new folder Hello, World. Keep all the files associated with the Hello, World project in this folder.

Create a New Project

To create your first program, double-click on the THINK Pascal application in the THINK Pascal folder. The first thing you'll see is the **Open Project** dialog box (Figure 2.6).

Click on the **New** button, and you should see the dialog box in Figure 2.7.

Use the standard Macintosh mechanisms to open the dialog to the Hello, World folder that you just created (move up once to the top of the hard drive, down once into the Development folder, and down once more into the Hello, World folder). Type Hello.π in the **Name Project** dialog box and click the **Create** button (use **Option-p** for π). The project window (titled Hello.π) will appear

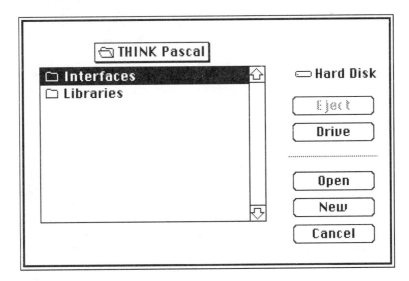

Figure 2.6 The **Open Project** dialog box.

33

(Figure 2.8). Notice that two files have been added to your project automatically. The file `Runtime.lib` gives your program access to the standard Pascal input and output routines. `Runtime.lib` is described on page 54 of the *User Manual*. The file `Interface.lib` contains the glue your program will need to access the Macintosh Toolbox routines built into ROM.

As you add your own files to your project, they will be added to the project window, with the object code size displayed in bytes.

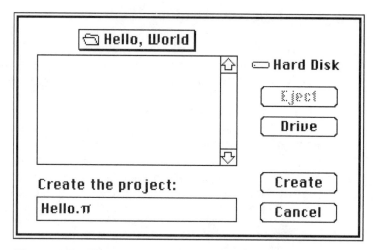

Figure 2.7   The Name Project dialog box.

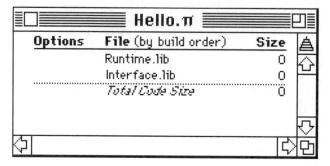

Figure 2.8   The Project window.

> As you may have noticed, we've snuck another naming convention in at this point. This one came directly out of the THINK Pascal *User Manual*. If you wish to keep consistency with our text, name your source code files x x x . p, your project files x x x . π, and your resource files x x x . π . r s r c. The π character is created by holding down the **Option** key and pressing *p*.

Now, you're ready to type in your first program.

> The Project file acts as an information center for all the files involved in building an application. It contains the names of all the source code and resource files necessary to run the application. In addition, the Project file contains information about the THINK Pascal environment, such as the preferred font and font size for printing source code. Projects are a THINK Pascal concept, not a Macintosh concept.

The Code

Pull down the **File** menu and select **New**. Figure 2.9 should show the result.

Now that you have a blank window, type in the following program:

```
program Hello;
begin
    ShowText;
    writeln('Hello, world!');
end.
```

The THINK Pascal editor checks your syntax as you type. It will catch most Pascal errors, displaying what it thinks is an illegal statement using an outline font style. The editor will automatically format your code, saving you lots of work and keystrokes. By selecting **Source Options...** from the **Edit** menu, you can customize the editor's formatting rules to suit your own tastes.

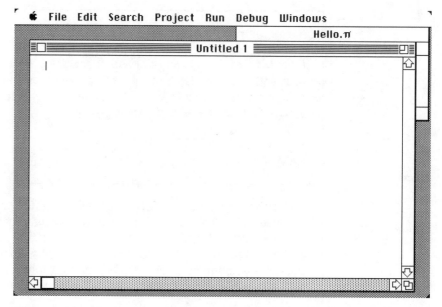

Figure 2.9   A new source code window.

Although the editor is pretty smart, it can be fooled. If the editor outlines an error that you're sure is correct, try deleting the line and retyping it. You might also check the lines before and after the outlined error, in case the error occurred there.

Check the code for typing errors. If everything looks all right, then select **Save As...** from the **File** menu. Call the file Hello.p. Then select the **Add Window** menu item from the **Project** menu to add Hello.p to the project.

If you typed in Hello.p. instead of Hello.p while following the preceding instructions, you share your inclination with many readers of earlier editions. To repeat: in this book, program files look like xxx.p and project files look like xxx.π and resource files (when we get to them in Chapter 3) look like xxx.π.rsrc and that's it. Periods are *not* used at the end of any file names in this book.

> The difference between **Add Window** and **Add File...** in the **Project** menu is that **Add Window** adds the frontmost window to the project, whereas **Add File...** allows you to select one or more files to add to the project.

Running Hello, World

Note that the Hello.p file is now displayed in the project window (Figure 2.10). Now try running the program by choosing **Go** from the **Run** menu, or by keying ⌘**G** (pronounced "command-G"). THINK Pascal will load the two libraries and compile Hello.p. Note that the libraries are loaded only the first time you try to compile a project.

If the compiler encounters an error, it will do its best to describe the problem to you. For example, Figure 2.11 shows the result when

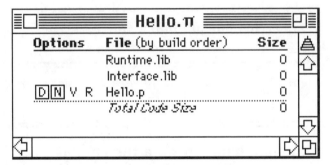

Figure 2.10   Hello.p added to the Project window.

Figure 2.11   The Editor detects a missing semicolon.

the semicolon is left off the end of the call to ShowText. Notice that the call to writeln is outlined.

When you attempt to compile Hello.p, the compiler will point out the line with the error and display an error message in a window. For the error in Figure 2.11, the error message in Figure 2.12 appeared.

To make the error message window go away, just click the mouse button.

Once you've removed the errors, THINK Pascal will give you a chance to save any changes you've made since the last time you saved your source code file (Figure 2.13). Make sure you click **Yes** to save your changes.

Once you've saved your changes, THINK Pascal will run your program. The call to ShowText brings up THINK Pascal's built-in text window. The call to WriteLn writes the string Hello, world! in the window (Figure 2.14). Congratulations! You've just completed your very first Macintosh program.

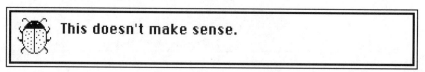

Figure 2.12   A helpful THINK Pascal error message.

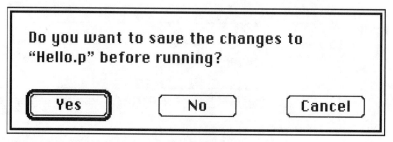

Figure 2.13   The save changes dialog box.

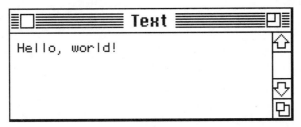

Figure 2.14   Hello, World in action!

You might be wondering about the [icon] or the [D][N] V R in the project window. Well, the [icon] icon shows you that the files are listed in the **build order,** the order in which they will be compiled. Click on the icon and it will change to [icon] and sort the file listing to show how the project is segmented. The [D][N] V R refers to THINK Pascal testing options for that file. There's more information about this on pages 93–105 in the THINK Pascal *User Manual.* For your purposes now, the default settings need not be changed.

The Problem with Hello, World

We don't want to get you too excited about this version of Hello, World. Although it does illustrate how to use THINK Pascal, it does not make use of the Macintosh Toolbox. The first program in Chapter 3 is a Macintized version of Hello, World called Hello2.

In Review

In Chapter 2, you installed THINK Pascal and created your first project. Chapter 3 looks at the basics of Mac programming: QuickDraw, windows, and resources. It also presents four applications that demonstrate the versatility of the Macintosh.

It's almost too late to turn back. To all those who have come from other environments: Beware! QuickDraw is addictive!

3

Drawing on the Macintosh

On the Macintosh, the Toolbox routines that are responsible for all drawing are collectively known as QuickDraw. Now that you have installed THINK Pascal, you can start programming. A good starting point is the unique routines that define the Macintosh graphic interface.

Introduction

QuickDraw IS THE Macintosh drawing environment. With it, you can draw rectangles and other shapes and fill them with different patterns. You can draw text in different fonts and sizes. The windows, menus, and dialogs that are displayed on the Macintosh screen are all created using QuickDraw routines.

In this chapter, we'll show you how to create your own windows and draw in them with QuickDraw. Let's start by examining the QuickDraw coordinate system, the mathematical basis for QuickDraw.

The QuickDraw Coordinate System

QuickDraw drawing operations are all based on a two-dimensional grid coordinate system. The grid is finite, running from (−32,767, −32,767) to (32,767, 32,767), as shown in Figure 3.1.

Every Macintosh screen is actually an array of pixels aligned to the grid. The lines of the grid surround the pixels. The grid point labeled (0,0) is just above, and to the left of, the upper left-hand corner of the Mac screen (Figure 3.2).

(-32,767, -32,767)

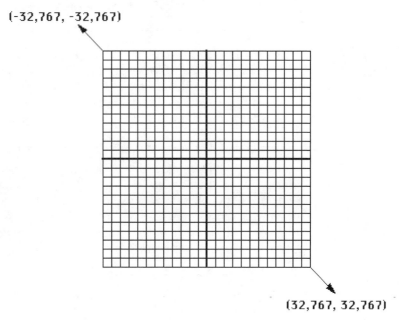

(32,767, 32,767)

Figure 3.1   The grid.

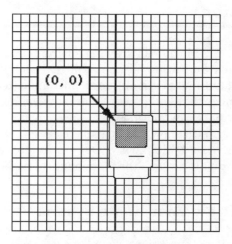

Figure 3.2   The Macintosh screen on the grid.

A screen measuring 32,768 pixels x 32,768 pixels with a screen resolution of 1 pixel = 1/72 inch would be 38 feet wide and 38 feet tall. The Mac Plus and SE monitors are 512 x 342 pixels. Apple's Mac 13" color monitor is 640 x 480 pixels.

The grid is also referred to as the **global coordinate system.**[*] Each window defines a rectangle in global coordinates. Every rectangle has a top, left, bottom, and right. For example, the window depicted in Figure 3.3 defines a rectangle whose top is 80, left is –50, bottom is 220, and right is 300.

Interestingly, the window does not have to be set up within the boundaries of the screen. You can set up a window whose left is –50, top is 100, bottom is 200, and right is 800. On a Mac Plus, this window would extend past the left and right sides of the screen (Figure 3.4)! This is known as the Big Long Window Technique. Use of the Big Long Window Technique is discouraged.

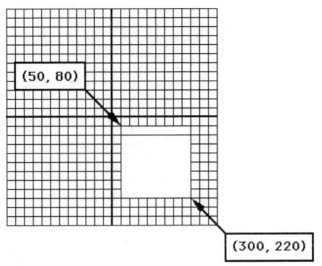

Figure 3.3 A window on the grid.

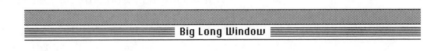

Figure 3.4 A big long window.

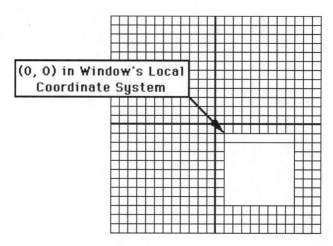

Figure 3.5   Local coordinates.

When drawing inside a window, you'll always draw with respect to the window's **local coordinate system**. The upper left-hand corner of a window lies at coordinate (0,0) in that window's local coordinate system (Figure 3.5).

To draw a rectangle inside your window, specify the top, left, bottom, and right in your window's local coordinates (Figure 3.6). Even if you move your window to a different position on the screen, the rectangle coordinates stay the same. That's because the rectangle was specified in local coordinates.

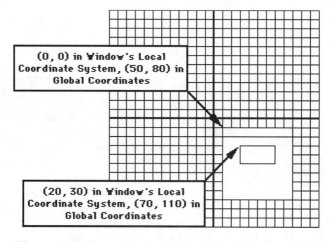

Figure 3.6   Rectangle drawn in window's local coordinates.

Local coordinates are really handy! Suppose you write an application that puts up a window and draws a circle in the window (Figure 3.7). Then, the user of your application drags the window to a new position (Figure 3.8).

You still know exactly where that circle is, even though its window has been moved. That's because you specified your circle in the window's local coordinates.

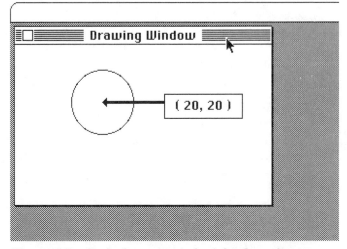

Figure 3.7 Circle drawn in window's local coordinates.

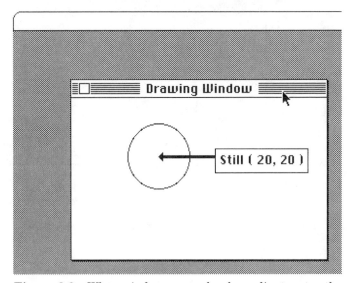

Figure 3.8 When window moves, local coordinates stay the same.

On the Macintosh, text and graphics created by your programs will be displayed in windows. Windows are the device that Macintosh programs use to present information to a user.

Because we need windows to draw in, let's look more closely at windows and the Window Manager.

Window Management

When you draw graphics and text on the Macintosh, you draw them inside a window. The **Window Manager** is the collective name for all the routines that allow you to display and maintain the windows on your screen. Window Manager routines are called whenever a window is moved, resized, or closed.

Window Parts

Although windows can be defined to be any shape you choose, the standard Macintosh window is rectangular. Figure 3.9 shows the parts of a typical window.

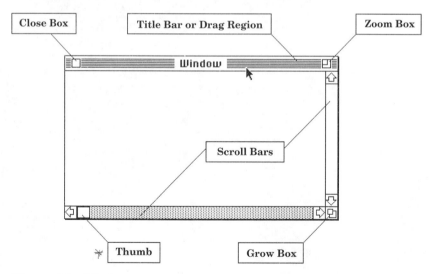

Figure 3.9   Window components.

The **close box** is used when you wish to close the window. The **drag region** is where you grab the window to move it around the screen; this region also contains the window's title. **Scroll bars** are used to examine parts of the window content not currently in view. The **thumb** may be dragged within the scroll bar to display the corresponding part of the window content. The **grow box** (also known as the **size box**) lets you resize the window. The **zoom box** toggles the window between its standard size and a predefined size, normally about the size of the full screen.

There are several types of windows. The window in Figure 3.9 is known as a **document window**. When you use desk accessories or print documents, you will notice other kinds of windows. These windows may not have all the same components as the standard window, but they operate in the same fashion.

Window Types

Six standard types of windows are defined by the Window Manager. Each type has a specific use. In this section, each type is described and its use is discussed.

The documentProc window, shown in Figure 3.10, is the standard window used in applications. This one has a size box, so it is resizable; it has a close box in the upper left-hand corner that closes the window.

The noGrowDocProc window (shown in Figure 3.11), is the standard window without scroll bars or a grow box. Use this window for

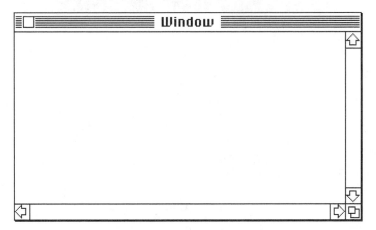

Figure 3.10   The documentProc window.

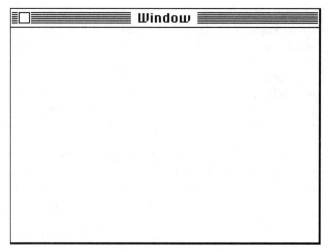

Figure 3.11   The noGrowDocProc window.

information that has a fixed size. The rDocProc window (shown in Figure 3.12), has a black title bar; it has no scroll bars or grow box. This window is most often used with desk accessories.

The remaining three types of windows are all dialog box windows: dBoxProc, plainDBox, and altDBoxProc (Figure 3.13). Dialog boxes will be discussed in Chapter 6.

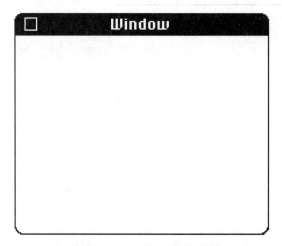

Figure 3.12   The rDocProc window.

Figure 3.13   The dBoxProc, plainDBox, and altDBoxProc windows.

The windows described here are the standard models. You can customize them by adding a few options. For example, most of the window types supported by the Mac can come either with or without the close box (also known as the go-away box). You can specify whether or not the window has a size box (grow box). A zoom box can be added to documentProc and noGrowDocProc windows (see Chapter 4). We'll show you everything you need to know to create exactly the type of window you want for your application.

Setting Up a Window for Your Application

If you plan to use one of the standard window designs for your applications, creating a window is easy. First, build a WIND resource using ResEdit (if you're not familiar with ResEdit, turn to Chapter 8). The WIND resource requires the information shown in Figure 3.14. Use this resource ID within your application to refer to your WIND resource.

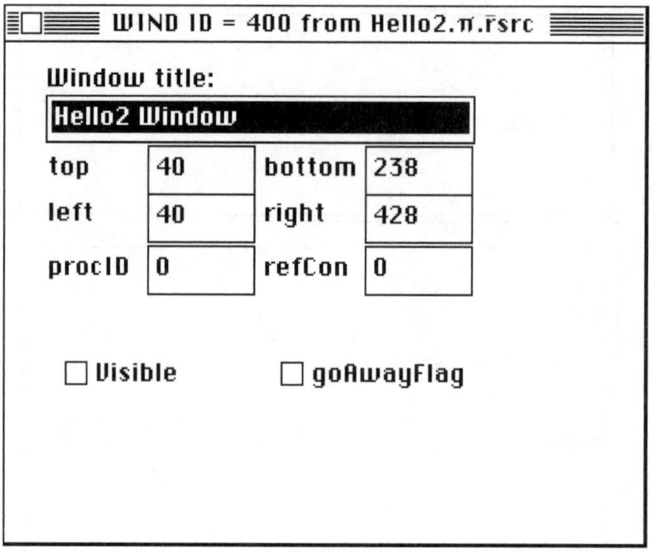

Figure 3.14 WIND resource fields.

Once your WIND resource is built, you're ready to start coding. One of the first things your program will do is initialize the Toolbox. The Window Manager is initialized at this point.

Next, load your WIND resource from the resource file, using the GetNewWindow Toolbox routine:

```
( pictureWindow := GetNewWindow( windowID,
                               wStorage, behind);
```

GetNewWindow loads the WIND resource that has a resource ID of WindowID. The WIND information is stored in memory at the space pointed to by wStorage. The Window Manager will automatically allocate its own memory if you pass nil as your wStorage parameter. For now, this technique is fine. As your applications get larger, you'll want to consider developing your own memory management scheme. The parameter behind determines whether your window is placed in front of or behind any other windows. If the value is nil, it goes to the back; WindowPtr(-1) puts it in front. For example:

```
theWindow := GetNewWindow( 400, nil,
                          WindowPtr(-1) );
```

loads a window with a resource ID of 400, asks the Window Manager to allocate storage for the window record, and puts the window in front of all other windows. <u>A pointer to the window data is returned in the variable theWindow.</u>

Pascal is a strongly typed language. Basically, this means that the compiler is extremely cautious when it comes to passing parameters and assigning values of one type to variables of another type. The expression WindowPtr(-1) asks the compiler to make the constant -1 look like a WindowPtr so that it can be passed as a parameter to GetNewWindow. This technique, known as type-casting, is critical to programming on the Mac. For more information on type-casting, refer to page 285 in the THINK Pascal *User Manual*.

When you create the WIND resource with ResEdit, you are given a choice of making the window visible or not. Visible windows appear as soon as they are loaded from the resource file with GetNewWindow. If the visible flag is not set, you can use ShowWindow to make the window visible:

```
ShowWindow( theWindow );
```

where theWindow is the pointer you got from GetNewWindow. Most applications start with invisible windows and use ShowWindow when they want the window to appear. The Window Manager routine HideWindow makes the window invisible again. In general, you'll use ShowWindow and HideWindow to control the visibility of your windows.

At this point, you've learned the basics of the Window Manager. You can create a window resource using ResEdit, load the resource using GetNewWindow, and make the window appear and disappear using ShowWindow and HideWindow. This technique will be illustrated shortly. After you have put up the kind of window you want, you can start drawing in it. The next section shows you how to use QuickDraw routines to draw in your window.

Drawing in Your Window: The QuickDraw Toolbox Routines

There are many QuickDraw drawing routines. They can be conveniently divided into four groups: routines that draw lines, shapes, text, and pictures. These routines do all their drawing using a graphics "pen." The pen's characteristics affect all drawing, whether the drawing involves lines, shapes, or text.

Before starting to draw, you have to put the pen somewhere (MoveTo), define the size of the line it will draw (PenSize), choose the pattern used to fill thick lines (PenPat), and decide how the line you are drawing changes what's already on the screen (PenMode). Figure 3.15 shows how changing the graphics pen changes the drawing effect.

Every window you create has its own pen. The location of a window's pen is defined in the window's local coordinate system. Once a window's pen characteristics have been defined, they will stay defined until you change them.

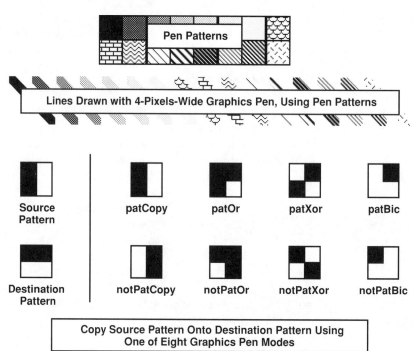

Figure 3.15 Graphics pen characteristics.

Setting the Current Window

Because your application can have more than one window open at the same time, you must first tell QuickDraw which window to draw in. This is done with a call to `SetPort`:

```
theWindow := GetNewWindow( 400, nil,
                             WindowPtr(-1) );
SetPort( theWindow );
```

In this example, `SetPort` made `theWindow` the current window. Until the next call to `SetPort`, all QuickDraw drawing operations will occur in `theWindow`, using `theWindow`'s pen. Once you've called `SetPort` and set the window's pen attributes, you're ready to start drawing.

The basic data structure behind all QuickDraw operations is the `GrafPort`. When you call `SetPort`, you are actually setting the current `GrafPort` (I:271). Since every window has a `GrafPort` data structure associated with it, in effect you are setting the current window. The `GrafPort` data structure contains fields like `pnSize` and `pnLoc`, which define the `GrafPort` pen's current size and location. QuickDraw routines like `PenSize` modify the appropriate field in the current `GrafPort` data structure.

Drawing Lines

The `LineTo` routine allows you to draw lines from the current pen position (which you have set with `MoveTo`) to any point in the current window. For example, a call to:

```
theWindow := GetNewWindow( 400, nil,
                             WindowPtr(-1) );
SetPort( theWindow );
MoveTo( 39, 47 );
LineTo( 407, 231 );
```

would draw a line from (37, 47) to (407, 231) in `theWindow`'s local coordinate system (Figure 3.16).

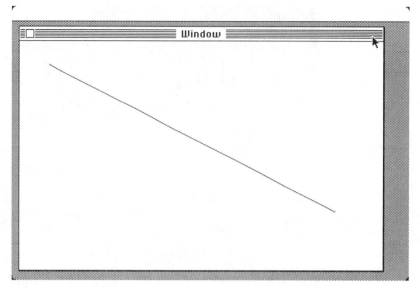

Figure 3.16 Drawing a line with QuickDraw.

It is perfectly legal to draw a line outside the current boundary of a window. QuickDraw will clip it automatically so that only the portion of the line within the window is drawn. QuickDraw will keep you from scribbling outside the window boundaries. This is true for all the QuickDraw drawing routines.

The last program in this chapter is the Flying Line, an extensive example of what you can do using the QuickDraw line-drawing routines.

Drawing Shapes

QuickDraw has a set of drawing routines for each of the following shapes: rectangles, ovals, rounded-corner rectangles, and arcs. Each shape can be drawn filled, inverted, or as an outline (Figure 3.17).

The current pen's characteristics are used to draw each shape, where appropriate. For example, the current fill pattern will have no effect on a framed rectangle. The current `PenMode` setting, however, will affect all drawing. The second program in this chapter, Mondrian, shows you how to create different shapes with QuickDraw (Figure 3.18). It also demonstrates the different pen modes.

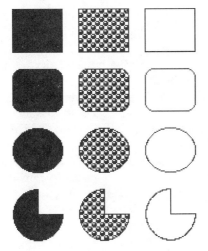

Figure 3.17   Some QuickDraw shapes.

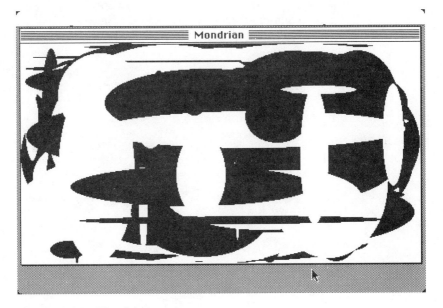

Figure 3.18   Mondrian.

Drawing Text

QuickDraw allows you to draw different text formats easily on the screen. QuickDraw can vary text by font, style, size, spacing, and mode. Let's examine each one of the text characteristics.

Font refers to the typeface of the text you are using. Courier, Helvetica, and Geneva are some of the typefaces available on the Macintosh. **Style** refers to the appearance of the typeface, (**bold**, *italic*, <u>underline</u>, etc.). The **size** of text on the Macintosh is measured in points, where a point is equal to 1/72 inch. **Spacing** defines the average number of pixels in the space between letters on a line of text. Figure 3.19 shows some of these characterics of QuickDraw text.

The **mode** of text is similar to the mode of the pen. The text mode defines the way drawn text interacts with text and graphics already drawn. Text can be defined to overlay the existing graphics (`srcOr`); text can be inverted as it is placed on the existing graphics (`srcXor`); or text can simply paint over the existing graphics (`srcCopy`). The other modes described in QuickDraw shapes (`srcBic`, `notSrcCopy`, `notSrcOr`, etc.) can also be used with text. Figure 3.20 demonstrates how text mode affects appearance.

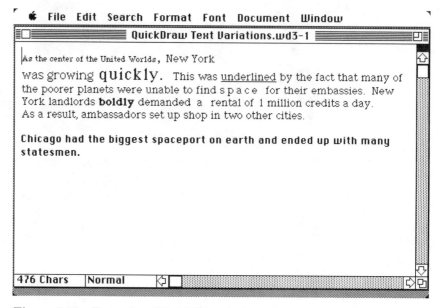

Figure 3.19   Examples of QuickDraw text.

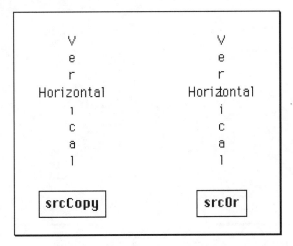

Figure 3.20   The two most popular QuickDraw text modes.

Drawing Pictures

QuickDraw can save text and graphics created with the drawing routines as picture resources called `PICT`s. You can create a picture (using a program like MacPaint or MacDraw), copy the picture to the clipboard, and paste it into a `PICT` resource using ResEdit. Later in the chapter, you'll see how to make use of `PICT` resources in the ShowPICT program.

About Regions

QuickDraw allows you to define a collection of lines and shapes as a **region**. You can then perform operations on the entire region, as shown in Figure 3.21.

By now most of you are probably itching to start coding. First, let's look at the basic Mac programming structure used in this chapter's programs. Then, we'll hit the keyboards!

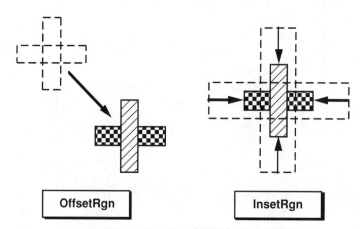

Figure 3.21 Two QuickDraw region operations.

Basic Mac Program Structure

We've looked at a general outline of the QuickDraw and Window routines necessary to make a Macintosh application go. The basic algorithm used in each of the Chapter 3 programs goes something like this:

```
program MyApp;
begin
    DoInitialization;
    DoPrimeDirective;

    while (not Button) do
        begin
        end
end.
```

As you'd expect, the first thing the program does is initialize variables and such. One nice feature of THINK Pascal is that it automatically initializes the Macintosh Toolbox for you. All you have to worry about is any program-specific initialization, such as loading windows or pictures from the resource file. Next, the program performs its prime directive. In the case of the Hello, World program, the prime directive is drawing a text string in a window. Finally, the program waits for the mouse button to be pressed. This format is very basic: Except for clicking the button, there is no interaction between the user and the program. This will be added in the next chapter.

Danger, Will Robinson! Normal Macintosh applications do not exit with a click of the mouse button. Mac programs are interactive. They use menus, dialogs, and events. We'll add these features later. For the purpose of demonstrating QuickDraw, we'll bend the rules a bit.

The QuickDraw Programs

The following programs each demonstrate different parts of the Toolbox. The Hello2 program demonstrates some of the QuickDraw routines related to text; Mondrian displays QuickDraw shapes and modes; ShowPICT loads a `PICT` resource and draws the picture in a window. Finally, you'll code the Flying Line, an intriguing program that can be used as a screen saver.

Let's look at another version of the Hello, World program presented in Chapter 2.

Hello2

The new Hello2 program will do the following:

- Load a resource window, show it, and make it the current port.
- Draw the string `'Hello, World!'` in the window.
- Quit when the mouse button is pressed.

To get started, create a folder in the `Development` folder and call it `Hello2`. This is where you'll build your first Macintosh application.

Create a resource of type `WIND`. The `WIND` resource allows you to define a window with the appearance and size that you desire. Use the tutorial in Chapter 8 if you feel hesitant about using ResEdit.

To build the `WIND` resource, run ResEdit. Select **New** from the **File** menu and create a file named `Hello2.π.rsrc` (remember, π is **option-p**). Make sure you save your resource file inside your newly created `Hello2` folder (Figure 3.22).

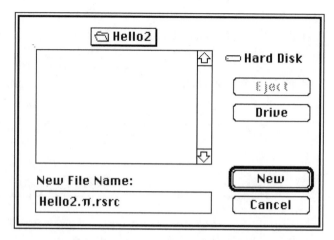

Figure 3.22   ResEdit, naming the new resource file.

Once you've named the new resource file, a window listing all of its resources will appear automatically. Because you just created the file, no resources are listed. Select **Create New Resource** from the **Resource** menu. When prompted to select a resource type, select **WIND** from the scrolling list and click **OK** (you could also have typed in **WIND** and clicked **OK**). Two new windows should appear, a window listing all of the **WIND** resources and, on top of that, a window showing the newly created **WIND** (Figure 3.23).

First, define the coordinates of the window. Pull down the **WIND** menu and choose the menu item **Display as Text**. Then, fill out the fields as shown in Figure 3.24.

Next, select **Get Resource Info** from the **Resource** menu. When the resource information window appears (Figure 3.25), set the **WIND**'s resource ID to **400** and make sure the **Purgeable** checkbox is checked. Checking the **Purgeable** checkbox allows the Macintosh Memory Manager to purge the **WIND** resource from memory once it's not needed anymore. This approach maximizes the amount of memory available for your application.

Choose **Quit** from the **File** menu. When prompted to save the file, click **Yes**. Now you're ready to start up THINK Pascal.

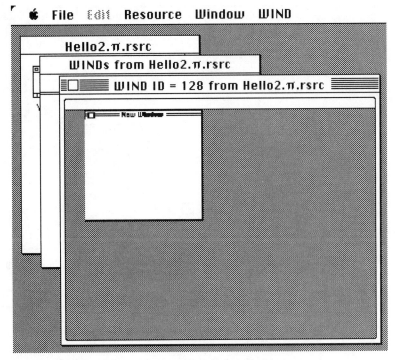

Figure 3.23 The newly created WIND resource.

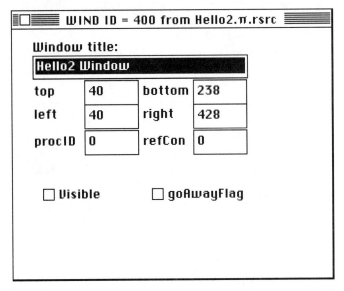

Figure 3.24 The WIND resource, displayed as text.

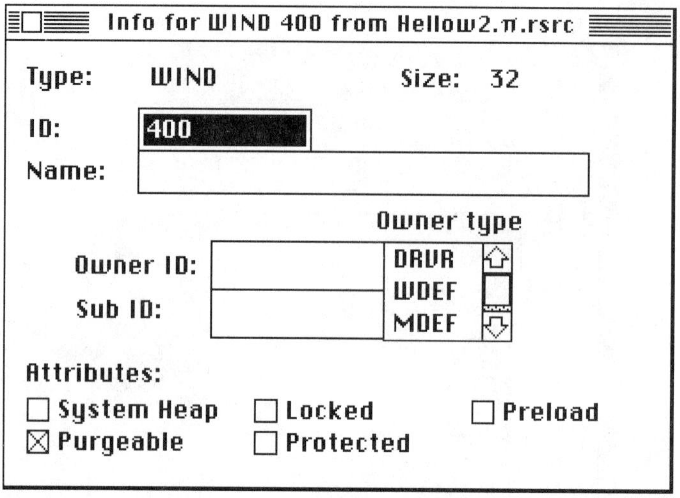

Figure 3.25   The resource information window for W I N D.

Some of you may note that the **Size:** field in Figure 3.25 has a number different from that in the W I N D you just made. That's usually okay. Different versions of ResEdit make resources of slightly different sizes, so if you get 36 instead of 32, don't worry. This will be true for all the resources in this book, so stay calm if the sizes shown in the figures don't match up exactly with what you get at home or at work.

The Hello2 Project

Get into THINK Pascal and create a new project in the Hello2 folder. If you need help creating a new project, refer to Chapter 2 or just review the THINK Pascal documentation. Call the project Hello2.π (remember, π is **option-p**). Next, select **New** from the **File** menu and type the following source code into the window that appears:

```
program Hello2;
   const
      BASE_RES_ID = 400;
      HORIZONTAL_PIXEL = 30;
      VERTICAL_PIXEL = 50;
```

```
{------------------->     WindowInit  <--}

    procedure WindowInit;
        var
            helloWindow: WindowPtr;
    begin
        helloWindow := GetNewWindow(BASE_RES_ID,
                nil, WindowPtr(-1));
        ShowWindow(helloWindow);
        SetPort(helloWindow);
        MoveTo(HORIZONTAL_PIXEL, VERTICAL_PIXEL);
        DrawString('Hello, world!');
    end;


{------------------->     Hello2      <--}

begin
    WindowInit;
    while (not Button) do
        begin
        end;
end.
```

Select **Save As...** from the **File** menu and save your source code as Hello2.p. Select **Add Window** from the **Project** menu to add Hello2.p to the project. When you're done, the Project window should look like Figure 3.26.

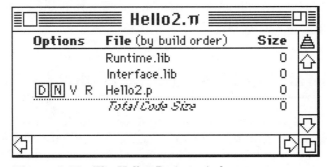

Figure 3.26 The Hello2 Project window.

Adding the Resource File

Before you run the program, you have to tell THINK Pascal to use your newly created resource file. Select **Run Options...** from the **Run** menu. The **Run-time Environment Settings** window will appear.

Click your mouse on the Use resource file checkbox. When the file selection window appears, select the file Hello2.π.rsrc from your project folder. If you can't find your resource file, you probably don't have your project file (Hello2.π) and the resource file (Hello2.π.rsrc) in the same folder at the same level. Quit THINK Pascal, drag them into the same folder and try again. Your **Run-time Environment Settings** window should look like Figure 3.27. Click **OK** to save the settings.

Running Hello2

Now you're ready to run Hello2. Select **Go** from the **Run** menu. You may get a complaint about a syntax error or two. If so, just retype the line the compiler points to.

If you make any changes to Hello2.p, you'll be asked whether you'd like to **Save changes before running?**. Click **Yes**.

Once you've gotten Hello2 to compile without a hitch, it will automatically start running, as shown in Figure 3.28. *Voila!* The new Hello, World should display a window with the text Hello, world! in it. Quit the program by clicking the mouse button.

Let's look at how the code works.

If Hello2 compiles, but the Hello2 window fails to appear, it may indicate a problem with the resource file. If the WIND resource has been entered correctly, try reselecting the resource file in the **Run Options...** dialog box. Also make sure that the resource file is in the same folder as Hello.p.

Walking Through the Hello2 Code

We'll be walking through the source code of each of the programs presented in the *Mac Primer*. We'll start with each program's global const and var declarations. Next, we'll dig into the main routine (usually found at the very bottom of the source code file) and discuss each routine in the order called.

The Hello2 program starts off with some constant declarations. The constant BASE_RES_ID allows all resource references in the program to refer to the same starting ID. By convention, all of our resources start at 400 and go up from there. For example, if we had three WIND resources, they'd most likely be numbered 400, 401, and 402.

The constants HORIZONTAL_PIXEL and VERTICAL_PIXEL will determine where the top left-hand corner of the window is placed on the screen.

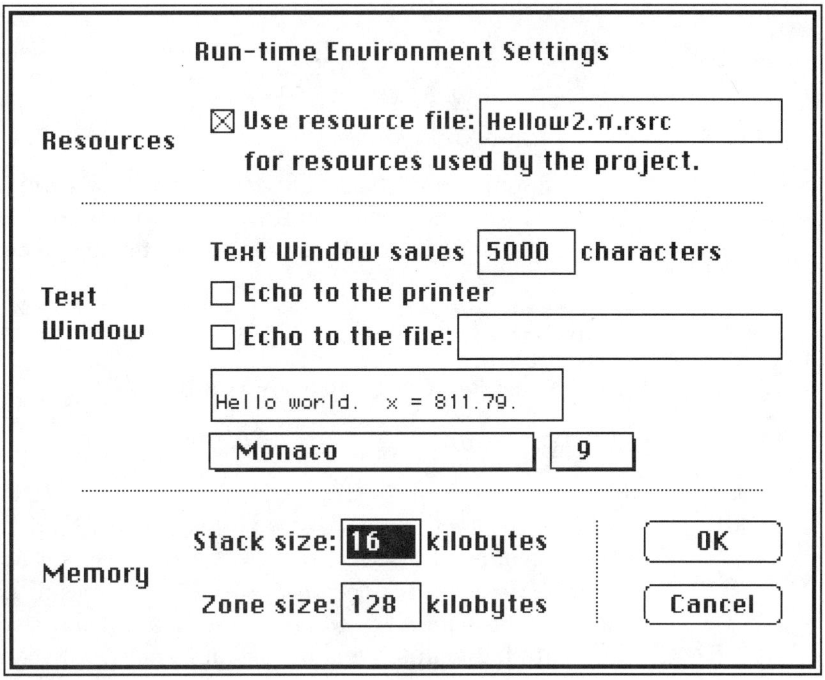

Run-time Environment Settings

Resources

⊠ **Use resource file:** `Hellow2.π.rsrc`
for resources used by the project.

Text Window

Text Window saves `5000` **characters**
☐ **Echo to the printer**
☐ **Echo to the file:**

`Hello world.  x = 811.79.`

`Monaco` `9`

Memory

Stack size: `16` **kilobytes**

Zone size: `128` **kilobytes**

OK

Cancel

Figure 3.27 Adding the resource file to the project.

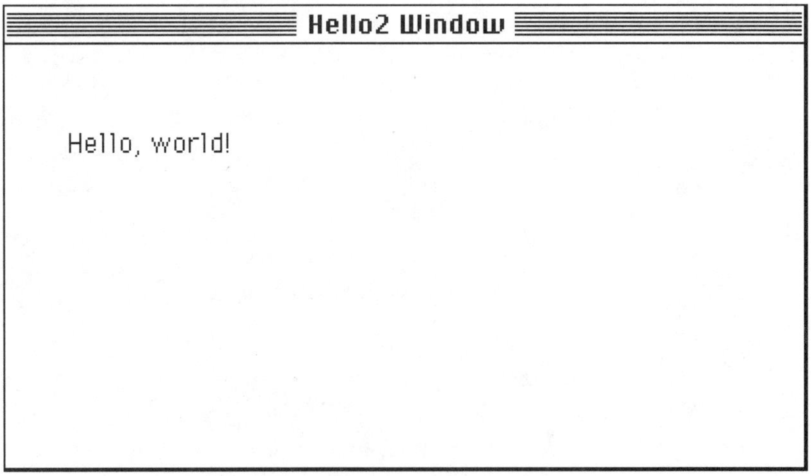

Hello2 Window

Hello, world!

Figure 3.28 The new Hello, World.

```
program Hello2;
   const
      BASE_RES_ID = 400;
      HORIZONTAL_PIXEL = 30;
      VERTICAL_PIXEL = 50;
```

The main routine starts with a call to `WindowInit`. Hello2 then waits in an indefinite loop until the Toolbox routine `Button` returns `true`. `Button` will return true when the mouse button is pressed.

```
{------------------->   Hello2   <--}
begin
   WindowInit;
   while (not Button) do
      begin
      end;
end.
```

`WindowInit` calls `GetNewWindow` to load the `WIND` resource with resource `ID = BASE_RES_ID` from your resource file. The first parameter specifies the resource ID. The second parameter tells the Toolbox how memory for the new window data structure should be allocated. Because you passed `nil` as the second parameter, the Toolbox will allocate the memory for you. Finally, the third parameter to `GetNewWindow` tells the Window Manager to create this window in front of any of the application's open windows.

`GetNewWindow` returns a pointer to the new window data structure. Next, `WindowInit` calls `ShowWindow` to make the window visible. It is at this point that the window actually appears on the screen. The call to `SetPort` makes `helloWindow` the current window. All subsequent QuickDraw drawing operations will take place in `helloWindow`. Next, `helloWindow`'s pen is moved to the local coordinates 50 down and 30 across from the upper left-hand corner of `helloWindow`, and the string `Hello, world!` is drawn.

```
{------------------->   WindowInit <--}

procedure WindowInit;
   var
      helloWindow: WindowPtr;
begin
   helloWindow := GetNewWindow(BASE_RES_ID,
         nil, WindowPtr(-1));
   ShowWindow(helloWindow);
   SetPort(helloWindow);
   MoveTo(HORIZONTAL_PIXEL, VERTICAL_PIXEL);
   DrawString('Hello, world!');
end;
```

Unlike many programming environments, THINK Pascal takes care of initializing the Toolbox for you. If you wanted to initialize the Toolbox yourself, you'd use a routine that looked like this:

```
{----------------->       ToolboxInit<--}
   procedure ToolboxInit;
   begin
      InitGraf( @thePort );
      InitFonts;
      InitWindows;
      InitMenus;
      TEInit;
      InitDialogs( nil );
      MaxApplZone;
   end;
```

Each call initializes a different part of the Macintosh interface. The call to `InitGraf` initializes QuickDraw.

The following global variables are initialized by `InitGraf` and can be used in your routines:

- `thePort` always points to the current GrafPort. Because it is the first QuickDraw global, passing its address to `InitGraf` tells QuickDraw where in memory all the QuickDraw globals are located.

- `white` is a pattern variable set to a white fill; `black`, `gray`, `ltGray`, and `dkGray` are initialized as different shades between black and white.

- `arrow` is set as the standard cursor shape, an arrow. You can pass `arrow` as an argument to QuickDraw's cursor-handling routines.

- `screenBits` is a data structure that describes the main Mac screen. The field `screenBits.bounds` is declared as a `Rect` and contains a rectangle that encloses the main Mac screen.

- `randSeed` is used as a seed by the Macintosh random number generator (we'll show you how to use the seed in this chapter).

InitFonts initializes the Font Manager and loads the system font into memory. Because the Window Manager uses the Font Manager (to draw the window's title, for example), you must initialize fonts first. InitWindows initializes the Window Manager and draws the desktop and the empty menu bar. InitMenus initializes the Menu Manager so you can use menus. (Chapter 5 shows how to use the Menu Manager.)

InitWindows and InitMenus both draw the empty menu bar. This is done intentionally by the ROM programmers for a reason that is such a dark secret that they didn't even document it in *Inside Macintosh*.

TEInit initializes TextEdit, the Text-Editing Manager built right into the Toolbox. InitDialogs initializes the Dialog Manager (illustrated in Chapter 6). MaxAppleZone maximizes the size of the application's memory area.

As far as the *Primer* code is concerned, you needn't concern yourself with initialization procedures. If you're porting code from other Pascal programming environments, remove Toolbox initialization code, as it will crash your Mac. Alternatively, you can disable the automatic initialization (see page 142 of the THINK Pascal *User Manual*).

The new Hello, World can easily be turned into a stand-alone application. Pull down the **Project** menu and select **Build Application....** When the Build Application dialog box appears, type in the name of your application and press return. THINK Pascal will build a stand-alone application out of Hello2. If you'd like to add a custom icon to Hello2, take a quick tour through Chapter 8.

Variants

This section presents some variants to the Hello2 program. We'll start by changing the font used to draw Hello, World. Next, we'll modify the style of the text, using **boldface**, *italics*, and so on. We'll also show you how to change the size of your text. Finally, we'll experiment with different window types.

Changing the Font

Every window has an associated font. You can change the current window's font by calling `TextFont`, passing an integer that represents the font you'd like to use:

```
var
    myFontNumber : INTEGER;

begin
    TextFont( myFontNumber );
end;
```

Macintosh font numbers start at zero and count up from there. THINK Pascal has predefined a number of font names with which you can experiment. The best way to make use of a specific font is to pass its name as a parameter to the Toolbox routine `GetFNum`. `GetFNum` will return the font number associated with that name. You can then pass the font number to `TextFont`.

Did someone in the back ask, "How can you tell which fonts have been installed in the system?" An excellent question! Not every Mac has the same set of fonts installed. Some folks have the LaserWriter font set; others a set of fonts for their ImageWriter. Some people might even have a complete set of foreign language fonts. For the most part, your applications shouldn't care which fonts are installed. There are, however, two exceptions to this rule. All dialog boxes and menus are drawn in the **system font**, which defaults to font number 0. The default font for applications is called the **application font**, usually font number 1. In the United States, the system font is Chicago, and the application font is Geneva.

For now, put the `GetFNum` and `TextFont` calls before your call to `DrawString` and after your call to `SetPort`, and try different font names (use the Key Caps desk accessory for a list of font names on your Mac).

```
{-------------> WindowInit <--}

procedure WindowInit;
    var
        helloWindow: WindowPtr;
        fontNum : INTEGER;
```

```
begin
   helloWindow := GetNewWindow(BASE_RES_ID,
          nil, WindowPtr(-1));
   ShowWindow(helloWindow);
   SetPort(helloWindow);
   MoveTo(HORIZONTAL_PIXEL, VERTICAL_PIXEL);
   GetFNum( 'Monaco', fontNum );
   TextFont( fontNum );
   { Try other font names!!!  }
   DrawString('Hello, world!');
end;
```

Changing Text Style

The Macintosh supports seven font styles: **bold**, *italic*, underlined, outline, shadow, condensed, and e x t e n d e d , or any combination of these. Chapter 5 shows you how to set text styles using menus. For now, try inserting the call TextFace(style) before the call to DrawString. Here's one example:

```
{---------------> WindowInit <--}

procedure WindowInit;
   var
      helloWindow: WindowPtr;
begin
   helloWindow := GetNewWindow(BASE_RES_ID,
          nil, WindowPtr(-1));
   ShowWindow(helloWindow);
   SetPort(helloWindow);
   MoveTo(HORIZONTAL_PIXEL, VERTICAL_PIXEL);
   TextFace( [bold] );
   { Try the other predefined styles!!!  }
   DrawString('Hello, world!');
end;
```

Here's a list of predefined QuickDraw styles:

- bold
- italic
- underline
- outline

- shadow
- condense
- extend

You can also combine styles; try TextFace([bold, italic]) or some other combination.

Changing Text Size

It's also easy to change the size of the fonts, using the `TextSize` Toolbox routine:

```
var
    myFontSize : INTEGER;

begin
    TextSize( myFontSize );
end;
```

The number you supply as an argument to `TextSize` is the font size that will be used the next time text is drawn in the current window. The Font Manager will scale a font up to the size requested; this may result in a jagged character, as shown in Figure 3.29.

The default size is 0, which specifies that the system font size (12 point) be used. Try this variant in your code.

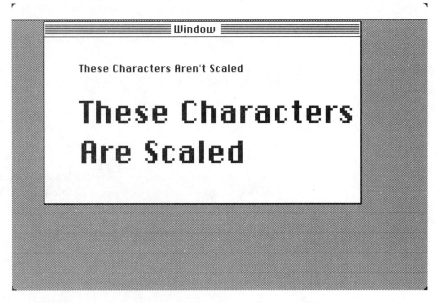

Figure 3.29 The result of font scaling.

```
{-------------------->     WindowInit  <--}

   procedure WindowInit;
      var
         helloWindow: WindowPtr;
   begin
      helloWindow := GetNewWindow(BASE_RES_ID,
               nil, WindowPtr(-1));
      ShowWindow(helloWindow);
      SetPort(helloWindow);
      MoveTo(HORIZONTAL_PIXEL, VERTICAL_PIXEL);
      TextSize( 24 );
      {  Try other pixel sizes!!!  You    }
      {  may have to change the value     }
      {  of VERTICAL_PIXEL     }
      DrawString('Hello, world!');
   end;
```

> If you're trying different font sizes and you can't get the font to be
> jagged, you could be running System 7, which has a much more
> powerful font scaling procedure. Adobe Type Manager, a utility
> program from Adobe, also prevents scaled font jaggies.

Changing the Hello2 Window

Another modification you can try involves changing the window type
from 0 to something else. Use ResEdit to change the WIND resource's
procID from 0 to 1. (See the section on window types earlier in this
chapter for other possibilities.)

Now that you have mastered QuickDraw's text-handling routines,
you're ready to exercise the shape-drawing capabilities of QuickDraw
with the next program: Mondrian.

Mondrian

The Mondrian program opens a window and draws randomly
generated ovals, alternately filled with white or black. Like Hello2,
Mondrian waits for a mouse press to exit. The program, with its
variants, demonstrates most of QuickDraw's shape-drawing
functionality.

Mondrian is made up of two steps:

- Initialize the window.
- Draw random QuickDraw shapes in a loop, until the mouse button is clicked.

First, create a new folder called `Mondrian` in the `Development` folder. Next, create the resources you need for the program, and then enter the code.

Resources

The Mondrian program needs a `WIND` resource, just as Hello2 did. In this case, create a new resource file called `Mondrian.π.rsrc` in the `Mondrian` folder you just made. Then create a window with the specifications shown in Figure 3.30. Before you close and save `Mondrian.π.rsrc`, go to **Get Resource Info**, change the resource ID of the new `WIND` to 400, and check the **Purgeable** checkbox. Quit ResEdit, saving your changes.

Next, go into THINK Pascal and create a new project called `Mondrian.π` inside the `Mondrian` folder. Then open up a new source code window and enter the program:

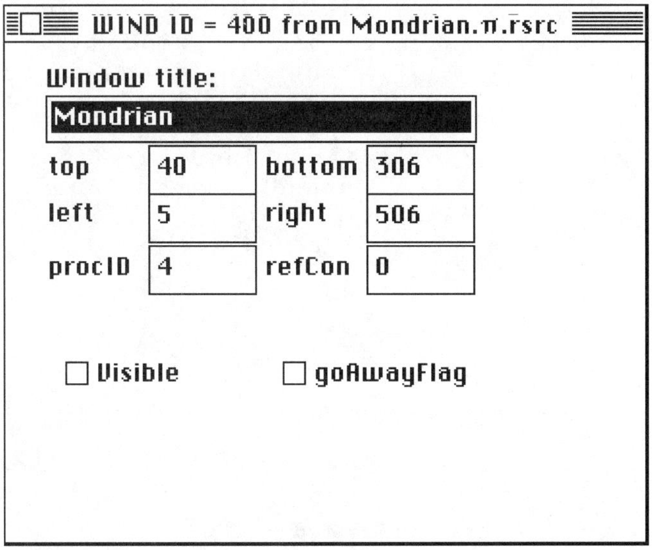

Figure 3.30 `WIND` parameters for Mondrian.

```
program Mondrian;
   const
      BASE_RES_ID = 400;

   var
      gDrawWindow: WindowPtr;
      gFillColor: LONGINT;


{------------------->   Randomize   <--}

   function Randomize (range: INTEGER): INTEGER;
      var
         rawResult: LONGINT;
   begin
      rawResult := Random;
      rawResult := abs(rawResult);

      Randomize := (rawResult * range) div 32768;
   end;


{------------------->   RandomRect <--}

   procedure RandomRect (var myRect: Rect; boundingWindow:
                         WindowPtr);
   begin
      myRect.left := Randomize(boundingWindow^.portRect.right -
                            boundingWindow^.portRect.left);
      myRect.right := Randomize(boundingWindow^.portRect.right -
                            boundingWindow^.portRect.left);
      myRect.top := Randomize(boundingWindow^.portRect.bottom -
                            boundingWindow^.portRect.top);
      myRect.bottom := Randomize(boundingWindow^.portRect.bottom -
                            boundingWindow^.portRect.top);
   end;


{------------------->   DrawRandomRect   <--}

   procedure DrawRandomRect;
      var
         myRect: Rect;
   begin
      RandomRect(myRect, gDrawWindow);
```

```
      ForeColor(gFillColor);
      PaintOval(myRect);
   end;


{----------------->   MainLoop    <--}

   procedure MainLoop;
   begin
      GetDateTime(randSeed);
      gFillColor := blackColor;

      while (not Button) do
         begin
            DrawRandomRect;
            if (gFillColor = blackColor) then
                  gFillColor := whiteColor
            else
                  gFillColor := blackColor
         end;
   end;


{----------------->   WindowInit  <--}

   procedure WindowInit;
   begin
      gDrawWindow := GetNewWindow(BASE_RES_ID, nil,
                              WindowPtr(-1));
      ShowWindow(gDrawWindow);
      SetPort(gDrawWindow);
   end;


{----------------->   Mondrian    <--}

begin
   WindowInit;
   MainLoop;
end.
```

Running Mondrian

Once you've finished typing in the code, save it as `Mondrian.p` and add it to the project using **Add Window**. Next, select **Run Options...** from the **Run** menu and tell the project to use the

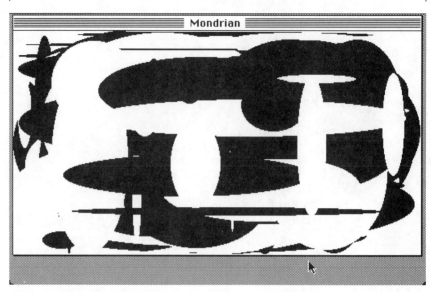

Figure 3.31   Running Mondrian.

resource file `Mondrian.π.rsrc`. Now, select **Go** from the **Run** menu. If everything went correctly, you should see something like Figure 3.31. The window should fill with overlapping black and white ovals until you click the mouse button. If you got a different result, then check out your resource; make sure the `WIND` resource has the correct resource ID. If your resource is all right, go through the code for typos.

Now let's look at the Mondrian code.

Walking Through the Mondrian Code

The *Mac Primer* uses the convention of starting resource ID numbers at `400`, adding one each time a new resource ID is needed. Use any number you wish (as long as it's between 128 and 32,767). The constant `BASE_RES_ID` used in Mondrian is identical to that used in Hello2. The global variable `gDrawWindow` is Mondrian's main window. Each shape you draw will be filled with the color in `gFillColor`, which is initialized as `blackColor`.

```
program Mondrian;
   const
      BASE_RES_ID = 400;

   var
      gDrawWindow: WindowPtr;
      gFillColor: LONGINT;
```

Mondrian's main routine calls `WindowInit`, then `MainLoop`.

```
{---------------> Mondrian <--}

begin
   WindowInit;
   MainLoop;
end.
```

`WindowInit` loads `WIND` number `400` from the resource file, storing a pointer to it in `gDrawWindow`. Next, `ShowWindow` is called to make the window visible, and `SetPort` is called to make `gDrawWindow` the current window.

```
{---------------> WindowInit <--}

   procedure WindowInit;
   begin
      gDrawWindow := GetNewWindow (BASE_RES_ID,
      nil, WindowPtr (-1));
      ShowWindow (gDrawWindow);
      SetPort (gDrawWindow);
   end;
```

`MainLoop` starts by using the current time (in seconds since January 1, 1904) to seed the Mac random number generator. The QuickDraw global `randSeed` is used as a seed by the random number generator. If you didn't modify `randSeed`, you'd generate the same patterns every time you ran Mondrian.

Next, `gFillColor` is initialized to `blackColor`. This means that the first oval will be filled with black. Next, `MainLoop` loops, waiting for the press of the mouse button. In the loop, `DrawRandomRect` is called, first generating a random rectangle inside the window, then drawing an oval in the rectangle. Next, `gFillColor` is flipped from black to white or from white to black.

```
{------------------->      MainLoop    <--}

    procedure MainLoop;
    begin
        GetDateTime(randSeed);
        gFillColor := blackColor;

        while (not Button) do
            begin
                DrawRandomRect;
                if (gFillColor  = blackColor) then
                        gFillColor := whiteColor
                else
                        gFillColor := blackColor
            end;
    end;
```

DrawRandomRect controls the actual drawing of the ovals in the
window. RandomRect generates a random rectangle inside
gDrawWindow, ForeColor sets the current drawing color to
gFillColor, and PaintOval paints the oval inside the generated
rectangle.

```
{------------------> DrawRandomRect <--}

    procedure DrawRandomRect;
        var
            myRect: Rect;
    begin
        RandomRect(myRect, gDrawWindow);
        ForeColor(gFillColor);
        PaintOval(myRect);
    end;
```

RandomRect sets up the rectangle to be used in drawing the oval.
Each of the four sides of the rectangle is generated as a random
number between the right and left (or top and bottom, as
appropriate) sides of the input parameter, boundingWindow.

The notation myRecordPtr^.myField refers to the field
myField in the record pointed to by myRecordPtr.

Every window data structure has a field named portRect that
defines the boundary of the content region of the window. Because
boundingWindow is a pointer to a window data structure, you use
boundingWindow˘.portRect to access this rectangle.

```
{------------------->        RandomRect  <--}

    procedure RandomRect (var myRect: Rect;
        boundingWindow: WindowPtr);
    begin
       myRect.left := Randomize
          (boundingWindow^.portRect.right -
          boundingWindow^.portRect.left);
       myRect.right :=
Randomize(boundingWindow^.portRect.right -
          boundingWindow^.portRect.left);
       myRect.top :=
Randomize(boundingWindow^.portRect.bottom -
          boundingWindow^.portRect.top);
       myRect.bottom :=
Randomize(boundingWindow^.portRect.bottom -
          boundingWindow^.portRect.top);
    end;
```

Randomize takes an integer argument and returns a positive
integer greater than or equal to 0 and less than the argument. This is
accomplished via a call to the Random Toolbox utility, which returns
a random number in the range –32,767 through 32,767. You may find
Randomize helpful in your own applications.

```
{------------------->        Randomize  <--}

    function Randomize (range: INTEGER): INTEGER;
       var
          rawResult: LONGINT;
    begin
       rawResult := Random;
       rawResult := abs(rawResult);

       Randomize := (rawResult * range) div 32768;
    end;
```

Variants

Here are some variants of Mondrian. The first few change the shape
of the repeated figure in the window from ovals to some other shapes.

Your first new shape will be a rectangle. This one's easy: Just
change the PaintOval call to PaintRect. When you run this, you
should see rectangles instead of ovals.

Your next new shape is the rounded rectangle. You'll need two new parameters for `PaintRoundRect`: `ovalWidth` and `ovalHeight`. Declare them as constants, each with a value of 20:

```
const
   OVAL_WIDTH = 20;
   OVAL_HEIGHT = 20;
```

Now, change the `DrawRandomRect` routine, as follows:

```
{---------------->  DrawRandomRect   <--}

   procedure DrawRandomRect;
      var
         myRect: Rect;
   begin
      RandomRect(myRect, gDrawWindow);
      ForeColor(gFillColor);
      PaintRoundRect( myRect, OVAL_WIDTH,
                      OVAL_HEIGHT );
   end;
```

You should see something like Figure 3.32 if you run this variation.

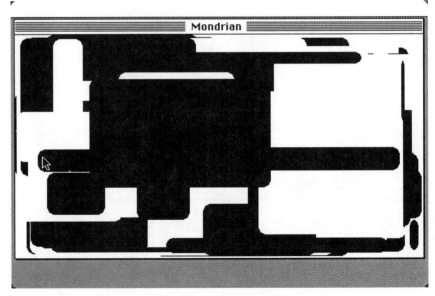

Figure 3.32   Mondrian with rounded rectangles.

Instead of filling the rectangles, try using `FrameRoundRect` to draw just the outline of your rectangles:

```
{---------------> DrawRandomRect   <--}

    procedure DrawRandomRect;
        var
            myRect: Rect;
    begin
        RandomRect(myRect, gDrawWindow);
        ForeColor(gFillColor);
        FrameRoundRect( myRect, OVAL_WIDTH,
                    OVAL_HEIGHT );
    end;
```

The framing function is more interesting if you change the state of your pen: The default setting for your pen is a size of 1 pixel wide by 1 pixel tall, and the pattern is black. Change it by modifying `WindowInit` as follows:

```
{---------------> WindowInit <--}

    procedure WindowInit;
    begin
        gDrawWindow := GetNewWindow(BASE_RES_ID,
                    nil, WindowPtr(-1));
        ShowWindow(gDrawWindow);
        SetPort(gDrawWindow);

        PenSize( PEN_WIDTH, PEN_HEIGHT );
        PenPat( gray );
    end;
```

Here, you changed the pen pattern to `gray`. Don't forget to declare the constants `PEN_WIDTH` and `PEN_HEIGHT`. We used values of 10 and 2, respectively (Figure 3.33).

While you're at it, try using `InvertRountRect` instead of `FrameRoundRect`. `InvertRoundRect` will invert the pixels in its rectangle. The arguments are handled in the same way (Figure 3.34).

Next, try using `FrameArc` in place of `InvertRoundRect`. `FrameArc` requires two new parameters. The first defines the arc's starting angle, and the second defines the size of the arc. Both are expressed in degrees (Figure 3.35).

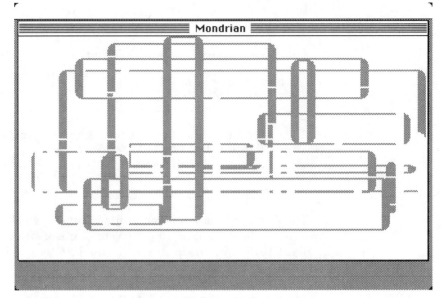

Figure 3.33   Mondrian with framed, gray, rounded rectangles.

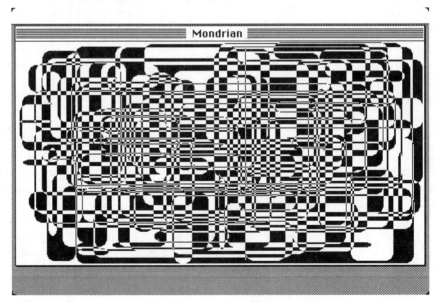

Figure 3.34   Mondrian with inverted, rounded rectangles.

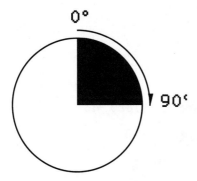

Figure 3.35   Figuring your arc.

Change `DrawRandomRect` as follows:

```
{---------------->  DrawRandomRect   <--}

    procedure DrawRandomRect;
        var
            myRect: Rect;
    begin
        RandomRect(myRect, gDrawWindow);
        ForeColor(gFillColor);
        FrameArc( myRect, START_DEGREES,
                ARC_DEGREES );
    end;
```

Don't forget to declare the constants `START_DEGREES` and `ARC_DEGREES`. Try using values of `0` and `270`. Experiment with `PaintArc` and `InvertArc`.

We'll do one final variation with QuickDraw. This one is useful only for people with color monitors. If you change the `ForeColor` arguments in `MainLoop`, you can see colored filled ovals (or whatever your program is currently producing). Modify your `MainLoop` routine as follows:

```
{----------------->        MainLoop    <--}

    procedure MainLoop;
    begin
       GetDateTime(randSeed);
       gFillColor := redColor;

       while (not Button) do
          begin
             DrawRandomRect;
             if ( gFillColor = redColor) then
                   gFillColor := yellowColor
             else
                   gFillColor := redColor
          end;
    end;
```

The following colors have already been defined for you:
blackColor, whiteColor, redColor, yellowColor,
greenColor, blueColor, cyanColor, and magentaColor. These
colors are part of Classic QuickDraw—the original, eight-color
QuickDraw model that was part of the original Macintosh. Newer
Macs support a new version of QuickDraw called Color QuickDraw,
which supports millions of different colors. (Color QuickDraw is
discussed in Volume II of the *Mac Primer*.) The programs you write
using the eight colors of Classic QuickDraw will run on any Macintosh
(even the Macintosh II Series).

The next program demonstrates how to load QuickDraw picture
resources and draw them in a window.

ShowPICT

ShowPICT will take your favorite artwork (in the form of a PICT
resource) and display it in a window. You can create a PICT resource
by copying any graphic to the Mac clipboard and then pasting it into
a ResEdit PICT window. We'll show you how a little later on. We
copied our artwork from the scrapbook that comes with the
Macintosh System disks.

ShowPICT is made up of four distinct steps:

1. Load a resource window, show it, and make it the current port.
2. Load a resource picture.
3. Center the picture, then draw it in the window.
4. Wait for the mouse button to be pressed.

Resources

Start by creating a new folder, called ShowPICT, in the Development folder. Next, using ResEdit, create a new resource file called ShowPICT.π.rsrc in the ShowPICT folder. Create a WIND resource using the specifications shown in Figure 3.36. Select **Get Resource Info** from the **Resource** menu, set the resource ID of your new WIND to 400, and check the **Purgeable** checkbox.

Next, create your PICT resource. Close the WIND list, so you get back to the main ShowPICT.π.rsrc window. Pull down the menu and select the **Scrapbook**. Find a picture that is of type PICT—you can tell by checking the label on the bottom right of the **Scrapbook** window—pull down the **Edit** menu, and select **Copy**. Now close the **Scrapbook** and return to ResEdit. Finally, select Paste; ResEdit will create a PICT resource and put the picture in it. Figure 3.37 details this process.

Now, click on your picture and select **Get Resource Info** from the **Resource** menu. Set the resource ID of the PICT to 400 and set the **Purgeable** checkbox. Finally, quit ResEdit, saving your changes to ShowPICT.π.rsrc.

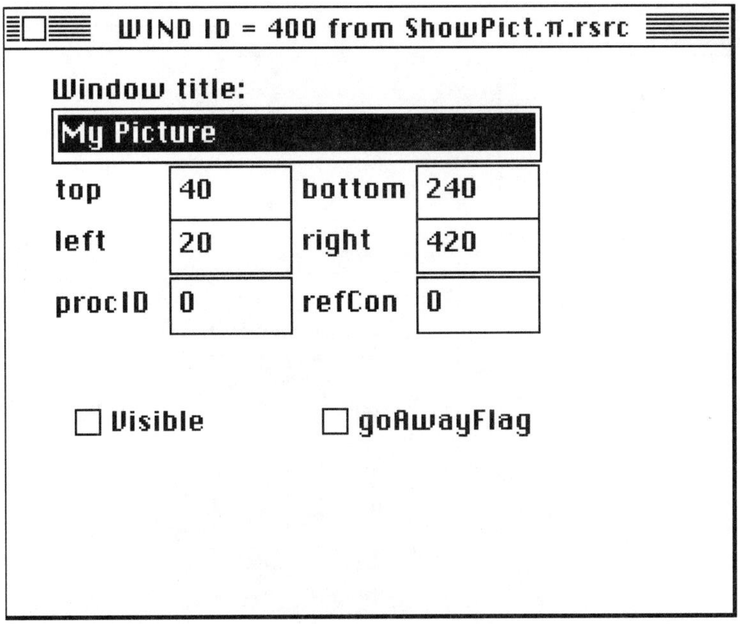

Figure 3.36 WIND parameters for ShowPICT.

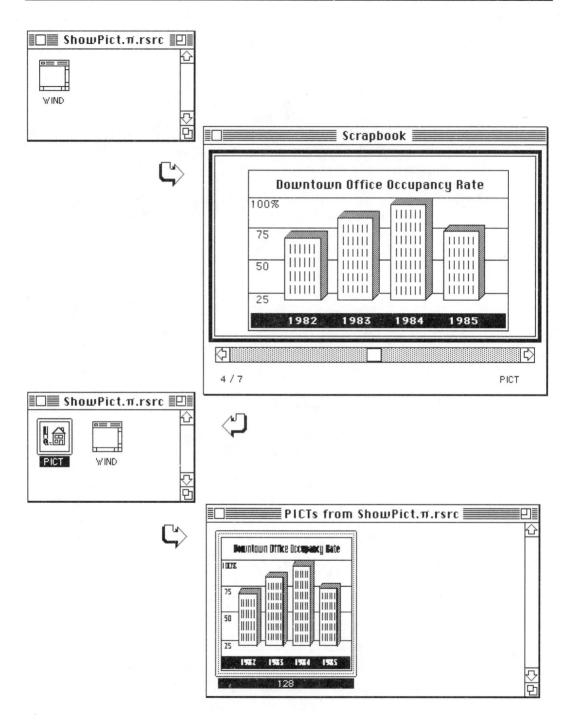

Figure 3.37   PICT from ScrapBook to resource file.

Next, go into THINK Pascal and create a new project called ShowPICT.π inside the ShowPICT folder. Select **New** from the **File** menu and enter the following code:

```
program ShowPICT;
   const
      BASE_RES_ID = 400;

   var
      gPictureWindow: WindowPtr;


{----------------->    CenterPict    <--}

   procedure CenterPict (thePicture: PicHandle; var myRect:
Rect);
      var
         windRect, pictureRect: Rect;
   begin
      windRect := myRect;
      pictureRect := thePicture^^.picFrame;
      myRect.top := (windRect.bottom - windRect.top -
      (pictureRect.bottom - pictureRect.top)) div 2 +
      windRect.top;
      myRect.bottom := myRect.top + (pictureRect.bottom -
         pictureRect.top);
      myRect.left := (windRect.right - windRect.left -
      (pictureRect.right - pictureRect.left)) div 2 +
      windRect.left;
      myRect.right := myRect.left + (pictureRect.right -
         pictureRect.left);
   end;


{----------------->    DrawMyPicture    <--}

   procedure DrawMyPicture (pictureWindow: WindowPtr);
      var
         myRect: Rect;
         thePicture: PicHandle;
   begin
      myRect := pictureWindow^.portRect;

      thePicture := GetPicture(BASE_RES_ID);

      CenterPict(thePicture, myRect);
      DrawPicture(thePicture, myRect);
   end;
```

```
{----------------->      WindowInit  <--}

   procedure WindowInit;
   begin
      gPictureWindow := GetNewWindow(BASE_RES_ID, nil,
                                     WindowPtr(-1));
      ShowWindow(gPictureWindow);
      SetPort(gPictureWindow);
   end;


{----------------->      ShowPICT    <--}

begin
   WindowInit;
   DrawMyPicture(gPictureWindow);

   while (not Button) do
      begin
      end;
end.
```

Running ShowPICT

After you've finished typing in the code, save the file as ShowPICT.p and add it to your project. Next, select **Run Options...** from the **Run** menu and tell THINK Pascal to use ShowPICT.π.rsrc as the resource file. Next, select **Go** from the **Run** menu. If everything went well, you should get something like Figure 3.38. Your PICT should appear in your window. If it does not, check the resource ID of your PICT. Did your PICT make it into ShowPICT.π.rsrc? Check your WIND resource and your code for typos.

Walking Through the ShowPICT Code

The constant BASE_RES_ID performs the same function as it does in earlier programs. The global gPictureWindow acts as a pointer to the PICT window.

```
   program ShowPICT;
       const
           BASE_RES_ID = 400;

       var
           gPictureWindow: WindowPtr;
```

Figure 3.38 Running ShowPICT.

ShowPICT's main routine sets up the window, draws the picture, and then waits for the mouse click before exiting.

```
{------------------>        ShowPICT    <--}

begin
    WindowInit;
    DrawMyPicture(gPictureWindow);

    while (not Button) do
        begin
        end;
end.
```

The window initialization code is the same as that in Hello2. (If you are cutting and pasting, note that the variable name has changed to gPictureWindow.)

```
{----------------->          WindowInit      <--}

   procedure WindowInit;
   begin
       gPictureWindow := GetNewWindow(BASE_RES_ID,
               nil, WindowPtr(-1));
       ShowWindow(gPictureWindow);
       SetPort(gPictureWindow);
   end;
```

DrawMyPicture sets up a Rect the size of pictureWindow
(the window passed in as a parameter). Then, it loads the picture with
a call to GetPicture. Next, it passes thePicture and the Rect to
CenterPict. Finally, DrawMyPicture draws thePicture in the
newly centered Rect.

```
{----------------->          DrawMyPicture     <--}

   procedure DrawMyPicture (pictureWindow:
                                  WindowPtr);
       var
       myRect: Rect;
       thePicture: PicHandle;
   begin
       myRect := pictureWindow^.portRect;

       thePicture := GetPicture(BASE_RES_ID);

       CenterPict(thePicture, myRect);
       DrawPicture(thePicture, myRect);
   end;
```

CenterPict takes a PicHandle (thePicture) and a Rect
(myRect) as input parameters. thePicture is a **handle** to the
picture to be centered in myRect. CenterPict constructs a new
Rect the size of thePicture, centering it in the original Rect.

A **Handle** is a specialized pointer to a pointer. Handles are a necessary part of the Mac's memory management scheme. They allow the Macintosh Memory Manager to relocate blocks of memory as it needs to, without disturbing your program.

If you have a pointer to an object, when the Mac moves the object in memory, your pointer becomes invalid. If, however, you use a Handle (pointer to a pointer) to an object, then, when the Mac moves the object, as long as it updates the pointer, your handle remains valid.

We'll show you some of the basics of using handles, but we won't spend a lot of time on them (there's an entire chapter dedicated to handles and related topics in Volume II of the *Mac Primer*). You should read up on handles and the Mac memory management scheme because eventually you'll want to write code that takes advantage of handles.

In `ShowPICT`, we declare a handle to a picture (pointer to a pointer to a picture). We then set the handle to the value returned by `GetPicture`:

```
    thePicture : PicHandle;
    thePicture := GetPicture( BASE_RES_ID );
```

Like most of the Toolbox functions that return handles, `GetPicture` actually allocates the memory for the picture itself, as well as the memory for the pointer to the picture. The great thing about handles is that you hardly know they're there.

In this program, `CenterPict` is used to center a picture in a window. The original `Rect` is copied into the local variable `windRect`. Then, the picture's frame `Rect` is copied to the local variable `pictureRect`. Finally, each field in the original `Rect` is modified, based on the corresponding fields in `windRect` and `pictureRect`. For example, `myRect.top` is adjusted to become the new top of the picture.

`CenterPict` is a useful utility routine. You'll be seeing it again in other chapters.

```
{------------------>        CenterPict     <--}
procedure CenterPict (thePicture: PicHandle; var myRect: Rect);
                var
                windRect, pictureRect: Rect;
```

```
begin
    windRect := myRect;
    pictureRect := thePicture^^.picFrame;
    myRect.top := (windRect.bottom - windRect.top -
                (pictureRect.bottom - pictureRect.top))
                div 2 + windRect.top;
    myRect.bottom := myRect.top + (pictureRect.bottom -
                                pictureRect.top);
    myRect.left := (windRect.right - windRect.left -
                (pictureRect.right - pictureRect.left))
                div 2 + windRect.left;
    myRect.right := myRect.left + (pictureRect.right -
                                pictureRect.left);
end;
```

Variants

Try using different pictures, either from the Scrapbook or from MacPaint or some other Macintosh graphics program. With a little experimentation, you should be able to copy and paste these files into your resource file. In Chapter 4, you'll see an enhanced ShowPICT program.

Screen Saver: The Flying Line Program

The Flying Line is the last program in the QuickDraw chapter. Although it does demonstrate the use of line drawing in QuickDraw, we included it mostly because it's fun. The Flying Line draws a set of lines that move across the screen with varying speeds, directions, and orientations. The program can be used as a screen saver (we even show you how to hide the menu bar).

The Flying Line program consists of three steps:

1. Set up the Flying Line window.
2. Initialize the Flying Line data structure, drawing it once.
3. Redraw the Flying Line inside a loop until a mouse click occurs.

Create a folder called Flying Line inside your Development folder. Flying Line needs no resources, so go into THINK Pascal and create a new project called Flying Line.π inside the Flying

Line folder. Select **New** from the **File** menu to open a new window for the Flying Line source code:

```
program FlyingLine;
    const
        NUM_LINES = 50;
        NIL_STRING = '';
        NIL_TITLE = '';
        VISIBLE = TRUE;
        NO_GO_AWAY = FALSE;
        NIL_REF_CON = 0;

    type
        IntPtr = ^INTEGER;

    var
        gLineWindow: WindowPtr;
        gLines: array[1..NUM_LINES] of Rect;
        gDeltaTop, gDeltaBottom: INTEGER;
        gDeltaLeft, gDeltaRight: INTEGER;
        gOldMBarHeight: INTEGER;
        gMBarHeightPtr: IntPtr;


{------------------->        DrawLine          <--}

    procedure DrawLine (i: INTEGER);
    begin
        MoveTo(gLines[i].left, gLines[i].top);
        LineTo(gLines[i].right, gLines[i].bottom);
    end;


{------------------->        RecalcLine         <--}

    procedure RecalcLine (i: INTEGER);
    begin
        gLines[i].top := gLines[i].top + gDeltaTop;
        if ((gLines[i].top < gLineWindow^.portRect.top) |
            (gLines[i].top > gLineWindow^.portRect.bottom)) then
            gDeltaTop := gDeltaTop * (-1);
        gLines[i].top := gLines[i].top + 2 * gDeltaTop;

        gLines[i].bottom := gLines[i].bottom + gDeltaBottom;
        if ((gLines[i].bottom < gLineWindow^.portRect.top) |
            (gLines[i].bottom > gLineWindow^.portRect.bottom))
                then
            gDeltaBottom := gDeltaBottom * (-1);
        gLines[i].bottom := gLines[i].bottom + 2 * gDeltaBottom;
```

```
        gLines[i].left := gLines[i].left + gDeltaLeft;
        if ((gLines[i].left < gLineWindow^.portRect.left) |
            (gLines[i].left > gLineWindow^.portRect.right))
            then
          gDeltaLeft := gDeltaLeft * (-1);
        gLines[i].left := gLines[i].left + 2 * gDeltaLeft;

        gLines[i].right := gLines[i].right + gDeltaRight;
        if ((gLines[i].right < gLineWindow^.portRect.left) |
            (gLines[i].right > gLineWindow^.portRect.right))
            then
          gDeltaRight := gDeltaRight * (-1);
        gLines[i].right := gLines[i].right + 2 * gDeltaRight;
    end;


{----------------->          MainLoop          <--}

    procedure MainLoop;
        var
            i: INTEGER;

    begin
        while (not Button) do
            begin
                DrawLine(NUM_LINES);
                for i := NUM_LINES downto 2 do
                    gLines[i] := gLines[i - 1];
                RecalcLine(1);
                DrawLine(1);
                gMBarHeightPtr^ := gOldMBarHeight;
            end;
    end;


{----------------->          Randomize          <--}

    function Randomize (range: INTEGER): INTEGER;
        var
            rawResult: LONGINT;

    begin
        rawResult := Random;
        rawResult := abs(rawResult);

        Randomize := (rawResult * range) div 32768;
    end;
```

```
{------------------->          RandomRect          <--}

    procedure RandomRect (var myRect: Rect; boundingWindow:
                        WindowPtr);
    begin
       myRect.left := Randomize(boundingWindow^.portRect.right -
                            boundingWindow^.portRect.left);
       myRect.right := Randomize(boundingWindow^.portRect.right -
                            boundingWindow^.portRect.left);
       myRect.top := Randomize(boundingWindow^.portRect.bottom -
                            boundingWindow^.portRect.top);
       myRect.bottom := Randomize(boundingWindow^.portRect.bottom -
                            boundingWindow^.portRect.top);
    end;


{------------------->          LinesInit          <--}

    procedure LinesInit;
       var
          i: INTEGER;

    begin
       gDeltaTop := 3;
       gDeltaBottom := 3;
       gDeltaLeft := 2;
       gDeltaRight := 6;

       HideCursor;
       GetDateTime(randSeed);
       RandomRect(gLines[1], gLineWindow);
       DrawLine(1);

       for i := 2 to NUM_LINES do
          begin
             gLines[i] := gLines[i - 1];
             RecalcLine(i);
             DrawLine(i);
          end;
    end;


{------------------->          WindowInit          <--}

    procedure WindowInit;
       var
          totalRect, mBarRect: Rect;
          mBarRgn: RgnHandle;
```

```
begin
   gMBarHeightPtr := IntPtr($baa);
   gOldMBarHeight := gMBarHeightPtr^;
   gMBarHeightPtr^ := 0;
   gLineWindow := NewWindow(nil, screenBits.bounds,
      NIL_TITLE, VISIBLE, plainDBox, WindowPtr(-1),
      NO_GO_AWAY, NIL_REF_CON);
   SetRect(mBarRect, screenBits.bounds.left,
      screenBits.bounds.top, screenBits.bounds.right,
      screenBits.bounds.top + gOldMBarHeight);
   mBarRgn := NewRgn;
   RectRgn(mBarRgn, mBarRect);
   UnionRgn(gLineWindow^.visRgn, mBarRgn,
      gLineWindow^.visRgn);
   DisposeRgn(mBarRgn);
   SetPort(gLineWindow);
   FillRect(gLineWindow^.portRect, black);
         { Change black to ltGray, }
   PenMode(patXor); {   <-- and comment out this line  }
end;


{------------------>          FlyingLine         <--}

begin
   WindowInit;
   LinesInit;
   MainLoop;
end.
```

Running Flying Line

After you've finished typing in the code, save it as Flying Line.p.
Add the file to the project. Select **Go** from the **Run** menu. If
everything went well, you should see something like Figure 3.39. The
window will be completely black except for the flying line; the menu
bar should be hidden. Now, let's take a look at the code.

Figure 3.39   Running Flying Line.

Walking Through the Flying Line Code

Most of Flying Line should be familiar to you. The biggest change is in `WindowInit`, where you create a window from scratch and hide the menu bar. We won't go into exhaustive detail on the Flying Line algorithm, because it has little to do with the Toolbox. This one's just for fun!

`NUM_LINES` defines the number of lines in the Flying Line. The rest of the constants will be used as parameters later on in the program.

```
program FlyingLine;
    const
        NUM_LINES = 50;
        NIL_STRING = '';
        NIL_TITLE = '';
        VISIBLE = TRUE;
        NO_GO_AWAY = FALSE;
        NIL_REF_CON = 0;
```

The type `IntPtr` is used to declare the global `gMBarHeightPtr` as a pointer to an `INTEGER`. `gMBarHeightPtr` will give us access to one of the Macintosh System's internal globals.

> Although it's important to understand the technique involved here, it is even more important to remember that it's generally bad practice to mess with system globals. They are likely to change when new system versions come out. We use system globals in Flying Line because Apple doesn't make it easy to hide the menu bar, mainly because they don't want programmers to do it. Because a screen saver has to hide the menu bar, Flying Line uses a system global. Make sure you have good reasons to use system globals.

```
type
      IntPtr = ^INTEGER;
```

`gDeltaBottom`, `gDeltaTop`, `gDeltaLeft`, and `gDeltaRight` are all tuning parameters. Play around with their values until you get just the right Flying Line.

The Flying Line is drawn in `gLineWindow`. The array `gLines` holds all of the individual lines in the Flying Line. Finally, `gOldMBarHeight` saves the menu bar height when you start, so you can restore it when the application quits.

```
var
    gLineWindow: WindowPtr;
    gLines: array[1..NUM_LINES] of Rect;
    gDeltaTop, gDeltaBottom: INTEGER;
    gDeltaLeft, gDeltaRight: INTEGER;
    gOldMBarHeight: INTEGER;
    gMBarHeightPtr: IntPtr;
```

Flying Line sets up its window, initializes its line data structure, then enters the main loop.

```
{---------------> FlyingLine <--}

begin
    WindowInit;
    LinesInit;
    MainLoop;
end.
```

The window initialization code for Flying Line is unusual because the window itself is unusual. Normally, Mac programs display a menu bar. Flying Line, however, will not. Flying Line hides the menu bar (by making it 0 pixels tall) and creates a window that covers the entire screen.

The call to `NewWindow` is an alternative to `GetNewWindow`. `GetNewWindow` creates a window using the information specified in a `WIND` resource. `NewWindow` also creates a window, but gets the window specifications from its parameter list:

```
FUNCTION NewWindow( wStorage : Ptr; boundsRect
                    : Rect;
    title : Str255; visible : BOOLEAN; procID :
            INTEGER;
    behind : WindowPtr; goAwayFlag : BOOLEAN;
    refCon : LONGINT ) : WindowPtr;
```

The program next specifies the size of the window as a `Rect`, using the QuickDraw global `screenBits.bounds` to create a window the size of the current screen.

```
{------------------->          WindowInit <--}

    procedure WindowInit;
        var
            totalRect, mBarRect: Rect;
            mBarRgn: RgnHandle;

    begin
        gMBarHeightPtr := IntPtr($baa);
        gOldMBarHeight := gMBarHeightPtr^;
        gMBarHeightPtr^ := 0;
        gLineWindow := NewWindow(nil,
screenBits.bounds, NIL_TITLE,
    VISIBLE, plainDBox, WindowPtr(-1),
    NO_GO_AWAY, NIL_REF_CON);
```

The next bit of code is tricky. It calls `SetRect` to create a rectangle surrounding the normal menu bar. Next, it uses this `Rect` to create a new region, and then it adds this region to the visible region of your window. As a result of this hocus-pocus, your window can overlap the menu bar, taking up the entire screen. If this makes you uncomfortable, don't panic. The call to `NewWindow` is normally all you'll need in your applications. This extra code is just here to allow your window to obscure the menu bar.

```
SetRect(mBarRect, screenBits.bounds.left,
    screenBits.bounds.top,
    screenBits.bounds.right,
    screenBits.bounds.top + gOldMBarHeight);
mBarRgn := NewRgn;
RectRgn(mBarRgn, mBarRect);
UnionRgn(gLineWindow^.visRgn, mBarRgn,
    gLineWindow^.visRgn);
DisposeRgn(mBarRgn);
```

Next, the program calls `SetPort` so that all its drawing will occur in `gLineWindow`. Then, it fills the window with the black pattern. It sets the `PenMode` to `patXor`. Try some other pen modes, too. We suggest changing the second `FillRect` parameter to `ltGray`, and commenting out the call to `PenMode`.

```
SetPort(gLineWindow);
FillRect(gLineWindow^.portRect, black);
        { Change black to ltGray,}
PenMode(patXor); {<-- and comment out this line} end;
```

Don't be fooled by imitations. The second parameter to `FillRect` is a pattern, not a color. These are the fill patterns you normally associate with the paint bucket in MacPaint, not the eight colors of Classic QuickDraw. You can experiment with colors by using a call to `PaintRect`.

`LinesInit` starts off by hiding the cursor. Next, it seeds the random number generator with the current date (*à la* Mondrian). Finally, it generates the first line of the Flying Line, draws it, and then generates the rest of the lines and draws them.

```
{-------------->     LinesInit    <--}

procedure LinesInit;
    var
        i: INTEGER;

begin
    gDeltaTop := 3;
    gDeltaBottom := 3;
    gDeltaLeft := 2;
    gDeltaRight := 6;
```

```
HideCursor;
GetDateTime(randSeed);
RandomRect(gLines[1], gLineWindow);
DrawLine(1);

for i := 2 to NUM_LINES do
    begin
        gLines[i] := gLines[i - 1];
        RecalcLine(i);
        DrawLine(i);
    end;
end;
```

You've seen this routine in Mondrian:

```
{-------------->      Randomize   <--}

function Randomize (range: INTEGER): INTEGER;
    var
        rawResult: LONGINT;

begin
    rawResult := Random;
    rawResult := abs(rawResult);

    Randomize := (rawResult * range) div 32768;
end;
```

Another routine you've seen before:

```
{-------------->      RandomRect <--}

procedure RandomRect (var myRect: Rect;
boundingWindow: WindowPtr);
begin
    myRect.left :=
Randomize(boundingWindow^.portRect.right -
    boundingWindow^.portRect.left);
    myRect.right :=
Randomize(boundingWindow^.portRect.right -
    boundingWindow^.portRect.left);
    myRect.top :=
Randomize(boundingWindow^.portRect.bottom -
    boundingWindow^.portRect.top);
    myRect.bottom :=
Randomize(boundingWindow^.portRect.bottom -
boundingWindow^.portRect.top);
end;
```

DrawLine draws line number i, using the coordinates stored in gLines[i]. Because the pen mode is set to patXor, this may actually have the effect of erasing the line.

```
{-------------->  DrawLine     <--}

   procedure DrawLine (i: INTEGER);
   begin
      MoveTo(gLines[i].left, gLines[i].top);
      LineTo(gLines[i].right, gLines[i].bottom);
   end;
```

The ReCalc routine determines where to draw the next line:

```
{-------------->  RecalcLine  <--}

   procedure RecalcLine (i: INTEGER);
   begin
      gLines[i].top := gLines[i].top + gDeltaTop;
      if ((gLines[i].top < gLineWindow^.portRect.top) |
         (gLines[i].top > gLineWindow^.portRect.bottom)) then
      gDeltaTop := gDeltaTop * (-1);
      gLines[i].top := gLines[i].top + 2 * gDeltaTop;

      gLines[i].bottom := gLines[i].bottom + gDeltaBottom;
      if ((gLines[i].bottom < gLineWindow^.portRect.top) |
         (gLines[i].bottom > gLineWindow^.portRect.bottom)) then
         gDeltaBottom := gDeltaBottom * (-1);
      gLines[i].bottom := gLines[i].bottom + 2 * gDeltaBottom;

      gLines[i].left := gLines[i].left + gDeltaLeft;
      if ((gLines[i].left < gLineWindow^.portRect.left) |
         (gLines[i].left > gLineWindow^.portRect.right)) then
         gDeltaLeft := gDeltaLeft * (-1);
      gLines[i].left := gLines[i].left + 2 * gDeltaLeft;

      gLines[i].right := gLines[i].right + gDeltaRight;
      if ((gLines[i].right < gLineWindow^.portRect.left) |
         (gLines[i].right > gLineWindow^.portRect.right)) then
         gDeltaRight := gDeltaRight * (-1);
      gLines[i].right := gLines[i].right + 2 * gDeltaRight;
   end;
```

MainLoop sets up a loop that falls through when the mouse button is pressed. At the end of the loop, the menu bar height is restored. If you don't do this, you won't be able to pick from the menu bar when you exit the program. Oops! (If by accident, you don't reset the menu bar height, it won't come back when you return to the Finder. Restart your Mac to reset the menu bar height.)

Inside the loop, the program erases and redraws each line in the Flying Line. It erases lines by redrawing them in exactly the same position. Because the pen mode is set to `patXor`, this has the effect of erasing the line. Thus, the first call to `DrawLine` in `MainLoop` erases the last line in the `gLines` array. This simulates the line moving across the screen.

```
{-------------->     MainLoop    <--}

procedure MainLoop;
    var
        i: INTEGER;

begin
    while (not Button) do
        begin
            DrawLine(NUM_LINES);
            for i := NUM_LINES downto 2 do
                gLines[i] := gLines[i - 1];
            RecalcLine(1);
            DrawLine(1);
            gMBarHeightPtr^ := gOldMBarHeight;
        end;
end;
```

In Review

Whew! We've covered a lot in this chapter. We examined the basic Macintosh drawing model, QuickDraw, and showed you how to use many of the QuickDraw Toolbox routines. Now, you can read the QuickDraw chapter in *Inside Macintosh,* Volume I. Experiment with the programs presented here and try using some of the other QuickDraw routines. They're just as easy to use as the ones already covered.

We've also shown you different ways of using resources in your programs. If you haven't already, you may want to skip ahead to Chapter 8, to read up on ResEdit. Build a stand-alone application; then add an icon to your application. Chapter 8 will show you how.

Now that you understand how the Mac draws to the screen, you're ready to learn how the Mac interacts with users. Chapter 4 looks at the Event Manager—the manager that stage-directs operations.

4

The Event Mechanism

In this chapter, we'll tell you about events, the Mac's mechanism for describing the user's actions to your application. When the mouse button is clicked, a key is pressed, or a disk is inserted in the floppy drive, the operating system lets your program know by queueing an event.

ONE OF THE basic differences between programming on the Mac and programming on other machines lies in the use of events. **Events** are descriptions of actions taken by the user of your application. For example, when a key is pressed on the keyboard, a piece of the Mac operating system (known as the **Event Manager**) captures some important information about the keystroke in an `EventRecord`. As more keys are pressed, more `EventRecords` are created and joined to the first, forming the **event queue** (Figure 4.1).

The event queue is a FIFO (First In, First Out) queue: The event at the front of the queue is the oldest event in the queue. As you can see in Figure 4.1, different types of events live together in the same event queue. All events, no matter what their type, pass under the watchful eye of the Event Manager.

The Event Manager gets events from many different sources, queues them up, and passes them to your application, one at a time.

Your application can get at this information by retrieving `EventRecords` from the event queue, one at a time. If the retrieved `EventRecord` describes a keystroke, your application can jump to some code that handles keystrokes. If it describes the pressing of the mouse button, it can jump to some code that deals with the mouse button. Let's look at the mouse button case.

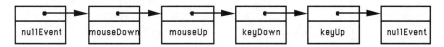

Figure 4.1 The event queue.

When the mouse button is pressed, what does it mean to the application? Maybe the user wants to select from a menu. Maybe the user is clicking on a window to bring it to the front, or has clicked in a scroll bar to move up or down in the document. One way to tell what the user is trying to accomplish is to compare the location of the mouse when its button was pressed with the locations of the menu bar, the windows on the screen, scroll bars, and so on.

If the user clicked in the menu bar, you can jump to some code that handles menu selection. If the user clicked on a scroll bar, you can jump to the scroll bar handling routine.

Event Types

The Event Manager handles 15 distinct events (V:249):

- **nullEvent**: This event is queued when the Event Manager has no other events to report.

- **mouseDown**: mouseDown events are queued whenever the mouse button is pressed. Note that the button doesn't have to be released for the event to qualify as a mouseDown.

- **mouseUp**: mouseUps are queued whenever the mouse button is released.

- **keyDown**: keyDown events are queued every time a key is pressed. Like mouseDowns, keyDowns are queued even if the key has not yet been released.

- **keyUp**: keyUps are queued whenever a key is released.

- **autoKey**: autoKey events are queued when a key is held down for a certain length of time (beyond the autoKey threshhold). Usually, an autoKey event is treated just like a keyDown.

- **updateEvt**: updateEvts are queued whenever a window needs redrawing. They are always associated with a specific window. This usually happens when a window is partially obscured and the obstruction is moved, revealing more of the window, as shown in Figure 4.2.

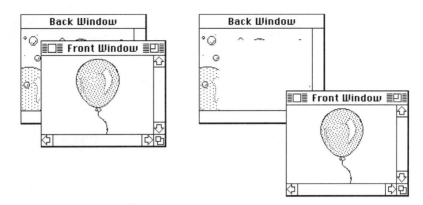

Figure 4.2 FrontWindow is moved down and to the right, generating an updateEvt for BackWindow.

The autoKey threshhold represents the time from the first keyDown until the autoKey event is generated. The default value is 16 ticks (sixtieths of a second). The autoKey rate is the interval between autoKeys. The default autoKey rate is 4 ticks. The user can change both of these from the control panel desk accessory. Their values are stored in the system global variables KeyThresh and KeyRepThresh.

- **diskEvt**: diskEvts are queued whenever a disk is inserted into a disk drive, or when an action is taken that requires that a volume be mounted. Don't worry too much about these right now. We'll tell you how to deal with disks and files in Chapter 7.

- **activateEvt**: activateEvts are also associated with windows. An activateEvt is queued whenever a window is activated (made to come to the front) or deactivated (replaced as the frontmost window by another window). As you might guess, activateEvts always occur in pairs (Figures 4.3 and 4.4).

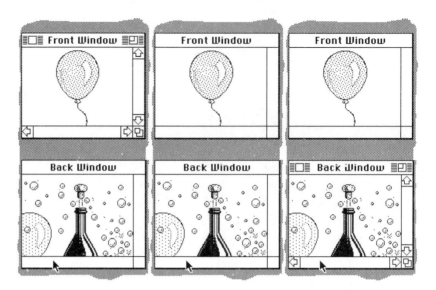

Figure 4.3 BackWindow is selected, an activateEvt is generated to deactivate FrontWindow, and an activateEvt is generated to activate BackWindow.

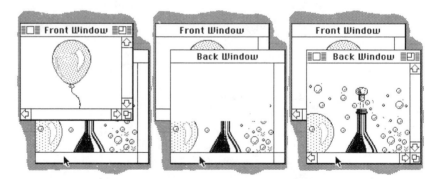

Figure 4.4 BackWindow is selected, an activateEvt is generated to deactivate FrontWindow, an activateEvt is generated to activate BackWindow, and an updateEvt is generated to redraw BackWindow.

- **networkEvt**: `networkEvts` are <u>no</u> <u>longer</u> <u>used</u>.

- **driverEvt**: `driverEvts` are used by device drivers to signal special conditions. They (and device drivers in general) are beyond the scope of this book.

- **app1Evt, app2Evt, app3Evt**: These events are defined by your application and can be used for just about anything. With the advent of MultiFinder, the use of application-defined events is discouraged.

- **app4Evt (Suspend/Resume/mouseMoved events)**: The `app4Evt` has been reserved by Apple for use with MultiFinder. MultiFinder will post an `app4Evt` just before it moves your application into the background (suspends it) and just after it brings your application back to the foreground (resumes it). You can also set your application up to receive `mouseMoved` events. `mouseMoved` events are posted when the user moves the cursor outside a predefined region (such as a text-editing window) or back in again. When your application receives a `mouseMoved` event, it can change the cursor to one appropriate to that region. We'll discuss `app4Evts` in more detail later in the chapter.

The next section discusses a new Macintosh application model based on event handling. After that, we'll present `EventTutor`, this book's first event-based application.

The Structure of a Mac Program: New and Improved

In Chapter 3, we presented a very primitive Macintosh application model that looked like this:

```
program MyApp;
begin
    DoInitialization;
    DoPrimeDirective;

    while (not Button) do
        begin
        end;
end.
```

First, the application model takes care of any program-specific initialization, such as loading windows or pictures from the resource file. Next, the model performs its "prime directive." In the case of ShowPict, the prime directive was drawing a PICT in the main application. Finally, the model waits for the mouse button to be pressed.

There is one basic problem with this model: It does not reflect reality. Macintosh applications do not exit when the mouse button is pressed. Clearly, we need a better model.

The new model does things a little differently:

MODEL for Ap Program

(g— = global VAR)

```
program MyApp;
    var
        gTheEvent : EventRecord;
        gDone : BOOLEAN;

procedure HandleEvent;
    var
        gotOne : BOOLEAN;
begin
    if waitNextEventIsInstalled then
        gotOne := WaitNextEvent( everyEvent, gTheEvent,
                                 sleepValue, mouseRgn )
    else
        begin
            SystemTask;
            gotOne := GetNextEvent( everyEvent, gTheEvent );
        end;

    if gotOne then
        case gTheEvent.what of
            mouseDown:
                        .
                        .
                        .
                    if ... then
                        gDone := TRUE;
            end;
end;

procedure MainLoop;
begin
    gDone := FALSE;
    while gDone = FALSE do
        HandleEvent;
end;
```

New Systems

OLD Systems

```
begin
    DoInitialization;
    MainLoop
end.
```

This model starts off the same way as the basic model, with calls to the initialization routines. The difference lies in the call of `MainLoop`. `MainLoop` contains the **main event loop**. The main event loop is part of the basic structure of any Mac program. Each time through the loop, your program retrieves an event from the event queue and processes the event.

> As we'll explain in the next section, events are retrieved in one of two ways. If the Toolbox routine `WaitNextEvent` is available (it isn't on older systems), it gets called. If `WaitNextEvent` isn't available, the older Toolbox routine, `GetNextEvent`, is used.

Eventually, some event will cause `HandleEvent` to set `gDone` to `TRUE`, and the program will end. This might be the result of a `mouseDown` in the menu bar (selecting **Quit** from the **File** menu) or a `keyDown` (typing the key sequence ⌘**Q**). You can design your ending conditions any way you like.

> We should warn you that Apple has a little-known squad of mercenaries who seek out and eradicate applications that don't meet the user interface guidelines. Beware!

Retrieving Events from the Event Queue

In the early days of Mac programming, the Toolbox routine `GetNextEvent` was used to retrieve events from the event queue. `GetNextEvent` worked just fine until MultiFinder was introduced. MultiFinder is a set of operating system functions that extend the capabilities of the Macintosh. Most notably, MultiFinder allows the Macintosh to run several applications at the same time.

Figure 4.5 shows MultiFinder in action. Notice that only one application at a time can be "in front." Notice also that the Finder is one of the applications under MultiFinder. To bring an application to the front, you click on one of its windows.

One of the nicest features of MultiFinder is its ability to run applications in the background. Figure 4.5 shows the alarm clock desk accessory running in the background. Even though the alarm clock window is not the frontmost window, the time is updated because the alarm clock is running in the background.

`GetNextEvent` was written with the Finder in mind. When MultiFinder was introduced, Apple added a new routine to the Toolbox to handle things like background processing more efficiently. The new routine is called `WaitNextEvent`.

As you'll see when you get to the EventTutor application, your programs should always check to see if `WaitNextEvent` is installed before they call it. If it isn't installed, the program should call `GetNextEvent` instead.

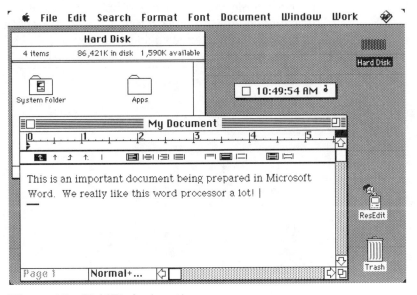

Figure 4.5 MultiFinder in action.

You may have noticed a call to the Toolbox routine `SystemTask` just before the call to `GetNextEvent` in the new application model. `SystemTask` gives the Mac operating system a slice of time to do things like update desk accessories (such as the alarm clock), process AppleTalk messages, and so on. `WaitNextEvent` has this functionality built right in, so an accompanying call to `SystemTask` isn't necessary.

Calling GetNextEvent and WaitNextEvent

The first parameter to both `GetNextEvent` and `WaitNextEvent` is an event mask, used to limit the types of events your program will handle. Figure 4.6 contains a list of predefined event mask constants. If your program needs only `mouseDowns` and `keyDowns`, for example, you might use the following call:

```
gTheEvent : EventRecord;
gotOne : BOOLEAN;

gotOne := GetNextEvent( (mDownMask |
        keyDownMask), &gTheEvent );
```

```
const
    mDownMask = 2;
    mUpMask = 4;
    keyDownMask = 8;
    keyUpMask = 16;
    autoKeyMask = 32;
    updateMask = 64;
    diskMask = 128;
    activMask = 256;
    networkMask = 1024;
    driverMask = 2048;
    app1Mask = 4096;
    app2Mask = 8192;
    app3Mask = 16384;
    app4Mask = -32768;
    everyEvent = -1;
```

Figure 4.6 Event masks predefined in THINK Pascal.

In this case, `GetNextEvent` will return only `mouseDown`, `keyDown`, or `nullEvent` information. `nullEvents` are never masked out. To handle all possible events, pass the predefined constant `everyEvent` as the `eventMask` parameter. *Inside Mac* recommends that you use `everyEvent` as your event mask in all your applications unless there's a specific reason not to do so.

The second parameter to both `GetNextEvent` and `WaitNextEvent` is `gTheEvent`, declared as an `EventRecord`. Here's the type definition of an `EventRecord`:

```
type EventRecord = RECORD
     what : INTEGER;
     message : LONGINT;
     when : LONGINT;
     where : Point;
     modifiers : INTEGER
end;
```

Here's a description of each of the fields:

- **what**: What type of event just occurred? Was it a `nullEvent`, `keyDown`, `mouseDown`, or `updateEvt`?

- **message**: This part of the `EventRecord` is specific to the event. For `keyDown` events, the `message` field contains information about the actual key that was pressed (the key code) and the character that key represents (the character code). For `activateEvts` and `updateEvts`, the message field contains a pointer to the affected window.

- **when**: When did the event occur? The Event Manager tells you, in ticks since the system was last started up (or booted).

- **where**: Where was the mouse when the event occurred? This information is specified in global coordinates (see Chapter 3).

- **modifiers**: This part of the `EventRecord` describes the state of the mouse button and the modifier keys (the Shift, Option, Control, Command, and Caps Lock keys) when the event occurred.

The third parameter to `WaitNextEvent` is the `sleep` parameter. `sleep` is a `LONGINT` specifying the amount of time (in clock ticks) your application is willing not to perform any background processing while waiting for an event. *Inside Mac* recommends a value of at least `60` for `sleep`, to be truly MultiFinder friendly. If you pass a value of `0` for `sleep`, you're telling `WaitNextEvent` to hog the processor. Pretty unfriendly!

The fourth parameter to `WaitNextEvent` is the `mouseRgn` parameter, used to simplify cursor tracking. If your application requires different cursors, depending on which part of the screen the cursor is in, the `mouseRgn` parameter is essential. With it, you can specify the screen region appropriate to the current cursor. Whenever the mouse is outside that region, the Event Manager queues up a `mouseMoved` event. When your program receives the `mouseMoved` event, the region is changed to reflect the new mouse position and is passed as a parameter to the next `WaitNextEvent` call.

Calling `WaitNextEvent` with a `sleep` value of `60` and a `mouseRgn` of `nil` is exactly equivalent to calling `SystemTask` and `GetNextEvent`. The programs presented throughout the rest of the book will do just that. The *Programmer's Guide to MultiFinder* includes a program that uses the `sleep` and `mouseRgn` parameters of `WaitNextEvent`. The program was written by Apple's Macintosh Technical Support Group. The *Programmer's Guide to MultiFinder*, published by Apple, is essential reading for writing truly MultiFinder-friendly applications.

Handling Events

Once you've retrieved an event via `GetNextEvent` or `WaitNextEvent`, your next step is to process it. If the event is a `mouseDown` event, figure out where the mouse was clicked. If the mouse was clicked in a window's drag region, as shown in Figure 4.7, you can call a Toolbox routine that handles window dragging. If the event is an `updateEvt`, you might want to redraw the window pointed to by `theEvent.message`.

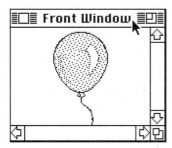

Figure 4.7 Arrow cursor in window's drag region.

If this sounds vague, don't worry. The concept of events may be unfamiliar to you, but it will be easier to understand once you see it in operation. This chapter's program, EventTutor, will show you how all types of events are handled.

EventTutor: The Return of ShowPICT

Back in Chapter 3, we presented a program called ShowPICT, which works like this:

- It loads a resource window, shows it, and makes it the current port.
- It loads a resource picture.
- It centers the picture, then draws it in the window.
- It waits for the mouse button to be pressed.

The new program presented here, EventTutor, adds a main event loop to this model. EventTutor also adds a new window, gEventWindow. gEventWindow keeps a scrolling list of events, updated as the events occur. You can also drag both windows around the screen, as well as zoom and grow the picture window. EventTutor works like this:

- It loads the picture and event windows from the resource file, shows them, and makes gEventWindow the current port.
- It loads a picture from the resource file.
- While (gdone = FALSE), EventTutor handles events.
- As events occur, it displays their names in gEventWindow, then calls the appropriate routines to process them.

Setting Up the EventTutor Project

Start by creating a new project folder, called EventTutor, inside your Development folder. Use ResEdit to create a new file inside this folder called EventTutor.π.rsrc.

Resources

Create three new resources. The first two are WINDs with resource IDs 400 and 401. Figure 4.8 shows the specifications for these WINDs. When you set the resource IDs in the Get Resource Info window, make sure you make both WINDs purgeable.

The third resource is a PICT. In our example, we use the champagne picture from the standard Scrapbook, but feel free to use any PICT you'd like. Make sure you change the resource ID to 400 and make the resource purgeable.

Next, start up THINK Pascal. When prompted, create a new project inside the EventTutor folder. Call the project EventTutor.π. Select **New** from the **File** menu to create a new source code file. Type the code listing in and save the file inside the EventTutor folder as EventTutor.p. Select **Add Window** from the **Project** menu to add EventTutor.p to the project. The Project window should now look like Figure 4.9.

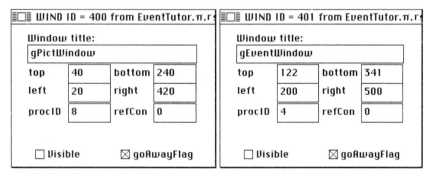

Figure 4.8 EventTutor WIND specifications.

Macintosh Programming Primer

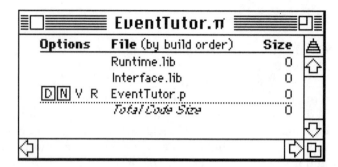

Figure 4.9 EventTutor's project window.

Here's the source code for `EventTutor.p`:

```
program EventTutor;
    const
        BASE_RES_ID = 400;
        LEAVE_WHERE_IT_IS = FALSE;
        NORMAL_UPDATES = TRUE;
        SLEEP = 60;
        WNE_TRAP_NUM = $60;
        UNIMPL_TRAP_NUM = $9F;
        SUSPEND_RESUME_BIT = $0001;
        ACTIVATING = 1;
        RESUMING = 1;
        TEXT_FONT_SIZE = 12;
        DRAG_THRESHOLD = 30;
        MIN_WINDOW_HEIGHT = 50;
        MIN_WINDOW_WIDTH = 50;
        SCROLL_BAR_PIXELS = 15;
        ROWHEIGHT = 15;
        LEFTMARGIN = 10;
        STARTROW = 0;
        HORIZONTAL_OFFSET = 0;

    var
        gPictWindow, gEventWindow : WindowPtr;
        gDone, gWNEImplemented: BOOLEAN;
        gTheEvent: EventRecord;
        gCurRow, gMaxRow: INTEGER;
        gSizeRect: Rect;


{---------------> CenterPict <--}
    procedure CenterPict (thePicture: PicHandle;
                          var myRect: Rect);
        var
```

```
            windRect, pictureRect: Rect;

    begin
        windRect := myRect;
        pictureRect := thePicture^^.picFrame;
        myRect.top := (windRect.bottom - windRect.top -
            (pictureRect.bottom -
            pictureRect.top)) div 2 + windRect.top;
        myRect.bottom := myRect.top + (pictureRect.bottom -
            pictureRect.top);
        myRect.left := (windRect.right - windRect.left -
            (pictureRect.right -
            pictureRect.left)) div 2 + windRect.left;
        myRect.right := myRect.left + (pictureRect.right -
            pictureRect.left);
    end;


{---------------> DrawMyPicture  <--}

    procedure DrawMyPicture (drawingWindow: WindowPtr);
        var
            drawingClipRect, myRect: Rect;
            oldPort: GrafPtr;
            tempRgn: RgnHandle;
            thePicture: PicHandle;
    begin
        GetPort(oldPort);
        SetPort(drawingWindow);
        tempRgn := NewRgn;
        GetClip(tempRgn);
        EraseRect(drawingWindow^.portRect);
        DrawGrowIcon(drawingWindow);

        drawingClipRect := drawingWindow^.portRect;
        drawingClipRect.right := drawingClipRect.right -
            SCROLL_BAR_PIXELS;
        drawingClipRect.bottom := drawingClipRect.bottom -
            SCROLL_BAR_PIXELS;
        myRect := drawingWindow^.portRect;

        thePicture := GetPicture(BASE_RES_ID);
        CenterPict(thePicture, myRect);
        ClipRect(drawingClipRect);
        DrawPicture(thePicture, myRect);

        SetClip(tempRgn);
        DisposeRgn(tempRgn);
        SetPort(oldPort);
    end;
```

```
{--------------> HandleMouseDown    <--}

    procedure HandleMouseDown;
        var
            whichWindow: WindowPtr;
            thePart: INTEGER;
            windSize: LONGINT;
            oldPort: GrafPtr;
    begin
        thePart := FindWindow(gTheEvent.where, whichWindow);
        case thePart of
            inSysWindow:
                SystemClick(gTheEvent, whichWindow);
            inDrag:
                DragWindow(whichWindow, gTheEvent.where,
                    screenBits.bounds);
            inContent:
                if whichWindow <> FrontWindow then
                    SelectWindow(whichWindow);
            inGrow:
                begin
                    windSize := GrowWindow(whichWindow,
                        gTheEvent.where, gSizeRect);
                    if (windSize <> 0) then
                        begin
                            GetPort(oldPort);
                            SetPort(whichWindow);
                            EraseRect(whichWindow^.portRect);
                            SizeWindow(whichWindow,
                                LoWord(windSize),
                                HiWord(windSize),
                                NORMAL_UPDATES);
                            InvalRect(whichWindow^.portRect);
                            SetPort(oldPort);
                        end;
                end;
            inGoAway:
                gDone := TRUE;
            inZoomIn, inZoomOut:
                if TrackBox(whichWindow, gTheEvent.where,
                    thePart) then
                    begin
                        GetPort(oldPort);
                        SetPort(whichWindow);
                        EraseRect(whichWindow^.portRect);
                        ZoomWindow(whichWindow, thePart,
                            LEAVE_WHERE_IT_IS);
                        InvalRect(whichWindow^.portRect);
                        SetPort(oldPort);
                    end;
        end;
    end;
```

```
{----------------> ScrollWindow    <--}

    procedure ScrollWindow;
        var
            tempRgn: RgnHandle;
    begin
        tempRgn := NewRgn;
        ScrollRect(gEventWindow^.portRect, HORIZONTAL_OFFSET, -
                    ROWHEIGHT, tempRgn);
        DisposeRgn(tempRgn);
    end;


{----------------> DrawEventString    <--}

    procedure DrawEventString (s: Str255);
    begin
        if (gCurRow > gMaxRow) then
            ScrollWindow
        else
            gCurRow := gCurRow + ROWHEIGHT;

        MoveTo(LEFTMARGIN, gCurRow);
        DrawString(s);
    end;


{----------------> HandleEvent<--}

    procedure HandleEvent;
        var
            gotOne: BOOLEAN;
    begin
        if gWNEImplemented then
            gotOne := WaitNextEvent(everyEvent, gTheEvent,
                        SLEEP, nil)
        else
            begin
                SystemTask;
                gotOne := GetNextEvent(everyEvent, gTheEvent);
            end;

        if gotOne then
            case gTheEvent.what of
                nullEvent:
                    begin
                        {   DrawEventString('nullEvent');        }
                {Uncomment the previous line for a burst of flavor! }
                    end;
                mouseDown:
```

```
            begin
                DrawEventString('mouseDown');
                HandleMouseDown;
            end;
        mouseUp:
            DrawEventString('mouseUp');
        keyDown:
            DrawEventString('keyDown');
        keyUp:
            DrawEventString('keyUp');
        autoKey:
            DrawEventString('autoKey');
        updateEvt:
            if (WindowPtr(gTheEvent.message) =
            gPictWindow) then
                begin
DrawEventString('updateEvt: gPictWindow');
BeginUpdate(WindowPtr (gTheEvent.message));
DrawMyPicture(WindowPtr (gTheEvent.message));
EndUpdate(WindowPtr (gTheEvent.message));
                end
            else
                begin
                    DrawEventString('updateEvt:
                                    gEventWindow');
                    BeginUpdate(WindowPtr
                                (gTheEvent.message));
{   We won't handle updates to gEventWindow,   }
{   but we still need to empty the gEventWindow}
{   Update Region so the Window Manager will stop}
{   queing UpdateEvts. We do this with calls to }
{   BeginUpdate and EndUpdate.                  }
                    EndUpdate(WindowPtr
                                (gTheEvent.message));
                end;
        diskEvt:
            DrawEventString('diskEvt');
        activateEvt:
            if (WindowPtr(gTheEvent.message) =
                        gPictWindow) then
                begin
                    DrawGrowIcon(WindowPtr
                                (gTheEvent.message));
                    if (BitAnd(gTheEvent.modifiers,
                        activeFlag) = ACTIVATING) then
            DrawEventString
                ('activateEvt: activating gPictWindow')
                    else
            DrawEventString
                ('activateEvt: deactivating gPictWindow');
                end
```

```
    else
        begin
            if (BitAnd(gTheEvent.modifiers, activeFlag) =
                ACTIVATING) then
        DrawEventString('activateEvt: activating gEventWindow')
    else
        DrawEventString('activateEvt: deactivating gEventWindow');
            end;
                networkEvt:
                    DrawEventString('networkEvt');
                driverEvt:
                    DrawEventString('driverEvt');
                app1Evt:
                    DrawEventString('app1Evt');
                app2Evt:
                    DrawEventString('app2Evt');
                app3Evt:
                    DrawEventString('app3Evt');
                app4Evt:
                    if (BitAnd(gTheEvent.message,
                        SUSPEND_RESUME_BIT) = RESUMING) then
                        DrawEventString('Resume event')
                    else
                        DrawEventString('Suspend event');
            end;
    end;


{---------------->  MainLoop   <--}

    procedure MainLoop;
    begin
        gDone := FALSE;
        gWNEImplemented := (NGetTrapAddress(WNE_TRAP_NUM,
ToolTrap) <> NGetTrapAddress(UNIMPL_TRAP_NUM, ToolTrap));

        while gDone = FALSE do
            HandleEvent;
    end;


{---------------->  SetUpSizeRect <--}

    procedure SetUpSizeRect;
    begin
        gSizeRect.top := MIN_WINDOW_HEIGHT;
        gSizeRect.left := MIN_WINDOW_WIDTH;

        gSizeRect.bottom := 32767;
        gSizeRect.right := 32767;
    end;
```

```
{---------------> SetupEventWindow   <--}

    procedure SetupEventWindow;
        var
            eventRect: Rect;
            fontNum: INTEGER;
    begin
        eventRect := gEventWindow^.portRect;
        gMaxRow := eventRect.bottom - eventRect.top -
                    ROWHEIGHT;
        gCurRow := STARTROW;

        SetPort(gEventWindow);
        GetFNum('monaco', fontNum);
        TextFont(fontNum);
        TextSize(TEXT_FONT_SIZE);
    end;


{---------------> WindowInit <--}

    procedure WindowInit;
    begin
        gPictWindow := GetNewWindow(BASE_RES_ID, nil,
                        WindowPtr(-1));
        gEventWindow := GetNewWindow(BASE_RES_ID + 1, nil,
                        WindowPtr(-1));
        SetupEventWindow;

        ShowWindow(gEventWindow);
        ShowWindow(gPictWindow);
    end;


{---------------> EventTutor <--}

begin
    WindowInit;
    SetUpSizeRect;

    MainLoop;
end.
```

Running EventTutor

Now that your source code is entered, you're ready to run EventTutor. Select **Go** from the **Run** menu. THINK Pascal will start the compilation process. If you run into any compilation errors, try the debugging tips discussed in Appendix C.

Once the code compiles, you'll be asked whether you'd like to **Save changes before running**. Click **Yes**, and EventTutor will execute. Figure 4.10 shows EventTutor running under the Finder.

EventTutor puts two windows up on the screen. The background window, `gPictWindow`, should display your centered picture. The foreground window, `gEventWindow`, should already list three events:

- `activateEvt: activating gEventWindow`: This event was caused by your code. You called `SelectWindow`, requesting that `gEventWindow` be made the frontmost window.

- `updateEvt: gEventWindow`.

- `updateEvt: gPictWindow`: The Window Manager automatically generates an `updateEvt` for each of its windows as soon as they are drawn for the first time.

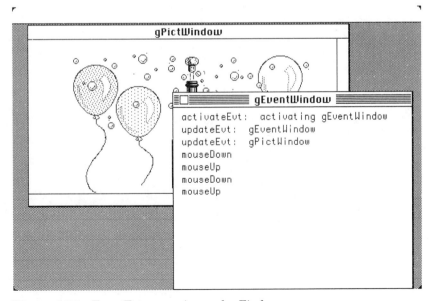

Figure 4.10   EventTutor running under Finder.

When the Window Manager draws a window, it first draws the window frame. The window frame includes the border, as well as a drag region, zoom box, and a go-away box, if appropriate. Next, it generates an `updateEvt` for the window, so the application will draw the window contents.

Press the mouse button in the middle of `gEventWindow`. Now release the mouse button. You should see first a `mouseDown` and then a `mouseUp` event. Press the mouse button in the `gEventWindow` drag region (you'll see a `mouseDown`) and drag `gEventWindow` down and to the right. You should see an `updateEvt` for `gPictWindow`. This is because you just revealed a piece of `gPictWindow` that was covered before. The reason you didn't get a `mouseUp` when you released the mouse button is that the `mouseUp` was swallowed by the system routine that handles window dragging. This is also true when you zoom or resize a window.

In Chapter 3 we established a standard of starting our program global variable names with the letter g. This led to `WindowPtrs` named `gEventWindow` and `gPictWindow`. For clarity, we used these variable names as titles for their respective windows, but we could have used any titles we wanted.

Click the mouse button in the center of `gPictWindow`. You should see a `mouseDown`, a deactivate event for `gEventWindow`, an activate event for `gPictWindow`, an update event for `gPictWindow` (assuming that you clicked on it while it was still at least partially covered by `gEventWindow`), and a `mouseUp` (Figure 4.11).

There is no such thing as a `deactivateEvt`. We use the term **deactivate event** to indicate an `activateEvt` with the `activeFlag` cleared. There's an example of this in the code.

Try clicking in `gPictWindow`'s zoom box. The picture should remain centered in `gPictWindow`. Click in the zoom box again. `gPictWindow` should return to its original size. Resize `gPictWindow`

Figure 4.11 After g P i c t W i n d o w is activated.

by clicking and dragging the grow box. Keep an eye on g E v e n t W i n d o w. As you create events, review the list of event types presented earlier in the chapter. All these features were made possible by the use of events. Now, let's take a look at the code.

Writing MultiFinder-friendly applications is not extremely difficult. We will try to get the basics across in our code, but we again recommend that you read the *Programmer's Guide to MultiFinder* from Apple for a thorough background (oops!) in MultiFinder programming.

For starters, you can get your program to handle suspend and resume events by creating a resource of type S I Z E. For a quick tutorial in creating a S I Z E resource, check out Chapter 8. Once your S I Z E resource is in place, your program will receive suspend and resume events when you send it to the background and bring it back again under MultiFinder.

In Chapter 5, you'll build a clock that runs in the background under MultiFinder, and in Chapter 6, you'll build a countdown timer that also runs in the background under MultiFinder.

Walking Through the EventTutor Code

Figure 4.12 shows EventTutor's software architecture. As we did in Chapter 3, we'll present the routines in the order they are called, not in the order they appear in the source code. Don't worry, we won't leave any of them out.

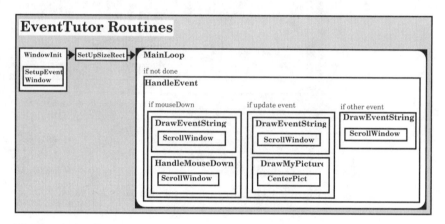

Figure 4.12 EventTutor's architecture.

EventTutor starts with a slew of constants, some of which should be familiar from Chapter 3. We'll discuss each constant as it appears in the code:

```
program EventTutor;
    const
        BASE_RES_ID = 400;
        LEAVE_WHERE_IT_IS = FALSE;
        NORMAL_UPDATES = TRUE;
        SLEEP = 60;
        WNE_TRAP_NUM = $60;
        UNIMPL_TRAP_NUM = $9F;
        SUSPEND_RESUME_BIT = $0001;
        ACTIVATING = 1;
        RESUMING = 1;
        TEXT_FONT_SIZE = 12;
        DRAG_THRESHOLD = 30;
        MIN_WINDOW_HEIGHT = 50;
```

```
MIN_WINDOW_WIDTH = 50;
SCROLL_BAR_PIXELS = 15;
ROWHEIGHT = 15;
LEFTMARGIN = 10;
STARTROW = 0;
HORIZONTAL_OFFSET = 0;
```

gPictWindow and gEventWindow are pointers to the two program windows. gDone is initialized to FALSE and checked each time through the main event loop. If anyone sets gDone to TRUE, the program exits. gWNEImplemented is a BOOLEAN you'll set to TRUE if WaitNextEvent is implemented in the current version of the system. gTheEvent is your EventRecord. Whenever you retrieve an event from the event queue, use gTheEvent to hold the event information. gCurRow holds the vertical pixel coordinate (in gEventWindow's local coordinate system) for drawing the next event string in gEventWindow. gMaxRow is the maximum value allowed for gCurRow. If gCurRow gets bigger than gMaxRow, you'll scroll the text in gEventWindow. gSizeRect controls the size of a window.

```
var
    gPictWindow, gEventWindow : WindowPtr;
    gDone, gWNEImplemented: BOOLEAN;
    gTheEvent: EventRecord;
    gCurRow, gMaxRow: INTEGER;
    gSizeRect: Rect;
```

EventTutor's main procedure starts by calling the window initialization routine. Next, it calls SetUpSizeRect to set up a Rect for resizing our windows (see HandleMouseDown). Finally, EventTutor enters the main event loop by calling MainLoop.

```
{---------------> EventTutor <--}

begin
  WindowInit;
  SetUpSizeRect;

  MainLoop;
end.
```

WindowInit starts by loading the two windows from the resource file. Next, gEventWindow is made the current window, and its attributes are set via the call to SetupEventWindow. Both windows are made visible with ShowWindow.

```
{---------------->    WindowInit <--}

    procedure WindowInit;
    begin
        gPictWindow := GetNewWindow(BASE_RES_ID, nil,
                    WindowPtr(-1));
        gEventWindow := GetNewWindow(BASE_RES_ID + 1,
                    nil, WindowPtr(-1));

        SetupEventWindow;

        ShowWindow(gEventWindow);
        ShowWindow(gPictWindow);
    end;
```

SetupEventWindow sets some of the gEventWindow global variables. eventRect is a placeholder for gEventWindow's boundary rectangle. gMaxRow is set to the maximum row you'll draw into (in gEventWindow's local coordinates). gCurRow holds the current row number (also in local coordinates). gEventWindow's font is set to 12-point Monaco.

```
{---------------->    SetupEventWindow <--}

    procedure SetupEventWindow;
        var
            eventRect: Rect;
            fontNum: INTEGER;
    begin
        eventRect := gEventWindow^.portRect;
        gMaxRow := eventRect.bottom -
                    eventRect.top - ROWHEIGHT;
        gCurRow := STARTROW;

        SetPort(gEventWindow);
        GetFNum('monaco', fontNum);
        TextFont(fontNum);
        TextSize(TEXT_FONT_SIZE);
    end;
```

SetUpSizeRect sets up a resizing rectangle for your call to GrowWindow (see HandleMouseDown). gSizeRect.top defines the minimum number of pixels allowed for window height. gSizeRect.left defines the minimum number of pixels allowed for window width. gSizeRect.bottom defines the maximum number of pixels allowed for window height, and gSizeRect.right defines the maximum number for width. By using a really large value for the maximum width and height, you make sure that your window can be grown as big as the biggest possible monitor.

```
{----------------->      SetUpSizeRect     <--}

     procedure SetUpSizeRect;
     begin
          gSizeRect.top := MIN_WINDOW_HEIGHT;
          gSizeRect.left := MIN_WINDOW_WIDTH;

          gSizeRect.bottom := 32767;
          gSizeRect.right := 32767;
     end;
```

MainLoop starts by initializing gDone. Your application will exit when gDone is set to TRUE. Next, check to see if WaitNextEvent is installed. Essentially, you're checking to see if WaitNextEvent and an unimplemented Toolbox routine have the same address in memory. If so, you know that WaitNextEvent is not implemented in the currently booted system.

> This piece of code has changed several times since WaitNextEvent was first made available. To be on the safe side, get the very latest copy of the *Programmer's Guide to MultiFinder* from APDA. In the back, you'll see an example of a program that reflects Apple's current thinking on WaitNextEvent. By following this example, you'll minimize the chances of your program breaking under future releases of the Mac operating system.

Finally, MainLoop loops on HandleEvent until gDone is set to TRUE.

```
{-----------------> MainLoop    <--}

     procedure MainLoop;
     begin
```

```
                              gDone := FALSE;
                              gWNEImplemented := (NGetTrapAddress
                                              (WNE_TRAP_NUM, ToolTrap) <>
                        NGetTrapAddress(UNIMPL_TRAP_NUM, ToolTrap));

                              while gDone = FALSE do
                                  HandleEvent;
                        end;
```

HandleEvent starts with a call to either WaitNextEvent (if it's implemented), or SystemTask and GetNextEvent. Either way, gTheEvent gets filled with the latest event info. Each event is handled by drawing the name of the event in gEventWindow using DrawEventString. If you uncomment the code in the nullEvent case, you'll get a feel for the number of nullEvents the system generates.

---

nullEvents offer an excellent opportunity to do things like cursor tracking and internal housekeeping. For example, Chapter 5's Timer program updates a clock window when it gets a nullEvent.

```
{----------------> HandleEvent <--}

procedure HandleEvent;
    var
        gotOne: BOOLEAN;
begin
    if gWNEImplemented then
        gotOne := WaitNextEvent(everyEvent,gTheEvent,
                SLEEP,nil)
    else
        begin
            SystemTask;
            gotOne := GetNextEvent(everyEvent,
                    gTheEvent);
        end;

    if gotOne then
        case gTheEvent.what of
            nullEvent:
            begin
            {DrawEventString('nullEvent');}
            {Uncomment the previous line for a burst of flavor}
            end;
```

```
mousedown:
    begin
        DrawEventString('mouseDown');
        HandleMouseDown;
    end;
mouseUp:
    DrawEventString('mouseUp')
keyDown:
    DrawEventString('keyDown')
keyUp:
    DrawEventString('keyUp');
autoKey:
    DrawEventString('autoKey');
```

updateEvts are handled in a special way. First, figure out which window is affected by the updateEvt. The Event Manager stores a pointer to the window requiring updating in gTheEvent.message. By comparing this pointer to gEventWindow and gPictWindow, you can tell which window is for the updateEvt. If the updateEvt is for gPictWindow, draw the appropriate event string into gEventWindow, and then call BeginUpdate.

BeginUpdate tells the Event Manager that you're about to take care of the condition that caused the update. In this case, you'll redraw the picture in gPictWindow using DrawMyPicture. Finally, call EndUpdate to let the Event Manager know you're done.

If you commented out the calls to BeginUpdate and EndUpdate, you'd get an unending stream of updateEvts for gPictWindow. The Event Manager, thinking you were ignoring the ones you'd already retrieved, would just keep generating them. Try it for yourself.

You won't redraw the contents of gEventWindow in response to updateEvts. If you want to add this capability, add a data structure to the program that keeps track of all the strings currently in the window and redraw them whenever an updateEvt occurs for gEventWindow. In this version, you'll just call DrawEventString to add the updateEvt to your list of events, and you'll call BeginUpdate and EndUpdate to let the Window Manager know that you've responded to the updateEvt.

Every window has an update region associated with it. When a previously covered section of a window is uncovered, the uncovered area is added to the window's update region. The Window Manager is constantly on the lookout for windows with nonempty update regions. When it finds one, it generates an `updateEvt` for that window. `BeginUpdate`, as part of its processing, replaces the update region of the specified window with the empty region. Therefore, if you don't call `BeginUpdate`, you'll never empty the window's update region, and the Window Manager will never stop generating `updateEvt`s for the window.

If you have not done so already, you absolutely should read the Window Manager chapter of *Inside Macintosh* (Volume I, Chapter 9). The information presented in the Window Manager chapter is crucial to writing proper Macintosh applications.

Before `BeginUpdate` empties the update region, it replaces the visible region of the window (called the `visRgn`) with the intersection of the `visRgn` and the update region (see Figure 4.13). The application then redraws the contents of the window. If it wants to, it can use this newly cropped `visRgn` to help reduce the amount of drawing necessary. For now, you'll just redraw the entire contents of the window. Finally, `EndUpdate` is called. `EndUpdate` replaces the original version of the `visRgn`. A call to `BeginUpdate` without a corresponding call to `EndUpdate` will leave your window in an unpredictable state.

```
updateEvt:
    if (WindowPtr(gTheEvent.message) = gPictWindow) then
        begin
            DrawEventString('updateEvt: gPictWindow');
            BeginUpdate(WindowPtr(gTheEvent.message));
            DrawMyPicture(WindowPtr(gTheEvent.message));
            EndUpdate(WindowPtr(gTheEvent.message));
        end
    else
        begin
            DrawEventString('updateEvt: gEventWindow');
            BeginUpdate(WindowPtr(gTheEvent.message));
```

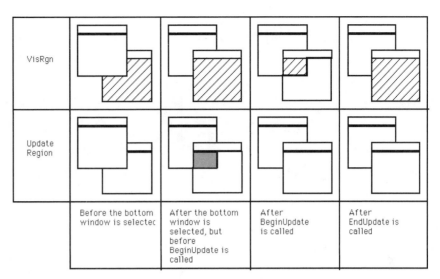

Figure 4.13 `BeginUpdate` in action.

```
{   We won't handle updates to gEventWindow,       }
{   but we still need to empty the gEventWindow    }
{   Update Region so the Window Manager will stop  }
{   queueing UpdateEvts.  We do this with calls to }
{   BeginUpdate and EndUpdate.                      }
            EndUpdate(WindowPtr(gTheEvent.message));
        end;
diskEvt:
    DrawEventString('diskEvt');
```

Another special case is the `activateEvt`. As you did with `updateEvt`, first check to see which window is affected by the `activateEvt`. If the `activateEvt` is for `gPictWindow`, call `DrawGrowIcon` to redraw the grow box and the empty scroll bar areas. The grow box looks different depending on whether the window was activated or deactivated (see Figure 4.14). `DrawGrowIcon` is smart enough to draw the grow box correctly.

Next, check a bit in the modifiers field to see if the event was an activate or a deactivate event. Remember, `activateEvts` usually occur in pairs: First, the frontmost window is deactivated and then the new front window is activated. Also draw the appropriate strings for `networkEvts`, `driverEvts`, and `app1` through `app3Evts`, although you probably won't get any of these.

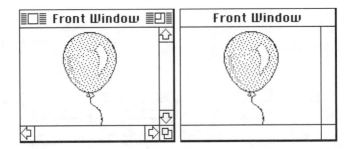

Figure 4.14   The grow box — activated and deactivated.

```
activateEvt:
    if (WindowPtr(gTheEvent.message) = gPictWindow) then
        begin
            DrawGrowIcon(WindowPtr(gTheEvent.message));
            if (BitAnd(gTheEvent.modifiers, activeFlag) =
                ACTIVATING) then
                DrawEventString
                    ('activateEvt: activating gPictWindow')
            else
                DrawEventString
                    ('activateEvt: deactivating gPictWindow');
        end
    else
        begin
            if (BitAnd(gTheEvent.modifiers, activeFlag) =
                ACTIVATING) then
                DrawEventString
                    ('activateEvt: activating gEventWindow')
else
    DrawEventString('activateEvt: deactivating gEventWindow');
end;
        networkEvt:
            DrawEventString('networkEvt');
        driverEvt:
            DrawEventString('driverEvt');
        app1Evt:
            DrawEventString('app1Evt');
        app2Evt:
            DrawEventString('app2Evt');
        app3Evt:
            DrawEventString('app3Evt');
```

If you handle resume and suspend events, you'll get them in the form of an app4Evt. The SUSPEND_RESUME_BIT is set if the event is a resume event and cleared if the event is a suspend event.

Remember, you won't get resume or suspend events if you're not in MultiFinder, or if you haven't put a SIZE resource in your application. For more information, read the discussion of the SIZE resource in Chapter 8.

```
app4Evt:
    if (BitAnd(gTheEvent.message,
        SUSPEND_RESUME_BIT) = RESUMING) then
            DrawEventString('Resume event')
    else
            DrawEventString('Suspend event');
    end;
end;
```

DrawEventString handles the text positioning in gEventWindow. If the QuickDraw pen is near the bottom of the window, ScrollWindow is called. The string is drawn with DrawString. ROWHEIGHT is the height in pixels of a single row of text. LEFTMARGIN is the pixel coordinate (in gEventWindow's local coordinate system) of the left margin of the text in gEventWindow.

```
{----------------> DrawEventString    <--}

    procedure DrawEventString (s: Str255);
    begin
        if (gCurRow > gMaxRow) then
            ScrollWindow
        else
            gCurRow := gCurRow + ROWHEIGHT;

        MoveTo(LEFTMARGIN, gCurRow);
        DrawString(s);
    end;
```

ScrollWindow calls ScrollRect to scroll the pixels in gEventWindow up one row. ScrollRect scrolls the contents of the current GrafPort (in this case, gEventWindow) within the rectangle specified in the first parameter. The rectangle is scrolled to the right by the number of pixels specified in the second parameter and down by the number of pixels specified in the third parameter. Because you specified a negative third parameter, the contents of gEventWindow will be scrolled up.

The last parameter to ScrollRect is a RgnHandle, or a handle to a region. Regions are collections of drawn lines, shapes, and curves, as shown in Figure 4.15 (we discussed them briefly in Chapter 3). After the pixels in the rectangle are scrolled, ScrollRect will fill the vacated area of the rectangle with the GrafPort's background pattern. Then, these new areas are collected into the region handled by RgnHandle (Figure 4.16).

Many programs use this region as a guide to redrawing the window so that they don't have to redraw the entire window. This is especially useful if your window is extremely complex and takes a long time to redraw. In that case, a handle to the window's updateRgn is passed to ScrollRect. Whenever the Window Manager detects that a window's updateRgn is nonempty, the Window Manager generates an updateEvt for the window. As part of its processing, BeginUpdate sets the specified window's updateRgn to the empty region.

Figure 4.15   A region.

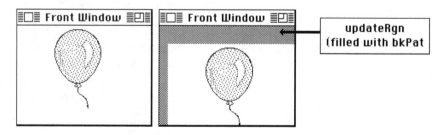

Figure 4.16   FrontWindow's updateRgn after ScrollRect (r, 10, 20, updateRgn).

Because you're not redrawing `gEventWindow` in response to `updateEvts`, you'll use a temporary region (`tempRgn`) as a parameter to `ScrollRect`. Deallocate the `tempRgn`'s memory by calling `DisposeRgn`.

```
{------------------>      ScrollWindow      <--}

    procedure ScrollWindow;
        var
            tempRgn: RgnHandle;
    begin
        tempRgn := NewRgn;
        ScrollRect(gEventWindow^.portRect,  HORIZONTAL_OFFSET,
                   - ROWHEIGHT, tempRgn);
        DisposeRgn(tempRgn);
    end;
```

Handling mouseDown Events

When you receive a `mouseDown` event, the first thing to do is find out which window the mouse was clicked in, by calling the Toolbox routine `FindWindow`. `FindWindow` takes, as input, a point on the screen; it returns, in the parameter `whichWindow`, a `WindowPtr` to the window containing the point. In addition, `FindWindow` returns an integer part code that describes the part of the window in which the point was located.

Once you have your part code, compare it to the predefined Toolbox part codes (you can find a list of legal part codes in I:287). The part code `inSysWindow` means that the mouse was clicked in a system window, very likely a desk accessory. (Because `EventTutor` doesn't support desk accessories, you probably won't see any `inSysWindow` `mouseDowns`, but you will see them in Chapter 5.) The appropriate thing to do in this case is to pass the event and the `WindowPtr` to the system so that it can handle the event. Do this with the Toolbox routine `SystemClick`.

The part code `inDrag` indicates a mouse click in `whichWindow`'s drag region. Handle this with a call to the Toolbox routine `DragWindow`. `DragWindow` wants a `WindowPtr`, the point on the screen where the mouse was clicked, and a boundary rectangle. `DragWindow` will allow the user to drag the window anywhere on the screen as long as it's within the boundary rectangle. Use `screenBits.bounds`, which will let you drag the window pretty much anywhere.

The inContent part code represents the part of the window in which you draw. When you detect a mouse click inContent, call SelectWindow. If the mouse click was not in the frontmost window, SelectWindow deactivates the frontmost window and activates the clicked-in window. A call to SelectWindow usually results in a pair of activateEvts.

```
{----------------> HandleMouseDown        <--}

procedure HandleMouseDown;
    var
        whichWindow: WindowPtr;
        thePart: INTEGER;
        windSize: LONGINT;
        oldPort: GrafPtr;
begin
    thePart := FindWindow(gTheEvent.where, whichWindow);
    case thePart of
        inSysWindow:
            SystemClick(gTheEvent, whichWindow);
        inDrag:
            DragWindow(whichWindow, gTheEvent.where,
                        screenBits.bounds);
        inContent:
            if whichWindow <> FrontWindow then
                SelectWindow(whichWindow);
```

A click in the grow box is handled by a call to GrowWindow, which takes the same arguments as DragWindow but allows the window to grow and shrink instead of move. GrowWindow returns a long integer composed of two words (four bytes) that define the number of pixels the window will grow or shrink in each direction. These words are passed to SizeWindow, causing the window to be resized accordingly. The last parameter to SizeWindow tells the Window Manager to accumulate any newly created content region into the update region. This means that the Window Manager will generate an update event whenever the window is made either taller or wider.

The update event strategy is fairly simple. Use the routine InvalRect to add the entire contents of the window to the window's updateRgn, guaranteeing that an updateEvt will be generated whether or not the window was grown. When you plan your applications, spend some time working out an appropriate update strategy. If redrawing the contents of your windows will be fairly easy and won't take too long, you may want to use the InvalRect approach. However, if the contents of your window are potentially complex (as is true of many drawing and CAD packages), you'll probably want to avoid the call to `InvalRect` and, instead, use the shape of the update region to aid you in updating your window efficiently.

```
inGrow:
    begin
        windSize := GrowWindow(whichWindow,
                    gTheEvent.where, gSizeRect);
        if (windSize <> 0) then
            begin
                GetPort(oldPort);
                SetPort(whichWindow);
                EraseRect(whichWindow^.portRect);
                SizeWindow(whichWindow,
                        LoWord(windSize),
                        HiWord(windSize),
                        NORMAL_UPDATES);
                InvalRect(whichWindow^.portRect);
                SetPort(oldPort);
            end;
    end;
```

A click in the go-away box of either window will result in `gdone`'s being set to `TRUE`. This will cause the program to exit.

```
inGoAway:
    gDone := TRUE;
```

A note from the thought police: A proper Macintosh application would never think of exiting just because someone clicked in the close box of a window! When we get to menu handling in Chapter 5, we'll show you the correct way to Quit.

If the mouse is clicked in the zoom box, respond by calling `TrackBox`, which will return `TRUE` if the mouse button is released while the mouse is still in the zoom box. `ZoomWindow` zooms the window in or out, depending on the part code passed as a parameter. The constant `LEAVE_WHERE_IT_IS` tells `ZoomWindow` to leave the window in front if it was in front when the zoom box was pressed and in back if the window was in back when the zoom box was pressed. Just as you did with `SizeWindow`, call `InvalRect` to guarantee that an `updateEvt` is generated when the window is zoomed in or out.

```
inZoomIn, inZoomOut:
    if TrackBox(whichWindow, gTheEvent.where, thePart)
    then
        begin
            GetPort(oldPort);
            SetPort(whichWindow);
            EraseRect(whichWindow^.portRect);
            ZoomWindow(whichWindow, thePart,
                    LEAVE_WHERE_IT_IS);
            InvalRect(whichWindow^.portRect);
            SetPort(oldPort);
        end;
    end;
end;
```

DrawMyPicture will draw the picture handled by thePicture in the window pointed to by drawingWindow, clipping the drawing so that the scroll bar and grow areas aren't overwritten. Copy drawingWindow's portRect to drawingClipRect, and adjust the left and bottom to clip the two scroll bar areas. Use this new Rect as a parameter to ClipRect so that when you draw your picture, it gets clipped properly.

Start by saving a pointer to the current GrafPort in oldPort so that you can restore it at the end of DrawMyPicture. Next, make drawingWindow the current GrafPort so that the picture will be drawn in the correct window:

```
{---------------> DrawMyPicture        <--}

procedure DrawMyPicture
    (drawingWindow: WindowPtr);
    var
        drawingClipRect, myRect: Rect;
        oldPort: GrafPtr;
        tempRgn: RgnHandle;
        thePicture: PicHandle;
begin
    GetPort(oldPort);
    SetPort(drawingWindow);
```

Then, allocate memory for a region to save a copy of the current clip region. Call GetClip to copy the current clip region into tempRgn. NewRgn allocates enough memory for the minimum-sized region. GetClip resizes the region to accommodate the current clip region.

```
tempRgn := NewRgn;
GetClip(tempRgn);
```

> If you created a region in the shape of a star and used SetClip to set the clip region to your star region, all drawing in that window would be clipped in the shape of a star. You can read more about regions in *Inside Macintosh* (I:141–142 and I:166–167).

Next, erase the whole window with a call to EraseRect. You've just erased the GrowIcon, so call DrawGrowIcon to redraw it. Next, set up your clipping Rect, drawingClipRect, so that it excludes the right and bottom scroll bar areas (and, as a result, the grow area). Then, set myRect to the drawingWindow portRect. You'll use myRect as a parameter to CenterPict, where it will be adjusted to reflect the size of the picture, centered in the input Rect.

At this point, you have not changed the clip region of drawingWindow. You are about to do so. Call ClipRect to set the clipping region to the rectangle defined by drawingClipRect. Now, draw the picture with DrawPicture.

```
EraseRect(drawingWindow^.portRect);
DrawGrowIcon(drawingWindow);

drawingClipRect := drawingWindow^.portRect;
drawingClipRect.right := drawingClipRect.right -
    SCROLL_BAR_PIXELS;
drawingClipRect.bottom := drawingClipRect.bottom
-
    SCROLL_BAR_PIXELS;
myRect := drawingWindow^.portRect;

thePicture := GetPicture(BASE_RES_ID);
CenterPict(thePicture, myRect);
ClipRect(drawingClipRect);
DrawPicture(thePicture, myRect);
```

Finally, reset the ClipRect to the setting saved in tempRgn, release the memory allocated to tempRgn, and set the current GrafPort back to the original setting.

```
    SetClip(tempRgn);
    DisposeRgn(tempRgn);
    SetPort(oldPort);
end;
```

CenterPict is the same as in Chapter 3's ShowPict program:

```
{-----------------> CenterPict      <--}

    procedure CenterPict (thePicture: PicHandle; var myRect:
                          Rect);
        var
            windRect, pictureRect: Rect;

    begin
        windRect := myRect;
        pictureRect := thePicture^^.picFrame;
        myRect.top := (windRect.bottom - windRect.top -
(pictureRect.bottom - pictureRect.top)) div 2 + windRect.top;
        myRect.bottom := myRect.top + (pictureRect.bottom -
pictureRect.top);
        myRect.left := (windRect.right - windRect.left -
(pictureRect.right - pictureRect.left)) div 2 + windRect.left;
        myRect.right := myRect.left + (pictureRect.right -
pictureRect.left);
    end;
```

If you'd like to learn more about event handling, read the Toolbox Event Manager chapter of *Inside Macintosh* (I:241–266).

In Review

At the heart of every Macintosh application is the main event loop. Mac applications are built around this loop. Each pass through the main event loop consists of the retrieval of an event from the event queue and the processing of the event.

The Window Manager plays an important role in the handling of events by generating updateEvts as a means of getting the application to draw (or update) the contents of a window. In addition, Window Manager routines like FindWindow offer a mechanism for linking an event to a window.

An underlying theme of this chapter is a concern for good user interface design. When you set out to build an application, concentrate on the user's view of your application. Use the main event loop in this chapter as your basic skeleton. Then, determine how you will handle each of the different events your user might initiate.

In Chapter 5, you'll learn all about menus. You'll learn how to design and implement regular menus, hierarchical menus, and pop-up menus!

5

Menu
Management

This chapter explains the use of menus in your programs. We'll show you how to install menus via MBAR *and* MENU *resources, and we'll describe the routines available from the Menu Manager. We'll also discuss the best way to support desk accessories and do event handling with menus.*

MACINTOSH MENUS HAVEN'T been the same since the advent of the Mac SE and the Mac II. The classic Mac menu was the pull-down menu—the strip at the top of the screen with options that, when clicked on, displayed the possibilities available to each program (Figure 5.1). The situation has changed for the better with two additional menu types: the **hierarchical** menu and the **pop-up** menu. We'll discuss and illustrate both. But first, let's look at the standard parts of all menu systems.

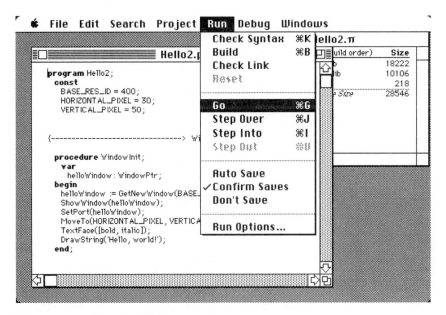

Figure 5.1 Classic pull-down menu.

151

Menu Components

Before we discuss the structure of menus, let's examine the parts of a menu and their functions. Figure 5.2 shows the main parts of Macintosh menus. We'll discuss the parts of the classic menu first, then discuss differences in the new menu types in the section devoted to each type.

The menu bar displayed at the top of the Mac screen is normally 20 pixels high. The font type and size are always the same as the system font. The menu bar height may be changed, using the global variable `MBarHeight`, as we saw in Chapter 3's screen saver program, the Flying Line.

On the menu bar, each list of choices is known as a **menu**. The , **File**, and **Edit** menus are found in most Macintosh applications. Menus are dimmed, or disabled, when none of their options is available.

Menu items are the choices that are available in a given menu. For example, the **File** menu items in MacPaint are shown in Figure 5.3.

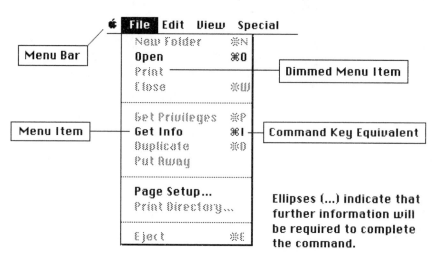

Figure 5.2   Components of Macintosh menus.

```
┌─────────────────────────────┐
│ File                        │
│  New              ⌘N        │
│  Open...          ⌘O        │
│  Close            ⌘W        │
│                             │
│  Save             ⌘S        │
│  Save As...                 │
│  Revert To Saved            │
│                             │
│  Take Snapshot    ⌘Y        │
│  Throw Away Snapshot        │
│                             │
│  Page Setup...              │
│  Print...                   │
│  Print Selection...         │
│                             │
│  Quit             ⌘Q        │
└─────────────────────────────┘
```

Figure 5.3   MacPaint **File** menu.

A menu item is selected if the mouse button is released while the item is still highlighted. Individual items may also be disabled (dimmed). An icon or a check mark can be placed to the left of an item's text. The font and size of the item may be varied; command key equivalents may be placed to the right of a menu item. If a menu item list becomes too long for the screen, which is not uncommon on a compact Mac, the last item that would normally be seen is replaced with a downward-pointing arrow [▼]. If the user drags the mouse cursor down farther, more menu items will scroll into view.

The menu is different in several respects from the other menus in the menu bar. By convention, the first item in the menu is used by your application to display information (an **about box**) about itself. The remaining menu items make up a list of available desk accessories (Figure 5.4).

Let's take a look at the classic pull-down menu and how it works.

Figure 5.4   The menu.

The Pull-Down Menu

The **pull-down menu**, displayed at the top of the screen, is standard for most Macintosh applications. Pull down menus are created by the Menu Manager, which also takes care of drawing the menu items; handling menu selection (as well as command key equivalents); and, finally, restoring the screen when the menu is released. All you have to do is provide the menu information in the form of two resources, MBAR and MENU, and call them with Menu Manager routines. The MBAR resource contains a list of the menus that will be displayed on the menu bar. Each MENU resource contains information about the individual menu items.

On the Mac II, menus and menu items can also be displayed in different colors (V:235).

The Hierarchical Menu

The **hierarchical menu** came on board in 1987, when it was added to the Toolbox. It was needed for the new, complex programs that had become available for the Mac. As more bells and whistles were added to Mac applications, it became harder to find a place for them on the menu bar. Hierarchical menus made it possible to put a whole menu into one item without inconveniencing the user (Figure 5.5).

Menu items that have a hierarchical submenu associated with them have a small right-pointing triangle (▶) on their right side. When the menu item is selected, the hierarchical submenu is displayed. The user then moves the arrow over to the item desired on the hierarchical menu.

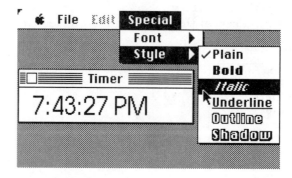

Figure 5.5 Hierarchical menu.

154

The Pop-Up Menu

The **pop-up menu** is the only menu that can be placed anywhere on the screen. This menu is similar to a hierarchical menu, except that pop-up menus can be placed in windows, dialog boxes, even on the desktop.

A pop-up menu appears when a `mouseDown` occurs in an area defined by an application. Once the pop-up menu appears, the user can select an item by moving the cursor up or down (Figure 5.6). When the mouse button is released, the selection is processed. Pop-up menu routines require a little more work than the other menu types, but the additional functionality makes a big difference to your users. We will build a pop-up menu project at the end of this chapter.

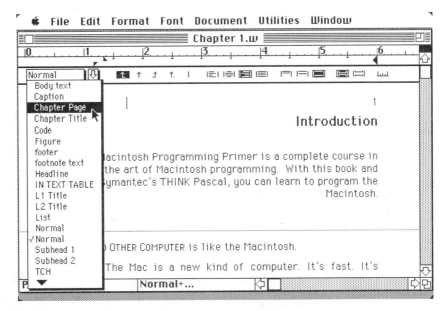

Figure 5.6 Application with pop-up menu (Microsoft Word 4).

Other Kinds of Menus

As with most other parts of the interface, you can make your own unique menus that use the same calls yet look very different from the three kinds of menus already described. Building your own menus, however, is more complicated than using the standards. And because many current applications don't even make good use of pop-up and hierarchical menus, there's no need to rush out and create something new (though if you'd like to, we show you how to create a different type of menu in Volume II of the *Primer*.)

Another type of Macintosh menu that has become quite popular is the **tear-off menu**, which appears to be a regular menu but which can be torn off the menu bar and moved around the screen like a window. Its use in HyperCard and MacPaint 2.0 guaranteed its enshrinement in the System 7 Toolbox. Examine Volume VI of *Inside Macinosh* if you'd like to use tear-off menus.

Menu formats from MS-DOS programs or other non-Macintosh systems are sometimes ported to the Macintosh. A result of this might be something like Figure 5.7. These MS-DOS style menus do not follow the Macintosh user interface guidelines. Don't use them or associate with developers that do.

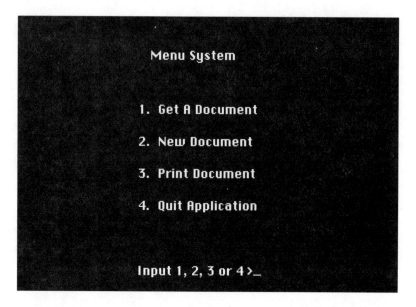

Figure 5.7   MS-DOS menu.

Putting Menus into Your Programs

There are a number of ways to add menus to the applications you create: You can insert menus at the end of the current menu bar (for example, desk accessories like QuickDex or DiskTop), you can build a new set of menus from scratch right inside your program, or you can create your menus in ResEdit and load them into your program. We're going to do it the last way, which makes for clean programming and easy changes without recompiling.

We'll use two menu resources: MENU and MBAR. The MBAR resource contains a list of all of the MENU resources that will be used to draw the menu bar. The MBAR resource also controls the order in which the menus are drawn on the menu bar. Each MENU resource contains a menu title, a list of the menu items, and detailed information about the display of each item.

Now, let's look at **Timer**, our first program with menus.

Timer

Timer displays the current time in a window and refreshes the time once per second. The standard , **File**, and **Edit** menus are supported as well as an additional menu, **Special**. The **Special** menu has two hierarchical submenus, which allow you to change the display's font and style.

Timer's menu supports desk accessories. The **File** menu has a single item, **Quit**. The **Edit** menu is disabled but is provided as a service to desk accessories. Every Macintosh application you write should support the standard **Edit** menu, as it is part of the Macintosh interface standards.

Timer works like this:

1. It loads the MBAR and MENU resources.

2. It initializes the Timer window.

3. It displays the time in the window.

4. It handles events for the menus and the window, refreshing the Timer window once per second.

Setting Up the Project

Create a folder called Timer inside your Development folder; keep your project and resource files inside the folder.

Resources

Now, add the resources you'll need for your Timer program. Create a file in your new Timer folder using ResEdit. Call it Timer.π.rsrc. Then build a WIND with ID = 400, with the specifications as shown in Figure 5.8.

Don't forget to make the WIND resource purgeable. In general, you'll want to make resources in your applications purgeable, so that the Macintosh Memory Manager can do a better job if memory gets tight. However, unlike all other resources discussed in this book, *NEVER* make MENU resources purgeable (I:344). We won't mention making resources purgeable again in this chapter. As you create resources, just click the checkbox in the **Get Resource Info** dialog box.

Next, you need an MBAR resource that lists the resource IDs of the four MENUs that will be part of Timer's menu bar. Create a new MBAR resource inside Timer.π.rsrc. You should see something like Figure 5.9. Click on the row of asterisks and select **Add Resource** from the **Resource** menu. A field for the first menu should appear, as well as a new row of asterisks. Create three more menu fields and fill all four as shown in Figure 5.10. Finally, change the MBAR resource ID to 400. Close the MBAR window. Now, you need to create four MENU resources (with ID numbers from 400 to 403. See?).

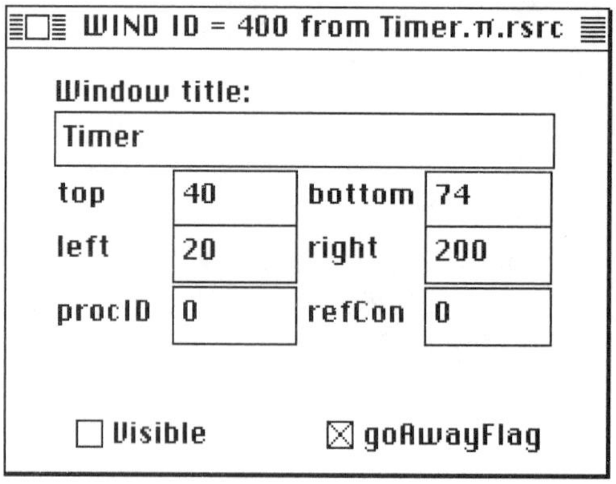

Figure 5.8   Timer WIND specifications.

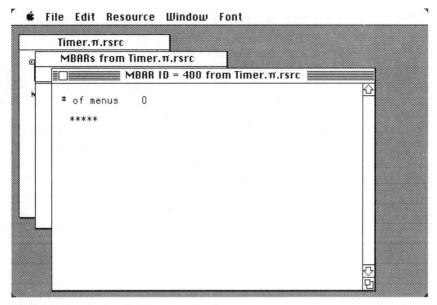

Figure 5.9   A new MBAR resource.

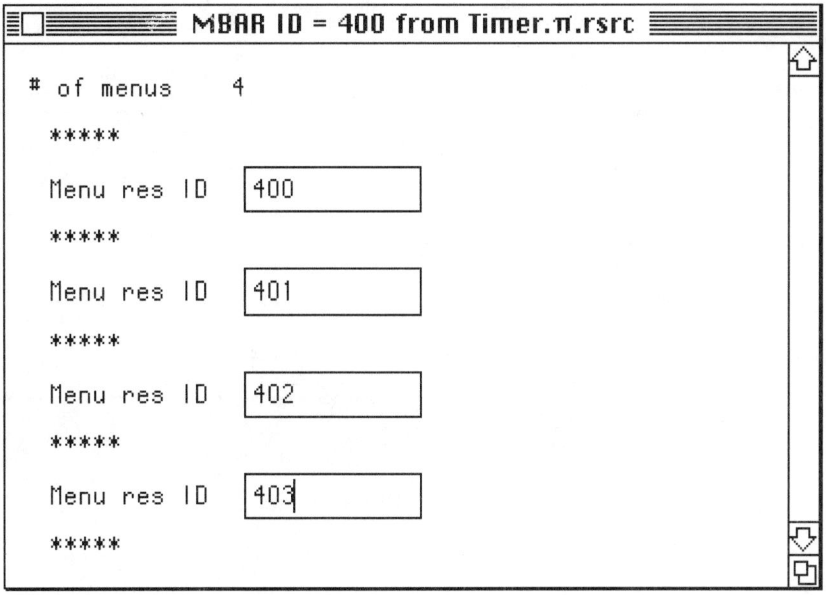

Figure 5.10   Completed MBAR resource.

To build the first MENU resource, for the menu, start by creating a new resource, then typing in or selecting MENU from the scrolling list.

The MENU editor in ResEdit 2 is a lot slicker than earlier versions. The new edit window for your MENU resource displays all the options available for menus, such as whether your MENU should be enabled or dimmed, and the coloring of the text and background of menu items. For now, just use the defaults.

Click on the radio button labeled **(Apple menu)** (Figure 5.11). This is what creates the title of the menu for you. Use **Get Resource Item** to set the Resource ID to 400. (Remember, NEVER make MENU resources purgeable (I:344).)

Then, select **Create New Item** from the **Resource** Menu and type in the text **About Timer**. Finally, select **Create New Item** and click on the radio button labeled **(separator line)**. Creation of the two menu items is shown in Figure 5.12.

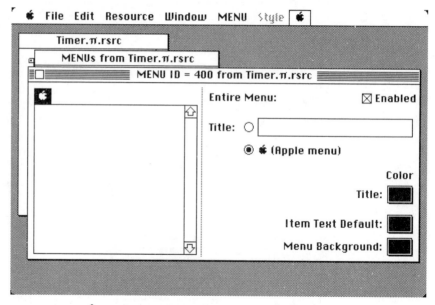

Figure 5.11 MENU specifications.

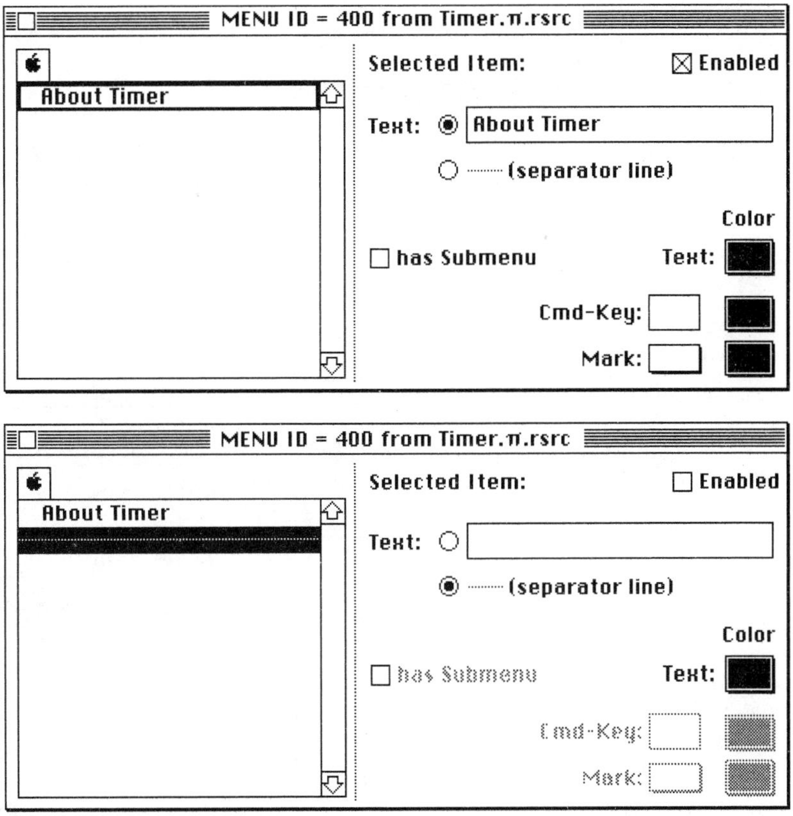

Figure 5.12 Creating menu items.

In the same fashion, create another MENU resource with resource ID of 401. This resource will be used to create the **File** menu. As shown above, create one text menu item labeled **Quit**. This time, add a command key equivalent to the **Quit** menu by typing in a **Q** in the **Cmd-Key** editable text field (Figure 5.13).

Close the **File** menu resource window (did you give it a resource number of 401?). Now, open a new MENU resource for the **Edit** menu information. Give it a resource ID of 402 and fill it in as shown in Figure 5.14.

The completed **Edit** menu now follows Mac interface guidelines. Figure 5.15 shows how the **Edit** menu looks when it is not disabled. The **Edit** menu is different from the first two menus in that it is disabled. To disable it, select the title of the menu on the left (**Edit**) and toggle off the checkbox labeled **Enabled**.

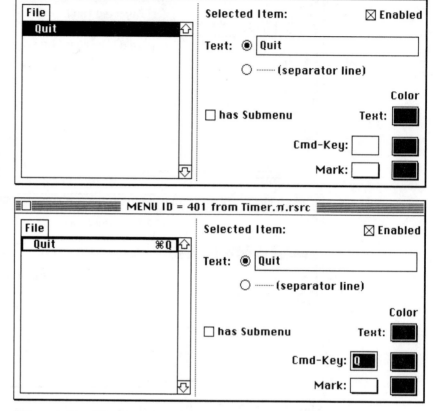

Figure 5.13 File MENU specifications.

Because it is a little harder to read the menu items when they are disabled, try typing them all in and assigning their command key equivalents before deselecting them. The completed **Edit** menu should look like Figure 5.16.

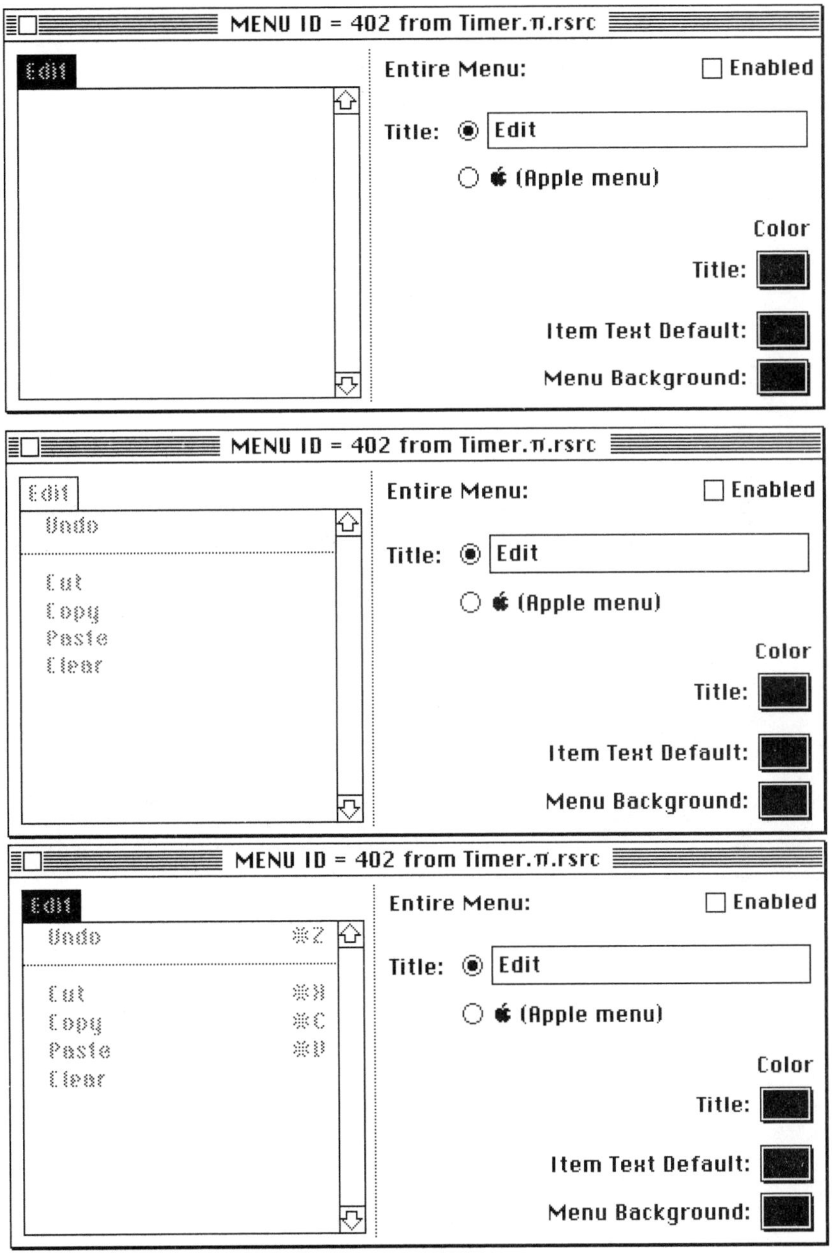

Figure 5.14 Edit MENU specifications.

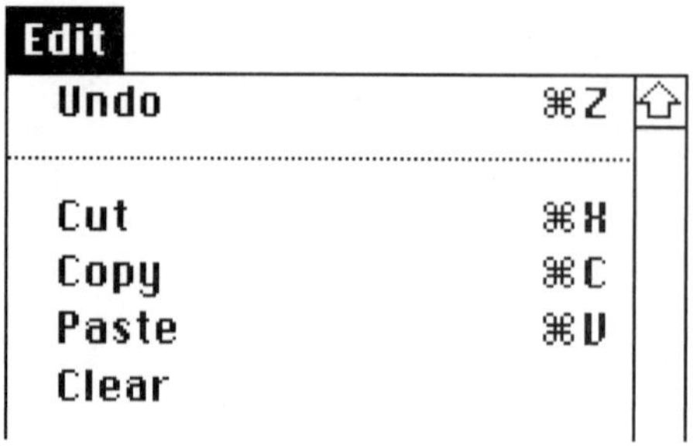

Edit		
Undo	⌘Z	⬆
Cut	⌘H	
Copy	⌘C	
Paste	⌘U	
Clear		

Figure 5.15   Standard **Edit** MENU specifications.

The Timer application does not use the **Edit** menu at all. So why add it? The reason is that although your application may not use the **Edit** menu, the desk accesories you support may. Many desk accessories expect an **Edit** menu on a Mac application. If you don't put one there, the desk accessory may not be able to function properly.

Now, add the **Special** menu. Open up a new MENU resource (Resource ID of 403) and fill it as shown in Figure 5.16. The **Special** menu has two menu items, both of which have submenus, which means that hierarchical menus will be attached to them.

The Menu Manager will look for a MENU resource with ID = 100 to use as the Font hierarchical submenu. In the same way, the Menu Manager will look for a MENU resource with ID = 101 for the **Style** hierarchical submenu. Now let's build these submenus.

Here's why you don't use 404 and 405 instead of 100 and 101 for hierarchical submenu resource IDs. The hierarchical menu structure was defined in Volume V of *Inside Macintosh.* Only two bytes are used as a pointer to the hierarchical menus in the menu structure. Because the biggest two-digit hexadecimal number is FF, or 255 decimal, that's the biggest hierarchical menu number that you can use.

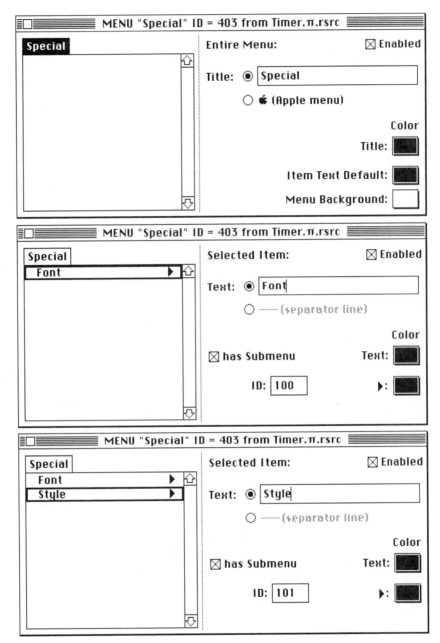

Figure 5.16   The completed **Special** menu (finale).

Close the **Special** menu window. Create a new MENU resource and fill it as shown in Figure 5.17. Note that the **Font** menu has no menu items. As with the menu, the items will be inserted from within the program. Change the Font menu resource ID to 100. Create another new MENU resource for the **Style** menu and fill it as shown in Figure 5.18.

The text style of the menu items in the **Style** menu has been changed to reflect the operation it performs in Timer. For example, the bold menu item is actually **bolded** in the menu itself. This is done by selecting **Bold** from ResEdit's **Style** menu; the bold affects only the appearance of the menu item. The Timer code will actually do the work of setting the text style, as we will see shortly. Make sure the **Style** menu resource ID is 101.

When you're finished with the **Style** menu, close and save your work.

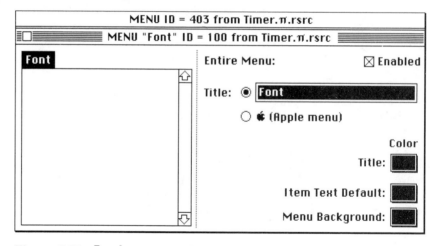

Figure 5.17 **Font** menu specifications.

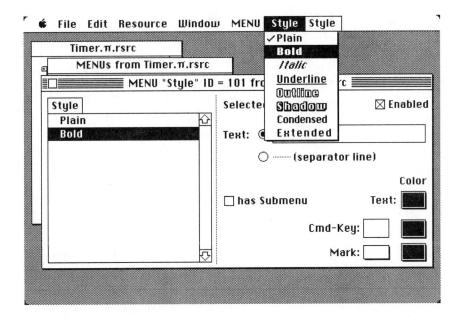

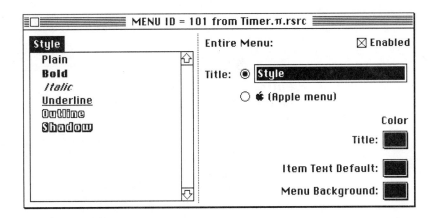

Figure 5.18 **Style** menu specifications.

You've completed the resources necessary for the window and menus of Timer. Now, you'll create an alert that is displayed when **About Timer** is selected from the menu. For the moment, don't worry too much about the alert mechanism (the ALRT and DITL resources). We'll cover alerts in Chapter 6.

Create a DITL resource (select **Create New Resource** and enter DITL). The DITL (for Dialog ITem List) contains the list of items you want to appear in your alert. By convention, the first item is always the **OK** button that the user clicks to make the alert disappear. Create a new item by selecting **Create New Dialog Item** from the **Resource** menu, making it look like Figure 5.19. Close the Item #1 window and create a second item, making it look like Figure 5.20.

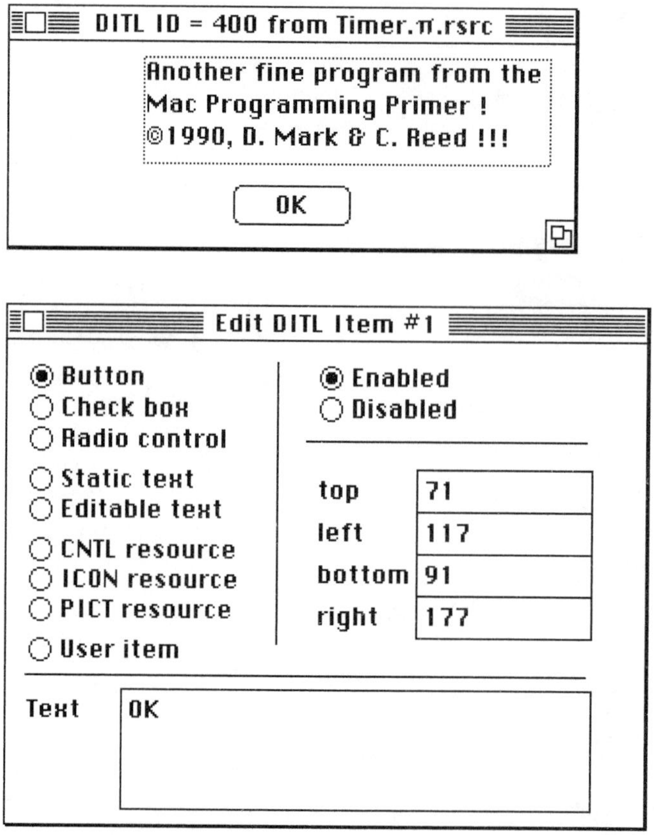

Figure 5.19   The **OK** button.

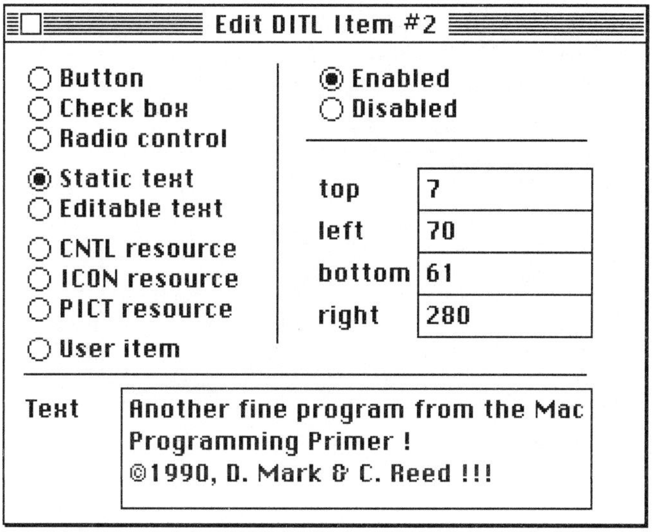

Figure 5.20   The About Box text.

Close the Item #2 window. Now, choose **Get Resource Info** from the **Resource** menu and change the DITL resource ID to 400.

Finally, make an alert template to display the DITL items. Create a new ALRT resource. A new ALRT menu should appear in ResEdit's menu bar. Select **Display as Text** from the **ALRT** menu. Change the alert fields so they look like those in Figure 5.21. Finally, change the ALRT resource ID to 400.

All the resources are now done. Select **Save** from the **File** menu to finish up.

This has been a pretty extensive resource editing session, so let's just make sure the resources went in like they were supposed to. Open up your resources as a final check. You should see something like Figure 5.22.

One ALRT, one DITL, one MBAR, one WIND, six MENUs: You're ready to code!

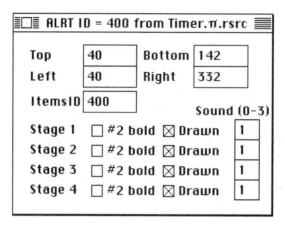

Figure 5.21 The About Alert, displayed as text.

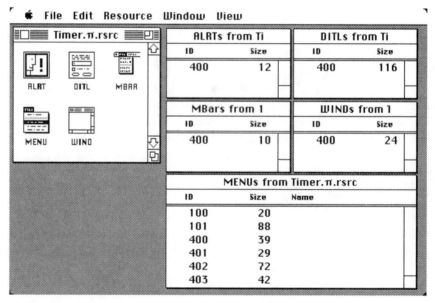

Figure 5.22 Timer resources.

Timer Code

Some of this code can be cannibalized from EventTutor. Just be careful with variable names and the like.

Get into THINK Pascal and start a new project in the `Timer` folder. Call the project `Timer.π`. Now, add the code.

```
program Timer;
    const
        BASE_RES_ID = 400;

        PLAIN = [];
        PLAIN_ITEM = 1;
        BOLD_ITEM = 2;
        ITALIC_ITEM = 3;
        UNDERLINE_ITEM = 4;
        OUTLINE_ITEM = 5;
        SHADOW_ITEM = 6;

        INCLUDE_SECONDS = TRUE;

        ADD_CHECK_MARK = TRUE;
        REMOVE_CHECK_MARK = FALSE;

        DRAG_THRESHOLD = 30;

        SLEEP = 60;
        WNE_TRAP_NUM = $60;
        UNIMPL_TRAP_NUM = $9F;

        QUIT_ITEM = 1;
        ABOUT_ITEM = 1;

        NOT_A_NORMAL_MENU = -1;
        APPLE_MENU_ID = BASE_RES_ID;
        FILE_MENU_ID = BASE_RES_ID + 1;
        FONT_MENU_ID = 100;
        STYLE_MENU_ID = 101;

        CLOCK_LEFT = 12;
        CLOCK_TOP = 25;
        CLOCK_SIZE = 24;

        ABOUT_ALERT = 400;

    var
        gClockWindow: WindowPtr;
        gDone, gWNEImplemented: BOOLEAN;
        gCurrentTime, gOldTime: LONGINT;
        gTheEvent: EventRecord;
```

```
        gLastFont: INTEGER;
        gCurrentStyle: Style;


{---------------> HandleStyleChoice    <--}

    procedure CheckStyles;
        var
            styleMenu: MenuHandle;
    begin
        styleMenu := GetMHandle(STYLE_MENU_ID);
        CheckItem(styleMenu, PLAIN_ITEM, (gCurrentStyle =
            PLAIN));
        CheckItem(styleMenu, BOLD_ITEM, (bold in gCurrent
            Style));
        CheckItem(styleMenu, ITALIC_ITEM, (italic in gCurrent
            Style));
        CheckItem(styleMenu, UNDERLINE_ITEM, (underline in
            gCurrentStyle));
        CheckItem(styleMenu, OUTLINE_ITEM, (outline in
            gCurrentStyle));
        CheckItem(styleMenu, SHADOW_ITEM, (shadow in
            gCurrentStyle));
    end;


{---------------> HandleStyleChoice    <--}

    procedure HandleStyleChoice (theItem: INTEGER);
    begin
        case theItem of
            PLAIN_ITEM:
                gCurrentStyle := PLAIN;
            BOLD_ITEM:
                if bold in gCurrentStyle then
                    gCurrentStyle := gCurrentStyle - [bold]
                else
                    gCurrentStyle := gCurrentStyle + [bold];
            ITALIC_ITEM:
                if italic in gCurrentStyle then
                    gCurrentStyle := gCurrentStyle - [italic]
                else
                    gCurrentStyle := gCurrentStyle + [italic];
            UNDERLINE_ITEM:
                if underline in gCurrentStyle then
                    gCurrentStyle := gCurrentStyle -
                    [underline]
                else
        gCurrentStyle := gCurrentStyle +
        [underline];
```

```
            OUTLINE_ITEM:
                if outline in gCurrentStyle then
                    gCurrentStyle := gCurrentStyle - [outline]
                else
                    gCurrentStyle := gCurrentStyle + [outline];
            SHADOW_ITEM:
                if shadow in gCurrentStyle then
                    gCurrentStyle := gCurrentStyle - [shadow]
                else
                    gCurrentStyle := gCurrentStyle + [shadow];
        end;
        CheckStyles;
        TextFace(gCurrentStyle);
    end;


{---------------> HandleFontChoice    <--}

    procedure HandleFontChoice (theItem: INTEGER);
        var
            fontNumber: INTEGER;
            fontName: Str255;
            fontMenu: MenuHandle;
    begin
        fontMenu := GetMHandle(FONT_MENU_ID);
        CheckItem(fontMenu, gLastFont, REMOVE_CHECK_MARK);
        CheckItem(fontMenu, theItem, ADD_CHECK_MARK);
        gLastFont := theItem;
        GetItem(fontMenu, theItem, fontName);
        GetFNum(fontName, fontNumber);
        TextFont(fontNumber);
    end;


{---------------> HandleFileChoice    <--}

    procedure HandleFileChoice (theItem: INTEGER);
    begin
        case theItem of
            QUIT_ITEM:
                gDone := TRUE;
        end;
    end;


{---------------> HandleAppleChoice    <--}

    procedure HandleAppleChoice (theItem: INTEGER);
        var
            accName: Str255;
            accNumber, itemNumber, dummy: INTEGER;
```

```
            appleMenu: MenuHandle;
    begin
        case theItem of
            ABOUT_ITEM:
                dummy := NoteAlert(ABOUT_ALERT, nil);
            otherwise
                begin
                    appleMenu := GetMHandle(APPLE_MENU_ID);
                    GetItem(appleMenu, theItem, accName);
                    accNumber := OpenDeskAcc(accName);
                end;
        end;
    end;


{----------------> HandleMenuChoice      <--}

    procedure HandleMenuChoice (menuChoice: LONGINT);
        var
            theMenu, theItem: INTEGER;
    begin
        if menuChoice <> 0 then
            begin
                theMenu := HiWord(menuChoice);
                theItem := LoWord(menuChoice);

                case theMenu of
                    APPLE_MENU_ID:
                        HandleAppleChoice(theItem);
                    FILE_MENU_ID:
                        HandleFileChoice(theItem);
                    FONT_MENU_ID:
                        HandleFontChoice(theItem);
                    STYLE_MENU_ID:
                        HandleStyleChoice(theItem);
                end;

                HiliteMenu(0);
            end;
    end;


{----------------> HandleMouseDown      <--}

    procedure HandleMouseDown;
        var
            whichWindow: WindowPtr;
            thePart: INTEGER;
            menuChoice, windSize: LONGINT;
    begin
        thePart := FindWindow(gTheEvent.where, whichWindow);
```

```
            case thePart of
                inMenuBar:
                    begin
                        menuChoice := MenuSelect(gTheEvent.where);
                        HandleMenuChoice(menuChoice);
                    end;
                inSysWindow:
                    SystemClick(gTheEvent, whichWindow);
                inDrag:
                    DragWindow(whichWindow, gTheEvent.where,
                    screenBits.bounds);
                inGoAway:
                    gDone := TRUE;
            end;
    end;


{---------------> DrawClock <--}

    procedure DrawClock (theWindow: WindowPtr);
        var
            myTimeString: Str255;
        begin
            IUTimeString(gCurrentTime, INCLUDE_SECONDS,
            myTimeString);
            EraseRect(theWindow^.portRect);
            MoveTo(CLOCK_LEFT, CLOCK_TOP);
            DrawString(myTimeString);
            gOldTime := gCurrentTime;
        end;


{---------------> HandleNull    <--}

    procedure HandleNull;
        begin
            GetDateTime(gCurrentTime);
            if gCurrentTime <> gOldTime then
                DrawClock(gClockWindow);
        end;


{---------------> HandleEvent    <--}

    procedure HandleEvent;
        var
            theChar: CHAR;
            dummy: BOOLEAN;
        begin
            if gWNEImplemented then
```

```
            dummy := WaitNextEvent(everyEvent, gTheEvent,
                SLEEP, nil)
        else
            begin
                SystemTask;
                dummy := GetNextEvent(everyEvent, gTheEvent);
            end;

        case gTheEvent.what of
            nullEvent:
                HandleNull;
            mouseDown:
                HandleMouseDown;
            keyDown, autoKey:
                begin
                    theChar := CHR(BitAnd(gTheEvent.message,
                        charCodeMask));
                    if (BitAnd(gTheEvent.modifiers, cmdKey) <>
                        0) then
                            HandleMenuChoice(MenuKey(theChar));
                end;
            updateEvt:
                begin
                    BeginUpdate(WindowPtr(gTheEvent.message));
                    EndUpdate(WindowPtr(gTheEvent.message));
                end;
        end;
    end;


{---------------> MainLoop    <--}

    procedure MainLoop;
    begin
        gDone := FALSE;
        gWNEImplemented := (NGetTrapAddress(WNE_TRAP_NUM,
            ToolTrap) <> NGetTrapAddress(UNIMPL_TRAP_NUM,
            ToolTrap));
        while (gDone = FALSE) do
            HandleEvent;
    end;


{---------------> MenuBarInit<--}

    procedure MenuBarInit;
        var
            myMenuBar: Handle;
            aMenu: MenuHandle;
    begin
        myMenuBar := GetNewMBar(BASE_RES_ID);
```

```
        SetMenuBar(myMenuBar);
        DisposHandle(myMenuBar);

        aMenu := GetMHandle(APPLE_MENU_ID);
        AddResMenu(aMenu, 'DRVR');

        aMenu := GetMenu(FONT_MENU_ID);
        InsertMenu(aMenu, NOT_A_NORMAL_MENU);
        AddResMenu(aMenu, 'FONT');

        aMenu := GetMenu(STYLE_MENU_ID);
        InsertMenu(aMenu, NOT_A_NORMAL_MENU);
        CheckItem(aMenu, PLAIN_ITEM, TRUE);

        DrawMenuBar;
        gLastFont := 1;
        gCurrentStyle := PLAIN;
        HandleFontChoice(gLastFont);
    end;


{---------------> WindowInit <--}

    procedure WindowInit;
    begin
        gClockWindow := GetNewWindow(BASE_RES_ID, nil,
                                    WindowPtr(-1));
        SetPort(gClockWindow);
        ShowWindow(gClockWindow);

        TextSize(CLOCK_SIZE);
    end;


{---------------> Timer   <--}

begin
    WindowInit;
    MenuBarInit;

    MainLoop;
end.
```

Running Timer

Now that your source code is in, you're ready to run Timer. Select **Go** from the **Project** menu. If you run into any compilation problems, check for typing errors, or consult the debugging tips found in the appendix. When asked to "Save changes before running," click **Yes**. Timer should be up and running (see Figure 5.23).

Timer should display the time in a window in the upper left-hand corner of the screen. The menu bar should display the , **File**, **Edit**, and **Special** menus. Desk accessories should work. The **File** menu has just one option, **Quit**, which should be operational. The **Edit** menu contains the standard menu items but is dimmed. The **Special** menu contains two hierarchical menu items: **Font** and **Style**. If you select **Font**, the hierarchical **Font** submenu should be displayed (top of Figure 5.24). If you select **Style**, the hierarchical **Style** submenu should be displayed (bottom of Figure 5.24). Both hierarchical menus should show a check mark next to the currently used font and style. If you change the style or font with the menus, the appearance of the timer window should change appropriately. Selecting **About Timer** from the menu should bring up the alert that you just created. Click on the **OK** button (or press **Return**) to make the alert disappear.

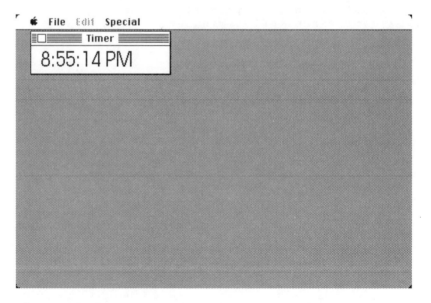

Figure 5.23   Running Timer.

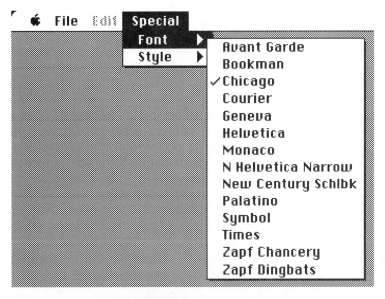

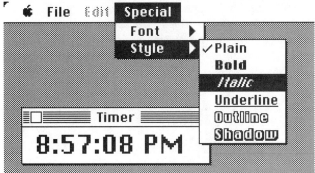

Figure 5.24   Timer hierarchical menus.

Choose **Quit** from the **File** menu. Let's look at the code.

> If you make Timer an application and run it, you'll notice that, if you're running in MultiFinder, the time is updated only when Timer is in the foreground, not when another application is active. This is because Timer does not have a SIZE resource (EventTutor had the same problem). See Chapter 8 if you'd like to add background functionality to Timer.

Timer consists of 13 procedures, as shown in Figure 5.25.

The figure displays where each routine is called. `WindowInit` runs, then `MenuBarInit`, then `MainLoop`. `MainLoop` calls `HandleEvent`, which runs until the user quits.

`HandleNull` and `HandleMouseDown` handle the two events used in Timer: null events and mouseDown events. `HandleNull` calls `DrawClock` if the time needs to be redrawn. `HandleMouseDown` calls `HandleMenuChoice` if the mouse is clicked in the menu bar. Then, different routines handle the different menus. The last routine, `CheckStyles`, is called within `HandleStyleChoices`.

We'll discuss the Timer code following the order of Figure 5.25, in that routines are discussed in their order of operation, as they were in the discussion of Chapter 4's EventTutor.

Timer starts off with a set of constants, which we will discuss when they are used in the routines. The first global, `gClockWindow`, is the pointer to Timer's clock window. `gDone`, `gTheEvent`, and `gWNEImplemented` are the same as they are in Chapter 4's EventTutor. `gCurrentTime` and `gOldTime` are used to determine when to change the clock display. `gLastFont` is used to determine the current font number in use, and `gCurrentStyle` contains the current style used by Timer.

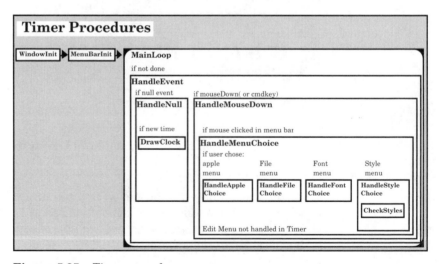

Figure 5.25 Timer procedures.

```
program Timer;
    const
        BASE_RES_ID = 400;

        PLAIN = [];
        PLAIN_ITEM = 1;
        BOLD_ITEM = 2;
        ITALIC_ITEM = 3;
        UNDERLINE_ITEM = 4;
        OUTLINE_ITEM = 5;
        SHADOW_ITEM = 6;

        INCLUDE_SECONDS = TRUE;

        ADD_CHECK_MARK = TRUE;
        REMOVE_CHECK_MARK = FALSE;

        DRAG_THRESHOLD = 30;

        SLEEP = 60;
        WNE_TRAP_NUM = $60;
        UNIMPL_TRAP_NUM = $9F;

        QUIT_ITEM = 1;
        ABOUT_ITEM = 1;

        NOT_A_NORMAL_MENU = -1;
        APPLE_MENU_ID = BASE_RES_ID;
        FILE_MENU_ID = BASE_RES_ID + 1;
        FONT_MENU_ID = 100;
        STYLE_MENU_ID = 101;

        CLOCK_LEFT = 12;
        CLOCK_TOP = 25;
        CLOCK_SIZE = 24;

        ABOUT_ALERT = 400;

    var
        gClockWindow: WindowPtr;
        gDone, gWNEImplemented: BOOLEAN;
        gCurrentTime, gOldTime: LONGINT;
        gTheEvent: EventRecord;
        gLastFont: INTEGER;
        gCurrentStyle: Style;
```

Timer starts by initializing the window and menu bar, then starts the `MainLoop`:

```
{----------------> Timer <--}

begin
    WindowInit;
    MenuBarInit;

    MainLoop;
end.
```

`WindowInit` is straightforward. A pointer to the new window is put into `gClockWindow`, its characteristics set up by the `WIND` resource. The clock window is made the current port and displayed with `ShowWindow`. Then, the standard text size is set to `CLOCK_SIZE`.

```
{----------------> WindowInit <--}

    procedure WindowInit;
    begin
        gClockWindow := GetNewWindow
        (BASE_RES_ID, nil, WindowPtr(-1));
        SetPort(gClockWindow);
        ShowWindow(gClockWindow);

        TextSize(CLOCK_SIZE);
    end;
```

An initialization routine called `MenuBarInit` is now called. `MenuBarInit` starts off by calling `GetNewMBar` to load the `MBAR` resource you created into memory. `GetNewMBar` automatically loads the individual `MENU`s pointed to by the `MBAR`.

Then `SetMenuBar` tells the system to use the `MBAR` handled by `myMenuBar` as the current menu bar. (The phrase, "xxx is handled by `myMenuBar`" really means that `myMenuBar` is a handle to xxx.)

```
{----------------> MenuBarInit<--}

    procedure MenuBarInit;
            var
                    myMenuBar: Handle;
                    aMenu: MenuHandle;
```

```
begin
      myMenuBar := GetNewMBar(BASE_RES_ID);
      SetMenuBar(myMenuBar);
      DisposHandle(myMenuBar);

      aMenu := GetMHandle(APPLE_MENU_ID);
      AddResMenu(aMenu, 'DRVR');

      aMenu := GetMenu(FONT_MENU_ID);
      InsertMenu(aMenu, NOT_A_NORMAL_MENU);
      AddResMenu(aMenu, 'FONT');

      aMenu := GetMenu(STYLE_MENU_ID);
      InsertMenu(aMenu, NOT_A_NORMAL_MENU);
      CheckItem(aMenu, PLAIN_ITEM, TRUE);

      DrawMenuBar;
      gLastFont := 1;
      gCurrentStyle := PLAIN;
      HandleFontChoice(gLastFont);
end;
```

After that, the menu and the hierarchical menus (**Font** and
Style) are set to handle their respective MENU data structures.
InsertMenu is called to add the **Font** hierarchical submenu to the
Menu Manager's list of available menus. The NOT_A_NORMAL_MENU
parameter tells the Menu Manager not to place the **Font** menu
directly on the menu bar. AddResMenu adds the name of all
resources of type FONT to the **Font** menu. Next, InsertMenu is
called for the **Style** hierarchical submenu. A check mark is placed
next to the **Plain** item on the **Style** menu with the call to
CheckItem. You use the handle to the menu so that you can add
desk accessories to it via the call to AddResMenu. All desk
accessories are resources of type DRVR. AddResMenu looks for all
resources of the specified type (we specified DRVR) and adds the
resource names found to the specified menu.

Next, DrawMenuBar draws the menu bar, and
HandleFontChoice sets the current font to the first font on the
Font menu.

MainLoop is the same as it is in Chapter 4:

```
{----------------> MainLoop    <--}

procedure MainLoop;
begin
      gDone := FALSE;
```

```
        gWNEImplemented := (NGetTrapAddress
               (WNE_TRAP_NUM, ToolTrap) <>
   NGetTrapAddress(UNIMPL_TRAP_NUM, ToolTrap));
        while (gDone = FALSE) do
             HandleEvent;
  end;
```

HandleEvent is similar to the version in Chapter 4. Start by checking for the existence of WaitNextEvent and then make the appropriate call. Then, switch on gTheEvent.what. The routine HandleNull handles nullEvents. As usual, mouseDowns are handled by HandleMouseDown. keyDown and autoKey events are handled by the same code. In either case, check to see if the Command key was depressed when the event occurred. If it was, convert the keystroke to a menu selection via MenuKey and pass that result to HandleMenuChoice. Finally, handle updateEvts by calling BeginUpdate and EndUpdate.

Because updateEvts have a higher priority than nullEvts, it is imperative that you respond to every updateEvt by calling BeginUpdate and EndUpdate. If you didn't, the Window Manager would keep queueing updateEvts, thinking you hadn't received them, and no nullEvts would ever make it into the event queue. One type of event can prevent another from making it into the event queue because the queue is finite. If the queue is big enough for 20 events, and 20 updateEvts are pending, there's no room for even one nullEvt.

You may notice that the update loop isn't used to redraw the window in Timer. Instead, the timer is redrawn in the HandleNull routine every second. Generally, you should use updateEvts as the place to redraw. Timer is coded like this to demonstrate one way to use null events.

```
{---------------> HandleEvent <--}

    procedure HandleEvent;
        var
            theChar: CHAR;
            dummy: BOOLEAN;
    begin
        if gWNEImplemented then
            dummy := WaitNextEvent(everyEvent, gTheEvent,
                    SLEEP, nil)
        else
            begin
                SystemTask;
                dummy := GetNextEvent(everyEvent, gTheEvent);
            end;

        case gTheEvent.what of
            nullEvent:
                HandleNull;
            mouseDown:
                HandleMouseDown;
            keyDown, autoKey:
                begin
                    theChar := CHR(BitAnd(gTheEvent.message,
                            charCodeMask));
                    if (BitAnd(gTheEvent.modifiers, cmdKey) <>
                        0) then
                        HandleMenuChoice(MenuKey(theChar));
                end;
            updateEvt:
                begin
                    BeginUpdate(WindowPtr(gTheEvent.message));
                    EndUpdate(WindowPtr(gTheEvent.message));
                end;
        end;
    end;
```

HandleNull is called whenever a nullEvent is retrieved from
the event queue. HandleNull checks the current time (in seconds)
and compares it to the last check performed. If the time has changed,
the clock window is refreshed.

```
{---------------> HandleNull      <--}

    procedure HandleNull;
    begin
        GetDateTime(gCurrentTime);
        if gCurrentTime <> gOldTime then
            DrawClock(gClockWindow);
    end;
```

DrawClock calls the International Utility IUTimeString to get the current time in a format suitable for display. Next, the window is erased, the pen is positioned, and the new time string is drawn. Finally, gOldTime is updated.

```
{---------------> DrawClock <--}

    procedure DrawClock (theWindow: WindowPtr);
        var
            myTimeString: Str255;
    begin
        IUTimeString(gCurrentTime, INCLUDE_SECONDS,
                    myTimeString);
        EraseRect(theWindow^.portRect);
        MoveTo(CLOCK_LEFT, CLOCK_TOP);
        DrawString(myTimeString);
        gOldTime := gCurrentTime;
    end;
```

HandleMouseDown is similar to its Chapter 4 counterpart. FindWindow is called, returning a part code that indicates the part of the window in which the mouseDown event occurred. In addition, FindWindow sets whichWindow to the window in which the mouseDown occurred.

If the mouseDown occurred in the menu bar, MenuSelect is called, allowing the user to make a selection from the menu bar. The user's selection is passed on to HandleMenuChoice.

The rest of the part codes are handled as they were in Chapter 4.

```
{---------------> HandleMouseDown       <--}

    procedure HandleMouseDown;
        var
            whichWindow: WindowPtr;
            thePart: INTEGER;
            menuChoice, windSize: LONGINT;
    begin
        thePart := FindWindow(gTheEvent.where, whichWindow);
        case thePart of
            inMenuBar:
                begin
                    menuChoice := MenuSelect(gTheEvent.where);
                    HandleMenuChoice(menuChoice);
                end;
            inSysWindow:
                SystemClick(gTheEvent, whichWindow);
```

```
            inDrag:
                DragWindow(whichWindow, gTheEvent.where,
                          screenBits.bounds);
            inGoAway:
                gDone := TRUE;
        end;
    end;
```

HandleMenuChoice takes a four-byte argument. The first two bytes contain the menu selected, and the last two bytes contain the item selected from that menu. theMenu is set to the first two bytes and theItem to the last two bytes using the Toolbox routines HiWord and LoWord. After that, theMenu is compared against the four MENU resource IDs to find which one was selected. A different routine exists for each of the four menus. When MenuSelect is called, the selected menu title is left inverted. When you finish processing the menu selection, the menu title is uninverted with a call to HiliteMenu(0) (I:357).

```
{---------------> HandleMenuChoice     <--}

    procedure HandleMenuChoice (menuChoice: LONGINT);
        var
            theMenu, theItem: INTEGER;
    begin
        if menuChoice <> 0 then
            begin
                theMenu := HiWord(menuChoice);
                theItem := LoWord(menuChoice);

                case theMenu of
                    APPLE_MENU_ID:
                        HandleAppleChoice(theItem);
                    FILE_MENU_ID:
                        HandleFileChoice(theItem);
                    FONT_MENU_ID:
                        HandleFontChoice(theItem);
                    STYLE_MENU_ID:
                        HandleStyleChoice(theItem);
                end;

                HiliteMenu(0);
            end;
    end;
```

HandleAppleChoice handles all menu selections. If the **About Timer** menu item is selected, the alert with resource ID = ABOUT_ALERT is drawn with NoteAlert. Alerts are discussed in more detail in Chapter 6. Any other item selected is assumed to be a desk accessory. The name of the desk accessory is retrieved with GetItem, and the desk accessory is opened with OpenDeskAcc.

```
{---------------> HandleAppleChoice    <--}

    procedure HandleAppleChoice (theItem: INTEGER);
        var
            accName: Str255;
            accNumber, itemNumber, dummy: INTEGER;
            appleMenu: MenuHandle;
    begin
        case theItem of
            ABOUT_ITEM:
                dummy := NoteAlert(ABOUT_ALERT, nil);
            otherwise
                begin
                    appleMenu := GetMHandle(APPLE_MENU_ID);
                    GetItem(appleMenu, theItem, accName);
                    accNumber := OpenDeskAcc(accName);
                end;
        end;
    end;
```

Because there's only one item under the **File** menu, the code for HandleFileChoice is pretty simple. The global variable gDone is set to TRUE if **Quit** is selected. The value of gDone is checked every time through the main loop. When gDone = TRUE, the program knows that it's time to exit.

```
{---------------> HandleFileChoice    <--}

    procedure HandleFileChoice (theItem: INTEGER);
    begin
        case theItem of
            QUIT_ITEM:
                gDone := TRUE;
        end;
    end;
```

The **Edit** menu is in this application only to support desk accessories. All items were dimmed when you created the MENU resource. Because you don't care what happens as far as your application is concerned, you need not do anything.

> Actually, we've done only half the job so far; although Timer allows the use of desk accessories, the Cut, Copy, and Paste commands are not yet supported. We'll add this in Chapter 7's WindowMaker program.

HandleFontChoice is called when the **Font** item in the **Special** menu is selected. First, we get the font's menu handle with GetMHandle (you could have used globals for the menu handles, but GetMHandle makes it easy to use local variables). Next, the first CheckItem call removes the check mark from whatever had been the last font selected. Then, the same call is used to place a check mark on the newly selected font. gLastFont is set to the selected item number. Next, the GetItem call returns the fontName for the menu selection that you picked. GetFNum provides the font number given the fontName, and finally the font of the text is changed with the **TextFont** call, given the font ID number.

```
{----------------> HandleFontChoice     <--}

    procedure HandleFontChoice (theItem: INTEGER);
        var
            fontNumber: INTEGER;
            fontName: Str255;
            fontMenu: MenuHandle;
    begin
        fontMenu := GetMHandle(FONT_MENU_ID);
        CheckItem(fontMenu, gLastFont, REMOVE_CHECK_MARK);
        CheckItem(fontMenu, theItem, ADD_CHECK_MARK);
        gLastFont := theItem;
        GetItem(fontMenu, theItem, fontName);
        GetFNum(fontName, fontNumber);
        TextFont(fontNumber);
    end;
```

The **Style** hierarchical submenu controls gCurrentStyle. When a style is selected, it must be checked against gCurrentStyle. If the style is currently in use, it must be removed, and vice versa (I:171). CheckStyles is then called to update the check marks on the **Style** menu. Finally, TextFace is called to implement the styles in gCurrentStyle.

```
{---------------> HandleStyleChoice    <--}

    procedure HandleStyleChoice (theItem: INTEGER);
    begin
        case theItem of
            PLAIN_ITEM:
                gCurrentStyle := PLAIN;
            BOLD_ITEM:
                if bold in gCurrentStyle then
                    gCurrentStyle := gCurrentStyle - [bold]
                else
                    gCurrentStyle := gCurrentStyle + [bold];
            ITALIC_ITEM:
                if italic in gCurrentStyle then
                    gCurrentStyle := gCurrentStyle - [italic]
                else
                    gCurrentStyle := gCurrentStyle + [italic];
            UNDERLINE_ITEM:
                if underline in gCurrentStyle then
                    gCurrentStyle := gCurrentStyle - [underline]
                else
                    gCurrentStyle := gCurrentStyle + [underline];
            OUTLINE_ITEM:
                if outline in gCurrentStyle then
                    gCurrentStyle := gCurrentStyle - [outline]
                else
                    gCurrentStyle := gCurrentStyle + [outline];
            SHADOW_ITEM:
                if shadow in gCurrentStyle then
                    gCurrentStyle := gCurrentStyle - [shadow]
                else
                    gCurrentStyle := gCurrentStyle + [shadow];
        end;
        CheckStyles;
        TextFace(gCurrentStyle);
    end;
```

CheckStyles steps through each item in the **Style** menu, placing a check mark next to those styles set in gCurrentStyle:

```
{---------------> HandleStyleChoice    <--}

    procedure CheckStyles;
        var
            styleMenu: MenuHandle;
    begin
        styleMenu := GetMHandle(STYLE_MENU_ID);
        CheckItem(styleMenu, PLAIN_ITEM, (gCurrentStyle =
                PLAIN));
```

```
      CheckItem(styleMenu, BOLD_ITEM, (bold in
         gCurrentStyle));
      CheckItem(styleMenu, ITALIC_ITEM, (italic in
         gCurrentStyle));
      CheckItem(styleMenu, UNDERLINE_ITEM, (underline in
         gCurrentStyle));
      CheckItem(styleMenu, OUTLINE_ITEM, (outline in
         gCurrentStyle));
      CheckItem(styleMenu, SHADOW_ITEM, (shadow in
         gCurrentStyle));
   end;
```

That's it for our discussion of Timer. With this code, you should be able to add pull down and hierarchical menus to your programs. The last menu type, pop-up menus, is explored in the next program.

Zinger

Zinger opens a window on the desktop and implements a pop-up menu of numbers inside the window. When a number is selected from the pop-up, Zinger beeps that number of times and resets the value on the face of the pop-up to reflect this selection.

Zinger works like this:

1. It initializes the window and the pop-up menu, drawing the pop-up for the first time.

2. It activates the pop-up menu when a `mouseDown` occurs in the menu rectangle and redraws the pop-up when an `updateEvt` occurs.

3. Finally, Zinger quits when the window's close box is clicked.

Because you've seen much of Zinger's code in previous chapters, we'll concentrate on the code that makes the pop-up menu work. Start by building a folder called `Zinger` for the project files.

Next, create a resource file called `Zinger.π.rsrc`. Then, build a resource of type `MENU` with `ID = 400` and with the specifications in Figure 5.26. Note that the resource is identical to a regular pull-down menu.

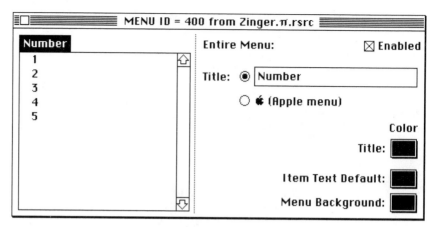

Figure 5.26   Zinger MENU specifications.

Now, build a WIND with the specifications of Figure 5.27.

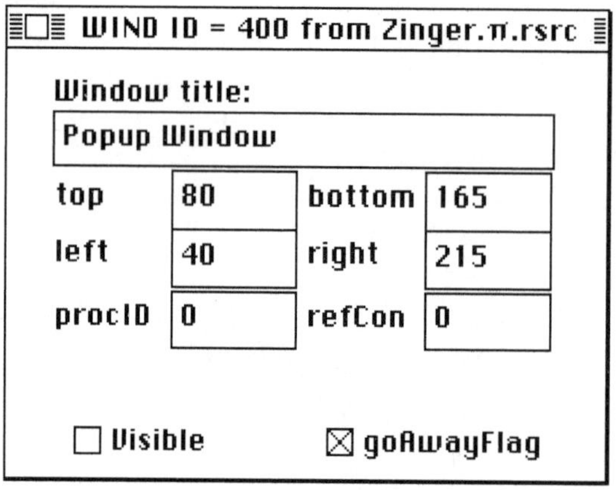

Figure 5.27   Zinger WIND resource.

Start a new project called Zinger.π, and type in the following code:

```
program Zinger;
    const
        BASE_RES_ID = 400;
        SLEEP = 60;
        DRAG_THRESHOLD = 30;
        WNE_TRAP_NUM = $60;
        UNIMPL_TRAP_NUM = $9F;
        POPUP_MENU_ID = BASE_RES_ID;
        NOT_A_NORMAL_MENU = -1;
        POPUP_LEFT = 100;
        POPUP_TOP = 35;
        POPUP_RIGHT = 125;
        POPUP_BOTTOM = 52;
        SHADOW_PIXELS = 1;
        RIGHT_MARGIN = 5;
        BOTTOM_MARGIN = 4;
        LEFT_MARGIN = 5;
        PIXEL_FOR_TOP_LINE = 1;

    var
        gDone, gWNEImplemented: BOOLEAN;
        gPopUpItem, gPopUpLabelWidth: INTEGER;
        gPopUpMenu: MenuHandle;
        gTheEvent: EventRecord;
        gPopUpRect, gLabelRect, gDragRect: Rect;
        gPopUpLabelH: StringHandle;

{---------------> DrawPopUpNumber        <--}

    procedure DrawPopUpNumber;
        var
            menuItem: Str255;
            itemLeftMargin: INTEGER;
    begin
        GetItem(gPopUpMenu, gPopUpItem, menuItem);
        itemLeftMargin := (gPopUpRect.right - gPopUpRect.left -
                        StringWidth(menuItem)) div 2;
        MoveTo(gPopUpRect.left + itemLeftMargin,
            gPopUpRect.bottom - BOTTOM_MARGIN);
        DrawString(menuItem);
    end;


{---------------> DrawPopUp   <--}

    procedure DrawPopUp;
    begin
        SetRect(gPopUpRect, POPUP_LEFT, POPUP_TOP, POPUP_RIGHT,
```

```
                POPUP_BOTTOM);
        FrameRect(gPopUpRect);

        MoveTo(gPopUpRect.left + SHADOW_PIXELS,
                gPopUpRect.bottom);
        LineTo(gPopUpRect.right, gPopUpRect.bottom);
        LineTo(gPopUpRect.right, gPopUpRect.top +
                SHADOW_PIXELS);

        MOVETO(GPOPUPRECT.LEFT - GPOPUPLABELWIDTH -
                RIGHT_MARGIN, GPOPUPRECT.BOTTOM - BOTTOM_MARGIN);
        HLock(Handle(gPopUpLabelH));
        DrawString(gPopUpLabelH^^);
        HUnlock(Handle(gPopUpLabelH));

        gLabelRect.top := gPopUpRect.top + PIXEL_FOR_TOP_LINE;
        gLabelRect.left := gPopUpRect.left - gPopUpLabelWidth -
                        LEFT_MARGIN - RIGHT_MARGIN;
        gLabelRect.right := gPopUpRect.left;
        gLabelRect.bottom := gPopUpRect.bottom;

        DrawPopUpNumber;
    end;



{---------------> HandleMouseDown        <--}

    procedure HandleMouseDown;
        var
            whichWindow: WindowPtr;
            thePart, i: INTEGER;
            theChoice: LONGINT;
            myPoint, popUpUpperLeft: Point;
    begin
        thePart := FindWindow(gTheEvent.where, whichWindow);
        case thePart of
            inContent:
                begin
                    myPoint := gTheEvent.where;
                    GlobalToLocal(myPoint);
                    if PtInRect(myPoint, gPopUpRect) then
                        begin
                            InvertRect(gLabelRect);
                            popUpUpperLeft.v := gPopUpRect.top +
                                PIXEL_FOR_TOP_LINE;
                            popUpUpperLeft.h := gPopUpRect.left;
                            LocalToGlobal(popUpUpperLeft);
                            theChoice := PopUpMenuSelect
                                (gPopUpMenu, popUpUpperLeft.v,
                                popUpUpperLeft.h, gPopUpItem);
                            InvertRect(gLabelRect);
```

```
                              if LoWord(theChoice) > 0 then
                                  begin
                                      gPopUpItem :=
                                          LoWord(theChoice);
                                      DrawPopUpNumber;
                                      for i := 0 to gPopUpItem -
                                          1 do
                                          SysBeep(20);
                                  end;
                          end;
              inSysWindow:
                  SystemClick(gTheEvent, whichWindow);
              inDrag:
                  DragWindow(whichWindow, gTheEvent.where,
                          screenBits.bounds);
              inGoAway:
                  gDone := TRUE;
          end;
      end;


{--------------> HandleEvent<--}

    procedure HandleEvent;
        var
            dummy: BOOLEAN;
    begin
        if gWNEImplemented then
            dummy := WaitNextEvent(everyEvent, gTheEvent,
                            SLEEP, nil)
        else
            begin
                SystemTask;
                dummy := GetNextEvent(everyEvent, gTheEvent);
            end;

        case gTheEvent.what of
            mouseDown:
                HandleMouseDown;
            updateEvt:
                begin
                    BeginUpdate(WindowPtr(gTheEvent.message));
                        DrawPopUp; EndUpdate
                        (WindowPtr(gTheEvent.message));
                    end;
                end;
            end;
```

```
{---------------> MainLoop   <--}

    procedure MainLoop;
    begin
        gDone := FALSE;
        gWNEImplemented := (NGetTrapAddress(WNE_TRAP_NUM,
        ToolTrap) <> NGetTrapAddress(UNIMPL_TRAP_NUM,
        ToolTrap));
        while gDone = FALSE do
            HandleEvent;
    end;


{---------------> MenuBarInit<--}

    procedure MenuBarInit;
    begin
        gPopUpMenu := GetMenu(POPUP_MENU_ID);
        InsertMenu(gPopUpMenu, NOT_A_NORMAL_MENU);
        gPopUpLabelH := GetString(BASE_RES_ID);
        HLock(Handle(gPopUpLabelH));
        gPopUpLabelWidth := StringWidth(gPopUpLabelH^^);
        HUnlock(Handle(gPopUpLabelH));
        gPopUpItem := 1;
    end;


{---------------> WindowInit  <--}

    procedure WindowInit;
        var
            popUpWindow: WindowPtr;
    begin
        popUpWindow := GetNewWindow(BASE_RES_ID, nil,
            WindowPtr(-1));
        SetPort(popUpWindow);
        ShowWindow(popUpWindow);

        TextFont(systemFont);
        TextMode(srcCopy);
    end;
{--------------> Zinger  <--}

    begin
        WindowInit;
        MenuBarInit;
        DrawPopUp;

        MainLoop;
    end.
```

Save your code as `Zinger.p` and add it to the project. When you run the program, you should get a window with a pop-up box in it (Figure 5.28). When you select a number on the menu, `SysBeep` should sound for the number of times that you selected. If you don't hear anything, check the volume in the control panel. If it's set above zero, and you don't have an external speaker attached to your Mac's sound port, check your code.

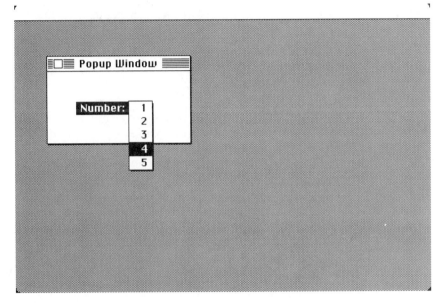

Figure 5.28 Zinger!

Walking Through the Zinger Code

Figure 5.29 displays where each routine is called. `WindowInit` runs, then `MenuBarInit`, then `DrawPopUp`, then `MainLoop`. `MainLoop` calls `HandleEvent`, which runs until the user quits.

`DrawPopUp` and `HandleMouseDown` handle two events used in Zinger, update events and `mouseDown` events. `HandleMouseDown` calls `DrawPopUpNumber` if an item is selected in the pop-up menu. `DrawPopUp` is called if an update event occurs.

We'll discuss the Zinger code following the order of Figure 5.29, so that routines are discussed in their order of operation.

Zinger starts, as usual, with constants, followed by declaration of its global variables:

```
const
        BASE_RES_ID = 400;
        SLEEP = 60;
        DRAG_THRESHOLD = 30;
        WNE_TRAP_NUM = $60;
        UNIMPL_TRAP_NUM = $9F;
        POPUP_MENU_ID = BASE_RES_ID;
        NOT_A_NORMAL_MENU = -1;
        POPUP_LEFT = 100;
        POPUP_TOP = 35;
        POPUP_RIGHT = 125;
        POPUP_BOTTOM = 52;
        SHADOW_PIXELS = 1;
        RIGHT_MARGIN = 5;
        BOTTOM_MARGIN = 4;
        LEFT_MARGIN = 5;
        PIXEL_FOR_TOP_LINE = 1;

var
        gDone, gWNEImplemented: BOOLEAN;
        gPopUpItem, gPopUpLabelWidth: INTEGER;
        gPopUpMenu: MenuHandle;
        gTheEvent: EventRecord;
        gPopUpRect, gLabelRect, gDragRect: Rect;
        gPopUpLabelH: StringHandle;
```

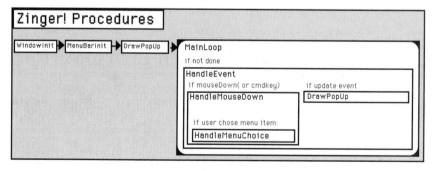

Figure 5.29   Zinger procedures.

Zinger starts like Timer, except that it calls `DrawPopUp` before it enters the `MainLoop`:

```
{----------------> Zinger        <--}

begin
    WindowInit;
    MenuBarInit;
    DrawPopUp;

    MainLoop;
end.
```

`WindowInit` may give you a sense of *déjà vu*, as well. `popUpWindow` is loaded, made visible, and made the current port. Next, the font is changed to `systemFont`, the same font used to draw the regular pull-down menus. The `srcCopy` text mode is used to simplify drawing of the pop-up menu item. With `srcCopy` enabled, text drawn in a window overlays existing graphics.

```
{----------------> WindowInit <--}

procedure WindowInit;
        var
                popUpWindow: WindowPtr;
        begin
                popUpWindow := GetNewWindow(BASE_RES_ID,
                                nil, WindowPtr(-1));
                SetPort(popUpWindow);
                ShowWindow(popUpWindow);

                TextFont(systemFont);
                TextMode(srcCopy);
        end;
```

In `MenuBarInit`, as in the routines in Zinger that handled the hierarchical menus, you load the `MENU` and add it to the menu list via the call to `InsertMenu`. Next, get the pop-up label from the menu data structure and calculate its width in pixels. You'll use this information later.

```
{----------------> MenuBarInit    <--}

procedure MenuBarInit;
begin
    gPopUpMenu := GetMenu(POPUP_MENU_ID);
    InsertMenu(gPopUpMenu, NOT_A_NORMAL_MENU);
    gPopUpLabelH := GetString(BASE_RES_ID);
    HLock(Handle(gPopUpLabelH));
```

```
        gPopUpLabelWidth := StringWidth(gPopUpLabelH^^);
        HUnlock(Handle(gPopUpLabelH));
        gPopUpItem := 1;
    end;
```

MainLoop works as it did in Timer:

```
{---------------> MainLoop <--}

    procedure MainLoop;
    begin
        gDone := FALSE;
        gWNEImplemented := (NGetTrapAddress(WNE_TRAP_NUM,
        ToolTrap) <> NGetTrapAddress(UNIMPL_TRAP_NUM,
        ToolTrap));
        while (gDone = FALSE) do
            HandleEvent;
    end;


---------------> HandleEvent    <--}

    procedure HandleEvent;
        var
            dummy: BOOLEAN;
    begin
        if gWNEImplemented then
            dummy := WaitNextEvent(everyEvent, gTheEvent,
                    SLEEP, nil)
        else
            begin
                SystemTask;
                dummy := GetNextEvent(everyEvent, gTheEvent);
            end;

        case gTheEvent.what of
            mouseDown:
                HandleMouseDown;
```

When Zinger gets an `updateEvt`, it redraws the pop-up menu:

```
        case updateEvt:
            updateEvt:
                begin
                  BeginUpdate(WindowPtr(gTheEvent.message));
                  DrawPopUp;
                  EndUpdate(WindowPtr(gTheEvent.message));
                end;
        end;
    end;
```

If the mouse was clicked in the window, copy the point, convert it to the window's local coordinate system, and check to see if it's inside `gPopUpRect`. If so . . .

```
{----------------> HandleMouseDown      <--}

    procedure HandleMouseDown;
        var
            whichWindow: WindowPtr;
            thePart, i: INTEGER;
            theChoice: LONGINT;
            myPoint, popUpUpperLeft: Point;
    begin
        thePart := FindWindow(gTheEvent.where, whichWindow);
        case thePart of
            inContent:
                begin
                    myPoint := gTheEvent.where;
                    GlobalToLocal(myPoint);
                    if PtInRect(myPoint, gPopUpRect) then
                        begin
```

. . . invert the label and use `gPopUpRect` to determine where the pop-up menu should appear. Because `PopUpMenuSelect` works with global coordinates, call `LocalToGlobal` to convert `popUpUpperLeft`. Next, call `PopUpMenuSelect` to implement the pop-up menu. Then, uninvert the label.

Finally, handle the selection by calling `SysBeep` the selected number of times. `gPopUpItem` is set to the selected item number, so the next time the pop-up appears, `gPopUpItem` will be the default.

Early versions of Apple's system 6 software had problems with the `SysBeep` call. If you experience problems with Zinger, make sure that you are not using System 6.0 or 6.1!

```
                            InvertRect(gLabelRect);
                            popUpUpperLeft.v := gPopUpRect.top +
                                PIXEL_FOR_TOP_LINE;
                            popUpUpperLeft.h := gPopUpRect.left;
                            LocalToGlobal(popUpUpperLeft);
                            theChoice := PopUpMenuSelect
                                (gPopUpMenu, popUpUpperLeft.v,
                                popUpUpperLeft.h, gPopUpItem);
                            InvertRect(gLabelRect);
                            if LoWord(theChoice) > 0 then
                                begin
```

```
                                        gPopUpItem := LoWord
                                            (theChoice);
                                        DrawPopUpNumber;
                                        for i := 0 to gPopUpItem -
                                            1 do
                                                SysBeep(20);
                                    end;
                            end;
                    end;
            inSysWindow:
                SystemClick(gTheEvent, whichWindow);
            inDrag:
                DragWindow(whichWindow, gTheEvent.where,
                        screenBits.bounds);
```

This is not the way "proper" Macintosh applications exit. Use a
Quit item in the **File** menu for your applications.

```
            inGoAway:
                gDone := TRUE;
        end;
    end;
```

DrawPopUp will draw the pop-up outline, its one-pixel drop
shadow, the pop-up label, and set gLabelRect, which you'll invert
when the pop-up is selected. DrawPopUp will also be called to
handle updateEvts. After the background is drawn, call
DrawPopUpNumber to draw the current menu value—in this case, a
number.

```
{---------------> DrawPopUp <--}

procedure DrawPopUp;
begin
    SetRect(gPopUpRect, POPUP_LEFT, POPUP_TOP, POPUP_RIGHT,
            POPUP_BOTTOM);
    FrameRect(gPopUpRect);

    MoveTo(gPopUpRect.left + SHADOW_PIXELS,
            gPopUpRect.bottom);
    LineTo(gPopUpRect.right, gPopUpRect.bottom);
    LineTo(gPopUpRect.right, gPopUpRect.top +
            SHADOW_PIXELS);

    MoveTo(gPopUpRect.left - gPopUpLabelWidth -
            RIGHT_MARGIN, gPopUpRect.bottom - BOTTOM_MARGIN);
    HLock(Handle(gPopUpLabelH));
    DrawString(gPopUpLabelH^^);
    HUnlock(Handle(gPopUpLabelH));
```

```
    gLabelRect.top := gPopUpRect.top + PIXEL_FOR_TOP_LINE;
    gLabelRect.left := gPopUpRect.left - gPopUpLabelWidth -
                    LEFT_MARGIN - RIGHT_MARGIN;
    gLabelRect.right := gPopUpRect.left;
    gLabelRect.bottom := gPopUpRect.bottom;

    DrawPopUpNumber;
end;
```

DrawPopUpNumber gets the menu item corresponding to gPopUpItem, calculates the margin, and draws it:

```
{----------------> DrawPopUpNumber        <--}

procedure DrawPopUpNumber;
    var
        menuItem: Str255;
        itemLeftMargin: INTEGER;
begin
    GetItem(gPopUpMenu, gPopUpItem, menuItem);
    itemLeftMargin := (gPopUpRect.right - gPopUpRect.left -
                    StringWidth(menuItem)) div 2;
    MoveTo(gPopUpRect.left + itemLeftMargin,
        gPopUpRect.bottom - BOTTOM_MARGIN);
    DrawString(menuItem);
end;
```

In Review

Menus are an intrinsic part of the Macintosh interface. Designing them correctly allows you to take advantage of the familiarity of users with standard Mac menus. The standard pull-down menu does the job for many applications, and hierarchical and pop-up menus bring freshness to the interface.

In Chapter 6, you'll learn about another essential part of the Mac interface: creating and controlling dialog boxes. While you're there, you'll also look at one of the newest managers on the Macintosh: the Notification Manager.

Working with Dialogs

In a dialog box, the computer presents a list of alternatives for the user to choose from. Alerts are simplified dialogs, used to report errors and give warnings to the user. Chapter 6 discusses both of these, along with the Notification Manager, Apple's background notification mechanism.

DIALOGS ARE AN important part of the Macintosh interface; they provide a friendly, standardized way of communicating and receiving feedback from the user. Some dialogs ask questions of the user. Others offer the user the opportunity to modify current program parameters (Figures 6.1 and 6.2). Some dialogs are the direct result of a user menu selection. For example, when you select **Print...** from within an application, the **Print Job dialog** appears (Figure 6.3).

Dialogs that appear as a direct result of menu commands give you a chance to change your mind (with the **Cancel** button), to continue on as planned (with the **OK** button), or to change things around a bit before continuing.

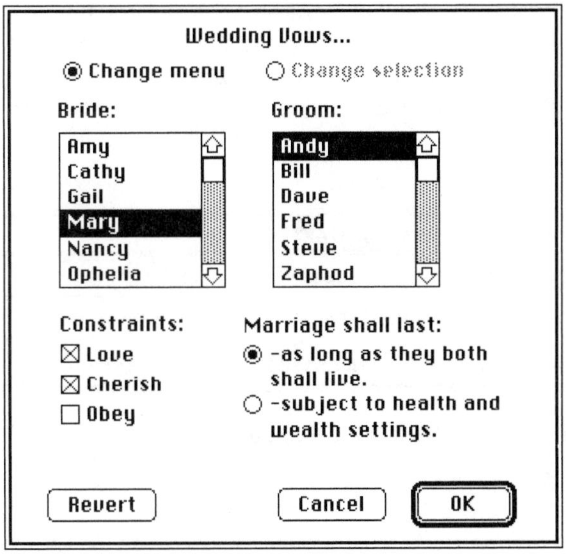

Figure 6.1 "Wedding Vow Options" dialog box.

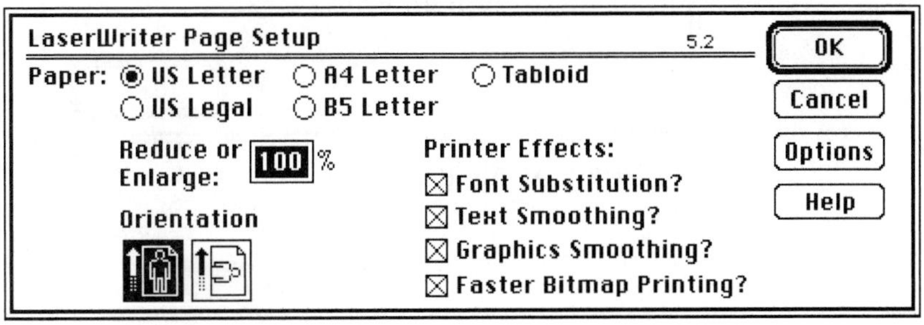

Figure 6.2 **Page Setup** dialog box.

> By convention, menu items that spawn dialog boxes always end with an ellipsis (**...**). For example, the **Print...** item on the **File** menu brings up a print dialog box.

Another important part of the Mac interface is the **alert mechanism**. **Alerts** (Figure 6.4) are simplified dialogs, used to report errors and give warnings to the user. From a programmer's point of view, alerts are easier to deal with than dialogs, so we'll use them when we can.

Chapter 6 also presents the Notification Manager, one of the newer additions to the Toolbox. The Notification Manager is designed to work with MultiFinder, so that a program not currently in the foreground has a way of notifying the user of an important event.

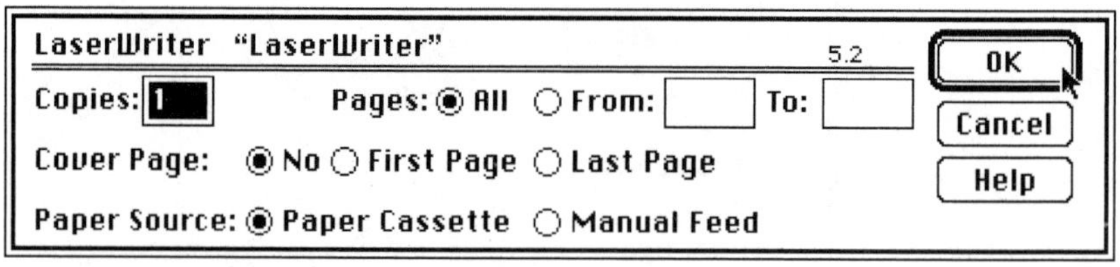

Figure 6.3 **Print Job** dialog box.

Figure 6.4 An Alert!

How Dialogs Work

Dialog boxes consist of a window and a list of dialog items. When the dialog first appears, each item on the dialog item list is drawn. Typical dialog items include checkboxes, radio buttons, and push buttons. These items are called **controls**. In addition, static text fields, editable text fields, `PICT`s, and `ICON`s may also be part of an item list (Figure 6.5). Every dialog box has at least one exit item (by convention, most dialog boxes offer an **OK** button for this purpose). There are two different kinds of dialogs: modal dialogs and modeless dialogs.

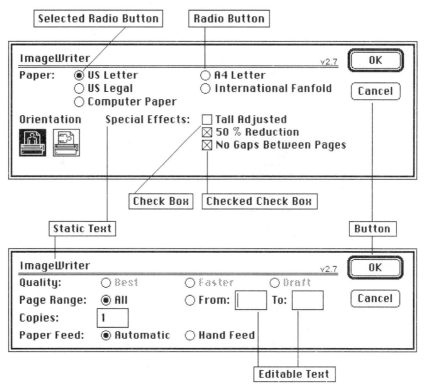

Figure 6.5 Dialog items.

Modal Dialogs

A **modal dialog** is one to which the user must respond before the program can continue. Modal dialogs are used for decisions that must be made immediately. They represent the vast majority of dialog boxes.

The Macintosh is generally a modeless machine. This means that most of the operations performed by an application are available to the user most of the time. For example, most of the operations performed by THINK Pascal are available via pull-down menus. Modal dialogs come into play when you must focus the user's attention on a specific task or issue. Alerts are always modal. Dialog boxes aren't always modal.

Modeless Dialogs

Modeless dialogs act more like regular windows; they appear to the user like any other window and can be brought to the front with a mouse click, or even dragged around the screen. Whereas modal dialogs require an immediate response from the user, modeless dialogs may be set aside until they are needed. The algorithms used to implement modal and modeless dialogs are quite different.

The Modal Dialog Algorithm

The algorithm for modal dialogs follows these steps:

1. First, load the dialog (including the dialog's item list) from the resource file using `GetNewDialog`.

2. Then, make the dialog window visible (just as you would a new window).

3. Next, enter a loop, first calling `ModalDialog` to find out which item the user selected, then processing that item. When an exit item (such as **OK** or **Cancel**) is selected, exit the loop.

The Modeless Dialog Algorithm

The algorithm for modeless diaglogs follows these steps:

1. First, load the dialog and make it visible (as was done with the modal dialog).

2. As an event is returned by `GetNextEvent` or `WaitNextEvent`, pass it on to `IsDialogEvent`.

3. If `IsDialogEvent` returns `FALSE`, the event is not related to the dialog and should be handled normally. Otherwise, the event should be passed to `DialogSelect`.

4. `DialogSelect` returns a pointer to the dialog box whose item was selected, as well as the number of the item selected by the user. Process the item as you would with `ModalDialog`.

Let's look at the types of items found in dialogs.

Dialog Items: Controls

One of the most important types of dialog items are controls. **Controls** are items that exist in at least two different states. For example, the checkbox can be checked or unchecked (Figure 6.6). Although controls may be defined by the program designer, four types of controls are already defined in the Toolbox. They are **buttons**, **checkboxes**, **radio buttons**, and **dials**.

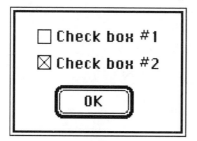

Figure 6.6 The checkbox

These controls fall under the jurisdiction of the **Control Manager**, which handles the creation, editing, and use of controls.

Buttons

The classic example of a button is the **OK** button found in most dialog boxes (Figure 6.7). When the mouse button is released with the cursor inside the button, the button's action is performed. For example, clicking an **OK** button might start a print job or save an application's data. Those of you who are familiar with HyperCard should note the similarity of HyperCard buttons to Toolbox buttons. Toolbox buttons have the shape of rounded-corner rectangles, whereas HyperCard buttons have more variation in shape and appearance.

Checkboxes

Checkboxes are generally used to set options or arguments of an action. For example, you might use a checkbox to determine whether the user wants sound turned on or off in an application (Figure 6.8).

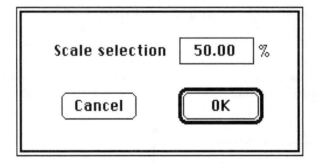

Figure 6.7 **Cancel** and **OK** buttons.

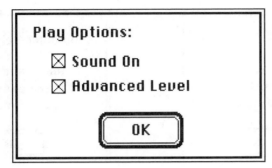

Figure 6.8 Checkbox example.

Radio Buttons

Radio buttons are similar to checkboxes in function, in that they also are generally used to set options or choices in a dialog box. Figure 6.9 shows some radio buttons. The difference between radio buttons and checkboxes is that the choices displayed in radio buttons are mutually exclusive. Radio buttons appear in sets, and one and only one radio button in a set may be on (or highlighted) at any given time (Figure 6.10).

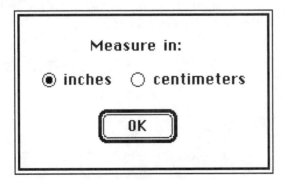

Figure 6.9 Radio button example.

Wrong Way: radio
buttons should indicate
mutually exclusive
options.

Right Way: only one
of these choices
would reasonable be
picked.

Figure 6.10 Radio button etiquette.

Dials

Dials are different from other controls: They display and supply
qualitative instead of off/on information. The only dial control type
predefined in the Toolbox is the **scroll bar** (Figure 6.11), which is an
integral part of many Mac application windows. In Chapter 7, we'll
show you how to set up a scroll bar.

Figure 6.11 Scroll bar example (from Pager in Chapter 7).

Other Dialog Items

Controls are only one type of item used in dialogs. You can display pictures (PICTs) and icons (resource type ICON) in dialog boxes. You can also add static and editable text fields, as well as user items, to your dialogs (Figure 6.12). User items designate an area of the dialog box that will be drawn in by a userItem procedure. If the procedure draws outside the user item Rect, the drawing is clipped. For example, you can define a clock-drawing procedure that gets updated each time ModalDialog is called.

ResEdit makes it easy to define a group of dialog items. Figure 6.13 shows how ResEdit allows you to graphically edit the appearance of a dialog and the items within it.

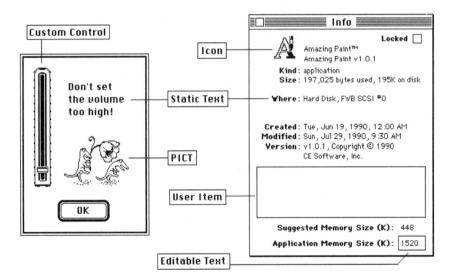

Figure 6.12 Other dialog items.

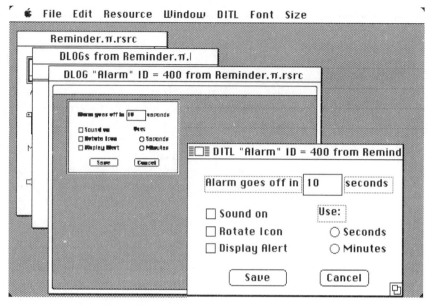

Figure 6.13 Making dialogs (in ResEdit).

Where do dialog items come from?

Some dialog items are controls, like check boxes and radio buttons. Other items, like **PICT**s and **ICON**s, are resources that may be used in both windows and dialogs. Finally, there are items like editable text and static text items that are created and managed by the dialog manager—you won't see them in regular windows.

Working with Alerts

Alerts are very much like dialogs: You build them using ResEdit, and they consist of a window and a dialog item list. However, alerts are self-contained and can be invoked with a single line of code. Whereas ModalDialog is called repeatedly inside a loop, the alert procedures are called once. Each alert routine takes care of its own housekeeping.

There are three standard types of alerts: note alerts, caution alerts, and stop alerts (Figure 6.14). **Note alerts** have an informative tone and are an easy way to tell the user something. **Caution alerts** tell the user that the next step taken should be considered carefully, as it may lead to unexpected results. **Stop alerts** indicate a critical situation, such as a fatal error, that must be brought to the user's attention.

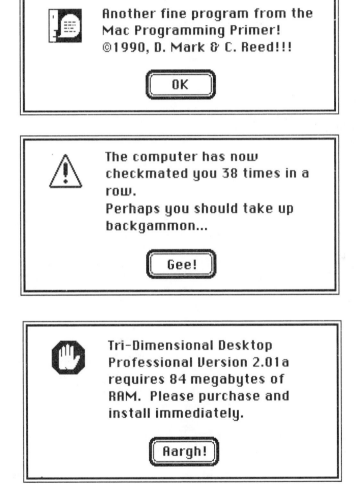

Figure 6.14 Note, caution, and stop alerts.

Each alert exists in stages. The first time an alert is presented, it is a stage 1 alert; the second time, a stage 2 alert; the third time, a stage 3 alert; the fourth and subsequent times, a stage 4 alert. You can design your alerts so that stage 1 alerts are silent but stage 2, 3, and 4 alerts beep when the alert is presented. You can also specify whether or not the alert is presented at different stages.

The Alert Algorithm

Working with alerts is easy. Build your alert with ResEdit by creating an `ALRT` and a `DITL`. Unlike regular dialogs, the only type of control you should put in your alert dialog item list is a button. The alert mechanism is as follows:

1. Load and present the alert with a call to `StopAlert`, `NoteAlert`, or `CautionAlert`.

2. Use the value returned from each of these functions to determine which item was hit (i.e., which button was pressed).

Adding Dialogs to Your Programs

In this chapter, we'll show you how to build modal dialog boxes and alerts through the use of `DLOG` and `DITL` resources. Although we could have created the dialog structure in THINK Pascal instead, we chose to emphasize the resource-based approach.

As was stated in the dialog algorithm, to put a dialog box in your application, you do the following things: initialize the Dialog Manager and load your dialog box resources, call `ModalDialog`, and respond to the events that occur in the dialog box window.

Here's an outline of the procedure. First, initialize the Dialog Manager (**THINK** Pascal does this for you):

```
InitDialogs( nil );
```

Then, load a dialog from your resource file with the `GetNewDialog` routine:

```
myDialog: = GetNewDialog( resource_ID,nil,
                    WindowPtr(-1);
```

Now, initialize each of your controls. Each control has a unique item number, defined in the DITL resource (Figure 6.15). Use GetDItem to get a handle to each control item in the dialog box; then use SetCtlValue to set the buttons, radio buttons, and check boxes to their initial values. For example, the following routine will fill the first radio button and clear the second radio button in a dialog box:

```
FIRST_RADIO := 2;
SECOND_RADIO := 3;

ON    := 1;
OFF :=      0;
.
.
.

GetDItem( myDialog, FIRST_RADIO, itemType,itemHandle,
         itemRect );
SetCtlValue( itemHandle, ON );
GetDItem( myDialog, SECOND_RADIO, itemType, itemHandle,
         itemRect );
SetCtlValue( itemHandle, OFF );
```

FIRST_RADIO and SECOND_RADIO are the radio button item numbers defined in the DITL resource. The first radio button will be set to ON, the second to OFF (Figure 6.16).

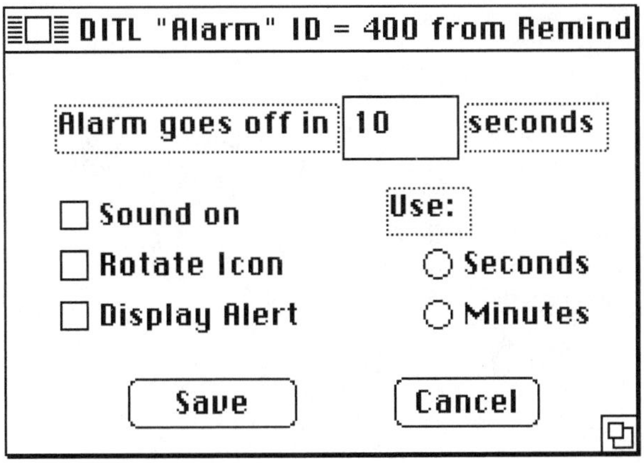

Figure 6.15 A sample DITL.

Figure 6.16 Radio buttons

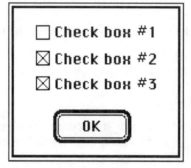

Figure 6.17 Three checkboxes.

Here's an example of initialization of a series of checkboxes. The code fragment clears the first checkbox and checks the second and third checkboxes (Figure 6.17).

```
FIRST_CHECKBOX   := 4;
SECOND_CHECKBOX  := 5;
THIRD_CHECKBOX   := 6;

ON   := 1;
OFF  := 0;
 .
 .
 .
```

```
GetDItem( myDialog, FIRST_CHECKBOX, itemType,
          itemHandle, itemRect );
SetCtlValue( itemHandle, OFF );
GetDItem( myDialog, SECOND_CHECKBOX, itemType,
          itemHandle, itemRect );
SetCtlValue( itemHandle, ON );
GetDItem( myDialog, THIRD_CHECKBOX, itemType,
          itemHandle, itemRect );
SetCtlValue( itemHandle, ON );
```

When you create your DLOG in ResEdit, make sure the Visible box is unchecked. That way, if you load your dialog at the beginning of your program, it won't appear until you're ready.

By the way, if you plan on drawing in the dialog box with QuickDraw (which you might want to do with a userItem procedure), make the dialog the current port:

```
SetPort( myDialog );
```

Then, when the dialog is made visible, draw away.

Make the dialog visible by calling ShowWindow. You're now ready to call ModalDialog to handle the events that occur in the dialog window.

```
dialogDone = FALSE;
ShowWindow( myDialog );
while dialogDone = FALSE do
    begin
        ModalDialog( nil, itemHit );
        case itemHit of
        OK_BUTTON:
            begin
                dialogDone := TRUE;
            end;
```

```
            FIRST_RADIO:
                begin
                    HandleRadio
                        ( SECOND_BUTTON );
                end;
            .
            .
            .
            THIRD_CHECKBOX :
                begin
                    HandleCheck
                        ( THIRD_CHECKBOX );
                end;
        end;
    end;
    HideWindow( myDialog );
```

When the user clicks the **OK** button, the dialog loop exits and the dialog window is made invisible again.

If you're dealing with more than one window, make sure you are aware of routines like `SelectWindow`, which brings the window specified in the parameter to the front. You may also want to consider hiding your other windows while your dialog box is visible, and then showing them when you drop out of the dialog loop.

Dialog items are either **enabled** or **disabled**. If an item is disabled, `ModalDialog` will not report mouse clicks in the item. In general, clicking `ICON`s and `PICT`s in a dialog box has no special significance, so disable both of these types of items.

Static text and **Editable text** fields are also usually disabled, although you may change them in response to other events. For example, a timer might display the time in minutes or seconds, depending on the value of a set of radio buttons (Figure 6.18). If the **Seconds** radio button is clicked, the static text field could read **Seconds**. If the **Minutes** radio button is clicked, the static text field could be changed to read **Minutes**. Use the routines `GetIText` and `SetIText` to read and set the values of static text fields.

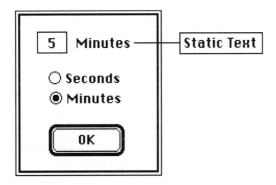

Figure 6.18 Static text.

ParamText allows you to create a set of four default strings that can be substituted in your static text fields. To specify them, call ParamText with four Str255s:

```
ParamText( 'the tiny republic of Togo',
           'porkpie hats', 'babar',
           'Altarian dog biscuits' );
```

From now on, whenever the strings "^0", "^1", "^2", or "^3" appear in a static text item, they will be replaced by the appropriate ParamText parameter. ParamText is used in Chapter 7's error-handling routines.

> You can store ParamText strings in your resource file as resources of type 'STR ' or inside a single 'STR#' resource, then read the strings in with GetResource or GetString, and finally, pass them to ParamText. If, during the course of running your program, you decide to change the values of your strings, you can write them back out to the resource file with WriteResource. This is a little tricky, but it gives you a great way to store program defaults. The mechanism for modifying resources is covered in *Inside Macintosh,* Volume I, pages 122–127.

GetIText and SetIText can also be used to modify the contents of an editable text field. Here's an example:

```
GetDItem( myDialog, TEXT_FIELD, itemType,
          itemHandle, itemRect );
GetIText( itemHandle, myString );
SetIText( itemHandle, 'I've been replaced!!!' );
```

> The last three arguments to GetDItem are placeholders. That is, they won't always be used, but you always need to provide a variable to receive the values returned. In the previous example, itemHandle was used, but itemType and itemRect were not.

Like ICONs and PICTs, editable and static text field items should be disabled so that mouse clicks are not reported. In the case of editable text fields, the dialog manager handles the mouse click for you.

The Notification Manager

The Notification Manager contains calls that allow applications running in the background to communicate with the user. The Notification Manager was first implemented in System 6.0. Because the Notification Manager is not described in *Inside Macintosh,* we've provided the following tech block. We warn you, though, that this is an experimental, highly classified, multipage tech block. Take your time. Remember, read *all* the directions before you start.

How the Notification Manager Works

The Notification Manager alerts the user that a background application requires the user's attention. The following notification techniques can be used. First, a small diamond-shaped mark (◆) may be placed on the notifying application's item in the menu.

Next, the icon may be rotated with another small icon (see Figure 6.19). Then, the user may be notified of the event by a sound designated by the background application. Finally, an alert can be displayed with a message regarding the event (see Figure 6.20). After the user clicks on the alert's **OK** button, a response procedure defined in the notifying application can be called.

Figure 6.19 Small icon rotation.

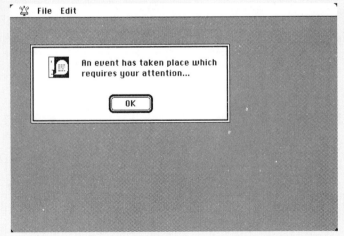

Figure 6.20 Alert message from the Notification Manager.

The Notification Manager will still run even if your program is not running under MultiFinder. Because your program can't run in the background, however, the Notification Manager's functionality will be limited.

The Notification Manager Structure

Each call to the Notification Manager makes use of the `NMRec` data structure:

```
TYPE NMRec = RECORD
   qLink:       QElemPtr;   {next queue entry}
   qType:       INTEGER;    {queue type — ORD(nmType)
                             = 8}
   nmFlags:     INTEGER;    {reserved}
   nmPrivate:   LONGINT;    {reserved}
   nmReserved:  INTEGER;    {reserved}
   nmMark:      INTEGER;    {item to mark in Apple
                             menu}
   nmSIcon:     Handle;     {handle to small icon}
   nmSound:     Handle;     {handle to sound record}
   nmStr:       StringPtr;  {string to appear in alert}
   nmResp:      ProcPtr;    {pointer to response
                             routine}
   nmRefCon:    LONGINT;    {for application use}
END;
```

Here's an explanation of the `NMRec` fields:

- `qLink`, `qType`, `nmFlags`, `nmPrivate`, and `nmReserved` are either reserved or contain information about the notification queue; you won't adjust these values.

- `nmMark`: If `nmMark` is 0, the (◆) will not be displayed in the menu when the notification occurs; if `nmMark` is 1, the application that is making the notifying call receives the mark. If you want a desk accessory to be marked, use the `refnum` of the desk accessory. Drivers should pass 0.

- `nmSIcon`: If `nmSIcon` is `nil`, no icon is used; otherwise, the handle to the small icon (`SICN` resource) to be used should be placed here.

- `nmSound`: if `nmSound` is 0, no sound is played; −1 will result in the system sound being played. To play an `'snd '` sound resource, put a handle to the resource here. The handle must be nonpurgeable.

- `nmStr` contains the pointer to the text string to be used in the alert box. Put in `nil` for no alert box.

- `nmResp` is a pointer to a response procedure that gets called once the notification is complete. We'll set `nmResp` to −1, which removes the request from the notification queue once the notification is complete.

There are only two calls in the Notification Manager. The first, `NMInstall`, adds the notification request to the Notification Queue, which is checked periodically:

```
FUNCTION NMInstall (nmReqPtr: QElemPtr) :
OSErr;
```

The second, `NMRemove`, removes the notification from the Notification Queue:

```
FUNCTION NMRemove (nmReqPtr: QElemPtr) :
OSErr;
```

The next section lists and describes Reminder, the biggest and most complex program in this book. Reminder will show you how to put together all the pieces we've talked about so far: windows, events, menus, fonts, dialogs, alerts, and the Notification Manager.

Reminder

Reminder sets a countdown timer and, when the time runs out, alerts the user of the event via the Notification Manager. Reminder also supports a dialog box that allows you to change some of its settings. Here's a quick look at the Reminder algorithm:

1. It checks for System 6.0 or later. If the System version is too old, it puts up an alert and exits.

2. It loads and initializes the settings dialog.

3. It loads the ⌘, **File**, and **Edit** menus.

4. It initializes the Notification Manager data structure.

5. It handles events.

6. If the **Change Settings** menu item is selected, it handles the settings dialog box.

7. If the **Start Countdown** menu item is selected, it pulls the number of seconds from the settings dialog, loads and shows the countdown window, counts down, and sets the notification.

8. If the **Kill Notification** menu item is selected, it removes the notification from the Notification Queue.

9. If the **Quit** menu item is selected, it exits.

Warning: This is the longest of all of the Primer programs. You can save a little time by using resources and code from Chapter 5, but it's still going to take a while. You may wish to take a brief recess.

Setting Up the Project

Start by creating your project files. You can save some time by copying your Timer folder from Chapter 5 and renaming it Reminder. But remember, if you do this, you'll need to change the source code file name, the project file name, and the resource file name. We'll assume you're starting from scratch.

Making the Resources for Reminder

Go into ResEdit and create a file named Reminder.π.rsrc. As has been discussed earlier, it's a good idea to set each resource (except MENUs) to be purgeable in the **Get Resource Info** dialog box. Create a DITL with the controls and fields shown in Figure 6.21. This DITL will have eleven items. The table in Figure 6.22 lists the values for these items.

Next, create a DITL with the information shown in Figure 6.23. You'll use this DITL in your About box alert. The About DITL has two items. Create them from the table shown in Figure 6.24.

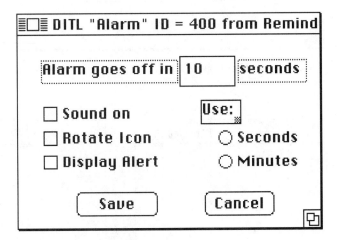

Figure 6.21 Settings DITL appearance.

Item#	Type	Enabled	Top	Left	Bottom	Right	Text/Resource ID
1	Button	Yes	130	50	150	120	Save
2	Button	Yes	130	160	150	220	Cancel
3	Static Text	No	20	20	40	138	Alarm goes off in
4	Editable Text	No	20	142	40	184	10
5	Static Text	No	20	189	40	249	seconds
6	Checkbox	Yes	55	20	75	102	Sound on
7	Checkbox	Yes	75	20	95	122	Rotate Icon
8	Checkbox	Yes	95	20	115	130	Display Alert
9	Radio Button	Yes	54	157	74	192	Use:
10	Radio Button	Yes	75	170	95	247	Seconds
11	Static Text	No	95	170	115	249	Minutes

Figure 6.22 Item specifications for settings D I T L.

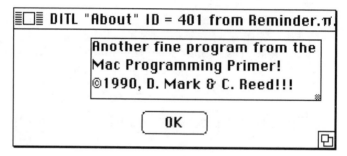

Figure 6.23 About box D I T L Get Info window.

Item#	Type	Enabled	Top	Left	Bottom	Right	Text/Resource ID
1	Button	Yes	71	117	91	177	OK
2	Static Text	No	7	70	61	280	Another fine program from the Macintosh Programming Primer © 1990 D. Mark & C. Reed!!!

Figure 6.24 Item specifications for About D I T L.

Finally, create a DITL similar to Figure 6.25. This DITL belongs to the alert shown for a system earlier than version 6.0. The Bad System DITL also has two items. Create them using the table in Figure 6.26.

Create an ALRT resource with ID = 401 that matches Figure 6.27. This snapshot was made by selecting **Display as Text** from the ALRT menu that appears when the ALRT is opened. Don't forget to set the **itemsID** field to 401. This links the ALRT to DITL 401.

Next, create an ALRT resource with ID = 402 that matches the table in Figure 6.28.

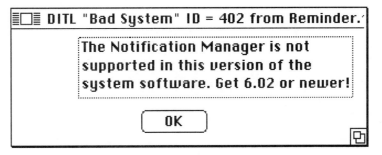

Figure 6.25 Bad System DITL.

Item#	Type	Enabled	Top	Left	Bottom	Right	Text/Resource ID
1	Button	Yes	71	117	91	177	OK
2	Static Text	No	7	70	61	280	The Notification Manager is not supported in this version of the system software. Get 6.02 or newer!!

Figure 6.26 Item specifications for Bad System DITL.

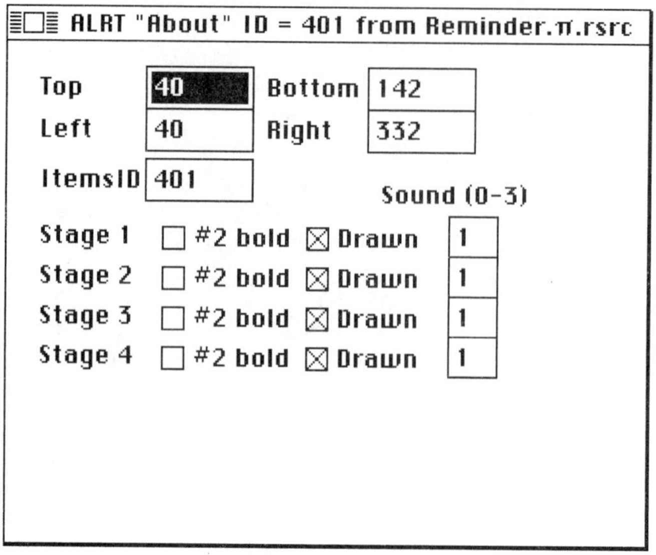

▤☐▤ ALRT "About" ID = 401 from Reminder.π.rsrc

Top	`40`	**Bottom**	`142`
Left	`40`	**Right**	`332`

ItemsID `401`

Sound (0-3)

Stage 1	☐ #2 bold	☒ Drawn	`1`
Stage 2	☐ #2 bold	☒ Drawn	`1`
Stage 3	☐ #2 bold	☒ Drawn	`1`
Stage 4	☐ #2 bold	☒ Drawn	`1`

Figure 6.27 The About Box A L R T, displayed as text.

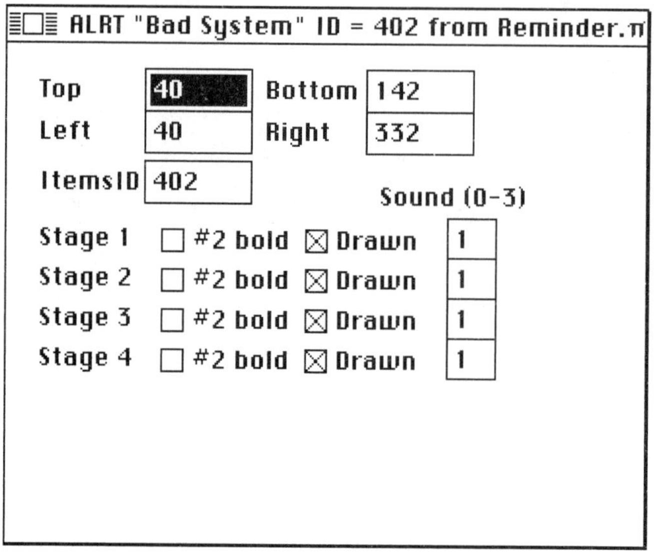

▤☐▤ ALRT "Bad System" ID = 402 from Reminder.π

Top	`40`	**Bottom**	`142`
Left	`40`	**Right**	`332`

ItemsID `402`

Sound (0-3)

Stage 1	☐ #2 bold	☒ Drawn	`1`
Stage 2	☐ #2 bold	☒ Drawn	`1`
Stage 3	☐ #2 bold	☒ Drawn	`1`
Stage 4	☐ #2 bold	☒ Drawn	`1`

Figure 6.28 The Bad System A L R T, displayed as text.

You're now ready to create your alarm settings dialog box. Create a DLOG with ID = 400 that matches Figure 6.29. Remember to set the procID to 1. This tells the Dialog Manager to draw the standard modal dialog type window.

Next, we'll create two 'STR ' resources to use in the Settings dialog. The first contains the default value to use when the time is displayed in seconds. The second contains the default value to use when the time is displayed in minutes. Figure 6.30a shows the value for 'STR ' 401, and Figure 6.30b shows the value for 'STR ' 402.

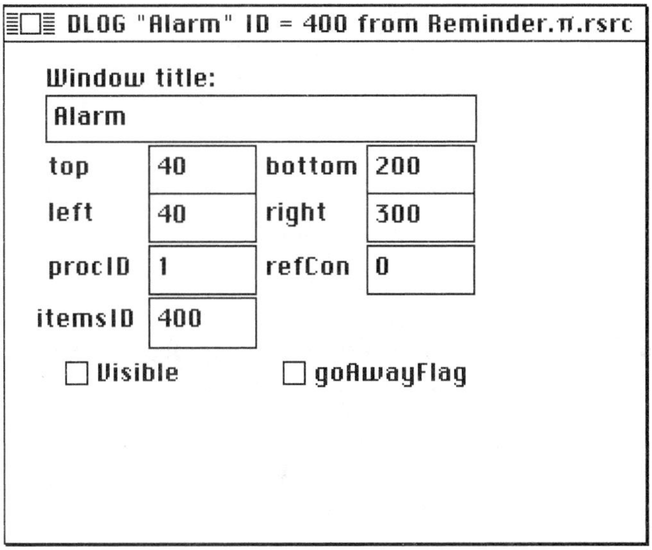

```
▤☐▤  DLOG "Alarm" ID = 400 from Reminder.π.rsrc

   Window title:
   ┌─────────────────────────────────────────────┐
   │ Alarm                                        │
   └─────────────────────────────────────────────┘

      top      ┌──────┐    bottom  ┌──────┐
               │ 40   │            │ 200  │
      left     │ 40   │    right   │ 300  │

      procID   │ 1    │    refCon  │ 0    │
               └──────┘            └──────┘
      itemsID  ┌──────┐
               │ 400  │
               └──────┘
          ☐ Visible          ☐ goAwayFlag

```

Figure 6.29 The Settings DLOG, displayed as text.

```
≣□≣ STR "Def. Secs." ID = 401 from Reminder.π.rsrc ≣
```

The String | 10
Data $ |

a

```
≣□≣ STR "Def. Mins." ID = 402 from Reminder.π.rsrc ≣
```

The String | 1
Data $ |

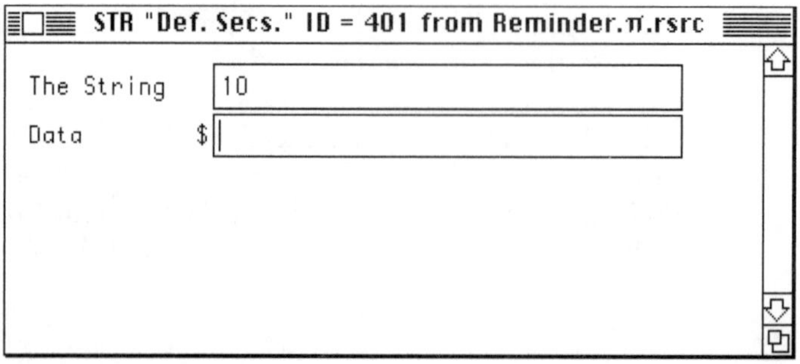

b

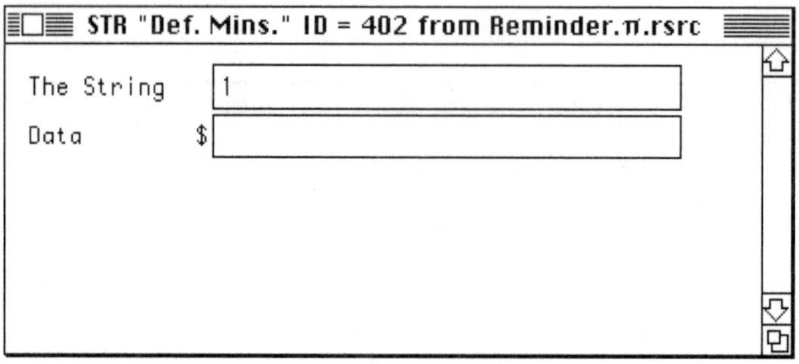

Figure 6.30 Default time 'STR' resources.

Setting Up the Notification Manager Resources

Now that you've finished with the dialog and alert resources, you
need to add three resources for the Notification Manager: a string, a
sound, and a small icon. First, create another 'STR ' resource, with
ID = 400, that the Notification Manager will use in the alert that
is presented to the user (Figure 6.31).

```
≣□≣         STR ID = 400 from Reminder.π.rsrc ≣
```

The String | Zounds!!! It's time...
Data $ |

Figure 6.31 The 'STR' resource for the Notification Manager.

Now, add the sound. There are a number of different sound resource types. The resource type needed is a 'snd ' (space at the end), with resource ID = 400. If you have a favorite sound from a HyperCard stack, you can copy it using ResEdit and paste it into Reminder.π.rsrc.

A good check to determine if the sound will work properly is to use the **play it** option in ResEdit's **snd** menu, which shows when you are editing 'snd ' resources. If that works, then the Notification Manager should be able to use it. If your 'snd ' is a large file, you may have some problems. Start with a small 'snd ' resource.

If you don't have a favorite sound, don't panic. Figure 6.32 shows the 'snd ' resources found in System 6.0.5. Open up your system file (Careful! Use a backup!) and copy the 'snd ' of your choice into your resource file. Change the ID of the 'snd ' to 400.

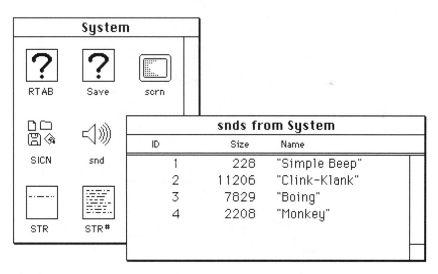

Figure 6.32 System 6.0.5 'snd' resources.

The final resource for the Notification Manager is the small icon that rotates with the menu icon. Ours is a little bell. Use it or create your own small icon. Create a resource of type SICN, with ID = 400. Figure 6.33 is a snapshot of our SICN editing session. To replicate the figure, just click on the "fat bits" in the 16-by-16 square of pixels to turn them on or off.

Adding the Menu Resources

Here's where cutting and pasting will reduce your time on this project. If you have the Timer project, copy the MBAR and MENU resources from it into the Reminder project. They are quite similar, except for the names of a few menu items.

If you don't have Timer resources, create the two menu resources. The first, MBAR, contains the three menu IDs (400, 401, and 402). Create a resource of type MBAR, with ID = 400 (Figure 6.34). Remember, to add a new menu to the list, click on the asterisks and select **Insert New Field** from the **Resource** menu.

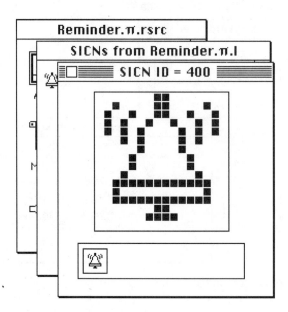

Figure 6.33 The SICN resource for the Notification Manager

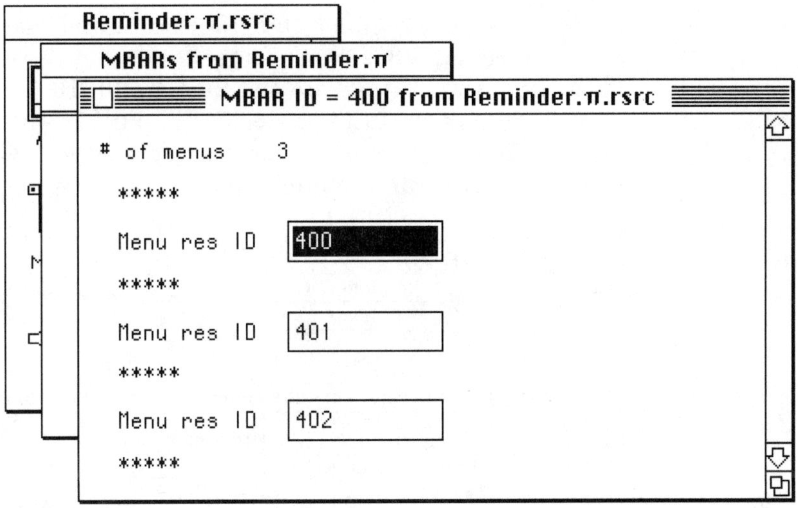

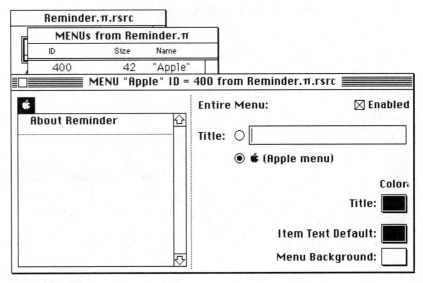

Figure 6.34 MBAR resource.

Now you need to create each menu with its items. Create the
MENU, ID = 400, and make it look like the menu in Figure 6.35.

Figure 6.35 MENU resources.

Next, create the **File** MENU, ID = 401, and make it look like the menu in Figure 6.36. (Don't forget to disable the **Kill Notification** menu item.) Finally, create the **Edit** MENU, ID = 402, and make it look like the menu in Figure 6.37. The **Edit** menu is disabled and is provided only as a courtesy for desk accessories. (Cut and paste this menu from Timer in Chapter 5.)

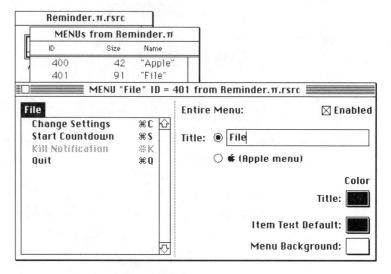

Figure 6.36 File MENU resource.

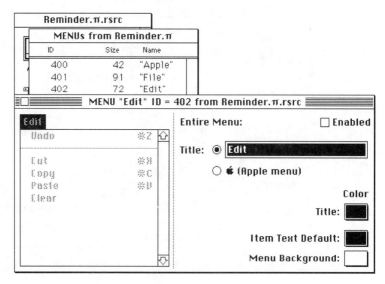

Figure 6.37 Edit MENU resource.

The Home Stretch

Finally, add the old WIND resource for your countdown window. Create a WIND, ID = 400, with the specifications in Figure 6.38. When you're done, save the resource file (whew!). Then, check it to see if you have all the resources listed in Figure 6.39. If you don't, go back and add them.

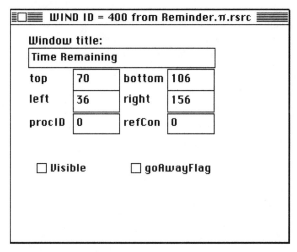

Figure 6.38 WIND resource for countdown window.

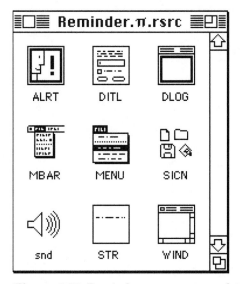

Figure 6.39 Reminder resources completed.

This is, by far, the biggest set of resources in the book. It is not uncommon at this point to start making mistakes (such as mangling your motherboard and switching on the TV), so you might want to take a break before you start entering the code.

The Reminder Code

If you haven't done so already, go into THINK Pascal and create a new project named `Reminder.π`. Next, create a new source code file named `Reminder.p` and add it to the project.

Some of the Reminder code can be copied from Chapter 5's Timer. Just be careful with variable names and the like.

```pascal
program Reminder;
    uses
        Notification;

    const
        BASE_RES_ID = 400;
        ABOUT_ALERT = 401;
        BAD_SYS_ALERT = 402;

        SLEEP = 60;

        SAVE_BUTTON = 1;
        CANCEL_BUTTON = 2;
        TIME_FIELD = 4;
        S_OR_M_FIELD = 5;
        SOUND_ON_BOX = 6;
        ICON_ON_BOX = 7;
        ALERT_ON_BOX = 8;
        SECS_RADIO = 10;
        MINS_RADIO = 11;

        DEFAULT_SECS_ID = 401;
        DEFAULT_MINS_ID = 402;

        ON = 1;
        OFF = 0;

        SECONDS_PER_MINUTE = 60;
```

```
                TOP = 25;
                LEFT = 12;

                MARK_APPLICATION = 1;

                APPLE_MENU_ID = BASE_RES_ID;
                FILE_MENU_ID = BASE_RES_ID + 1;
                ABOUT_ITEM = 1;

                CHANGE_ITEM = 1;
                START_STOP_ITEM = 2;
                KILL_ITEM = 3;
                QUIT_ITEM = 4;

                SYS_VERSION = 2;

        type
                Settings = record
                    timeString: Str255;
                    sound, icon, alert, secsRadio, minsRadio: INTEGER;
                end;

        var
                gSettingsDialog: DialogPtr;
                gDone, gCounting, gNotify_set: BOOLEAN;
                gSeconds_or_minutes: (seconds, minutes);
                gNotifyStrH,      gDefaultSecsH,      gDefaultMinsH:
        StringHandle;
                gMyNMRec: NMRec;
                gTheEvent: EventRecord;
                savedSettings: Settings;


        procedure HandleEvent;
        forward;


   {---------------> SetNotification      <--}

        procedure SetNotification;
            var
                itemType: INTEGER;
                itemRect: Rect;
                itemHandle: Handle;
                dummy: OSErr;
                fileMenu: MenuHandle;
        begin
            if gNotify_set then
                begin
                    dummy := NMRemove(QElemPtr(@gMyNMRec));
```

```
                    HUnlock(Handle(gNotifyStrH));
            end;

        GetDItem(gSettingsDialog, ICON_ON_BOX, itemType,
        itemHandle, itemRect);
        if GetCtlValue(ControlHandle(itemHandle)) = ON then
            gMyNMRec.nmSIcon := GetResource('SICN',
        BASE_RES_ID)
        else
            gMyNMRec.nmSIcon := nil;

        GetDItem(gSettingsDialog, SOUND_ON_BOX, itemType,
        itemHandle, itemRect);
        if GetCtlValue(ControlHandle(itemHandle)) = ON then
            gMyNMRec.nmSound := GetResource('snd ',
            BASE_RES_ID)
        else
            gMyNMRec.nmSound := nil;

        GetDItem(gSettingsDialog, ALERT_ON_BOX, itemType,
        itemHandle, itemRect);
        if GetCtlValue(ControlHandle(itemHandle)) = ON then
            begin
                MoveHHi(Handle(gNotifyStrH));
                HLock(Handle(gNotifyStrH));
                gMyNMRec.nmStr := gNotifyStrH^;
            end
        else
            gMyNMRec.nmStr := nil;

        dummy := NMInstall(QElemPtr(@gMyNMRec));
        fileMenu := GetMHandle(FILE_MENU_ID);
        EnableItem(fileMenu, KILL_ITEM);
        gNotify_set := TRUE;
    end;


{---------------> CountDown   <--}

    procedure CountDown (numSecs: LONGINT);
        var
            myTime, oldTime, difTime: LONGINT;
            myTimeString: Str255;
            countDownWindow: WindowPtr;
    begin
        countDownWindow := GetNewWindow(BASE_RES_ID, nil,
        WindowPtr(-1));
        SetPort(countDownWindow);
        ShowWindow(countDownWindow);
        TextFace([bold]);
        TextSize(24);
```

```
        GetDateTime(myTime);
        oldTime := myTime;

        if gSeconds_or_minutes = minutes then
            numSecs := numSecs * SECONDS_PER_MINUTE;

        gCounting := TRUE;

        while (numSecs > 0) and gCounting do
            begin
                HandleEvent;
                if gCounting then
                    begin
                        MoveTo(LEFT, TOP);
                        GetDateTime(myTime);
                        if myTime <> oldTime then
                            begin
                                difTime := myTime - oldTime;
                                numSecs := numSecs - difTime;
                                oldTime := myTime;
                                NumToString(numSecs,
                                        myTimeString);
                                EraseRect(countDownWindow^.
                                        portRect);
                                DrawString(myTimeString);
                            end;
                    end;
            end;

        if gCounting then
            SetNotification;

        gCounting := FALSE;

        DisposeWindow(countDownWindow);
    end;


{---------------> RestoreSettings      <--}

    procedure RestoreSettings;
        var
            itemType: INTEGER;
            itemRect: Rect;
            itemHandle: Handle;
    begin
        GetDItem(gSettingsDialog, TIME_FIELD, itemType,
                itemHandle, itemRect);
        SetIText(itemHandle, savedSettings.timeString);
        GetDItem(gSettingsDialog, SOUND_ON_BOX, itemType,
                itemHandle, itemRect);
```

```
            SetCtlValue(ControlHandle(itemHandle),
                    savedSettings.sound);
            GetDItem(gSettingsDialog, ICON_ON_BOX, itemType,
                    itemHandle, itemRect);
            SetCtlValue(ControlHandle(itemHandle),
                    savedSettings.icon);
            GetDItem(gSettingsDialog, ALERT_ON_BOX, itemType,
                    itemHandle, itemRect);
            SetCtlValue(ControlHandle(itemHandle),
                    savedSettings.alert);
            GetDItem(gSettingsDialog, SECS_RADIO, itemType,
                    itemHandle, itemRect);
            SetCtlValue(ControlHandle(itemHandle),
                    savedSettings.secsRadio);
            GetDItem(gSettingsDialog, MINS_RADIO, itemType,
                    itemHandle, itemRect);
            SetCtlValue(ControlHandle(itemHandle),
                    savedSettings.minsRadio);

            if savedSettings.secsRadio = ON then
                begin
                    GetDItem(gSettingsDialog, S_OR_M_FIELD,
                            itemType, itemHandle, itemRect);
                    SetIText(itemHandle, 'seconds');
                end
            else
                begin
                    GetDItem(gSettingsDialog, S_OR_M_FIELD,
                            itemType, itemHandle, itemRect);
                    SetIText(itemHandle, 'minutes');
                end;
        end;


    {----------------> SaveSettings    <--}

    procedure SaveSettings;
        var
            itemType: INTEGER;
            itemRect: Rect;
            itemHandle: Handle;
    begin
        GetDItem(gSettingsDialog, TIME_FIELD, itemType,
                itemHandle, itemRect);
        GetIText(itemHandle, savedSettings.timeString);
        GetDItem(gSettingsDialog, SOUND_ON_BOX, itemType,
                itemHandle, itemRect);
        savedSettings.sound := GetCtlValue
                            (ControlHandle(itemHandle));
        GetDItem(gSettingsDialog, ICON_ON_BOX, itemType,
                itemHandle, itemRect);
```

```
        savedSettings.icon := GetCtlValue
        (ControlHandle(itemHandle));
        GetDItem(gSettingsDialog, ALERT_ON_BOX, itemType,
                itemHandle, itemRect);
        savedSettings.alert := GetCtlValue
        (ControlHandle(itemHandle));
        GetDItem(gSettingsDialog, SECS_RADIO, itemType,
                itemHandle, itemRect);
        savedSettings.secsRadio := GetCtlValue
        (ControlHandle(itemHandle));
        GetDItem(gSettingsDialog, MINS_RADIO, itemType,
                itemHandle, itemRect);
        savedSettings.minsRadio := GetCtlValue
        (ControlHandle(itemHandle));
    end;


{----------------> HandleDialog    <--}

    procedure HandleDialog;
        var
            dialogDone: BOOLEAN;
            itemHit, itemType: INTEGER;
            alarmDelay: LONGINT;
            delayString: Str255;
            itemRect: Rect;
            itemHandle: Handle;
    begin
        ShowWindow(gSettingsDialog);
        SaveSettings;

        dialogDone := FALSE;
        while dialogDone = FALSE do
            begin
                ModalDialog(nil, itemHit);
                case itemHit of
                    SAVE_BUTTON:
                        begin
                            HideWindow(gSettingsDialog);
                            dialogDone := TRUE;
                        end;
                    CANCEL_BUTTON:
                        begin
                            HideWindow(gSettingsDialog);
                            RestoreSettings;
                            dialogDone := TRUE;
                        end;
                    SOUND_ON_BOX:
```

```
        begin
            GetDItem(gSettingsDialog, SOUND_ON_BOX, itemType,
                    itemHandle, itemRect);
            if GetCtlValue(ControlHandle (itemHandle)) = ON then
                SetCtlValue(ControlHandle (itemHandle), OFF)
            else
                SetCtlValue(ControlHandle (itemHandle), ON);
        end;
ICON_ON_BOX:
        begin
            GetDItem(gSettingsDialog, ICON_ON_BOX, itemType,
                    itemHandle, itemRect);
            if GetCtlValue(ControlHandle (itemHandle)) = ON then
                SetCtlValue(ControlHandle (itemHandle), OFF)
            else
                SetCtlValue(ControlHandle
                (itemHandle), ON);
        end;
ALERT_ON_BOX:
        begin
            GetDItem(gSettingsDialog, ALERT_ON_BOX, itemType,
                    itemHandle, itemRect);
            if GetCtlValue(ControlHandle (itemHandle)) = ON then
                SetCtlValue(ControlHandle (itemHandle), OFF)
            else
                SetCtlValue(ControlHandle (itemHandle), ON);
        end;
SECS_RADIO:
        begin
            gSeconds_or_minutes := seconds;
            GetDItem(gSettingsDialog, MINS_RADIO, itemType,
                    itemHandle, itemRect);
            SetCtlValue(ControlHandle (itemHandle), OFF);
            GetDItem(gSettingsDialog, SECS_RADIO, itemType,
                    itemHandle, itemRect);
            SetCtlValue(ControlHandle (itemHandle), ON);
            GetDItem(gSettingsDialog, S_OR_M_FIELD, itemType,
                    itemHandle, itemRect);
            SetIText(itemHandle, 'seconds');
            GetDItem(gSettingsDialog, TIME_FIELD, itemType,
                    itemHandle, itemRect);
            SetIText(itemHandle, gDefaultSecsH^^);
            end;
            MINS_RADIO:
                begin
                    gSeconds_or_minutes := minutes;
                    GetDItem(gSettingsDialog, SECS_RADIO, itemType,
                            itemHandle, itemRect);
                    SetCtlValue(ControlHandle (itemHandle), OFF);
                    GetDItem(gSettingsDialog, MINS_RADIO, itemType,
                            itemHandle, itemRect);
                    SetCtlValue(ControlHandle (itemHandle), ON);
```

```
                    GetDItem(gSettingsDialog, S_OR_M_FIELD, itemType,
                            itemHandle, itemRect);
                    SetIText(itemHandle, 'minutes');
                    GetDItem(gSettingsDialog, TIME_FIELD, itemType,
                            itemHandle, itemRect);
                    SetIText(itemHandle, gDefaultMinsH^^);
                end;
            end;
        end;
end;


{----------------> HandleFileChoice    <--}

    procedure HandleFileChoice (theItem: INTEGER);
        var
            timeString: Str255;
            countDownTime: LONGINT;
            itemType: INTEGER;
            itemRect: Rect;
            itemHandle: Handle;
            dummy: OSErr;
            fileMenu: MenuHandle;
    begin
        fileMenu := GetMHandle(FILE_MENU_ID);
        case theItem of
            CHANGE_ITEM:
                HandleDialog;
            START_STOP_ITEM:
                if gCounting then
                    begin
                        gCounting := FALSE;
                        SetItem(fileMenu, theItem, 'Start Countdown');
                                Countdown');
                    end
                else
                    begin
                        HiliteMenu(0);
                        GetDItem(gSettingsDialog, TIME_FIELD,
                                itemType, itemHandle, itemRect);
                        GetIText(itemHandle, timeString);
                        StringToNum(timeString, countDownTime);

                        DisableItem(fileMenu, CHANGE_ITEM);
                        SetItem(fileMenu, theItem, 'Stop Countdown');
                        CountDown(countDownTime);
                        EnableItem(fileMenu, CHANGE_ITEM);
                        SetItem(fileMenu, theItem, 'Start Countdown');
                                    Countdown');
                        end;
```

```
                    KILL_ITEM:
                        begin
                            dummy := NMRemove(QElemPtr(@gMyNMRec));
                            HUnlock(Handle(gNotifyStrH));
                            DisableItem(fileMenu, KILL_ITEM);
                            gNotify_set := FALSE;
                        end;
                    QUIT_ITEM:
                        begin
                            gCounting := FALSE;
                            gDone := TRUE;
                        end;
            end;
        end;


{---------------> HandleAppleChoice    <--}

    procedure HandleAppleChoice (theItem: INTEGER);
        var
            accName: Str255;
            accNumber, itemNumber, dummy: INTEGER;
            appleMenu: MenuHandle;
    begin
        case theItem of
            ABOUT_ITEM:
                dummy := NoteAlert(ABOUT_ALERT, nil);
            otherwise
                begin
                    appleMenu := GetMHandle(APPLE_MENU_ID);
                    GetItem(appleMenu, theItem, accName);
                    accNumber := OpenDeskAcc(accName);
                end;
        end;
    end;


{---------------> HandleMenuChoice    <--}

    procedure HandleMenuChoice (menuChoice: LONGINT);
        var
            theMenu, theItem: INTEGER;
    begin
        if menuChoice <> 0 then
            begin
                theMenu := HiWord(menuChoice);
                theItem := LoWord(menuChoice);

                case theMenu of
                    APPLE_MENU_ID:
                        HandleAppleChoice(theItem);
```

```
                           FILE_MENU_ID:
                              HandleFileChoice(theItem);
                       end;

                       HiliteMenu(0);
                  end;
            end;
      end;


{---------------> HandleMouseDown       <--}

      procedure HandleMouseDown;
            var
                whichWindow: WindowPtr;
                thePart: INTEGER;
                menuChoice, windSize: LONGINT;
      begin
            thePart := FindWindow(gTheEvent.where, whichWindow);
            case thePart of
                inMenuBar:
                    begin
                        menuChoice := MenuSelect(gTheEvent.where);
                        HandleMenuChoice(menuChoice);
                    end;
                inSysWindow:
                    SystemClick(gTheEvent, whichWindow);
                inDrag:
                    DragWindow(whichWindow, gTheEvent.where,
                            screenBits.bounds);
                inGoAway:
                    gDone := TRUE;
            end;
      end;


{---------------> HandleEvent<--}

      procedure HandleEvent;
            var
                theChar: CHAR;
                dummy: BOOLEAN;
      begin
            dummy := WaitNextEvent(everyEvent, gTheEvent, SLEEP, nil);

            case gTheEvent.what of
                mouseDown:
                    HandleMouseDown;
                keyDown, autoKey:
                    begin
                        theChar := CHR(BitAnd(gTheEvent.message,
                                charCodeMask));
```

```
                         if (BitAnd(gTheEvent.modifiers, cmdKey) <> 0) then
                             HandleMenuChoice(MenuKey(theChar));
                     end;
             end;
        end;


{---------------> MainLoop    <--}

    procedure MainLoop;
    begin
        gDone := FALSE;
        gCounting := FALSE;
        gNotify_set := FALSE;

        while gDone = FALSE do
            HandleEvent;
    end;


{---------------> NotifyInit <--}

    procedure NotifyInit;
    begin
        gNotifyStrH := GetString(BASE_RES_ID);
        gMyNMRec.qType := nmType;
        gMyNMRec.nmMark := MARK_APPLICATION;
        gMyNMRec.nmResp := nil;
    end;


{---------------> MenuBarInit<--}

    procedure MenuBarInit;
        var
            myMenuBar: Handle;
            aMenu: MenuHandle;
    begin
        myMenuBar := GetNewMBar(BASE_RES_ID);
        SetMenuBar(myMenuBar);
        DisposHandle(myMenuBar);

        aMenu := GetMHandle(APPLE_MENU_ID);
        AddResMenu(aMenu, 'DRVR');

        DrawMenuBar;
    end;
```

```
{----------------> DialogInit <--}

    procedure DialogInit;
        var
            itemType: INTEGER;
            itemRect: Rect;
            itemHandle: Handle;
    begin
        gDefaultSecsH := GetString(DEFAULT_SECS_ID);
        gDefaultMinsH := GetString(DEFAULT_MINS_ID);

        gSettingsDialog := GetNewDialog(BASE_RES_ID, nil,
                                        WindowPtr(-1));
        GetDItem(gSettingsDialog, SECS_RADIO, itemType,
                itemHandle, itemRect);
        SetCtlValue(ControlHandle(itemHandle), ON);
        GetDItem(gSettingsDialog, SOUND_ON_BOX, itemType,
                itemHandle, itemRect);
        SetCtlValue(ControlHandle(itemHandle), ON);
        GetDItem(gSettingsDialog, ICON_ON_BOX, itemType,
                itemHandle, itemRect);
        SetCtlValue(ControlHandle(itemHandle), ON);
        GetDItem(gSettingsDialog, ALERT_ON_BOX, itemType,
                itemHandle, itemRect);
        SetCtlValue(ControlHandle(itemHandle), ON);

        gSeconds_or_minutes := seconds;
    end;


{----------------> Sys6OrLater<--}

    function Sys6OrLater: BOOLEAN;
        var
            status: OSErr;
            SysEnvData: SysEnvRec;
            dummy: INTEGER;
    begin
        status := SysEnvirons(SYS_VERSION, SysEnvData);
        if (status <> noErr) or
           (SysEnvData.systemVersion < $0600) then
            begin
                dummy := StopAlert(BAD_SYS_ALERT, nil);
                Sys6OrLater := FALSE;
            end
        else
            Sys6OrLater := TRUE;
    end;
```

```
{---------------> Reminder    <--}
begin
    if Sys6OrLater then
        begin
            DialogInit;
            MenuBarInit;
            NotifyInit;

            MainLoop;
        end;
end.
```

Running Reminder

Now that your source code is updated, you're almost ready to run Reminder. You'll have to do something extra with this project because the Notification Manager requires some interface code that THINK Pascal doesn't normally use. Add `Notification.p` (it should be in THINK Pascal's `interface` folder) *before* `Reminder.p` in your project.

Because Reminder is more interesting if it works in the background, use Chapter 8 to put a `SIZE` resource in Reminder's resource file so that you can run it properly in MultiFinder.

Creating applications that are MultiFinder-friendly is very important. We've touched on the basics of MultiFinder friendliness by using `WaitNextEvent` and handling Suspend/Resume events, but there's a lot more to learn. If you want to write MultiFinder-friendly applications, read the *Programmer's Guide to MultiFinder* from Apple and APDA.

To be truly MultiFinder-friendly, Reminder would have to worry about things like scrap conversion (we discuss the scrap in Chapter 7), mouse regions, sleep times, and much more.

Select **Go** from the **Project** menu. If you run into any compilation problems, make sure that you put `Notification.p` before `Reminder.p` in the project listing. Consult the debugging tips found in Appendix C. When asked to save changes before running, click **Yes**. Reminder should be up and running (Figure 6.40).

Reminder does not display any windows initially. The **File** menu should display four menu items: **Change Settings, Start Countdown, Kill Notification,** and **Quit.** If **Change Settings** is selected, the alarm settings dialog box appears (Figure 6.41). You can

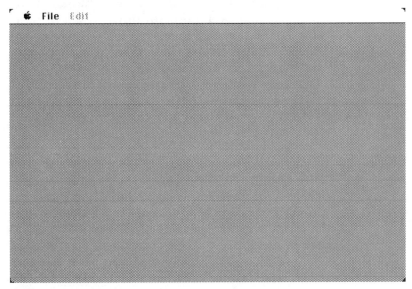

Figure 6.40 Running Reminder.

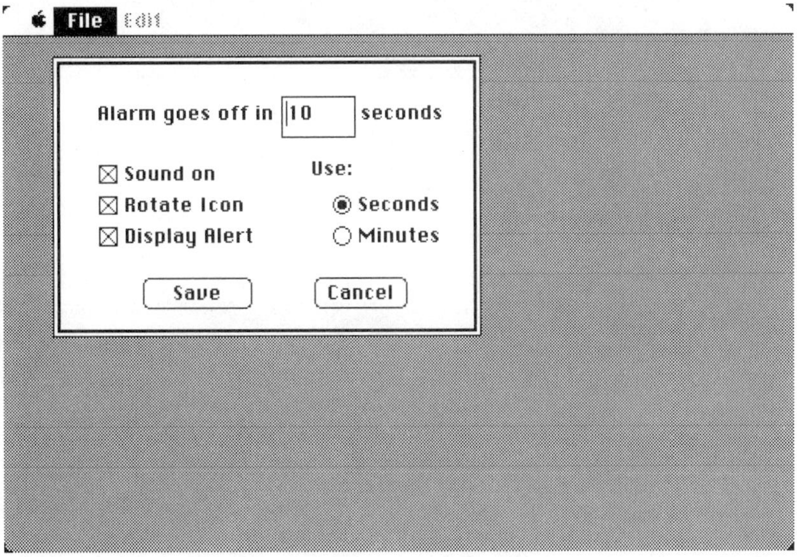

Figure 6.41 Using the **Change Settings** dialog box.

select the countdown time in minutes or seconds, and you can choose the method or methods by which you wish to be notified. **Saue** will keep the settings and close the dialog box. **Cancel** will restore the last saved settings and close the dialog box.

Start Countdown will begin the countdown: The countdown window is displayed, and the timer will count down in seconds. In the **File** menu, **Start Countdown** is changed to **Stop Countdown** and may be selected to cancel the countdown and close the countdown window. During countdown, the **Change Settings** item is dimmed. When the countdown reaches zero, up to three methods will be used to notify you that the time has been reached (Figure 6.42).

Once the notification is set, the **Kill Notification** item under the **File** menu will become available. When it is used to cancel a notification, it will become dim again.

If you installed a `SIZE` resource in your `Reminder.π.rsrc` file, compile Reminder as an application and run it under MultiFinder. Use **Change Settings** to set the countdown time to `20` seconds and then start the countdown. Before time runs out, click on another application's window (such as the Finder) so that the countdown window is in the background. The countdown should continue and, when it reaches zero, you should be notified. If this doesn't work, your `SIZE` resource may need to be checked.

Choose **Quit** from the **File** menu. Let's take a look at the code.

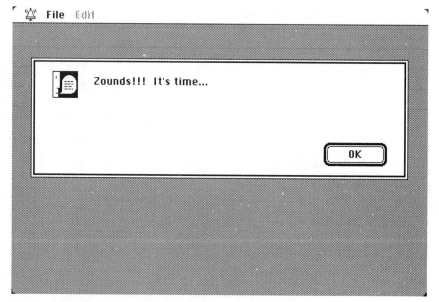

Figure 6.42 The Notification Manager comes through.

Walking Through the Reminder Code

First, look at the overall structure of Reminder as shown in Figure 6.43.

As we have in earlier chapters, we'll examine the code in the order that it executes.

First, set up your constants. Most of them relate to the Settings dialog box. Each dialog item is given an appropriate name. SAVE_BUTTON is dialog item number 1, CANCEL_BUTTON is dialog item number 2, and so on. DEFAULT_SECS_ID and DEFAULT_MINS_ID are the resource IDs of the 'STR ' resources used as second and minute defaults in the Settings dialog.

ON and OFF are set to 1 and 0 for ease of use in setting controls. SYS_VERSION is set to 2. You use this in the Sys6OrLater function to indicate which version of SysEnvirons to call.

> SysEnvirons fills out a record that describes the Mac operating
> environment. Most important, you can use it to tell what version of
> the system is running and, therefore, whether or not Toolbox
> routines like WaitNextEvent or the Notification Manager are
> present. SysEnvirons is described completely n *Inside
> Macintosh* (V:5).

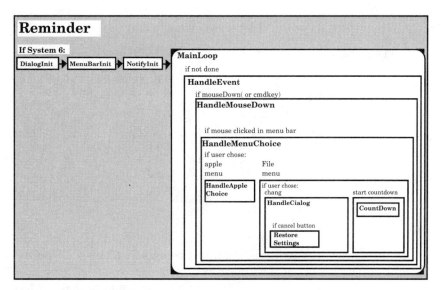

Figure 6.43 Reminder.

```
program Reminder;
    uses
        Notification;

const
    BASE_RES_ID = 400;
    ABOUT_ALERT = 401;
    BAD_SYS_ALERT = 402;

    SLEEP = 60;

    SAVE_BUTTON = 1;
    CANCEL_BUTTON = 2;
    TIME_FIELD = 4;
    S_OR_M_FIELD = 5;
    SOUND_ON_BOX = 6;
    ICON_ON_BOX = 7;
    ALERT_ON_BOX = 8;
    SECS_RADIO = 10;
    MINS_RADIO = 11;

    DEFAULT_SECS_ID = 401;
    DEFAULT_MINS_ID = 402;

    ON = 1;
    OFF = 0;

    SECONDS_PER_MINUTE = 60;

    TOP = 25;
    LEFT = 12;

    MARK_APPLICATION = 1;

    APPLE_MENU_ID = BASE_RES_ID;
    FILE_MENU_ID = BASE_RES_ID + 1;
    ABOUT_ITEM = 1;

    CHANGE_ITEM = 1;
    START_STOP_ITEM = 2;
    KILL_ITEM = 3;
    QUIT_ITEM = 4;

    SYS_VERSION = 2;
```

The variable gSettingsDialog will point to your Settings dialog. (Remember, you can treat a DialogPtr just like a WindowPtr. For example, you could pass gSettingsDialog as an argument to SetPort.)

When gDone is set to TRUE, the program will exit. gCounting is TRUE only when the countdown window is displayed. gNotify_set is TRUE when a notification has been set. gSeconds_or_minutes is set to seconds or minutes, depending on the setting in the Settings dialog. It is reset to FALSE when **Kill Notification** is selected from the **File** menu.

gDefaultSecsH and gDefaultMinsH are handles to the default time 'STR ' resources.dialog items. gNotifyStrH and gMyNMRec are used by the Notification Manager.

The settings structure is used to hold all the settings from the alarm settings dialog box, in case they need to be restored (if the user clicks the Cancel button).

```
type
    Settings = record
            timeString: Str255;
            sound, icon, alert, secsRadio,
            minsRadio: INTEGER;
        end;

var
    gSettingsDialog: DialogPtr;
    gDone, gCounting, gNotify_set: BOOLEAN;
    gSeconds_or_minutes: (seconds, minutes);
    gNotifyStrH, gDefaultSecsH, gDefaultMinsH: StringHandle;
    gMyNMRec: NMRec;
    gTheEvent: EventRecord;
    savedSettings: Settings;

    procedure HandleEvent;
    forward;
```

Reminder starts by testing to see if System 6.0 or later is installed. If it is, you can use the Notification Manager. Initialize your dialogs, your menus, and the notification data structure.

Finally, enter the MainLoop.

```
{---------------> Reminder    <--}

begin
    if Sys6OrLater then
        begin
            DialogInit;
            MenuBarInit;
            NotifyInit;
```

```
                    MainLoop;
              end;
        end.
```

Sys6OrLater will return TRUE if System version 6.0 or later is installed. Otherwise, it returns FALSE. The key to this function lies in the call to SysEnvirons. Pass in the version number of SysEnvirons that you'd like to use. In this case, use SYS_VERSION, which is set to 2. Apple will eventually add new features to the SysEnvirons call, but they'll always provide compatibility with older versions via the version parameter.

SysEnvData is a data structure that gets filled by SysEnvirons. One of the fields, systemVersion, gets filled with the current system version number. The first two bytes get the major version number, and the last two bytes get the minor version number. (In version 5.3, the major version number is 5, and the minor version number is 3.) As long as the version number is greater than $0600 (hex for 6*256), you know you have a system with a major version greater than 6.0.

If there is a problem, call StopAlert to put up your "You don't have version 6.0 or later" alert.

(Although Sys6OrLater tests for 6.0, you generally don't want users to run your programs on any version of System 6 older than 6.02.)

```
{----------------> Sys6OrLater      <--}

    function Sys6OrLater: BOOLEAN;
        var
            status: OSErr;
            SysEnvData: SysEnvRec;
            dummy: INTEGER;
    begin
        status := SysEnvirons(SYS_VERSION, SysEnvData);
        if (status <> noErr) or (SysEnvData.systemVersion
            < $0600) then
            begin
                dummy := StopAlert(BAD_SYS_ALERT, nil);
                Sys6OrLater := FALSE;
            end
        else
            Sys6OrLater := TRUE;
    end;
```

DialogInit starts by loading the default second and minute settings into the StringHandles gDefaultSecsH and gDefault MinsH. The Settings dialog is then loaded from the resource file. When you designed the dialog box in ResEdit, you set it up to be invisible. When the time is right, you can call ShowWindow to make it visible.

Call GetDItem and SetCtlValue in pairs to set the SECS_RADIO, SOUND_ON_BOX, ICON_ON_BOX, and ALERT_ON_BOX items to ON.

```
{----------------> DialogInit      <--}

    procedure DialogInit;
        var
            itemType: INTEGER;
            itemRect: Rect;
            itemHandle: Handle;
    begin
        gDefaultSecsH := GetString(DEFAULT_SECS_ID);
        gDefaultMinsH := GetString(DEFAULT_MINS_ID);

        gSettingsDialog := GetNewDialog(BASE_RES_ID, nil,
                                        WindowPtr(-1));
        GetDItem(gSettingsDialog, SECS_RADIO, itemType,
                itemHandle, itemRect);
        SetCtlValue(ControlHandle(itemHandle), ON);
        GetDItem(gSettingsDialog, SOUND_ON_BOX, itemType,
                itemHandle, itemRect);
        SetCtlValue(ControlHandle(itemHandle), ON);
        GetDItem(gSettingsDialog, ICON_ON_BOX, itemType,
                itemHandle, itemRect);
        SetCtlValue(ControlHandle(itemHandle), ON);
        GetDItem(gSettingsDialog, ALERT_ON_BOX, itemType,
                itemHandle, itemRect);
        SetCtlValue(ControlHandle(itemHandle), ON);

        gSeconds_or_minutes := seconds;
    end;
```

MenuBarInit is similar to the earlier menu routines you've seen. First, you load your MBAR resource (disposing of the handle after you use it), and then you get a handle to the menu so you can add all the desk accessories to it. Next, you get a handle to the **File** menu so you can change menu items later on. Finally, draw the menu bar:

```
{---------------> MenuBarInit  <--}

    procedure MenuBarInit;
        var
            myMenuBar: Handle;
            aMenu: MenuHandle;
    begin
        myMenuBar := GetNewMBar(BASE_RES_ID);
        SetMenuBar(myMenuBar);
        DisposHandle(myMenuBar);

        aMenu := GetMHandle(APPLE_MENU_ID);
        AddResMenu(aMenu, 'DRVR');

        DrawMenuBar;
    end;
```

> The Macintosh operating system, like most other operating
> systems, supports a set of operating system queues. You're
> already familiar with the Event Manager's queue. The Notification
> Manager maintains a queue, as well. Under MultiFinder, several
> applications might post notifications at the same time. Each
> notification request is handled by the operating system and posted
> on the Notification Manager's queue.

In `NotifyInit`, load the `'STR '` you want to appear in the notification alert with `GetString`. Then, `qType` is set to `nmType`. This
tells the part of the operating system that manages queues that this
request is destined for the Notification Manager's queue.

Next, `nmMark` is set to `MARK_APPLICATION`, which means the
(♦) will be placed next to Reminder in the Menu (if you're in
MultiFinder). `NMResp` is set to `nil`, which means you have no
response routine after the notification has been successfully made.

```
{---------------> NotifyInit   <--}

    procedure NotifyInit;
    begin
        gNotifyStrH := GetString(BASE_RES_ID);
        gMyNMRec.qType := nmType;
        gMyNMRec.nmMark := MARK_APPLICATION;
        gMyNMRec.nmResp := nil;
    end;
```

MainLoop initializes `gDone`, `gCounting`, and `gNotify_set`. It then loops on `HandleEvent`.

```
{--------------->   MainLoop   <--}

     procedure MainLoop;
     begin
         gDone := FALSE;
         gCounting := FALSE;
         gNotify_set := FALSE;

         while gDone = FALSE do
             HandleEvent;
     end;
```

The `HandleEvent` routine is set up much like `HandleEvent` in Chapter 5. Call `WaitNextEvent` to see what is in the event queue. (Because you're running System 6.0 or later, you know that `WaitNextEvent` is installed.) Use a switch to find out what the event was. If the mouse button is depressed, the `HandleMouseDown` routine is called. If a `keydown` or `autoKey` event occurs, check to see if the Command key was depressed. If so, the `HandleMenuChoice` routine is called. If you don't check for a `keydown` event first, you won't ever see the command key sequence (for example, when you type **Q** to `Quit`).

We've left out some of the standard event handling, such as `updateEvts`, to simplify the code. Don't worry—Reminder will work just fine without the extra code.

```
{--------------->  HandleEvent   <--}

procedure HandleEvent;
    var
        theChar: CHAR;
        dummy: BOOLEAN;
begin
    dummy := WaitNextEvent(everyEvent, gTheEvent, SLEEP, nil);

    case gTheEvent.what of
        mouseDown:
            HandleMouseDown;
        keyDown, autoKey:
            begin
                theChar := CHR(BitAnd(gTheEvent.message,
                            charCodeMask));
                if (BitAnd(gTheEvent.modifiers, cmdKey) <> 0) then
                    HandleMenuChoice(MenuKey(theChar));
            end;
    end;
end;
```

HandleMouseDown is the same as its Chapter 5 counterpart:

```
{---------------->  HandleMouseDown      <--}

    procedure HandleMouseDown;
        var
            whichWindow: WindowPtr;
            thePart: INTEGER;
            menuChoice, windSize: LONGINT;
    begin
        thePart := FindWindow(gTheEvent.where, whichWindow);
        case thePart of
            inMenuBar:
                begin
                    menuChoice := MenuSelect(gTheEvent.where);
                    HandleMenuChoice(menuChoice);
                end;
            inSysWindow:
                SystemClick(gTheEvent, whichWindow);
            inDrag:
                DragWindow(whichWindow, gTheEvent.where,
                        screenBits.bounds);
            inGoAway:
                gDone := TRUE;
        end;
    end;
```

HandleMenuChoice is also similar to its Chapter 5 counterpart:

```
{---------------->  HandleMenuChoice    <--}

    procedure HandleMenuChoice (menuChoice: LONGINT);
        var
            theMenu, theItem: INTEGER;
    begin
        if menuChoice <> 0 then
            begin
                theMenu := HiWord(menuChoice);
                theItem := LoWord(menuChoice);

                case theMenu of
                    APPLE_MENU_ID:
                        HandleAppleChoice(theItem);
                    FILE_MENU_ID:
                        HandleFileChoice(theItem);
                end;

                HiliteMenu(0);
            end;
    end;
```

It's *deja vu* all over again.

```
{----------------->  HandleAppleChoice   <--}

    procedure HandleAppleChoice (theItem: INTEGER);
        var
            accName: Str255;
            accNumber, itemNumber, dummy: INTEGER;
            appleMenu: MenuHandle;
    begin
        case theItem of
            ABOUT_ITEM:
                dummy := NoteAlert(ABOUT_ALERT, nil);
            otherwise
                begin
                    appleMenu := GetMHandle(APPLE_MENU_ID);
                    GetItem(appleMenu, theItem, accName);
                    accNumber := OpenDeskAcc(accName);
                end;
        end;
    end;
```

HandleFileChoice takes care of the four items under the **File** menu. If **Change Settings** is selected call HandleDialog. If **Start Countdown** (or its counterpart, **Stop Countdown**) is selected, check to see if you are currently counting down. If you are, then the menu item must have been **Stop Countdown**, so change the item back to **Start Countdown** and set gCounting to FALSE to stop the countdown.

If you were not counting down, **Start Countdown** was the item selected. In this case, unhighlight the **File** menu (try commenting this line to get a feel for why this is necessary). Then, pull the countdown time from the settings dialog and convert it to a number. Dim the **Change Settings** item (you don't want to change the settings while you're actually counting down), and change the **Start Countdown** menu item to **Stop Countdown.** Next, call CountDown. When CountDown returns, reenable the **Change Settings** item and change **Stop Countdown** to **Start Countdown.**

If the menu item selected was **Kill Notification**, call NMRemove to remove the notification from the Notification Manager's queue. Then, unlock the notification string you locked in SetNotification. (We discuss handle locking and unlocking in a Tech Block a little later on.) Also, dim the **Kill Notification** item, since the notification is no longer active. Finally, set gNotify_set to FALSE, so everyone else knows that the notification is no longer active.

If **Quit** is selected, set gCounting to FALSE so you'll drop out of the counting loop (if the selection was made during the countdown). In addition, set gDone to FALSE.

```
{---------------> HandleFileChoice      <--}

procedure HandleFileChoice (theItem: INTEGER);
    var
        timeString: Str255;
        countDownTime: LONGINT;
        itemType: INTEGER;
        itemRect: Rect;
        itemHandle: Handle;
        dummy: OSErr;
        fileMenu: MenuHandle;
begin
    fileMenu := GetMHandle(FILE_MENU_ID);
    case theItem of
        CHANGE_ITEM:
            HandleDialog;
        START_STOP_ITEM:
            if gCounting then
                begin
                    gCounting := FALSE;
                    SetItem(fileMenu, theItem, 'Start Countdown');
                end
            else
                begin
                    HiliteMenu(0);
                    GetDItem(gSettingsDialog, TIME_FIELD,
                            itemType, itemHandle, itemRect);
                    GetIText(itemHandle, timeString);
                    StringToNum(timeString, countDownTime);

                    DisableItem(fileMenu, CHANGE_ITEM);
                    SetItem(fileMenu, theItem, 'Stop Countdown');
                    CountDown(countDownTime);
                    EnableItem(fileMenu, CHANGE_ITEM);
                    SetItem(fileMenu, theItem, 'Start Countdown');
                end;
        KILL_ITEM:
            begin
                dummy := NMRemove(QElemPtr(@gMyNMRec));
                HUnlock(Handle(gNotifyStrH));
                DisableItem(fileMenu, KILL_ITEM);
                gNotify_set := FALSE;
            end;
        QUIT_ITEM:
            begin
```

```
            gCounting := FALSE;
            gDone := TRUE;
         end;
      end;
   end;
```

> As with Chapter 5's Timer, we still haven't added support for copy, cut, and paste operations to desk accessories. Look at WindowMaker in Chapter 7 to see how to support desk accessories with the **Edit** menu.

`HandleDialog` is the key to Reminder's modal dialog. As we discussed in the beginning of the chapter, modal dialogs are implemented in a loop. First `ModalDialog` is called, returning the number of the selected item. The selected item is processed and, if it was an exit item, the loop ends.

`HandleDialog` is a long routine, but it is not complex. Most of it is a big case statement with branches for most of the items in the dialog.

Start by making the Settings dialog visible and saving the settings you start off with (in case the user clicks on the **Cancel** button). You then enter the `ModalDialog` loop. If the user selects an exit item (in this case, **Save** or **Cancel**), `dialogDone` is set to `TRUE`. If the user selects the **Save** button, make the dialog window invisible and set `dialogDone` to `TRUE`.

If the user selects the **Cancel** button, make the dialog window invisible and restore the old settings. (We made the window invisible first because we didn't want the user to watch as we changed the items back. It's not a pretty sight.) Again, set `dialogDone` to `TRUE` to drop out of the while loop.

```
{---------------> HandleDialog   <--}

   procedure HandleDialog;
      var
         dialogDone: BOOLEAN;
         itemHit, itemType: INTEGER;
         alarmDelay: LONGINT;
         delayString: Str255;
         itemRect: Rect;
         itemHandle: Handle;
   begin
      ShowWindow(gSettingsDialog);
      SaveSettings;
```

```
dialogDone := FALSE;
while dialogDone = FALSE do
    begin
        ModalDialog(nil, itemHit);
        case itemHit of
            SAVE_BUTTON:
                begin
                    HideWindow(gSettingsDialog);
                    dialogDone := TRUE;
                end;
            CANCEL_BUTTON:
                begin
                    HideWindow(gSettingsDialog);
                    RestoreSettings;
                    dialogDone := TRUE;
                end;
```

If the user clicks in the sound, icon, or alert checkbox, set them to OFF if they were ON or to ON if they were OFF.

```
            SOUND_ON_BOX:
                begin
                    GetDItem(gSettingsDialog,
                    SOUND_ON_BOX, itemType, itemHandle,
                    itemRect);
                    if GetCtlValue(ControlHandle
                        (itemHandle)) = ON then
                        SetCtlValue(ControlHandle
                            (itemHandle), OFF)
                    else
                        SetCtlValue(ControlHandle
                            (itemHandle), ON);
                end;
            ICON_ON_BOX:
                begin
                    GetDItem(gSettingsDialog,
                    ICON_ON_BOX, itemType, itemHandle,
                    itemRect);
                    if GetCtlValue(ControlHandle
                        (itemHandle)) = ON then
                        SetCtlValue(ControlHandle
                            (itemHandle), OFF)
                    else
                        SetCtlValue(ControlHandle
                            (itemHandle), ON);
                end;
            ALERT_ON_BOX:
                begin
```

```
                GetDItem(gSettingsDialog,
                ALERT_ON_BOX, itemType, itemHandle,
                itemRect);
                if GetCtlValue(ControlHandle
                    (itemHandle)) = ON then
                    SetCtlValue(ControlHandle
                        (itemHandle), OFF)
                else
                    SetCtlValue(ControlHandle
                        (itemHandle), ON);
            end;
```

If the user clicks in the **Seconds** radio button, change the global gSeconds_or_minutes to seconds, turn off the **Minutes** radio button, and turn on the **Seconds** radio button. (It's important to turn off the old button and then turn on the new one, so the user never sees two radio buttons on at the same time.) Next, set the static text field to read **seconds**, and place the default value loaded into gDefaultSecsH in the editable text field (the resource was loaded in DialogInit). Lock the string handle, because you're passing a pointer to the string and not the string's handle to SetIText.

> Remember, a handle is a pointer to a pointer, allowing the system to move the data around in memory without changing the value of the handle. In this case, you need to use a pointer to your string instead of a handle to it, so you can't afford to let the system move your data around (relocate it). You can solve this problem in one of two ways. You can lock the handle and its data with HLock or you can make a copy of the data and dispose of the handle. Each of these techniques has its place. For simplicity, we used the HLock method, but this method is not necessarily the best. For more information, read about the Memory Manager in *Inside Macintosh* (II: 9–51).

If the user clicks in the **Minutes** radio button, you will go through a similar exercise, using a default value in gDefaultMinsH in the editable text field.

```
SECS_RADIO:
    begin
        gSeconds_or_minutes := seconds;
        GetDItem(gSettingsDialog,
        MINS_RADIO, itemType, itemHandle, itemRect);
```

```
                    SetCtlValue(ControlHandle (itemHandle), OFF);
                    GetDItem(gSettingsDialog, SECS_RADIO, itemType,
                            itemHandle, itemRect);
                    SetCtlValue(ControlHandle (itemHandle), ON);
                    GetDItem(gSettingsDialog, S_OR_M_FIELD,
                            itemType, itemHandle, itemRect);
                    SetIText(itemHandle, 'seconds');
                    GetDItem(gSettingsDialog, TIME_FIELD, itemType,
                            itemHandle, itemRect);
                    SetIText(itemHandle, gDefaultSecsH^^);
                end;
            MINS_RADIO:
                begin
                    gSeconds_or_minutes := minutes;
                    GetDItem(gSettingsDialog, SECS_RADIO, itemType,
                            itemHandle, itemRect);
                    SetCtlValue(ControlHandle (itemHandle), OFF);
                    GetDItem(gSettingsDialog, MINS_RADIO, itemType,
                            itemHandle, itemRect);
                    SetCtlValue(ControlHandle (itemHandle), ON);
                    GetDItem(gSettingsDialog, S_OR_M_FIELD,
                            itemType, itemHandle, itemRect);
                    SetIText(itemHandle, 'minutes');
                    GetDItem(gSettingsDialog, TIME_FIELD, itemType,
                            itemHandle, itemRect);
                    SetIText(itemHandle, gDefaultMinsH^^);
                end;
            end;
        end;
    end;
```

SaveSettings uses `GetDItem` and either `GetIText` or `GetCtlValue` to fill the `savedSettings` data structure with the values currently set in the settings dialog items.

```
{----------------> SaveSettings    <--}

procedure SaveSettings;
    var
        itemType: INTEGER;
        itemRect: Rect;
        itemHandle: Handle;
begin
    GetDItem(gSettingsDialog, TIME_FIELD, itemType,
            itemHandle, itemRect);
    GetIText(itemHandle, savedSettings.timeString);
    GetDItem(gSettingsDialog, SOUND_ON_BOX, itemType,
            itemHandle, itemRect);
```

```
        savedSettings.sound := GetCtlValue
                                (ControlHandle(itemHandle));
        GetDItem(gSettingsDialog, ICON_ON_BOX, itemType,
              itemHandle, itemRect);
        savedSettings.icon := GetCtlValue
                                (ControlHandle(itemHandle));
        GetDItem(gSettingsDialog, ALERT_ON_BOX, itemType,
              itemHandle, itemRect);
        savedSettings.alert := GetCtlValue
                                (ControlHandle(itemHandle));
        GetDItem(gSettingsDialog, SECS_RADIO, itemType,
              itemHandle, itemRect);
        savedSettings.secsRadio := GetCtlValue
                                (ControlHandle(itemHandle));
        GetDItem(gSettingsDialog, MINS_RADIO, itemType,
              itemHandle, itemRect);
        savedSettings.minsRadio := GetCtlValue
                                (ControlHandle(itemHandle));
    end;
```

RestoreSettings uses GetDItem, SetIText, and SetCtlValue to restore the settings dialog items to the values saved in the savedSettings data structure. Use the value saved in savedSettings.secsRadio to determine if the static text field should read **seconds** or **minutes**.

```
{---------------> RestoreSettings      <--}

procedure RestoreSettings;
    var
        itemType: INTEGER;
        itemRect: Rect;
        itemHandle: Handle;
begin
    GetDItem(gSettingsDialog, TIME_FIELD, itemType,
          itemHandle, itemRect);
    SetIText(itemHandle, savedSettings.timeString);
    GetDItem(gSettingsDialog, SOUND_ON_BOX, itemType,
          itemHandle, itemRect);
    SetCtlValue(ControlHandle(itemHandle),
            savedSettings.sound);
    GetDItem(gSettingsDialog, ICON_ON_BOX, itemType,
          itemHandle, itemRect);
    SetCtlValue(ControlHandle(itemHandle),
            savedSettings.icon);
    GetDItem(gSettingsDialog, ALERT_ON_BOX, itemType,
          itemHandle, itemRect);
    SetCtlValue(ControlHandle(itemHandle),
            savedSettings.alert);
```

```
        GetDItem(gSettingsDialog, SECS_RADIO, itemType,
                itemHandle, itemRect);
        SetCtlValue(ControlHandle(itemHandle),
                    savedSettings.secsRadio);
        GetDItem(gSettingsDialog, MINS_RADIO, itemType,
                itemHandle, itemRect);
        SetCtlValue(ControlHandle(itemHandle),
                    savedSettings.minsRadio);

        if savedSettings.secsRadio = ON then
            begin
                GetDItem(gSettingsDialog, S_OR_M_FIELD,
                itemType, itemHandle, itemRect);
                SetIText(itemHandle, 'seconds');
            end
        else
            begin
                GetDItem(gSettingsDialog, S_OR_M_FIELD,
                itemType, itemHandle, itemRect);
                SetIText(itemHandle, 'minutes');
            end;
    end;
```

CountDown takes the number of seconds (or minutes) to count down as its only argument, puts up the countdown window, and counts down in seconds.

Start by loading the countdown window from the resource file. Set the current GrafPort to the countdown window, and make it visible. Next, make the current font appear in **boldface**. Finally, set the current font's size to 24 point.

```
{----------------> CountDown <--}

procedure CountDown (numSecs: LONGINT);
    var
        myTime, oldTime, difTime: LONGINT;
        myTimeString: Str255;
        countDownWindow: WindowPtr;
begin
    countDownWindow := GetNewWindow(BASE_RES_ID, nil,
                                    WindowPtr(-1));
    SetPort(countDownWindow);
    ShowWindow(countDownWindow);
    TextFace([bold]);
    TextSize(24);
```

Your next step is to get the current time (in seconds since midnight, January 1, 1904), and to convert the countdown time from minutes to seconds, if necessary. Also, set the global gCounting to TRUE.

```
GetDateTime(myTime);
oldTime := myTime;

if gSeconds_or_minutes = minutes then
    numSecs := numSecs * SECONDS_PER_MINUTE;

gCounting := TRUE;
```

While you count down, call HandleEvent. This lets the user drag the countdown window around the screen or make menu selections while you count down. This is very important, because it keeps your program from falling into a mode. Users won't feel as though they're in countdown mode because they'll be able to pull down desk accessories and, if they're in MultiFinder, switch to other applications.

Every time myTime changes, a second has passed, and you have to redraw the countdown time. Call EraseRect to clear the window and redraw the time.

```
while (numSecs > 0) and gCounting do
    begin
        HandleEvent;
        if gCounting then
            begin
                MoveTo(LEFT, TOP);
                GetDateTime(myTime);
                if myTime <> oldTime then
                    begin
                        difTime := myTime - oldTime;
                        numSecs := numSecs - difTime;
                        oldTime := myTime;
                        NumToString(numSecs,
                                myTimeString);
                        EraseRect(countDownWindow^
                                .portRect);
                        DrawString(myTimeString);
                    end;
            end;
    end;
```

If gCounting is still TRUE, no one interrupted the countdown, and you can set your notification. Finally, set gCounting to FALSE and dispose of the countdown window.

```
        if gCounting then
            SetNotification;

        gCounting := FALSE;
        DisposeWindow(countDownWindow);
    end;
```

If a notification is already set, remove it so that you can set a new one. If appropriate, load the small icon ('SICN') from the resource file and put its handle in the notification data structure. Do the same for the 'snd ' resource and the string you loaded earlier.

Then, call NMInstall to set the notification. Also turn on the **Kill Notification** item in the **File** menu (after getting the handle for it). Finally, set gNotify_set to TRUE.

```
{---------------> SetNotification      <--}

    procedure SetNotification;
        var
            itemType: INTEGER;
            itemRect: Rect;
            itemHandle: Handle;
            dummy: OSErr;
            fileMenu: MenuHandle;
    begin
        if gNotify_set then
            begin
                dummy := NMRemove(QElemPtr(@gMyNMRec));
                HUnlock(Handle(gNotifyStrH));
            end;

        GetDItem(gSettingsDialog, ICON_ON_BOX, itemType,
                itemHandle, itemRect);
        if GetCtlValue(ControlHandle(itemHandle)) = ON then
            gMyNMRec.nmSIcon := GetResource('SICN',
                                            BASE_RES_ID)
        else
            gMyNMRec.nmSIcon := nil;

        GetDItem(gSettingsDialog, SOUND_ON_BOX, itemType,
                itemHandle, itemRect);
        if GetCtlValue(ControlHandle(itemHandle)) = ON then
            gMyNMRec.nmSound := GetResource('snd ',
                                            BASE_RES_ID)
        else
            gMyNMRec.nmSound := nil;

        GetDItem(gSettingsDialog, ALERT_ON_BOX, itemType,
                itemHandle, itemRect);
```

```
   if GetCtlValue(ControlHandle(itemHandle)) = ON then
      begin
         MoveHHi(Handle(gNotifyStrH));
         HLock(Handle(gNotifyStrH));
         gMyNMRec.nmStr := gNotifyStrH^;
      end
   else
      gMyNMRec.nmStr := nil;

   dummy := NMInstall(QElemPtr(@gMyNMRec));
   fileMenu := GetMHandle(FILE_MENU_ID);
   EnableItem(fileMenu, KILL_ITEM);
   gNotify_set := TRUE;
end;
```

Note that the routine `MoveHHi` was called before `gNotifyStrH` was locked. Normally, before you work with a pointer to a handled object, you `HLock` the handle. When you're done with the pointer, you `HUnlock` the handle again. As we mentioned earlier, `HLock` creates an obstruction in the middle of the application heap. If the handle will be `HLocked` only for a short period of time (a few lines of code), this won't be a problem. In Reminder, `gNotifyStrH` is kept `HLocked` from the time the notification is installed until the notification is removed. That's too long to keep a handle locked in the middle of the heap. `MoveHHi` reduces this problem by relocating the handled memory as high in the heap as possible. Locking the handle at this point creates an obstruction at one end of the heap instead of in the middle.

The topic of memory management on the Macintosh is important, but it is beyond the scope of this book. Volume II of the *Primer* contains a complete description of the Memory Manager. As your programs get larger and more sophisticated, you'll make more use of this part of the Toolbox.

In Review

This chapter examined some of the oldest parts of the Macintosh Toolbox (dialog boxes), together with some of the newest parts (`SysEnvirons` and the Notification Manager). You built an application that used most of the Toolbox routines presented in the previous three chapters.

In Chapter 7, we'll address some of the programming issues that we have not touched on so far, such as error-handling, managing multiple windows, using the clipboard, printing, and working with scroll bars. We'll end with a brief sojourn into the Macintosh Sound Manager.

Congratulations! The toughest part of the book is behind you.

Toolbox Potpourri

Congratulations! Now that you have the Macintosh interface under your belt, you'll see how to implement other traits that Mac programs should possess: multiple window handling, error-checking, the Clipboard, file and print management, scroll bars and sound.

THE FIRST APPLICATION, WindowMaker, shows you how to manage a dynamic windowing environment. In addition to supporting window creation, movement, and disposal, WindowMaker introduces an error-handling mechanism that you can use in your own applications.

Next, the desk scrap, more commonly known as the Clipboard, is introduced. The Scrap Manager utilities that support cut, copy, and paste operations are discussed. The second application, ShowClip, uses these routines to display the current scrap in a window.

The third application, PrintPICT, introduces the File Manager and the Printing Manager. You'll learn how to support the standard **Open**, **Save**, and **Save As... File** menu options in your own code.

Next, we present a discussion on the use of scroll bars. The fourth application, Pager, uses the Control Manager, as well as the Resource Manager, to build a kinescopic display of P I C T resources.

For the pièce de résistance, we present Sounder, an alternative to the dreary world of S y s B e e p.

Keeping Track of Windows: WindowMaker

Most applications on the Macintosh allow you to open more than one window at a time. **WindowMaker** lets you create as many windows as you desire. After they are created, you can select, move, and close any window.

WindowMaker Specifications

Here's how WindowMaker works:

1. It initializes the menu bar.

2. It loads a P I C T resource.

3. It enters the Main Event Loop and performs the following functions.

4. It creates a new window whenever the **New** menu item is selected, centering the P I C T in the window.

5. It closes the currently selected window whenever the **Close** menu item is selected.

6. It handles events for moving and updating windows.

7. It quits when the **Quit** menu item is selected.

WindowMaker is the first *Primer* program that does error-checking. Every time a Toolbox function is called, there is the possibility that it may not execute properly. For example, if you call `GetMenu` to load a `MENU` resource, and the operating system can't find the resource, the call returns an error code. Your program should check for and respond to these error codes. If you ignore Toolbox error codes, you do so at your own risk. Check Toolbox calls the way we do it in WindowMaker and the other programs in this chapter. WindowMaker also fully supports desk accessory editing operations.

Because WindowMaker uses the concepts of the previous chapters, and also handles error-checking and multiple windows, you should consider using it as the model for your own applications.

Setting up the WindowMaker Project

Create a folder called `WindowMaker` in your source code folder. Then use ResEdit to create a new file inside the new folder called `WindowMaker.π.rsrc`. Build a purgeable `WIND` with an ID of `400`. Figure 7.1 shows the specifications of the `WIND` you need.

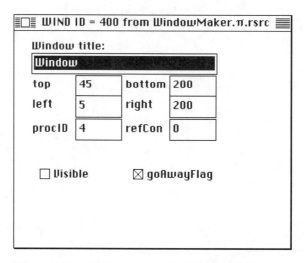

Figure 7.1 `WIND` resource for WindowMaker.

Now, create the menu resources. First, build the MBAR resource (Figure 7.2). Change the MBAR resource ID to 400. Now build the individual MENU items. Figure 7.3 displays the ⌘, **File**, and **Edit** menus for WindowMaker. (The **Edit** menu is the same as that in Chapter 5's Timer program and Chapter 6's Reminder program; copy resources from the older programs whenever possible.)

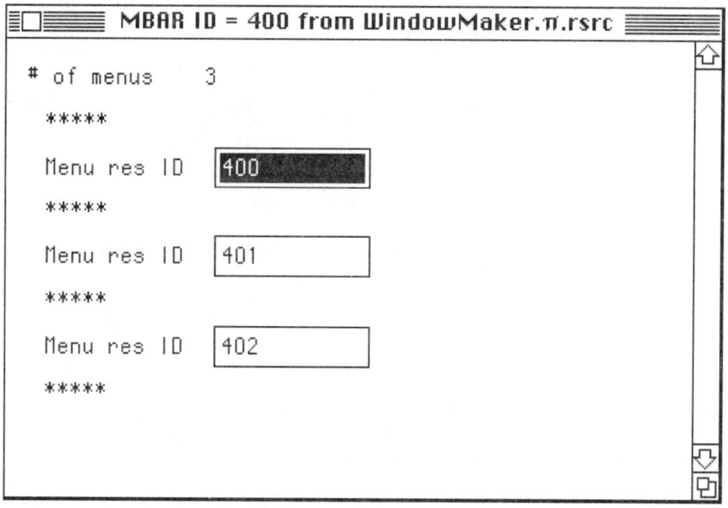

Figure 7.2 MBAR resource for WindowMaker.

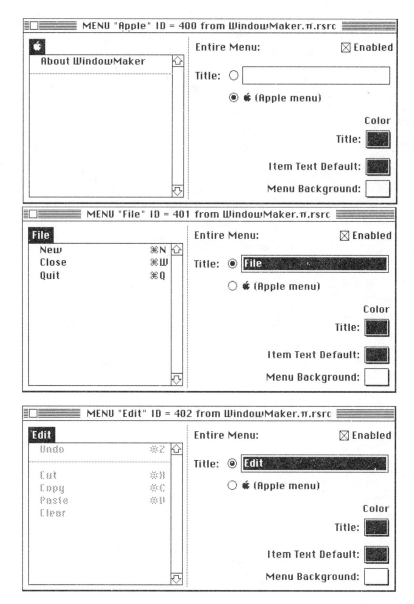

Figure 7.3 MENU resources for WindowMaker.

Next, create the two DITL resources, one for the about box, the other for the new error-checking routines. Change the resource IDs to the ones shown in Figure 7.4. To frame those two DITL resources, build the two ALRT resources shown in Figure 7.5.

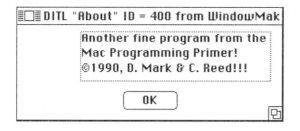

Item#	Type	Enabled	Top	Left	Bottom	Right	Text/Resource ID
1	Button	Yes	71	117	91	177	OK
2	Static Text	Yes	7	70	61	280	Another fine program from the Mac Programming Primer! ©1990, D. Mark & C. Reed!!!

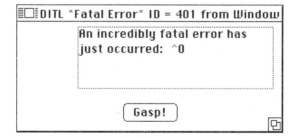

Item#	Type	Enabled	Top	Left	Bottom	Right	Text/Resource ID
1	Button	Yes	86	117	106	177	Gasp!
2	Static Text	Yes	5	67	71	283	An incredibly fatal error has just occurred: ^0

Figure 7.4 DITL resources for WindowMaker.

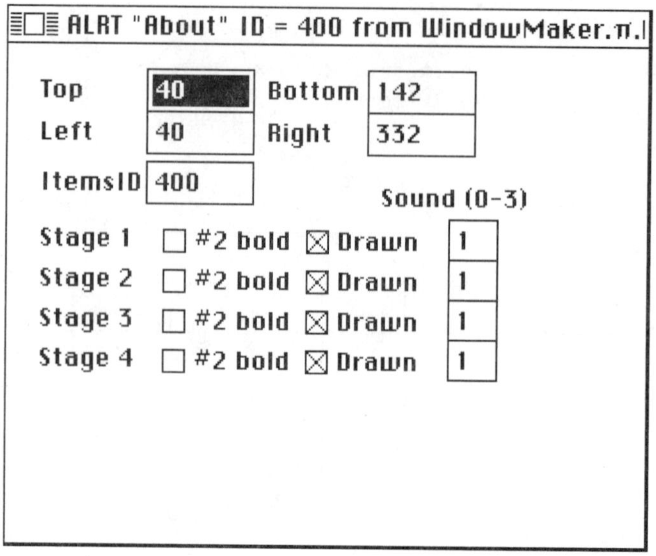

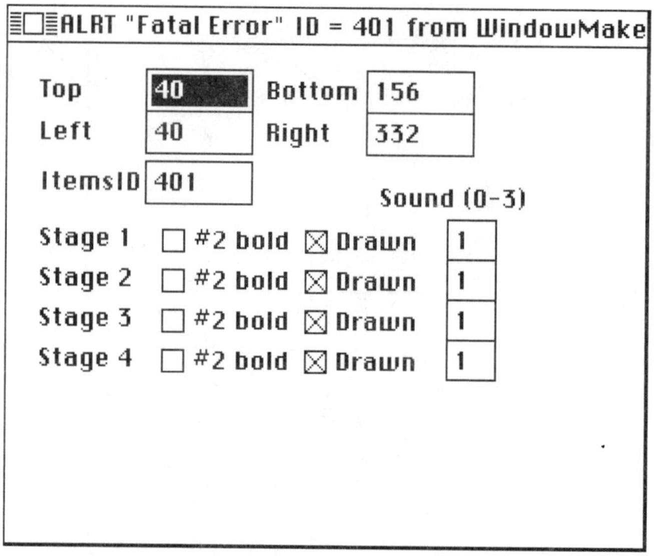

▤◻▤ ALRT "About" ID = 400 from WindowMaker.π.▐

Top   `40`   Bottom `142`
Left `40`   Right `332`

ItemsID `400`

                                    Sound (0-3)

Stage 1   ◻ #2 bold ⊠ Drawn   `1`
Stage 2   ◻ #2 bold ⊠ Drawn   `1`
Stage 3   ◻ #2 bold ⊠ Drawn   `1`
Stage 4   ◻ #2 bold ⊠ Drawn   `1`

▤◻▤ALRT "Fatal Error" ID = 401 from WindowMake

Top   `40`   Bottom `156`
Left `40`   Right `332`

ItemsID `401`

                                    Sound (0-3)

Stage 1   ◻ #2 bold ⊠ Drawn   `1`
Stage 2   ◻ #2 bold ⊠ Drawn   `1`
Stage 3   ◻ #2 bold ⊠ Drawn   `1`
Stage 4   ◻ #2 bold ⊠ Drawn   `1`

Figure 7.5   A L R T resources for WindowMaker.

All you need now are the PICT resources that you'll display in the WindowMaker windows and the STR resources that will be used in the error-checking routine. Use Chapter 3's ShowPICT PICT resource, or just cut and paste a picture from the Scrapbook. Be sure the resource ID for the PICT is 400 and mark the PICT as purgeable. Finally, add the four STR resources shown in Figure 7.6 to the WindowMaker.π.rsrc file. Again, be sure to change the resource IDs of each resource to those shown in the figure and mark each STR as **purgeable.** When you're done, the resource window of WindowMaker.π.rsrc should look like Figure 7.7.

```
STR "MBAR Error" ID = 400 from WindowMaker.π.rsrc

The String    Couldn't load the MBAR resource!
Data       $
```

```
STR "MENU Error" ID = 401 from WindowMaker.π.rsrc

The String    Couldn't load the MENU resource!
Data       $
```

```
STR "PICT Error" ID = 402 from WindowMaker.π.rsrc

The String    Couldn't load the PICT resource!
Data       $
```

```
STR "WIND Error" ID = 403 from WindowMaker.π.rsrc

The String    Couldn't load the WIND resource!
Data       $
```

Figure 7.6 STR resources for WindowMaker.

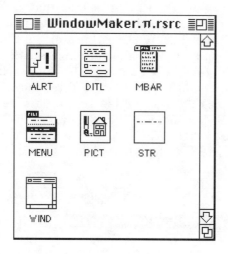

Figure 7.7 WindowMaker resources completed.

Now, you're ready to launch THINK Pascal. When prompted for a project to open, create a new project in the **WindowMaker** folder called WindowMaker.π. Next, use the **Run Options...** dialog box to add the resource file to the project.

Create a new source file (call it WindowMaker.p), and add it to WindowMaker.π. Here's the source code for WindowMaker.p:

```
program WindowMaker;
    const
        BASE_RES_ID = 400;
        APPLE_MENU_ID = 400;
        FILE_MENU_ID = 401;
        EDIT_MENU_ID = 402;

        ABOUT_ITEM = 1;
        ABOUT_ALERT = 400;
        ERROR_ALERT_ID = 401;

        NO_MBAR = BASE_RES_ID;
        NO_MENU = BASE_RES_ID + 1;
        NO_PICTURE = BASE_RES_ID + 2;
        NO_WIND = BASE_RES_ID + 3;

        NEW_ITEM = 1;
        CLOSE_ITEM = 2;
        QUIT_ITEM = 3;
```

```
        UNDO_ITEM = 1;
        CUT_ITEM = 3;
        COPY_ITEM = 4;
        PASTE_ITEM = 5;
        CLEAR_ITEM = 6;

        EDGE_THRESHOLD = 30;

        WINDOW_HOME_LEFT = 5;
        WINDOW_HOME_TOP = 45;
        NEW_WINDOW_OFFSET = 20;

        MIN_SLEEP = 60;

        LEAVE_WHERE_IT_IS = FALSE;

        WNE_TRAP_NUM = $60;
        UNIMPL_TRAP_NUM = $9F;

        NIL_STRING = '';
        HOPELESSLY_FATAL_ERROR = 'Game over, man!';

    var
        gDone, gWNEImplemented: Boolean;
        gTheEvent: EventRecord;
        gNewWindowLeft, gNewWindowTop: INTEGER;


{----------------->   ErrorHandler    <--}

    procedure ErrorHandler (stringNum: INTEGER);
        var
            errorStringH: StringHandle;
            dummy: INTEGER;
    begin
        errorStringH := GetString(stringNum);
        if errorStringH = nil then
            ParamText(HOPELESSLY_FATAL_ERROR, NIL_STRING,
            NIL_STRING, NIL_STRING)
        else
            ParamText(errorStringH^^, NIL_STRING, NIL_STRING,
            NIL_STRING);

        dummy := StopAlert(ERROR_ALERT_ID, nil);
        ExitToShell;
```

```
    end;
{---------------> CenterPict <--}

    procedure CenterPict (thePicture: PicHandle; var myRect:
    Rect);
        var
            windRect, pictureRect: Rect;
    begin
        windRect := myRect;
        pictureRect := thePicture^^.picFrame;
        myRect.top := (windRect.bottom - windRect.top -
            (pictureRect.bottom - pictureRect.top)) div 2 +
        windRect.top;
        myRect.bottom := myRect.top + (pictureRect.bottom -
            pictureRect.top);
        myRect.left := (windRect.right - windRect.left -
            (pictureRect.right - pictureRect.left)) div 2 +
        windRect.left;
        myRect.right := myRect.left + (pictureRect.right -
            pictureRect.left);
    end;


{---------------> DrawMyPicture  <--}

    procedure DrawMyPicture (pictureWindow: WindowPtr);
        var
            myRect: Rect;
            thePicture: PicHandle;
    begin
        myRect := pictureWindow^.portRect;

        thePicture := GetPicture(BASE_RES_ID);
        if thePicture = nil then
            ErrorHandler(NO_PICTURE);

        CenterPict(thePicture, myRect);
        SetPort(pictureWindow);
        DrawPicture(thePicture, myRect);
    end;


{---------------> CreateWindow   <--}

    procedure CreateWindow;
        var
            theNewestWindow: WindowPtr;
    begin
        theNewestWindow := GetNewWindow(BASE_RES_ID, nil,
            WindowPtr(-1));
        if theNewestWindow = nil then
            ErrorHandler(NO_WIND);
```

```
    if ((screenBits.bounds.right - gNewWindowLeft) <
        EDGE_THRESHOLD) or ((screenBits.bounds.bottom -
gNewWindowTop) < EDGE_THRESHOLD) then
        begin
            gNewWindowLeft := WINDOW_HOME_LEFT;
            gNewWindowTop := WINDOW_HOME_TOP;
        end;

    MoveWindow(theNewestWindow, gNewWindowLeft,
    gNewWindowTop, LEAVE_WHERE_IT_IS);
    gNewWindowLeft := gNewWindowLeft + NEW_WINDOW_OFFSET;
    gNewWindowTop := gNewWindowTop + NEW_WINDOW_OFFSET;
    ShowWindow(theNewestWindow);
end;


{----------------> HandleEditChoice     <--}

    procedure HandleEditChoice (theItem: INTEGER);
        var
            dummy: Boolean;
    begin
        dummy := SystemEdit(theItem - 1);
    end;


{----------------> HandleFileChoice     <--}

    procedure HandleFileChoice (theItem: INTEGER);
        var
            whichWindow: WindowPtr;
    begin
        case theItem of
            NEW_ITEM:
                CreateWindow;
            CLOSE_ITEM:
                begin
                    whichWindow := FrontWindow;
                    if whichWindow <> nil then
                        DisposeWindow(whichWindow);
                end;
            QUIT_ITEM:
                gDone := TRUE;
        end;
    end;
```

```
{----------------> HandleAppleChoice    <--}

    procedure HandleAppleChoice (theItem: INTEGER);
        var
            accName: Str255;
            accNumber, itemNumber, dummy: INTEGER;
            aMenu: MenuHandle;
    begin
        case theItem of
            ABOUT_ITEM:
                dummy := NoteAlert(ABOUT_ALERT, nil);
            otherwise
                begin
                    aMenu := GetMHandle(APPLE_MENU_ID);
                    GetItem(aMenu, theItem, accName);
                    accNumber := OpenDeskAcc(accName);
                end;
        end;
    end;


{----------------> HandleMenuChoice    <--}

    procedure HandleMenuChoice (menuChoice: LONGINT);
        var
            theMenu, theItem: INTEGER;
    begin
        if menuChoice <> 0 then
            begin
                theMenu := HiWord(menuChoice);
                theItem := LoWord(menuChoice);

                case theMenu of
                    APPLE_MENU_ID:
                        HandleAppleChoice(theItem);
                    FILE_MENU_ID:
                        HandleFileChoice(theItem);
                    EDIT_MENU_ID:
                        HandleEditChoice(theItem);
                end;

                HiliteMenu(0);
            end;
    end;
```

```
{--------------> IsDAWindow <--}

    function IsDAWindow (whichWindow: WindowPtr): BOOLEAN;
    begin
        if whichWindow = nil then
            IsDAWindow := FALSE
        else
            IsDAWindow := (WindowPeek(whichWindow)^.windowKind < 0);
    end;


{--------------> AdjustMenus <--}

    procedure AdjustMenus;
        var
            aMenu: MenuHandle;
    begin
        aMenu := GetMHandle(FILE_MENU_ID);
        if FrontWindow = nil then
            DisableItem(aMenu, CLOSE_ITEM)
        else
            EnableItem(aMenu, CLOSE_ITEM);

        aMenu := GetMHandle(EDIT_MENU_ID);
        if IsDAWindow(FrontWindow) then
            begin
                EnableItem(aMenu, UNDO_ITEM);
                EnableItem(aMenu, CUT_ITEM);
                EnableItem(aMenu, COPY_ITEM);
                EnableItem(aMenu, PASTE_ITEM);
                EnableItem(aMenu, CLEAR_ITEM);
            end
        else
            begin
                DisableItem(aMenu, UNDO_ITEM);
                DisableItem(aMenu, CUT_ITEM);
                DisableItem(aMenu, COPY_ITEM);
                DisableItem(aMenu, PASTE_ITEM);
                DisableItem(aMenu, CLEAR_ITEM);
            end;
    end;
```

```
{---------------> HandleMouseDown     <--}

    procedure HandleMouseDown;
        var
            whichWindow: WindowPtr;
            thePart: INTEGER;
            menuChoice, windSize: LONGINT;
    begin
        thePart := FindWindow(gTheEvent.where, whichWindow);
        case thePart of
            inMenuBar:
                begin
                    AdjustMenus;
                    menuChoice := MenuSelect(gTheEvent.where);
                    HandleMenuChoice(menuChoice);
                end;
            inSysWindow:
                SystemClick(gTheEvent, whichWindow);
            inDrag:
                DragWindow(whichWindow, gTheEvent.where,
                screenBits.bounds);
            inGoAway:
                DisposeWindow(whichWindow);
            inContent:
                SelectWindow(whichWindow);
        end;
    end;


{---------------> HandleEvent<--}

    procedure HandleEvent;
        var
            theChar: CHAR;
            dummy: BOOLEAN;
            oldPort: GrafPtr;
    begin
        if gWNEImplemented then
            dummy := WaitNextEvent(everyEvent, gTheEvent,
                                MIN_SLEEP, nil)
        else
            begin
                SystemTask;
                dummy := GetNextEvent(everyEvent, gTheEvent);
            end;
```

```
        case gTheEvent.what of
            mouseDown:
                HandleMouseDown;
            keyDown, autoKey:
                begin
                    theChar := CHR(BitAnd(gTheEvent.message,
                    charCodeMask));
                    if (BitAnd(gTheEvent.modifiers, cmdKey) <>
                    0) then
                        begin
                            AdjustMenus;
                            HandleMenuChoice(MenuKey(theChar));
                        end;
                end;
            updateEvt:
                if not IsDAWindow(WindowPtr(gTheEvent.message))
                then
                    begin
                        GetPort(oldPort);
                        SetPort(WindowPtr(gTheEvent.message));

                        BeginUpdate(WindowPtr(gTheEvent.message));

                        DrawMyPicture(WindowPtr(gTheEvent.message));
                        EndUpdate(WindowPtr(gTheEvent.message));
                        SetPort(oldPort);
                    end;
            end;
    end;


{----------------> MainLoop   <--}

    procedure MainLoop;
    begin
        gDone := FALSE;
        gNewWindowLeft := WINDOW_HOME_LEFT;
        gNewWindowTop := WINDOW_HOME_TOP;

        gWNEImplemented := (NGetTrapAddress(WNE_TRAP_NUM,
ToolTrap) <> NGetTrapAddress(UNIMPL_TRAP_NUM, ToolTrap));
        while (gDone = FALSE) do
            HandleEvent;
    end;
```

```
{---------------> MenuBarInit<--}

    procedure MenuBarInit;
        var
            myMenuBar: Handle;
            aMenu: MenuHandle;
    begin
        myMenuBar := GetNewMBar(BASE_RES_ID);
        if myMenuBar = nil then
            ErrorHandler(NO_MBAR);
        SetMenuBar(myMenuBar);

        aMenu := GetMHandle(APPLE_MENU_ID);
        if aMenu = nil then
            ErrorHandler(NO_MENU);

        AddResMenu(aMenu, 'DRVR');

        aMenu := GetMHandle(EDIT_MENU_ID);
        if aMenu = nil then
            ErrorHandler(NO_MENU);

        aMenu := GetMHandle(FILE_MENU_ID);
        if aMenu = nil then
            ErrorHandler(NO_MENU);

        DrawMenuBar;
    end;


{---------------> WindowMaker<--}

begin
    MenuBarInit;

    MainLoop;
end.
```

Running WindowMaker

Now that your source code is done, you're ready to run WindowMaker.
Select **Go** from the **Run** menu. If you run into any compilation
problems, consult the debugging tips found in Appendix C. When
asked if you want to save changes before running, click **Yes**. The menu
bar should display the , **File**, and **Edit** menus. Desk accessories
should work. The **File** menu should contain three new menu items:
New, **Close**, and **Quit**. The **Edit** menu contains the standard menu

items but is dimmed. Select **New** from the **File** menu a few times:
You should see something like Figure 7.8.

Each window can be selected and dragged around the screen.
Selecting **Close** closes the currently selected window.

Try selecting **New** about a dozen times (or until you've created
enough windows to cause window wrap). You should see something
like Figure 7.9. Each new window is placed below and to the right of
the previous window. When the new windows reach the bottom or the
right of the screen, the window wraps back to the top left corner.
Select a window and drag it partially off and then back onto the
screen. An `updateEvt` will cause the `PICT` to be redrawn. Click in
the close box of a window to close it. Now, choose **Quit** from the **File**
menu. Let's take a look at the code.

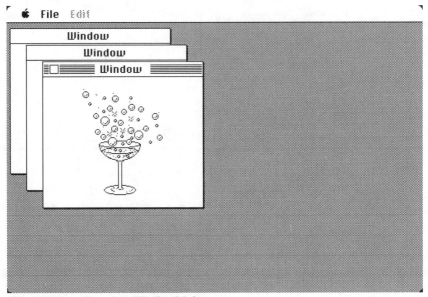

Figure 7.8   Running WindowMaker.

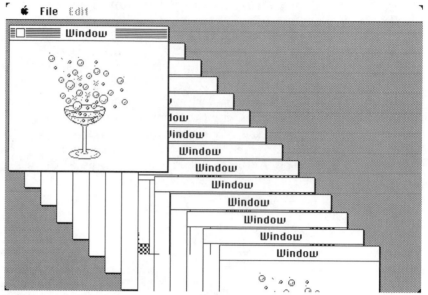

Figure 7.9   Window wrap in WindowMaker.

Walking Through the WindowMaker Code

Figure 7.10 shows a bird's-eye view of WindowMaker's software architecture.

WindowMaker.c starts off with constant declarations. BASE_RES_ID should be familiar to you. APPLE_MENU_ID, EDIT_MENU_ID, and FILE_MENU_ID are the resource ID numbers of the MENU resources. ABOUT_ITEM, ABOUT_ALERT, and ERROR_ALERT_ID are used to implement the program alerts. The names NO_MBAR, NO_MENU, NO_PICTURE, and NO_WIND are used to identify the resource ID of the four strings used in the error-handling routine. NEW_ITEM, CLOSE_ITEM, and QUIT_ITEM are used in the case statement in the menu-handling routines. UNDO_ITEM, CUT_ITEM, COPY_ITEM, PASTE_ITEM, and CLEAR_ITEM will be used to control the **Edit** menu items for desk accessories. EDGE_THRESHOLD sets the threshold from the edge, in pixels, before window wrap occurs. WINDOW_HOME_LEFT and WINDOW_HOME_TOP are the default positions for a new window on the screen. The NEW_WINDOW_OFFSET is set to the number of pixels

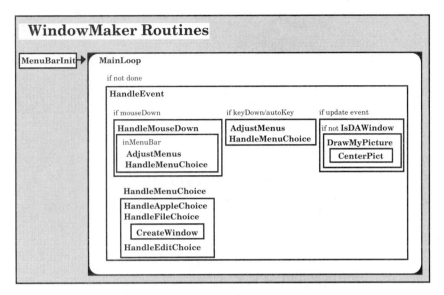

Figure 7.10   WindowMaker's software architecture.

that a new window will be offset from the previous window. `MIN_SLEEP` is provided as a parameter to `WaitNextEvent`; `LEAVE_WHERE_IT_IS` is a constant for `MoveWindow`. `WNE_TRAP_NUM` and `UNIMPL_TRAP_NUM` are used to determine the availability of `WaitNextEvent` on the user's Mac. Finally, set up `NIL_STRING` and `HOPELESSLY_FATAL_ERROR` for use in the error-handling alert.

```
  program WindowMaker;
const
   BASE_RES_ID = 400;

   APPLE_MENU_ID = 400;
   FILE_MENU_ID = 401;
   EDIT_MENU_ID = 402;

   ABOUT_ITEM = 1;
   ABOUT_ALERT = 400;
   ERROR_ALERT_ID = 401;

   NO_MBAR = BASE_RES_ID;
   NO_MENU = BASE_RES_ID + 1;
   NO_PICTURE = BASE_RES_ID + 2;
   NO_WIND = BASE_RES_ID + 3;
```

```
NEW_ITEM = 1;
CLOSE_ITEM = 2;
QUIT_ITEM = 3;

UNDO_ITEM = 1;
CUT_ITEM = 3;
COPY_ITEM = 4;
PASTE_ITEM = 5;
CLEAR_ITEM = 6;

EDGE_THRESHOLD = 30;

WINDOW_HOME_LEFT = 5;
WINDOW_HOME_TOP = 45;
NEW_WINDOW_OFFSET = 20;

MIN_SLEEP = 60;

LEAVE_WHERE_IT_IS = FALSE;

WNE_TRAP_NUM = $60;
UNIMPL_TRAP_NUM = $9F;

NIL_STRING = '';
HOPELESSLY_FATAL_ERROR = 'Game over, man!';
```

gDone, as always, is used as a flag for program completion. gWNEImplemented is the flag used when evaluating whether or not WaitNextEvent is available. gNewWindowLeft and gNewWindowTop are the left and top coordinates for new windows, which will be initialized for the first window.

```
   var
gDone, gWNEImplemented: Boolean;
gTheEvent: EventRecord;
gNewWindowLeft, gNewWindowTop: INTEGER;
```

WindowMaker starts with familiar calls to MenuInit and MainLoop.

```
{--------------->    WindowMaker  <--}

begin
    MenuBarInit;

    MainLoop;
end.
```

In `MenuBarInit`, load your menu resources and draw the menu bar. Everything is standard operating procedure except for the new error handling. If `GetNewMBar(BASE_RES_ID)` returns `nil`, it indicates that the operating system could not find the `MBAR` resource in your resource file; the error-handling routine, `ErrorHandler`, will then display an alert containing the string (`'STR '`) resource with an ID number of `NO_MBAR`. The same thing happens if the ⬤, **File**, or **Edit** menu resources cannot be found:

```
{---------------->    MenuBarInit  <--}

        procedure MenuBarInit;
            var
                myMenuBar: Handle;
                aMenu: MenuHandle;
        begin
            myMenuBar := GetNewMBar(BASE_RES_ID);
            if myMenuBar = nil then
                ErrorHandler(NO_MBAR);
            SetMenuBar(myMenuBar);

            aMenu := GetMHandle(APPLE_MENU_ID);
            if aMenu = nil then
                ErrorHandler(NO_MENU);

            AddResMenu(aMenu, 'DRVR');

            aMenu := GetMHandle(EDIT_MENU_ID);
            if aMenu = nil then
                ErrorHandler(NO_MENU);

            aMenu := GetMHandle(FILE_MENU_ID);
            if aMenu = nil then
                ErrorHandler(NO_MENU);

            DrawMenuBar;
        end;
```

`MainLoop` checks to see if `WaitNextEvent` is implemented.

```
{---------------->    MainLoop       <--}

    procedure MainLoop;
    begin
        gDone := FALSE;
        gNewWindowLeft := WINDOW_HOME_LEFT;
        gNewWindowTop := WINDOW_HOME_TOP;
```

```
      gWNEImplemented := (NGetTrapAddress(WNE_TRAP_NUM,
      ToolTrap) <> NGetTrapAddress(UNIMPL_TRAP_NUM,
      ToolTrap));
      while (gDone = FALSE) do
            HandleEvent;
end;
```

HandleEvent is similar to the earlier event handlers, except that cut, copy, and paste operations are now supported in desk accessories. AdjustMenus is now called if a Command key equivalent event has occurred, to change the state of the **Edit** menu. updateEvts are handled with a call to DrawMyPicture.

```
{----------------> HandleEvent    <--}

procedure HandleEvent;
    var
        theChar: CHAR;
        dummy: BOOLEAN;
        oldPort: GrafPtr;
    begin
    if gWNEImplemented then
        dummy := WaitNextEvent(everyEvent, gTheEvent,
        MIN_SLEEP, nil)
    else
        begin
            SystemTask;
            dummy := GetNextEvent(everyEvent, gTheEvent);
        end;

    case gTheEvent.what of
        mouseDown:
            HandleMouseDown;
        keyDown, autoKey:
            begin
                theChar := CHR(BitAnd(gTheEvent.message,
                            charCodeMask));
                if (BitAnd(gTheEvent.modifiers, cmdKey) <> 0)
                  then
                    begin
                        AdjustMenus;
                        HandleMenuChoice(MenuKey(theChar));
                    end;
            end;
        updateEvt:
            if not IsDAWindow(WindowPtr(gTheEvent.message))
then
```

```
            begin
                GetPort(oldPort);
                SetPort(WindowPtr(gTheEvent.message));

                BeginUpdate(WindowPtr(gTheEvent.message));

                DrawMyPicture(WindowPtr(gTheEvent.message));
                EndUpdate(WindowPtr(gTheEvent.message));
                SetPort(oldPort);
            end;
        end;
    end;
```

Now, `HandleMouseDown` supports desk accessory use of the **Edit**
menu. `AdjustMenus` is also called to activate the **Edit** menu if a
`mouseDown` has occurred in the menu bar. Clicking in the close box
calls `DisposeWindow`, which will close and free up the memory
used for the window.

```
{--------------->  HandleMouseDown     <--}

    procedure HandleMouseDown;
        var
            whichWindow: WindowPtr;
            thePart: INTEGER;
            menuChoice, windSize: LONGINT;
    begin
        thePart := FindWindow(gTheEvent.where, whichWindow);
        case thePart of
            inMenuBar:
                begin
                    AdjustMenus;
                    menuChoice := MenuSelect(gTheEvent.where);
                    HandleMenuChoice(menuChoice);
                end;
            inSysWindow:
                SystemClick(gTheEvent, whichWindow);
            inDrag:
                DragWindow(whichWindow, gTheEvent.where,
                screenBits.bounds);
            inGoAway:
                DisposeWindow(whichWindow);
            inContent:
                SelectWindow(whichWindow);
        end;
    end;
```

AdjustMenus and IsDAWindow work together: AdjustMenus enables and disables the items in the **Edit** menu, depending on whether the current window is a desk accessory window or a WindowMaker window. To determine this, look into the structure of the current window: One of the fields of a window, windowKind, is positive if the window is an application window and negative if it is a desk accessory window. So, in IsDAWindow, FALSE is returned if there is no window or if the window belongs to WindowMaker, and all items in the **Edit** menu are disabled (dimmed). If TRUE is returned, the **Edit** items are enabled so that desk accessories can use them.

```
{----------------> AdjustMenus <--}

procedure AdjustMenus;
    var
        aMenu: MenuHandle;
begin
    aMenu := GetMHandle(FILE_MENU_ID);
    if FrontWindow = nil then
        DisableItem(aMenu, CLOSE_ITEM)
    else
        EnableItem(aMenu, CLOSE_ITEM);

    aMenu := GetMHandle(EDIT_MENU_ID);
    if IsDAWindow(FrontWindow) then
        begin
            EnableItem(aMenu, UNDO_ITEM);
            EnableItem(aMenu, CUT_ITEM);
            EnableItem(aMenu, COPY_ITEM);
            EnableItem(aMenu, PASTE_ITEM);
            EnableItem(aMenu, CLEAR_ITEM);
        end
    else
        begin
            DisableItem(aMenu, UNDO_ITEM);
            DisableItem(aMenu, CUT_ITEM);
            DisableItem(aMenu, COPY_ITEM);
            DisableItem(aMenu, PASTE_ITEM);
            DisableItem(aMenu, CLEAR_ITEM);
        end;
end;
```

```
{----------------->      IsDAWindow   <--}

    function IsDAWindow (whichWindow: WindowPtr): BOOLEAN;
    begin
        if whichWindow = nil then
            IsDAWindow := FALSE
        else
            IsDAWindow := (WindowPeek(whichWindow)^.windowKind < 0);
    end;
```

HandleMenuChoice hasn't changed from the earlier programs with menus, except that you now handle **Edit** menu selections:

```
{----------------->      HandleMenuChoice   <--}

    procedure HandleMenuChoice (menuChoice: LONGINT);
        var
            theMenu, theItem: INTEGER;
    begin
        if menuChoice <> 0 then
            begin
                theMenu := HiWord(menuChoice);
                theItem := LoWord(menuChoice);

                case theMenu of
                    APPLE_MENU_ID:
                        HandleAppleChoice(theItem);
                    FILE_MENU_ID:
                        HandleFileChoice(theItem);
                    EDIT_MENU_ID:
                        HandleEditChoice(theItem);
                end;

                HiliteMenu(0);
            end;
    end;
```

HandleAppleChoice works the same way as Chapter 6's Reminder program. The about item calls NoteAlert, which displays the ALRT and the DITL you set up for the about box.

```
{----------------->      HandleAppleChoice      <--}

    procedure HandleAppleChoice (theItem: INTEGER);
        var
            accName: Str255;
            accNumber, itemNumber, dummy: INTEGER;
            aMenu: MenuHandle;
    begin
```

```
        case theItem of
            ABOUT_ITEM:
                dummy := NoteAlert(ABOUT_ALERT, nil);
            otherwise
                begin
                    aMenu := GetMHandle(APPLE_MENU_ID);
                    GetItem(aMenu, theItem, accName);
                    accNumber := OpenDeskAcc(accName);
                end;
        end;
    end;
```

HandleFileChoice takes care of the **File** menu choices. The
New menu item runs the routine CreateWindow, and the **Close**
menu item closes the active window by calling DisposeWindow.
Using the **Close** menu item is the same as clicking in the active
window's close box. **Quit** sets gDone to TRUE, which halts execution
of the main event loop.

```
{---------------->  HandleFileChoice  <--}

procedure HandleFileChoice (theItem: INTEGER);
    var
        whichWindow: WindowPtr;
begin
    case theItem of
        NEW_ITEM:
            CreateWindow;
        CLOSE_ITEM:
            begin
                whichWindow := FrontWindow;
                if whichWindow <> nil then
                    DisposeWindow(whichWindow);
            end;
        QUIT_ITEM:
            gDone := TRUE;
    end;
end;
```

HandleEditChoice calls SystemEdit. If the active window
belongs to a desk accessory, SystemEdit passes the appropriate edit
command to the accessory. Otherwise, it returns FALSE, and your
application should then handle the edit command. Because the **Edit**
menu items are disabled in WindowMaker, HandleEditChoice just
takes care of desk accessories.

```
{---------------->        HandleEditChoice   <--}

    procedure HandleEditChoice (theItem: INTEGER);
        var
            dummy: Boolean;
    begin
        dummy := SystemEdit(theItem - 1);
    end;
```

CreateWindow controls the creation and placing of new windows for WindowMaker. First, use GetNewWindow with your WIND resource to create a new window. If the WIND is missing, GetNewWindow returns nil, so you can call ErrorHandler with a 'STR ' resource of NO_WIND.

```
{---------------->        CreateWindow     <--}

    procedure CreateWindow;
        var
            theNewestWindow: WindowPtr;
    begin
        theNewestWindow := GetNewWindow(BASE_RES_ID, nil,
                            WindowPtr(-1));
        if theNewestWindow = nil then
            ErrorHandler(NO_WIND);
```

Normally, you'd use the position of a window as specified in the WIND resource. In this case, however, the position of each new window is defined by the globals gNewWindowLeft and gNewWindowTop. Whenever a new window is defined, MoveWindow is called to move the window from the original WIND-based position to the position described by gNewWindowLeft and gNewWindowTop. The final parameter to MoveWindow is a BOOLEAN that determines whether the window, once moved, is moved to the front of all other windows or is left in the same layer. LEAVE_WHERE_IT_IS tells MoveWindow not to move the window to the front. Because the window was created in the front, this parameter will have no effect.

Next, gNewWindowLeft and gNewWindowTop are incremented by NEW_WINDOW_OFFSET, so the next new window won't appear directly on top of the previous one. Finally, the window is made visible.

```
        if ((screenBits.bounds.right - gNewWindowLeft) <
          EDGE_THRESHOLD) or ((screenBits.bounds.bottom -
            gNewWindowTop) < EDGE_THRESHOLD) then
            begin
                gNewWindowLeft := WINDOW_HOME_LEFT;
                gNewWindowTop := WINDOW_HOME_TOP;
            end;
```

```
        MoveWindow(theNewestWindow, gNewWindowLeft,
               gNewWindowTop, LEAVE_WHERE_IT_IS);
        gNewWindowLeft := gNewWindowLeft + NEW_WINDOW_OFFSET;
        gNewWindowTop := gNewWindowTop + NEW_WINDOW_OFFSET;
        ShowWindow(theNewestWindow);
end;
```

DrawMyPicture passes thePicture to CenterPict and then draws the centered PICT in pictureWindow.

> The real value of parameter passing is seen here. By passing the WindowPtr embedded in gTheEvent.message as a parameter to DrawMyPicture, you avoid hard-coded variable names that would limit the flexibility of this routine.

```
{----------------->       DrawMyPicture      <--}

procedure DrawMyPicture (pictureWindow: WindowPtr);
    var
        myRect: Rect;
        thePicture: PicHandle;
begin
    myRect := pictureWindow^.portRect;
    thePicture := GetPicture(BASE_RES_ID);
    if thePicture = nil then
        ErrorHandler(NO_PICTURE);

    CenterPict(thePicture, myRect);
    SetPort(pictureWindow);
    DrawPicture(thePicture, myRect);
end;
```

CenterPict is the same routine you've used in your other PICT drawing programs:

```
{----------------->       CenterPict    <--}

procedure CenterPict (thePicture: PicHandle; var myRect:
Rect);
    var
        windRect, pictureRect: Rect;
begin
    windRect := myRect;
    pictureRect := thePicture^^.picFrame;
```

```
    myRect.top := (windRect.bottom - windRect.top -
        (pictureRect.bottom - pictureRect.top)) div 2 +
        windRect.top;
    myRect.bottom := myRect.top + (pictureRect.bottom -
        pictureRect.top);
    myRect.left := (windRect.right - windRect.left -
        (pictureRect.right - pictureRect.left)) div 2 +
        windRect.left;
    myRect.right := myRect.left + (pictureRect.right -
        pictureRect.left);
end;
```

Finally, there's the `ErrorHandler` routine. `ErrorHandler` takes an error ID as input, loads the `'STR '` resource with that ID, and uses `StopAlert` to display the error message. If the program can't find the `'STR '` resource it needs, it calls `StopAlert` with the `HOPELESSLY_FATAL_ERROR` string defined at the beginning of WindowMaker (`'Game over, man!'`), to inform the user that the situation is exceedingly grim.

Finally, `ExitToShell` returns control of the Macintosh to the Finder.

```
{---------------->      ErrorHandler      <--}

procedure ErrorHandler (stringNum: INTEGER);
    var
        errorStringH: StringHandle;
        dummy: INTEGER;
begin
    errorStringH := GetString(stringNum);
    if errorStringH = nil then
        ParamText(HOPELESSLY_FATAL_ERROR, NIL_STRING,
        NIL_STRING, NIL_STRING)
    else
        ParamText(errorStringH^^, NIL_STRING, NIL_STRING,
        NIL_STRING);

    dummy := StopAlert(ERROR_ALERT_ID, nil);
    ExitToShell;
end;
```

There are many solutions to error handling on the Macintosh. Whenever you make a Toolbox function call, check to see if an error has occurred. This is called passive error handling. Sometimes this is good enough; sometimes it's not.

You can also go out of your way to avoid errors by checking everything you can possibly check. For example, imagine adding a fourth MENU resource, to implement a **Utilities** menu. Assuming there is nothing special about the **Utilities** menu, you could get all the way through MenuBarInit without checking for the existence of the **Utilities** MENU resource. If the MENU is there, MenuBarInit will load the MENU automatically and make it available to your program. In this case, passive error handling worked fine.

Suppose, however, that the MENU resource were trashed or missing, preventing it from being loaded. Your program would not function properly and would most probably crash. Checking all your resources may be time-consuming, but in the end, it's well worth it.

You can take error handling one step further and also check your resources just before you use them. For example, you could call GetMHandle immediately before MenuSelect in case the MENU was somehow corrupted.

You'll decide on the appropriate amount of error handling to perform. Error handling adds bulk to code but provides a higher level of reliability for your program. We highly recommend the inclusion of error-handling code early in the programming cycle.

The Scrap Manager

Whenever you use the Mac's copy, cut, or paste facilities, you're making use of the **Scrap Manager**. The Scrap Manager manages the **desk scrap**, more commonly known as the **Clipboard**. The second program, **ShowClip**, will use the Scrap Manager Toolbox routines to open the Clipboard and display the contents in a window.

Scrap Manager Basics

Data copied to the desk scrap is stored in two basic flavors, TEXT and PICT. Data stored in TEXT format consist of a series of ASCII characters. Data stored in PICT format consist of a QuickDraw picture. ShowClip will handle both TEXT and PICT data types.

The Scrap Manager consists of six routines: InfoScrap, UnloadScrap, LoadScrap, ZeroScrap, PutScrap, and GetScrap. InfoScrap returns a pointer to a ScrapStuff record. Each of the other functions return a LONGINT containing a result code (I:457).

InfoScrap

InfoScrap is a function (of type PScrapStuff) that returns information about the desk scrap in a struct of type ScrapStuff:

```
TYPE PScrapStuff = ^ScrapStuff;
    ScrapStuff =
        RECORD
            scrapSize : LONGINT;    {size of desk scrap}
            scrapHandle : Handle;   {handle to desk scrap}
            scrapCount : INTEGER;   {count changed by ZeroScrap}
            scrapState : INTEGER;   {tells where the desk scrap is}
            scrapName : StringPtr   {scrap file name}
        END;
```

The scrapSize field contains the actual size, in bytes, of the desk scrap. The scrapHandle field contains a handle to the desk scrap (if it currently resides in memory). The scrapCount field is changed every time ZeroScrap is called (we'll get to ZeroScrap in a bit). The scrapState field is positive if the desk scrap is memory resident, zero if the scrap is on disk, and negative if the scrap has not yet been initialized. The scrapName field contains a pointer to the name of the scrap disk file (usually called Clipboard File).

UnloadScrap and LoadScrap

If the scrap is currently in memory, UnloadScrap copies the scrap to disk and releases the scrap's memory. If the scrap is currently disk-based, UnloadScrap does nothing.

If the scrap is currently on disk, LoadScrap allocates memory for the scrap and copies it from disk. If the scrap is currently memory-resident, LoadScrap does nothing.

ZeroScrap

If the desk scrap does not yet exist, ZeroScrap creates it in memory. If it does exist, ZeroScrap clears it. As we mentioned before, ZeroScrap always changes the scrapCount field of the ScrapStuff record.

PutScrap

`PutScrap` puts the data pointed to by `source` into the scrap:

```
FUNCTION PutScrap( length : LONGINT;
                        theType : ResType;
                        source : Ptr ) : LONGINT;
```

The parameter `length` specifies the length of the data, and `theType` specifies their type (whether they are `PICT` or `TEXT` data). You must call `ZeroScrap` immediately before each call to `PutScrap`.

GetScrap

`GetScrap` resizes the handle `hDest` and stores a copy of the scrap in this resized block of memory:

```
FUNCTION GetScrap( hDest : Handle;
                    theType : ResType;
                    VAR offset : LONGINT ) : LONGINT;
```

Specify the type of data you want in the parameter `theType`. The `offset` parameter is set to the returned data's offset in bytes from the beginning of the desk scrap. `GetScrap` returns a long containing the length of the data in bytes.

You can actually put and get data types other than `TEXT` and `PICT` to and from the scrap (I:461). For the most part, however, the `TEXT` and `PICT` data types should serve your needs.

ShowClip

The ability to use the Clipboard is basic to Mac applications. ShowClip shows you how to add this capability to your applications. If you cut or copy text or a picture in an application or in the Finder and then run ShowClip, it will display the cut or copied text in a window.

ShowClip Specifications

ShowClip works like this:

1. It initializes a window.
2. It puts whatever is in the Clipboard into the window.
3. It quits.

ShowClip also does error checking. It warns if the WIND resource is missing, or if the scrap is empty.

Setting Up the ShowClip Project

Start by creating a folder for this project, called ShowClip. Use ResEdit to create a new file called ShowClip.π.rsrc and, within that, a purgeable WIND with an ID of 400. Figure 7.11 shows the specifications of this WIND.

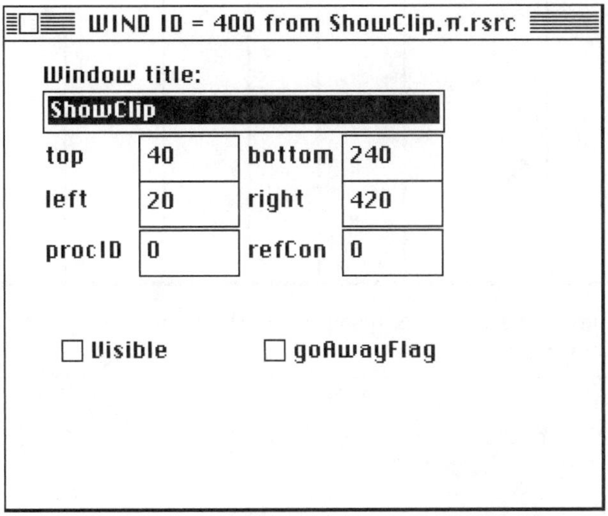

Figure 7.11 WIND specifications for ShowClip.

Add the DITL in Figure 7.12 (this is the same one as the "hopelessly fatal" DITL in WindowMaker, so use the WindowMaker DITL if you have it).

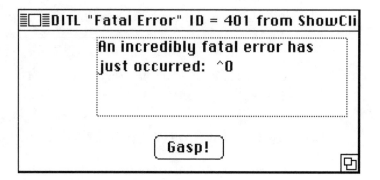

Item#	Type	Enabled	Top	Left	Bottom	Right	Text/Resource ID
1	Button	Yes	86	117	106	177	Gasp!
2	Static Text	Yes	5	67	71	283	An incredibly fatal error has just occurred: ^0

Figure 7.12   DITL resource for ShowClip.

Next, create a purgeable ALRT resource for your new error-checking routines (Figure 7.13). Add the two 'STR ' resources shown in Figure 7.14 to the ShowClip.π.rsrc file. Again, be sure to change the resource IDs of each resource to those shown in the figure and mark each as purgeable. When you're done, the resource list window from ShowClip.π.rsrc should look like Figure 7.15.

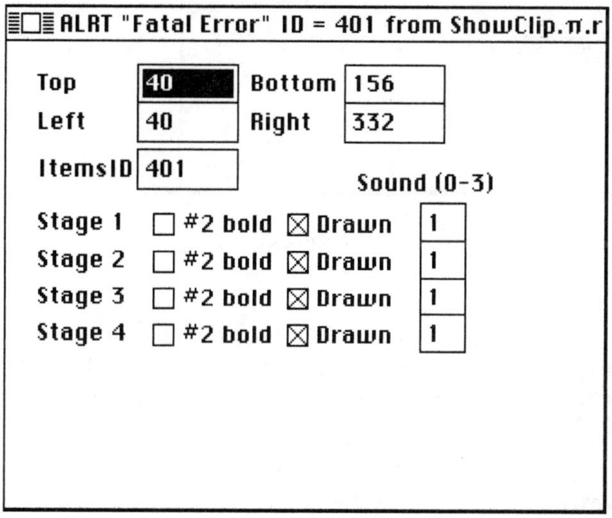

Figure 7.13 ALRT resource for ShowClip.

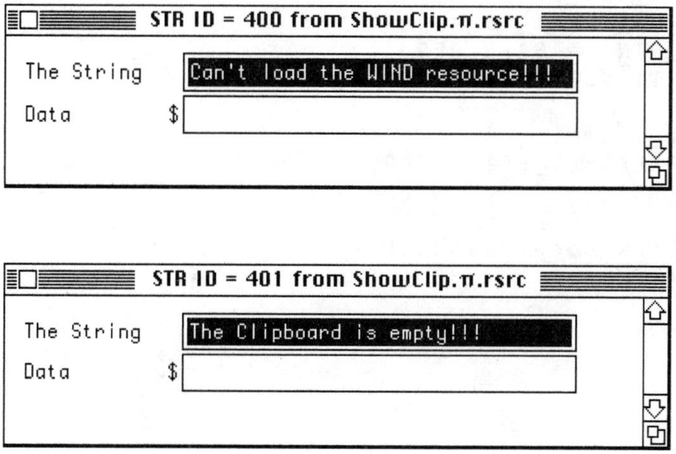

Figure 7.14 STR resources for ShowClip.

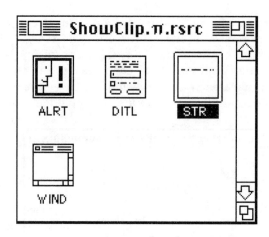

Figure 7.15   Resource list for ShowClip.

Now you're ready to launch THINK Pascal. When prompted for a project to open, create a new project in the `ShowClip` folder and call it `ShowClip.π`. Next, use the **Run Options...** dialog box to add the resource file to the project.

Create a new source file called `ShowClip.p` and add it to `ShowClip.π`. Here's the source code for `ShowClip.p`:

```
program ShowClip;
    const
        BASE_RES_ID = 400;
        ERROR_ALERT_ID = BASE_RES_ID + 1;
        NO_WIND = BASE_RES_ID;
        EMPTY_SCRAP = BASE_RES_ID + 1;

        NIL_STRING = '';
        HOPELESSLY_FATAL_ERROR = 'Game over, man!';

    var
        gClipWindow: WindowPtr;
```

```
{----------------> ErrorHandler   <--}

    procedure ErrorHandler (stringNum: INTEGER);
        var
            errorStringH: StringHandle;
            dummy: INTEGER;
    begin
        errorStringH := GetString(stringNum);
        if errorStringH = nil then
            ParamText(HOPELESSLY_FATAL_ERROR, NIL_STRING,
            NIL_STRING, NIL_STRING)
        else
            ParamText(errorStringH^^, NIL_STRING, NIL_STRING,
            NIL_STRING);

        dummy := StopAlert(ERROR_ALERT_ID, nil);
        ExitToShell;
    end;


{----------------> CenterPict   <--}

    procedure CenterPict (thePicture: PicHandle; var myRect:
    Rect);
        var
            windRect, pictureRect: Rect;
    begin
        windRect := myRect;
        pictureRect := thePicture^^.picFrame;
        myRect.top := (windRect.bottom - windRect.top -
            (pictureRect.bottom - pictureRect.top)) div 2 +
            windRect.top;
        myRect.bottom := myRect.top + (pictureRect.bottom -
            pictureRect.top);
        myRect.left := (windRect.right - windRect.left -
            (pictureRect.right - pictureRect.left)) div 2 +
            windRect.left;
        myRect.right := myRect.left + (pictureRect.right -
            pictureRect.left);
    end;


{----------------> MainLoop   <--}

    procedure MainLoop;
        var
            myRect: Rect;
            clipHandle: Handle;
            length, offset: LONGINT;
    begin
        clipHandle := NewHandle(0);
```

```
            length := GetScrap(clipHandle, 'TEXT', offset);
            if length < 0 then
                begin
                    length := GetScrap(clipHandle, 'PICT', offset);
                    if length < 0 then
                        ErrorHandler(EMPTY_SCRAP)
                    else
                        begin
                            myRect := gClipWindow^.portRect;
                            CenterPict(PicHandle(clipHandle),
                                myRect);
                            DrawPicture(PicHandle(clipHandle),
                                myRect);
                        end;
                end
            else
                begin
                    HLock(clipHandle);
                    TextBox(Ptr(clipHandle^), length,
                        thePort^.portRect, teJustLeft);
                    HUnlock(clipHandle);
                end;

        while not Button do
                begin
                end;
    end;


{---------------> WindowInit <--}

    procedure WindowInit;
    begin
        gClipWindow := GetNewWindow(BASE_RES_ID, nil,
        WindowPtr(-1));

        if gClipWindow = nil then
            ErrorHandler(NO_WIND);

        ShowWindow(gClipWindow);
        SetPort(gClipWindow);
    end;


{---------------> ShowClip   <--}

begin
    WindowInit;
    MainLoop;
end.
```

Running ShowClip

Now that your source code is done, you're ready to run ShowClip. Before you run the program, however, do a cut or copy operation on the `ShowClip.p` file, or copy a picture from the Scrapbook; otherwise, you'll get an alert telling you that the scrap is empty. Now run ShowClip. It should immediately display the text or picture that you cut or copied (Figure 7.16).

Quit by clicking the mouse. Try copying varying sizes of text or different pictures and running ShowClip again. This code should point out the ease with which you can add the Clipboard functions to your applications.

Now, let's see how it's done.

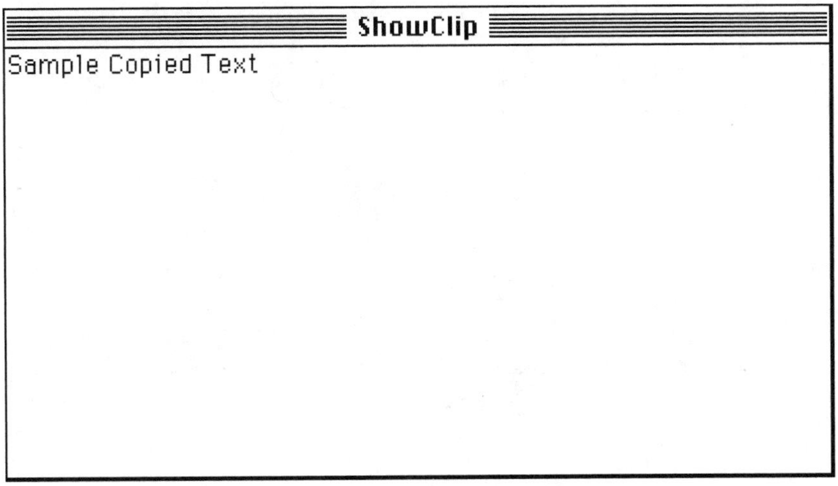

```
═══════════════ ShowClip ═══════════════
Sample Copied Text



```

Figure 7.16 Running ShowClip.

ShowClip.p starts off with the constant declarations. ShowClip's constants are similar to those declared in WindowMaker. The sole global variable, gClipWindow, points to the clipboard window.

```
program ShowClip;
    const
        BASE_RES_ID = 400;
        ERROR_ALERT_ID = BASE_RES_ID + 1;
        NO_WIND = BASE_RES_ID;
        EMPTY_SCRAP = BASE_RES_ID + 1;

        NIL_STRING = '';
        HOPELESSLY_FATAL_ERROR = 'Game over, man!';

    var
        gClipWindow: WindowPtr;
```

ShowClip calls WindowInit and then MainLoop. No excitement here.

```
{----------------->   ShowClip    <--}

begin
    WindowInit;
    MainLoop;
end.
```

In WindowInit, use GetNewWindow to load gClipWindow from the resource file. Then call ShowWindow to make gClipWindow visible and call SetPort so that all drawing is done in gClipWindow:

```
{----------------->   WindowInit <--}

    procedure WindowInit;
    begin
        gClipWindow := GetNewWindow(BASE_RES_ID, nil,
        WindowPtr(-1));

        if gClipWindow = nil then
            ErrorHandler(NO_WIND);

        ShowWindow(gClipWindow);
        SetPort(gClipWindow);
    end;
```

`MainLoop` is where the action is. You use `NewHandle` (II:32) to create minimum-size blocks of storage for your `PICT` and `TEXT` data. Remember, `GetScrap` will resize these memory blocks for you, as needed.

```
{----------------->   MainLoop   <--}

    procedure MainLoop;
        var
            myRect: Rect;
            clipHandle: Handle;
            length, offset: LONGINT;
    begin
        clipHandle := NewHandle(0);
```

Now, call `GetScrap`, looking first for some `TEXT` data. If there are no `TEXT` data in the scrap, call `GetScrap` to look for `PICT` data. If you find no `PICT` data, call `ErrorHandler` with the `EMPTY_SCRAP` string. If you do find `PICT` data, call `CenterPict` to center the picture in `gClipWindow`, and then call `DrawPicture` to draw the picture:

```
length := GetScrap(clipHandle, 'TEXT', offset);
if length < 0 then
    begin
        length := GetScrap(clipHandle, 'PICT', offset);
        if length < 0 then
            ErrorHandler(EMPTY_SCRAP)
        else
            begin
                myRect := gClipWindow^.portRect;
                CenterPict(PicHandle(clipHandle),
                myRect);
                DrawPicture(PicHandle(clipHandle),
                myRect);
            end;
    end
```

If you found the `TEXT` data in the scrap, lock `clipHandle` with `Hlock`, then call `TextBox` to draw the text in `gClipWindow`.

```
else
    begin
        HLock(clipHandle);
```

```
            TextBox(Ptr(clipHandle^), length,
            thePort^.portRect, teJustLeft);
            HUnlock(clipHandle);
      end;
```

Finally, wait for a mouse click to exit the program:

```
      while not Button do
            begin
            end;
      end;
```

CenterPict is the same routine you've used in the other *Primer* PICT drawing programs:

```
{----------------->    CenterPict    <--}

   procedure CenterPict (thePicture: PicHandle; var myRect:
   Rect);
      var
         windRect, pictureRect: Rect;
   begin
      windRect := myRect;
      pictureRect := thePicture^^.picFrame;
      myRect.top := (windRect.bottom - windRect.top -
         (pictureRect.bottom - pictureRect.top)) div 2 +
         windRect.top;
      myRect.bottom := myRect.top + (pictureRect.bottom -
         pictureRect.top);
      myRect.left := (windRect.right - windRect.left -
         (pictureRect.right - pictureRect.left)) div 2 +
         windRect.left;
      myRect.right := myRect.left + (pictureRect.right -
         pictureRect.left);
   end;
```

ErrorHandler is the same routine you encountered in WindowMaker. Here, you get the string you need and then display it with StopAlert. ExitToShell halts program execution and returns to the Finder.

```
{----------------->    ErrorHandler    <--}

   procedure ErrorHandler (stringNum: INTEGER);
      var
         errorStringH: StringHandle;
         dummy: INTEGER;
   begin
```

```
    errorStringH := GetString(stringNum);
    if errorStringH = nil then
        ParamText(HOPELESSLY_FATAL_ERROR,  NIL_STRING,
                  NIL_STRING, NIL_STRING)
    else
        ParamText(errorStringH^^,  NIL_STRING,  NIL_STRING,
                  NIL_STRING);

    dummy := StopAlert(ERROR_ALERT_ID, nil);
    ExitToShell;
end;
```

Inside the Printing and File Managers

The next program, PrintPICT, uses both the **Printing Manager** and the **File Manager**. PrintPICT uses the **Standard File Package** (IV:71) to prompt for the name of a PICT file to print. It opens the file, reads in a chunk of data, builds a page, and sends the page to the current printer. The power of the File and Printing Managers makes this task a simple one. Let's take a look at the Standard File Package.

The Standard File Package

The Standard File Package is used by most Macintosh applications to support the **Open, Save,** and **Save As... File** menu items. Figure 7.17 shows examples of calls to SFGetFile and SFPutFile. SFGetFile is used to get a file name from the user. It can be called with a list of file types, limiting the user's choices to files of the types specified on the list. PrintPICT prints a single PICT file. By calling SFGetFile, PrintPICT allows the user to select the print file from a list limited to PICT files.

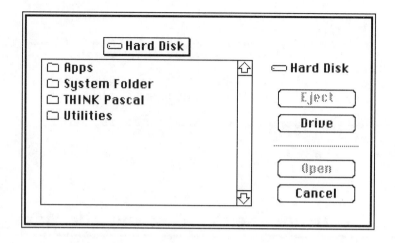

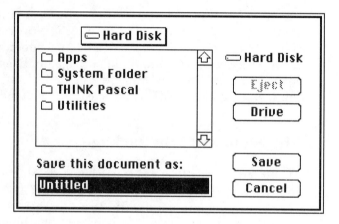

Figure 7.17   SFGetFile and SFPutFile.

The File Manager was totally remade when the Mac Plus came out. The original Macintosh Filing System (MFS) was inadequate to handle the number of files that hard disks could hold. The Hierarchical Filing System (HFS) replaced it, and Volume IV of *Inside Macintosh* details the new Toolbox calls. So, if you need information about the File Manager, use Chapter 19 of Volume IV, not Chapter 4 of Volume II.

Here's the calling sequence for SFGetFile:

```
PROCEDURE SFGetFile( where : Point;
                     prompt : Str255;
                     fileFilter : ProcPtr;
                     numTypes : INTEGER;
                     typeList : SFTypeList;
                     dlgHook : ProcPtr;
              VAR    reply : SFReply;
                     dlgID : INTEGER;
                     filterProc : ProcPtr );
```

SFGetFile displays the standard open dialog on the screen at the point where. The prompt string is ignored. numTypes and typeList allow you to specify up to four distinct file types (such as PICT or TEXT) for the user to choose from.

> Actually, you can specify as many file types as you like by creating your own data type, instead of SFTypeList. SFGetFile looks in typeList for numTypes types.

fileFilter is a pointer to a filtering routine called by SFGetFile after the file list is built from the typeList. This filtering routine can modify the file list before it's displayed to the user.

dlgHook also points to a function. The dlgHook function you write allows you to add extra items (such as pop-up menus) to the standard open dialog.

Once the user selects a file, SFGetFile fills in the struct pointed to by reply with information about the selected file:

```
TYPE SFReply = RECORD
         good : BOOLEAN;        {FALSE if ignore command}
         copy : BOOLEAN;        {not used}
         fType : OSType;        {file type or not used}
         vRefNum : INTEGER;     {volume reference number}
         version : INTEGER;     {file's version number}
         fName : STRING[63]     {file name}
     END;
```

The good field contains FALSE if the user pressed the **Cancel** button, TRUE otherwise. The copy field currently is not used. The fType field contains the file type selected (if the good field contains TRUE). The version field always contains 0. The vRefNum and fName fields specify the selected file. You'll see how to use these last two fields in the next section.

Using the File Manager

Once the user has picked a file to open (via `SFGetFile`), you'll use the File Manager routines `FSOpen` to open the file, `FSRead` to read a block of data, and `FSClose` to close the file.

You should know a few key terms before you use the File Manager. **Volumes** are the media used to store files. When the user presses the **Drive** button in the `SFGetFile` dialog box, the files on the next available volume are displayed. Macintosh floppy and hard disks are both examples of volumes. In the original Macintosh (the one with 64K ROMs), all the files on a volume were organized in a flat file format called the Macintosh File System (MFS) (Figure 7.18).

The concept of **folders** existed on these "flat" Macs, but internally the files on a volume were all stored in one big list. The folders were an illusion maintained by the Finder. On flat volumes, users can't have two files with the same name, even if they're in different folders. The Mac Plus (with 128K ROMs) introduced a new method for organizing files: the Hierarchical File System (HFS) (Figure 7.19).

Within each HFS volume is a set of files and directories. Within each directory, there can be still more files and directories. You'll use the File Manager Toolbox calls to open, read, write, and close these files and directories.

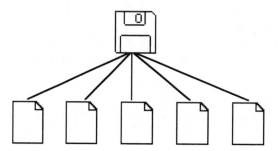

Figure 7.18   Flat files.

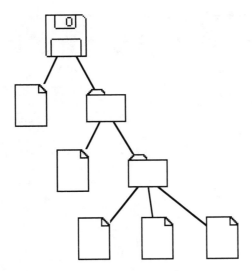

Figure 7.19 Hierarchical files.

FSOpen opens the specified file for reading and/or writing, depending on the file's open permission:

```
FUNCTION FSOpen( fileName : Str255;
                      vRefNum : INTEGER;
            VAR   refNum : INTEGER ) : OSErr;
```

SFGetFile translates the user's file selection into a vRefNum and an fName. The vRefNum specifies the file's volume and directory, and the fName specifies the file name. FSOpen gets open permission from a file control block stored on the file's volume.

Use the fileName and vRefnum fields of the reply record returned by SFGetFile as parameters to FSOpen. FSOpen will return a path reference number in the refNum parameter that you can use in FSRead:

```
FUNCTION FSRead( refNum : INTEGER;
            VAR count : LONGINT;
                  buffPtr : Ptr ) : OSErr;
```

> The refNum returned by FSOpen is known as an **access path**, specifying the file's volume and the file's location on the volume all in one variable.

Specify the file to be read from using the parameter refNum, and specify the number of bytes to be read using the parameter count. The bytes will be read into the space pointed to by the parameter buffPtr (make sure you allocate the memory to which buffPtr points), and the number of bytes actually read will be returned in count.

Finally, close the file by calling FSClose:

```
FUNCTION FSClose( refNum : INTEGER ) : OSErr;
```

Specify the file to be closed via the parameter refNum.

For a detailed discussion of the File Manager, turn to *Inside Macintosh* (Volume IV, Chapter 1) and *Tech Notes* 47, 77, 80, and 190. You'll need this for any substantial development effort.

Now, let's take a look at the Printing Manager.

Using the Printing Manager

Prepare the Printing Manager for use by calling PrOpen. Then, allocate a new print record using NewHandle. The print record contains information the Printing Manager needs to print your job, including **page setup** information and information specific to the **print job**.

You can prompt the user to fill in the page setup information by calling PrStlDialog. Prompt the user for job-specific information via a call to PrJobDialog. Each of these routines displays the appropriate dialog box and fills the newly allocated print record with the results.

Then, call PrOpenDoc to set up a printing grafPort. The printing grafPort is made up of pages. PrOpenDoc calls SetPort, so you don't need to do so. You'll call PrOpenPage to start a new page, and then make a set of QuickDraw calls (such as DrawPicture) to fill the page with graphics. Next, call PrClosePage to close the current page. Call PrOpenPage and PrClosePage for each page you want to create.

When you've drawn all your pages, close the document with a call to PrCloseDoc. Now, it's time to print your document. Do this with a call to PrPicFile. When you're done with the Printing Manager, call PrClose.

The Printing Manager is described in detail in *Inside Macintosh, Volume II,* Chapter 5. If you plan on writing an application that supports printing, read this chapter thoroughly.

Now, let's look at PrintPICT.

PrintPICT

Because the "paperless society" seems to be rapidly receding into the distance, it's reasonable to expect a Mac application to be able to print. PrintPICT shows you how to print PICT files.

> PrintPICT reads in the contents of a PICT file. Reading in the contents of a TEXT file is no different. Instead of interpreting the data as a PICT, you would run the data through a parser that handles pagination, line breaks, hyphenation, and so on, before you draw it on the print grafPort.

PrintPICT Specifications

PrintPICT works like this:

1. It uses the Standard File Package to locate a file of type PICT.

2. It uses the File Manager to open a file of type PICT.

3. It uses the Printing Manager to print the PICT file.

4. It quits.

PrintPICT also has error checking. It puts up an alert if the printing operation goes astray at a number of different points.

Setting Up PrintPICT Resources

Start by creating a folder for this project, called PrintPICT. Then, use ResEdit to create a new file called PrintPICT.π.rsrc.

Make sure all of the following resources are marked as purgeable. Create a DITL resource for your error alert (Figure 7.20). Add the same old ALRT (Figure 7.21). Next, add the six 'STR ' resources shown in Figure 7.22 to the PrintPICT.π.rsrc file. Be sure to change the resource IDs of each resource to those shown in the figures. When you're done, the resource window of PrintPICT.π.rsrc should look like Figure 7.23.

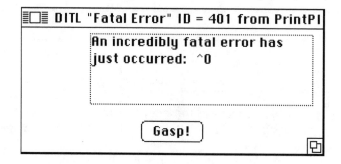

Item#	Type	Enabled	Top	Left	Bottom	Right	Text/Resource ID
1	Button	Yes	86	117	106	177	Gasp!
2	Static Text	Yes	5	67	71	283	An incredibly fatal error has just occurred: ^0

Figure 7.20   DITL resource for PrintPICT.

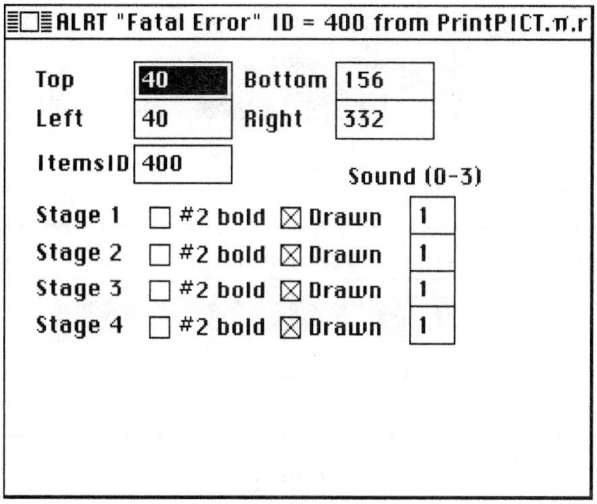

Figure 7.21 ALRT resource for PrintPICT.

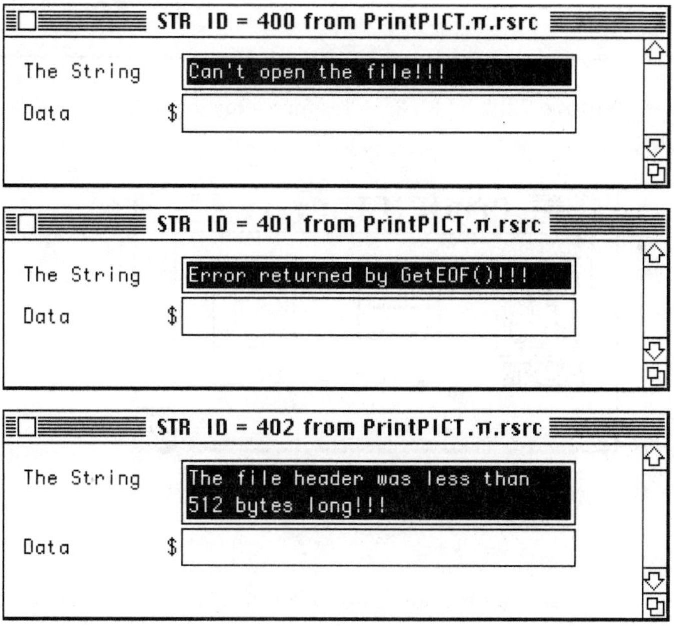

Figure 7.22 'STR ' resources for PrintPICT.

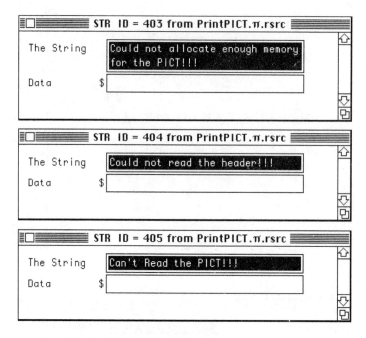

Figure 7.22   'STR ' resources for PrintPICT. (continued)

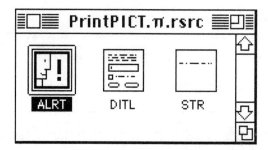

Figure 7.23   PrintPICT resources completed.

Once again, it's time to code.

Setting Up the PrintPICT Project

Start up THINK Pascal. Create a new project in the PrintPICT folder. Call it PrintPICT.π. Use the **Run Options...** dialog box to add the resource file to the project. Next, select **Add File...** from the

Project menu and add the two files that contain the Toolbox printing interface declarations and the interface routines. Both files can be found inside folders in the THINK Pascal folder. First, add the file Printing.p (you'll find it inside the Interfaces folder). Next, add the file PrintCalls.lib (you'll find it inside the Libraries folder).

Next, create a new source file called PrintPICT.p and add it to PrintPICT.π. Here's the source code for PrintPICT.p:

```pascal
program PrintPICT;
    uses
        Printing;

    const
        HEADER_SIZE = 512;
        BASE_RES_ID = 400;

        ERROR_ALERT_ID = BASE_RES_ID;
        CANT_OPEN_FILE = BASE_RES_ID;
        GET_EOF_ERROR = BASE_RES_ID + 1;
        HEADER_TOO_SMALL = BASE_RES_ID + 2;
        OUT_OF_MEMORY = BASE_RES_ID + 3;
        CANT_READ_HEADER = BASE_RES_ID + 4;
        CANT_READ_PICT = BASE_RES_ID + 5;

        NIL_STRING = '';
        IGNORED_STRING = NIL_STRING;
        HOPELESSLY_FATAL_ERROR = 'Game over, man!';

    var
        gPrintRecordH: THPrint;
        gReply: SFReply;


{---------------> ErrorHandler   <--}

    procedure ErrorHandler (stringNum: INTEGER);
        var
            errorStringH: StringHandle;
            dummy: INTEGER;
    begin
        errorStringH := GetString(stringNum);
        if errorStringH = nil then
            ParamText(HOPELESSLY_FATAL_ERROR, NIL_STRING,
            NIL_STRING, NIL_STRING)
        else
            ParamText(errorStringH^^, NIL_STRING, NIL_STRING,
            NIL_STRING);

        dummy := StopAlert(ERROR_ALERT_ID, nil);
        ExitToShell;
    end;
```

```
{----------------> PrintPictFile  <--}

    procedure PrintPictFile (reply: SFReply);
        var
            srcFile: INTEGER;
            printPort: TPPrPort;
            printStatus: TPrStatus;
            thePict: PicHandle;
            pictHeader: packed array[0..HEADER_SIZE] of CHAR;
            pictSize, headerSize: LONGINT;
            dummy: OSErr;
    begin
        if (FSOpen(reply.fName, reply.vRefNum, srcFile) <>
        noErr) then
            ErrorHandler(CANT_OPEN_FILE);

        if (GetEOF(srcFile, pictSize) <> noErr) then
            ErrorHandler(GET_EOF_ERROR);

        headerSize := HEADER_SIZE;
        if (FSRead(srcFile, headerSize, @pictHeader) <> noErr)
        then
            ErrorHandler(CANT_READ_HEADER);

        pictSize := pictSize - HEADER_SIZE;
        if pictSize <= 0 then
            ErrorHandler(HEADER_TOO_SMALL);

        thePict := PicHandle(NewHandle(pictSize));
        if thePict = nil then
            ErrorHandler(OUT_OF_MEMORY);

        HLock(Handle(thePict));

        if FSRead(srcFile, pictSize, Ptr(thePict^)) <> noErr
        then
            ErrorHandler(CANT_READ_PICT);

        dummy := FSClose(srcFile);

        printPort := PrOpenDoc(gPrintRecordH, nil, nil);
        PrOpenPage(printPort, nil);
        DrawPicture(thePict, thePict^^.picFrame);
        PrClosePage(printPort);
        PrCloseDoc(printPort);

        PrPicFile(gPrintRecordH, nil, nil, nil, printStatus);

        HUnlock(Handle(thePict));
    end;
```

```
{---------------> DoDialogs  <--}

    function DoDialogs: BOOLEAN;
        var
            keepGoing: BOOLEAN;
    begin
        keepGoing := PrStlDialog(gPrintRecordH);

        if keepGoing then
            DoDialogs := PrJobDialog(gPrintRecordH)
        else
            DoDialogs := FALSE;
    end;

{---------------> GetFileName <--}

    procedure GetFileName (var replyPtr: SFReply);
        var
            myPoint: Point;
            typeList: SFTypeList;
            numTypes: INTEGER;
    begin
        myPoint.h := 100;
        myPoint.v := 100;
        typeList[0] := 'PICT';
        numTypes := 1;
        SFGetFile(myPoint, IGNORED_STRING, nil, numTypes,
        typeList, nil, replyPtr);
    end;


{---------------> PrintInit  <--}

    procedure PrintInit;
    begin
        gPrintRecordH := THPrint(NewHandle(sizeof(TPrint)));
        PrOpen;
        PrintDefault(gPrintRecordH);
    end;


{---------------> PrintPICT  <--}

begin
    PrintInit;
    GetFileName(gReply);
    if gReply.good then
        begin
            if DoDialogs then
                PrintPictFile(gReply);
        end;
end.
```

Changing the Compilation Order

Notice that when you move the cursor over one of the file names in the Project window, the cursor turns into a hand. You can use the hand to drag files up and down, thus changing their compilation order. This is very important. Use the hand cursor to rearrange the files in the **Project** window so that they agree exactly with the order in Figure 7.24. If you don't do this, the program won't be able to resolve all of its references.

Running PrintPICT

Now that your source code is entered, you're ready to run PrintPICT. PrintPICT will bring up an SFGetFile dialog box (Figure 7.25).

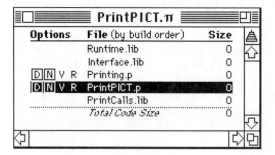

Figure 7.24   PrintPICT's Project window.

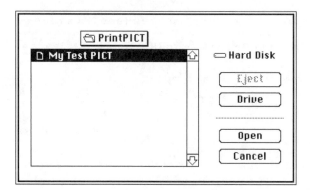

Figure 7.25   SFGetFile dialog box.

Select a PICT file to be printed. The **Page Setup** dialog box will then be displayed (Figure 7.26). After you click **OK**, the **Print Job** dialog box appears (Figure 7.27). If you click on **OK** or press Return, PrintPICT will print your PICT file and quit. Let's see how it's done

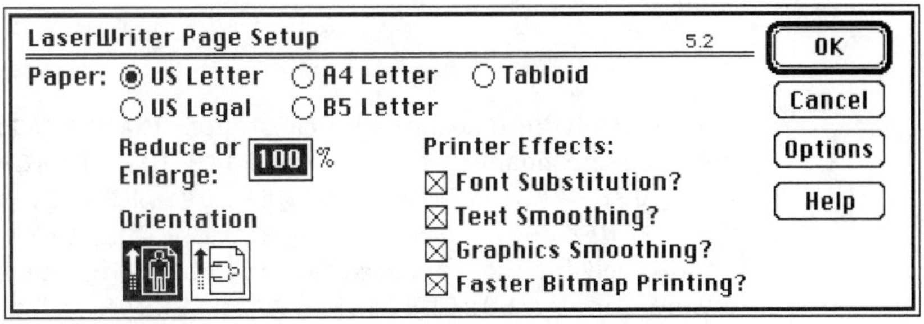

Figure 7.26 PrintPICT brings up the **Page Setup** dialog box.

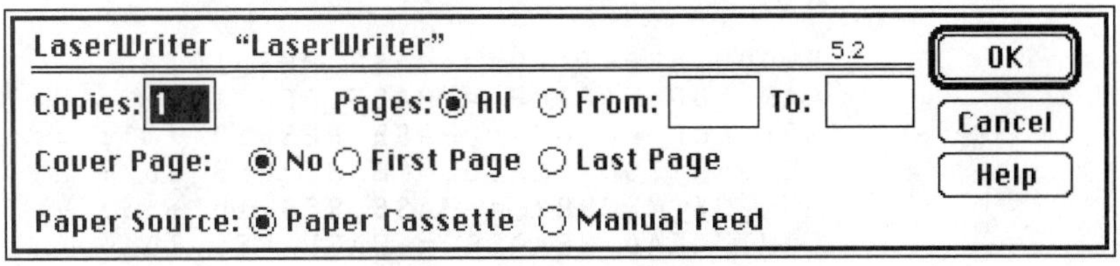

Figure 7.27 PrintPICT brings up the **Print Job** dialog box.

PrintPICT starts off with a `uses` statement, telling the compiler to give it access to the `Printing` unit. The `Printing` unit is found in the file `Printing.p` (which we added to the project earlier).

```
program PrintPICT;
    uses
        Printing;
```

Next, PrintPICT declares its constants. `HEADER_SIZE` is used for removing the header at the top of `PICT` files. `ERROR_ALERT_ID`, `CANT_OPEN_FILE`, `GET_EOF_ERROR`, `HEADER_TOO_SMALL`, `OUT_OF_MEMORY`, `CANT_READ_HEADER`, and `CANT_READ_PICT` are all used for the appropriate error strings in the error-handling routine. Finally, `HOPELESSLY_FATAL_ERROR` is for your `ALRT` of last resort.

```
const
    HEADER_SIZE = 512;
    BASE_RES_ID = 400;

    ERROR_ALERT_ID = BASE_RES_ID;
    CANT_OPEN_FILE = BASE_RES_ID;
    GET_EOF_ERROR = BASE_RES_ID + 1;
    HEADER_TOO_SMALL = BASE_RES_ID + 2;
    OUT_OF_MEMORY = BASE_RES_ID + 3;
    CANT_READ_HEADER = BASE_RES_ID + 4;
    CANT_READ_PICT = BASE_RES_ID + 5;

    NIL_STRING = '';
    IGNORED_STRING = NIL_STRING;
    HOPELESSLY_FATAL_ERROR = 'Game over, man!';
```

The global `gPrintRecordH` is the handle to the print record you'll create. `gReply` will hold the data returned by our call to `SFGetFile`.

```
var
    gPrintRecordH: THPrint;
    gReply: SFReply;
```

PrintPICT's main routine starts off with a call to `PrintInit`. Next, `GetFileName` is run and `SFGetFile` is invoked. If the user doesn't click on the **Cancel** button, `DoDialogs` is called. If `DoDialogs` returns `TRUE`, the file is printed via a call to `PrintPICTFile`.

```
{----------------->    PrintPICT   <--}

begin
    PrintInit;
    GetFileName(gReply);
    if gReply.good then
        begin
            if DoDialogs then
                PrintPictFile(gReply);
        end;
end.
```

The information entered by the user in the **Page Setup** and **Print Job** dialog boxes is stored in a print record. PrintDefault fills the print record with default print values. A handle to the print record is passed to PrPicFile at print time.

PrintInit uses NewHandle to allocate a block of memory the size of a print record and makes gPrintRecordH a handle to that memory. Call PrOpen to start up the Printing Manager, and then set the default print record to gPrintRecordH by calling PrintDefault. Doing this ensures that any changes you make to the **Page Setup** and **Print Job** dialogs will be implemented when you print.

```
{-----------------> PrintInit <--}

procedure PrintInit;
begin
    gPrintRecordH := THPrint(NewHandle(sizeof(TPrint)));
    PrOpen;
    PrintDefault(gPrintRecordH);
end;
```

GetFileName sets up the arguments and calls SFGetFile. numTypes was set to 1, so you need to set up a single entry in the typeList array. Display only files of type PICT. The pointer to the reply from SFGetFile will be placed in replyPtr:

```
{------------------>    GetFileName   <--}

    procedure GetFileName (var replyPtr: SFReply);
        var
            myPoint: Point;
            typeList: SFTypeList;
            numTypes: INTEGER;
    begin
        myPoint.h := 100;
        myPoint.v := 100;
        typeList[0] := 'PICT';
        numTypes := 1;
        SFGetFile(myPoint, IGNORED_STRING, nil, numTypes,
        typeList, nil, replyPtr);
    end;
```

DoDialogs calls PrStlDialog to do the **Page Setup** dialog,
then calls PrJobDialog to do the **Print Job** dialog. If the user hits
the **Cancel** button in the **Print Job** dialog box, DoDialogs returns
FALSE. The value returned by PrJobDialog is returned by
DoDialogs.

Normally, your application would bring up the **Page Setup** dialog
in response to a **Page Setup...** menu selection and the **Print
Job** dialog in response to a **Print...** menu selection. PrintPICT
calls both dialogs for demonstration purposes only.

```
{------------------>    DoDialogs   <--}

    function DoDialogs: BOOLEAN;
        var
            keepGoing: BOOLEAN;
    begin
        keepGoing := PrStlDialog(gPrintRecordH);

        if keepGoing then
            DoDialogs := PrJobDialog(gPrintRecordH)
        else
            DoDialogs := FALSE;
    end;
```

PrintPictFile starts off with a call to FSOpen to get the access
path of the file selected by SFGetFile. If the file can be opened,
GetEOF is called, returning the size of the file in the parameter
pictSize. Next, FSRead attempts to read the 512-byte header that

describes the rest of the file. The actual number of bytes read is returned in the parameter `headerSize`. If fewer than 512 bytes were read, or if you run out of memory while trying to read the picture, call the `ErrorHandler`. Because PrintPICT won't need the 512-byte `PICT` header, `pictSize` is decremented by 512. This reduced version of `pictSize` will be used to read in the headerless `PICT`.

```
{----------------->  PrintPictFile  <--}

    procedure PrintPictFile (reply: SFReply);
        var
            srcFile: INTEGER;
            printPort: TPPrPort;
            printStatus: TPrStatus;
            thePict: PicHandle;
            pictHeader: packed array[0..HEADER_SIZE] of CHAR;
            pictSize, headerSize: LONGINT;
            dummy: OSErr;
    begin
        if (FSOpen(reply.fName, reply.vRefNum, srcFile) <>
        noErr) then
            ErrorHandler(CANT_OPEN_FILE);

        if (GetEOF(srcFile, pictSize) <> noErr) then
            ErrorHandler(GET_EOF_ERROR);

        headerSize := HEADER_SIZE;
        if (FSRead(srcFile, headerSize, @pictHeader) <> noErr)
        then
            ErrorHandler(CANT_READ_HEADER);

        pictSize := pictSize - HEADER_SIZE;
        if pictSize <= 0 then
            ErrorHandler(HEADER_TOO_SMALL);

        thePict := PicHandle(NewHandle(pictSize));
        if thePict = nil then
            ErrorHandler(OUT_OF_MEMORY);
```

If you've passed through these trials successfully, you're ready to read in the `PICT` data. Because `FSRead` requires a pointer to the read buffer, and because you allocated a handle (`thePict`), you'll have to `HLock` the handle before you pass its pointer (`thePict^`) to `FSRead`. Call `FSRead` to read in the `PICT`. If this fails (IV:109), `ErrorHandler` is run yet again. Assuming that you finally have the `PICT` in memory at this point, close the `PICT` file with `FSClose`. Next, `PrOpenDoc` is called, returning a pointer (`printPort`) to the printing `grafPort`. Open a new page with `PrOpenPage`, and draw

the PICT with DrawPicture. When you're done, PrClosePage
closes the page and PrCloseDoc closes the printing grafPort.
Finally, print the file with PrPicFile.

```
HLock(Handle(thePict));

if FSRead(srcFile, pictSize, Ptr(thePict^)) <> noErr
then
    ErrorHandler(CANT_READ_PICT);

dummy := FSClose(srcFile);

printPort := PrOpenDoc(gPrintRecordH, nil, nil);
PrOpenPage(printPort, nil);
DrawPicture(thePict, thePict^^.picFrame);
PrClosePage(printPort);
PrCloseDoc(printPort);

PrPicFile(gPrintRecordH, nil, nil, nil, printStatus);

HUnlock(Handle(thePict));
end;
```

ErrorHandler is the same as in the earlier programs. Take the
alert string resource ID and set up ParamText with it. Then,
display the alert with StopAlert and quit with ExitToShell.

```
{---------------> ErrorHandler    <--}

procedure ErrorHandler (stringNum: INTEGER);
    var
        errorStringH: StringHandle;
        dummy: INTEGER;
begin
    errorStringH := GetString(stringNum);
    if errorStringH = nil then
        ParamText(HOPELESSLY_FATAL_ERROR, NIL_STRING,
        NIL_STRING, NIL_STRING)
    else
        ParamText(errorStringH^^, NIL_STRING, NIL_STRING,
        NIL_STRING);

    dummy := StopAlert(ERROR_ALERT_ID, nil);
    ExitToShell;
end;
```

Scroll Bars! We're Gonna Do Scroll Bars!

Scroll bars are a common control used in Macintosh applications (Figure 7.28). This section shows you how to set one up to control paging between a series of pictures in a window.

Making Use of Scroll Bars

The routines that create and control scroll bars are part of the Control Manager. `NewControl` is used to create a new control:

```
FUNCTION NewControl( theWindow : WindowPtr;
          boundsRect : Rect;
          title : Str255;
          visible : BOOLEAN;
          value : INTEGER;
          min,max : INTEGER;
          procID : INTEGER;
          refCon : LONGINT ) : ControlHandle;
```

The parameter `procID` specifies the type of control to be created. To create a new scroll bar, pass the constant `scrollBarProc` to `NewControl`. Every scroll bar has a minimum, maximum, and current `value`. For example, a scroll bar may go from 1 to 20, and may currently be at 10 (Figure 7.29).

Figure 7.28   Window with scroll bar (Pager).

339

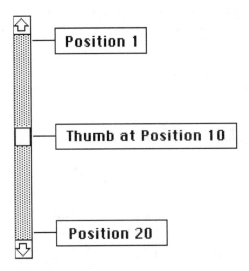

Figure 7.29   Scroll bar positioning.

Once the scroll bar is created, call `DrawControls` to draw it in your window:

```
PROCEDURE DrawControls( theWindow : WindowPtr );
```

> Because the calls to Window Manager routines (such as `ShowWindow` and `MoveWindow`) do not redraw controls in a window, `DrawControls` must be called whenever the window receives an update event.

When a `mouseDown` event occurs, `FindWindow` is called, returning a part code describing the part of the window in which the `mouseDown` occurred. If the `mouseDown` was `inContent`, call `FindControl`:

```
FUNCTION FindControl( thePoint : Point;
                            theWindow : WindowPtr;
                  VAR whichControl : ControlHandle ) :
                  INTEGER;
```

Like `FindWindow`, `FindControl` returns a part code. This time, the part code specifies which part of the scroll bar was clicked in (Figure 7.30). Pass the part code returned by `FindControl` to `TrackControl`:

```
FUNCTION TrackControl( theControl : ControlHandle;
               startPt : Point;
               actionProc : ProcPtr ) : INTEGER;
```

`TrackControl` will perform the action appropriate to that part of the scroll bar. For example, if the `mouseDown` was in the thumb of the scroll bar, an outline of the thumb is moved up and down (or across) the scroll bar until the mouse button is released. Once `TrackControl` returns, take the appropriate action, depending on the new value of the scroll bar.

Next, let's look at Pager, a program that uses a scroll bar to page between `PICT` drawings in a window.

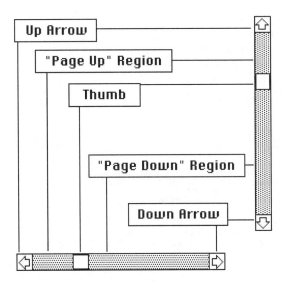

Figure 7.30   Parts of scroll bars.

Pager

Pager illustrates the use of scroll bars in a Macintosh application. It works like this:

1. It initializes a window.
2. It creates a new scroll bar, using the number of available `PICT` resources to determine the number of positions in the scroll bar.
3. When a `mouseDown` occurs in the scroll bar, it updates the value of the scroll bar, loads the appropriate `PICT`, and displays it in the window.
4. It quits when the close box is clicked.

Pager also warns if the `WIND` or `PICT` resources are unavailable.

Setting Up the Pager Project

Start by creating a folder for this project, called `Pager`. Use ResEdit to create a new file called `Pager.π.rsrc`. You might want to save some time by just copying and pasting the `WIND`, `ALRT`, and `DITL` resources from the `WindowMaker.π.rsrc` file. Remember to make each resource purgeable.

The `WIND` resource information appears in Figure 7.31.

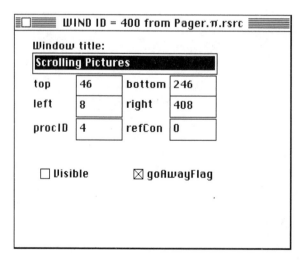

Figure 7.31 `WIND` resource for Pager.

Next, create a DITL resource (Figure 7.32). Add the ALRT (Figure 7.33). Then, add the three 'STR ' resources shown in Figure 7.34 to Pager.π.rsrc. Change the resource IDs of each resource to those shown in the figures and make each resource purgeable.

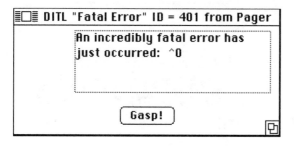

Item#	Type	Enabled	Top	Left	Bottom	Right	Text/Resource ID
1	Button	Yes	86	117	106	177	Gasp!
2	Static Text	Yes	5	67	71	283	An incredibly fatal error has just occurred: ^0

Figure 7.32 DITL resource for Pager.

ALRT "Fatal Error" ID = 401 from Pager.π.rsrc

Top	40	Bottom	156
Left	40	Right	332
ItemsID	401		

Sound (0-3)

Stage 1 ☐ #2 bold ☒ Drawn 1
Stage 2 ☐ #2 bold ☒ Drawn 1
Stage 3 ☐ #2 bold ☒ Drawn 1
Stage 4 ☐ #2 bold ☒ Drawn 1

Figure 7.33 ALRT resource for Pager.

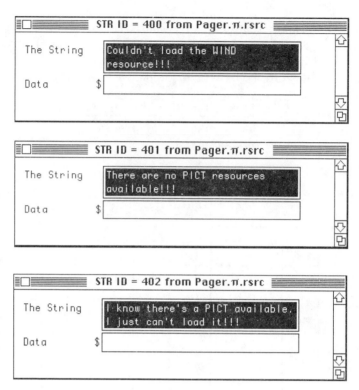

Figure 7.34   'STR ' resources for Pager.

Next, create some PICT resources from your favorite clip art and
paste them into the Pager.π.rsrc. Paste in as many as you like.
Don't worry about changing resource IDs for the PICT resources.
We'll display every available PICT, regardless of race, creed, or
resource ID. Remember to mark each PICT as purgeable. When
you're done, the resource window of Pager.π.rsrc should look like
Figure 7.35.

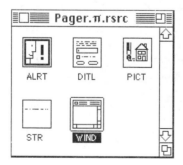

Figure 7.35   Pager resources completed.

Now you're ready to launch THINK Pascal. Create a new project in the `Pager` folder. Call it `Pager.π`. Create `Pager.p` and add it to `Pager.π`. Here's the source code for `Pager.p`:

```
program Pager;
    const
        BASE_RES_ID = 400;

        SCROLL_BAR_PIXELS = 16;

        MIN_SLEEP = 0;
        NIL_REF_CON = 0;

        WNE_TRAP_NUM = $60;
        UNIMPL_TRAP_NUM = $9F;

        ERROR_ALERT_ID = BASE_RES_ID + 1;
        NO_WIND = BASE_RES_ID;
        NO_PICTS = BASE_RES_ID + 1;
        CANT_LOAD_PICT = BASE_RES_ID + 2;

        NIL_STRING = '';
        NIL_TITLE = NIL_STRING;
        VISIBLE = TRUE;
        START_VALUE = 1;
        MIN_VALUE = 1;
        HOPELESSLY_FATAL_ERROR = 'Game over, man!';

    var
        gPictWindow: WindowPtr;
        gScrollBarHandle: ControlHandle;
        gDone, gWNEImplemented: BOOLEAN;
        gTheEvent: EventRecord;


{---------------> ErrorHandler   <--}

    procedure ErrorHandler (stringNum: INTEGER);
        var
            errorStringH: StringHandle;
            dummy: INTEGER;
    begin
        errorStringH := GetString(stringNum);
        if errorStringH = nil then
            ParamText(HOPELESSLY_FATAL_ERROR, NIL_STRING,
            NIL_STRING, NIL_STRING)
        else
            ParamText(errorStringH^^, NIL_STRING, NIL_STRING,
            NIL_STRING);
```

```
        dummy := StopAlert(ERROR_ALERT_ID, nil);
        ExitToShell;
    end;


{---------------> CenterPict <--}

    procedure CenterPict (thePicture: PicHandle; var myRect:
    Rect);
        var
            windRect, pictureRect: Rect;
    begin
        windRect := myRect;
        pictureRect := thePicture^^.picFrame;
        myRect.top := (windRect.bottom - windRect.top -
        (pictureRect.bottom - pictureRect.top)) div 2 +
        windRect.top;
        myRect.bottom := myRect.top + (pictureRect.bottom -
        pictureRect.top);
        myRect.left := (windRect.right - windRect.left -
        (pictureRect.right - pictureRect.left)) div 2 +
        windRect.left;
        myRect.right := myRect.left + (pictureRect.right -
        pictureRect.left);
    end;


{---------------> UpdateMyWindow <--}

    procedure UpdateMyWindow (drawingWindow: WindowPtr);
        var
            currentPicture: PicHandle;
            drawingClipRect, myRect: Rect;
            tempRgn: RgnHandle;
    begin
        tempRgn := NewRgn;
        GetClip(tempRgn);

        myRect := drawingWindow^.portRect;
        myRect.right := myRect.right - SCROLL_BAR_PIXELS;
        EraseRect(myRect);

        currentPicture := PicHandle(GetIndResource('PICT',
        GetCtlValue(gScrollBarHandle)));

        if currentPicture = nil then
            ErrorHandler(CANT_LOAD_PICT);

        CenterPict(currentPicture, myRect);

        drawingClipRect := drawingWindow^.portRect;
```

```
        drawingClipRect.right := drawingClipRect.right -
        SCROLL_BAR_PIXELS;
        ClipRect(drawingClipRect);

        DrawPicture(currentPicture, myRect);

        SetClip(tempRgn);
        DisposeRgn(tempRgn);
    end;


{--------------> ScrollProc <--}

    procedure ScrollProc (theControl: ControlHandle; theCode:
    INTEGER);
        var
            curControlValue, maxControlValue, minControlValue:
            INTEGER;
    begin
        maxControlValue := GetCtlMax(theControl);
        curControlValue := GetCtlValue(theControl);
        minControlValue := GetCtlMin(theControl);

        case theCode of
            inPageDown, inDownButton:
                if curControlValue < maxControlValue then
                    curControlValue := curControlValue + 1;
            inPageUp, inUpButton:
                if curControlValue > minControlValue then
                    curControlValue := curControlValue - 1;
        end;
        SetCtlValue(theControl, curControlValue);
    end;


{--------------> SetUpScrollBar <--}

    procedure SetUpScrollBar;
        var
            vScrollRect: Rect;
            numPictures: INTEGER;
    begin
        numPictures := CountResources('PICT');
        if numPictures <= 0 then
            ErrorHandler(NO_PICTS);
        vScrollRect := gPictWindow^.portRect;
        vScrollRect.top := vScrollRect.top - 1;
        vScrollRect.bottom := vScrollRect.bottom + 1;
        vScrollRect.left := vScrollRect.right -
SCROLL_BAR_PIXELS + 1;
        vScrollRect.right := vScrollRect.right + 1;
```

```
        gScrollBarHandle := NewControl(gPictWindow,
        vScrollRect, NIL_TITLE, VISIBLE, START_VALUE,
        MIN_VALUE, numPictures, scrollBarProc, NIL_REF_CON);
    end;


{---------------> HandleMouseDown  <--}

  procedure HandleMouseDown;
    var
      whichWindow: WindowPtr;
      thePart: INTEGER;
      thePoint: Point;
      theControl: ControlHandle;
  begin
    thePart := FindWindow(gTheEvent.where, whichWindow);
    case thePart of
      inSysWindow:
        SystemClick(gTheEvent, whichWindow);
      inDrag:
        DragWindow (whichWindow, gTheEvent.where, screenBits.bounds);
      inContent:
        begin
          thePoint := gTheEvent.where;
          GlobalToLocal(thePoint);
          thePart := FindControl(thePoint, whichWindow, theControl);
          if theControl = gScrollBarHandle then
            begin
              if thePart = inThumb then
                begin
                  thePart := TrackControl(theControl, thePoint, nil);
                  UpdateMyWindow(whichWindow);
                end
              else
                begin
                  thePart := TrackControl (theControl,thePoint,
                  @ScrollProc);
                  UpdateMyWindow(whichWindow);
                end;
            end;
        end;
      inGoAway:
        gDone := TRUE;
    end;
  end;
```

```
{---------------> HandleEvent <--}

    procedure HandleEvent;
        var
            dummy: BOOLEAN;
    begin
        if gWNEImplemented then
            dummy := WaitNextEvent(everyEvent, gTheEvent,
            MIN_SLEEP, nil)
        else
            begin
                SystemTask;
                dummy := GetNextEvent(everyEvent, gTheEvent);
            end;

        case gTheEvent.what of
            mouseDown:
                HandleMouseDown;
            updateEvt:
                begin
                    BeginUpdate(WindowPtr(gTheEvent.message));
                    DrawControls(WindowPtr(gTheEvent.message));

UpdateMyWindow(WindowPtr(gTheEvent.message));
                    EndUpdate(WindowPtr(gTheEvent.message));
                end;
        end;
    end;


{---------------> MainLoop   <--}

    procedure MainLoop;
    begin
        gDone := FALSE;
        gWNEImplemented := (NGetTrapAddress(WNE_TRAP_NUM,
            ToolTrap) <> NGetTrapAddress(UNIMPL_TRAP_NUM,
            ToolTrap));
        while (gDone = FALSE) do
            HandleEvent;
    end;


{---------------> WindowInit <--}

    procedure WindowInit;
    begin
        gPictWindow := GetNewWindow(BASE_RES_ID, nil,
        WindowPtr(-1));
```

```
        if gPictWindow = nil then
            ErrorHandler(NO_WIND);

        SelectWindow(gPictWindow);
        ShowWindow(gPictWindow);
        SetPort(gPictWindow);
    end;


{---------------->  Pager  <--}

begin
    WindowInit;
    SetUpScrollBar;

    MainLoop;
end.
```

Running Pager

When you've finished typing in your source code, run Pager. You should see something like Figure 7.28 (shown earlier), except that it will use the PICTs that you put in Pager.π.rsrc. The scroll bar should allow you to page back and forth between the PICTs. Clicking in the close box ends Pager's execution.

Walking Through the Pager Code

Figure 7.36 offers an overview of Pager's software architecture.

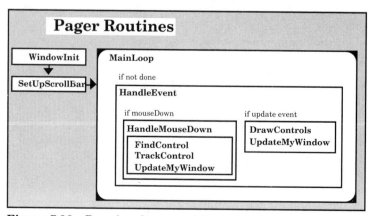

Figure 7.36   Pager's software architecture.

You've seen most of this program before. You'll create a window with `GetNewWindow` and get and handle events just as you did in WindowMaker. Now, let's look at the code.

Pager starts off with constant and global variable declarations. We'll discuss these in context.

```
program Pager;
    const
        BASE_RES_ID = 400;

        SCROLL_BAR_PIXELS = 16;

        MIN_SLEEP = 0;
        NIL_REF_CON = 0;

        WNE_TRAP_NUM = $60;
        UNIMPL_TRAP_NUM = $9F;

        ERROR_ALERT_ID = BASE_RES_ID + 1;
        NO_WIND = BASE_RES_ID;
        NO_PICTS = BASE_RES_ID + 1;
        CANT_LOAD_PICT = BASE_RES_ID + 2;

        NIL_STRING = '';
        NIL_TITLE = NIL_STRING;
        VISIBLE = TRUE;
        START_VALUE = 1;
        MIN_VALUE = 1;
        HOPELESSLY_FATAL_ERROR = 'Game over, man!';

    var
        gPictWindow: WindowPtr;
        gScrollBarHandle: ControlHandle;
        gDone, gWNEImplemented: BOOLEAN;
        gTheEvent: EventRecord;
```

Pager's main routine first calls `WindowInit`, next calls `SetUpScrollBar` to initialize the scroll bar control, and then runs `MainLoop` to start the main event loop.

```
{---------------->   Pager <--}

begin
    WindowInit;
    SetUpScrollBar;

    MainLoop;
end.
```

WindowInit is uneventful. The WIND resource is loaded and displayed, with the customary call to ErrorHandler if the WIND resource is missing.

```
{---------------->     WindowInit  <--}

    procedure WindowInit;
    begin
        gPictWindow := GetNewWindow(BASE_RES_ID, nil,
        WindowPtr(-1));

        if gPictWindow = nil then
            ErrorHandler(NO_WIND);

        SelectWindow(gPictWindow);
        ShowWindow(gPictWindow);
        SetPort(gPictWindow);
    end;
```

SetUpScrollBar calls CountResources to find out how many PICT resources are available.

Every application has access to resources from two different places: the resource fork of the application itself and the resource fork of the system file. In addition, an application may use the Resource Manager to open additional resource files. When looking for a resource, the Resource Manager searches the most recently opened resource file first.

If no PICT resources are available, the ErrorHandler is called. Otherwise, SetUpScrollBar creates a Rect the proper size for your scroll bar and then creates the scroll bar with a call to NewControl. The scroll bar ranges in value from MIN_VALUE to numPictures, the number of available PICT resources. START_VALUE is the initial value of the scroll bar and determines the initial position of the scroll bar thumb. The final parameter is a reference value available for your application's convenience. You can use these four bytes as scratch pad space.

```
{---------------> SetUpScrollBar <--}

    procedure SetUpScrollBar;
        var
            vScrollRect: Rect;
            numPictures: INTEGER;
    begin
        numPictures := CountResources('PICT');
        if numPictures <= 0 then
            ErrorHandler(NO_PICTS);
        vScrollRect := gPictWindow^.portRect;
        vScrollRect.top := vScrollRect.top - 1;
        vScrollRect.bottom := vScrollRect.bottom + 1;
        vScrollRect.left := vScrollRect.right -
        SCROLL_BAR_PIXELS + 1;
        vScrollRect.right := vScrollRect.right + 1;
        gScrollBarHandle := NewControl(gPictWindow,
        vScrollRect, NIL_TITLE, VISIBLE, START_VALUE,
        MIN_VALUE, numPictures, scrollBarProc, NIL_REF_CON);
    end;
```

> MainLoop sets the flag for GetNextEvent or WaitNextEvent,
> and then calls HandleEvent.

```
{---------------> MainLoop  <--}

    procedure MainLoop;
    begin
        gDone := FALSE;

        gWNEImplemented := (NGetTrapAddress(WNE_TRAP_NUM,
        ToolTrap) <> NGetTrapAddress(UNIMPL_TRAP_NUM,
        ToolTrap));
        while (gDone = FALSE) do
            HandleEvent;
    end;
```

> Pager handles two different events. mouseDowns are handled by
> HandleMouseDown. updateEvts are handled in line. First,
> BeginUpdate is called. Then, DrawControls draws the scroll bar
> with the thumb in the proper position. Finally, EndUpdate is called.

```
{---------------> HandleEvent    <--}

    procedure HandleEvent;
        var
            dummy: BOOLEAN;
    begin
        if gWNEImplemented then
```

```
                    dummy := WaitNextEvent(everyEvent, gTheEvent,
                                        MIN_SLEEP, nil)
            else
                begin
                    SystemTask;
                    dummy := GetNextEvent(everyEvent, gTheEvent);
                end;

            case gTheEvent.what of
                mouseDown:
                    HandleMouseDown;
                updateEvt:
                    begin
                        BeginUpdate(WindowPtr(gTheEvent.message));
                        DrawControls(WindowPtr(gTheEvent.message));

                        UpdateMyWindow(WindowPtr(gTheEvent.message));
                        EndUpdate(WindowPtr(gTheEvent.message));
                    end;
            end;
    end;
```

HandleMouseDown looks the same at the start:

```
{-----------------> HandleMouseDown      <--}

procedure HandleMouseDown;
    var
        whichWindow: WindowPtr;
        thePart: INTEGER;
        thePoint: Point;
        theControl: ControlHandle;
begin
    thePart := FindWindow(gTheEvent.where, whichWindow);
    case thePart of
        inSysWindow:
            SystemClick(gTheEvent, whichWindow);
        inDrag:
            DragWindow(whichWindow, gTheEvent.where,
            screenBits.bounds);
```

The big change comes when a mouseDown occurs in the content region (inContent) of a window. The mouseDown's location (gEvent.where) is translated into the window's local coordinate system. The localized point is passed to FindControl, which returns a Handle to the selected control (in the parameter theControl) and a part code indicating what part of the control was selected. If theControl is your scroll bar, find out if it was in the thumb. If it was, call TrackControl to drag an outline of the thumb up and down the scroll bar. When the thumb is released, update the window using the new scroll bar value. If any other part of the control was used, call `TrackControl` with a pointer to `ScrollProc`. `ScrollProc` scrolls the scroll bar until the mouse button is released.

Call `TrackControl` with a pointer to an action procedure if you want the control to change while the mouse button is still down. If you pass `nil` as an action proc, the control will animate, but its value will not change until the mouse button is released.

```
inContent:
  begin
    thePoint := gTheEvent.where;
    GlobalToLocal(thePoint);
    thePart := FindControl(thePoint, whichWindow, theControl);
    if theControl = gScrollBarHandle the begin
        if thePart = inThumb then
          begin
            thePart := TrackControl(theControl, thePoint, nil);
            UpdateMyWindow(whichWindow);
          end
        else
          begin
            thePart := TrackControl(theControl,
            thePoint,@ScrollProc);
            UpdateMyWindow(whichWindow);
          end;
      end;
    end;
  inGoAway:
    gDone := TRUE;
  end;
end;
```

`ScrollProc` handles `mouseDowns` in the page up, page down, up button, and down button regions of the scroll bar. `maxControlValue`, `curControlValue`, and `minControlValue` are set to the maximum, current, and minimum values of `theControl`. If the mouse click was `inPageDown` or `inDownButton`, increase the value of the control. If the mouse click was `inPageUp` or `inUpButton`, decrease the value of the control. Finally, update the control to this new value with `SetCtlValue`.

```
{----------------> ScrollProc      <--}

procedure ScrollProc (theControl: ControlHandle; theCode:
INTEGER);
    var
        curControlValue, maxControlValue, minControlValue:
        INTEGER;
begin
    maxControlValue := GetCtlMax(theControl);
    curControlValue := GetCtlValue(theControl);
    minControlValue := GetCtlMin(theControl);

    case theCode of
        inPageDown, inDownButton:
            if curControlValue < maxControlValue then
                curControlValue := curControlValue + 1;
        inPageUp, inUpButton:
            if curControlValue > minControlValue then
                curControlValue := curControlValue - 1;
    end;
    SetCtlValue(theControl, curControlValue);
end;
```

UpdateMyWindow works in a fashion similar to that of the
DrawPicture routine in EventTutor (Chapter 4). The algorithm
works as follows: Temporarily reset the window's clipping region so it
does not include the area covered by the scroll bar. Center the
picture, draw it, and reset the original clip region. The call to
GetIndResource uses the current value of the scroll bar
(GetCtlValue(gScrollBarHandle)) to load the appropriate
PICT resource.

For example, if there were 30 PICT resources available, the scroll
bar would run from 1 to 30. If the current thumb setting were 10, the
call to GetIndResource would return a handle to the tenth PICT
resource. Since GetIndResource returns a handle, you can use
Pascal's type-casting mechanism to convert it to a PicHandle.

Note that only one PICT at a time is ever loaded into memory.
When the scroll bar's value changes, a replacement PICT is loaded,
not an additional one.

```
{-----------------> UpdateMyWindow <--}

    procedure UpdateMyWindow (drawingWindow: WindowPtr);
        var
            currentPicture: PicHandle;
            drawingClipRect, myRect: Rect;
            tempRgn: RgnHandle;
    begin
        tempRgn := NewRgn;
        GetClip(tempRgn);

        myRect := drawingWindow^.portRect;
        myRect.right := myRect.right - SCROLL_BAR_PIXELS;
        EraseRect(myRect);

        currentPicture := PicHandle(GetIndResource('PICT',
        GetCtlValue(gScrollBarHandle)));

        if currentPicture = nil then
            ErrorHandler(CANT_LOAD_PICT);

        CenterPict(currentPicture, myRect);

        drawingClipRect := drawingWindow^.portRect;
        drawingClipRect.right := drawingClipRect.right -
        SCROLL_BAR_PIXELS;
        ClipRect(drawingClipRect);

        DrawPicture(currentPicture, myRect);

        SetClip(tempRgn);
        DisposeRgn(tempRgn);
    end;
```

CenterPict is the same as it ever was.

```
{-----------------> CenterPict     <--}

    procedure CenterPict (thePicture: PicHandle; var myRect:
    Rect);
        var
            windRect, pictureRect: Rect;
    begin
        windRect := myRect;
        pictureRect := thePicture^^.picFrame;
        myRect.top := (windRect.bottom - windRect.top -
        (pictureRect.bottom - pictureRect.top)) div 2 +
        windRect.top;
        myRect.bottom := myRect.top + (pictureRect.bottom -
        pictureRect.top);
```

```
      myRect.left := (windRect.right - windRect.left -
      (pictureRect.right - pictureRect.left)) div 2 +
      windRect.left;
      myRect.right := myRect.left + (pictureRect.right -
      pictureRect.left);
   end;
```

ErrorHandler should be familiar by now: ParamText to StopAlert to ExitToShell, leaving nothing to chance.

```
{----------------->  ErrorHandler  <--}

procedure ErrorHandler (stringNum: INTEGER);
   var
      errorStringH: StringHandle;
      dummy: INTEGER;
begin
   errorStringH := GetString(stringNum);
   if errorStringH = nil then
      ParamText(HOPELESSLY_FATAL_ERROR, NIL_STRING,
      NIL_STRING, NIL_STRING)
   else
      ParamText(errorStringH^^, NIL_STRING, NIL_STRING,
      NIL_STRING);

   dummy := StopAlert(ERROR_ALERT_ID, nil);
   ExitToShell;
end;
```

The Sound Manager

If you're tired of the same old SysBeep, there is an alternative. Within the system file is a set of 'snd ' resources, commonly known as beep sounds. The 'snd ' with resource ID = 1 is the familiar Beep. The current system comes with three additional 'snd 's: Monkey, Clink-Klank, and Boing. Hundreds more are available on electronic bulletin boards throughout the country.

Using the Sound Manager, you can add these sounds to your applications. The final *Mac Primer* application, Sounder, shows you how.

Sounder

Sounder works like this:

1. It loads the ' s n d ' resources from the system file.
2. It plays them (assuming you have the volume set above 0).
3. It quits.

Sounder also performs error checking. It puts up an alert if the ' s n d ' resources can't be accessed.

Setting Up the Sounder Project

Start by creating a folder for this project, called S o u n d e r. Use ResEdit to create a new file called S o u n d e r . π . r s r c. Sounder uses the same D I T L and A L R T resources as all the other Chapter 7 programs, so you can cut and paste if you've typed in the other programs. If not, use Figures 7.37 and 7.38 for those resources. Add the four ' S T R ' resources shown in Figure 7.39 to the S o u n d e r . π . r s r c file. Again, be sure to change the resource IDs of each resource to those shown in the figure. When you're done, the resource window of S o u n d e r . π . r s r c should look like Figure 7.40.

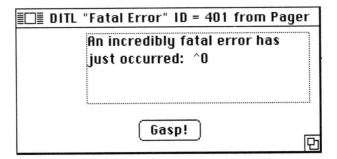

Figure 7.37   D I T L resource for Sounder.

Item#	Type	Enabled	Top	Left	Bottom	Right	Text/Resource ID
1	Button	Yes	86	117	106	177	Gasp!
2	Static Text	Yes	5	67	71	283	An incredibly fatal error has just occurred: ^0

Figure 7.37   D I T L resource for Sounder. (Continued)

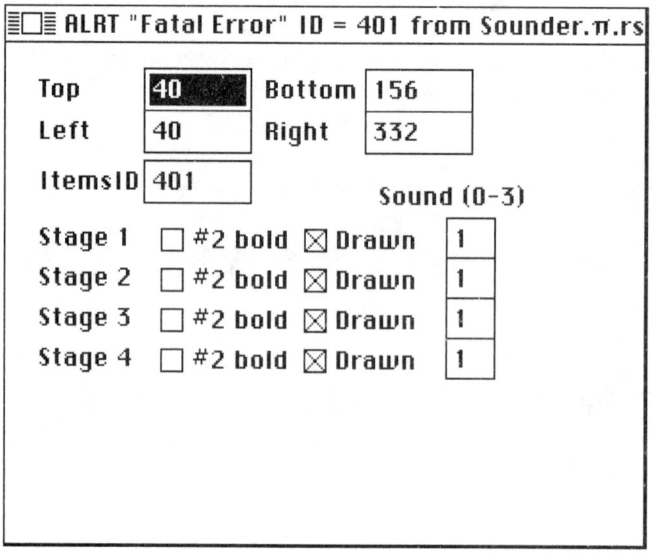

≡□≣ ALRT "Fatal Error" ID = 401 from Sounder.π.rs

Top	40	Bottom	156
Left	40	Right	332

ItemsID 401

Sound (0-3)

Stage 1   ☐ #2 bold ☒ Drawn   1
Stage 2   ☐ #2 bold ☒ Drawn   1
Stage 3   ☐ #2 bold ☒ Drawn   1
Stage 4   ☐ #2 bold ☒ Drawn   1

Figure 7.38   A L R T resource for Sounder.

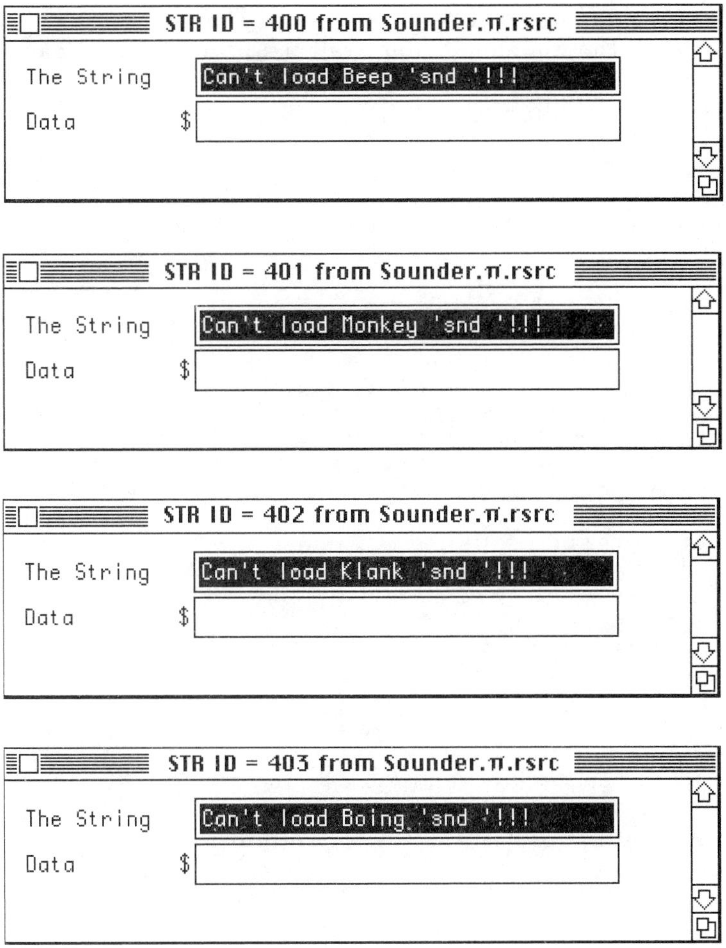

Figure 7.39   ' snd ' resources from Sounder.

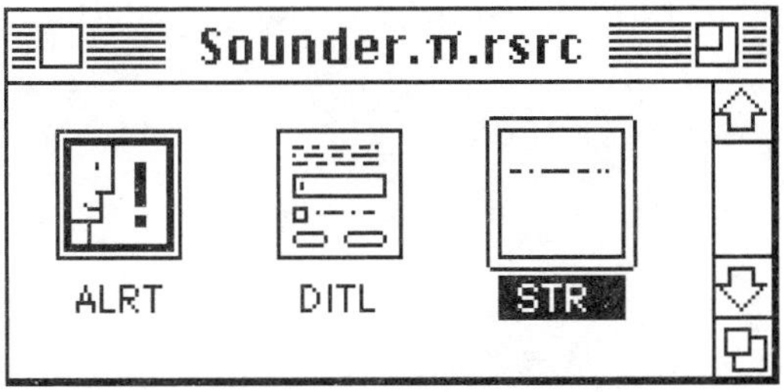

Figure 7.40   Pager resources completed.

Now you're ready to launch THINK Pascal. Create a new project in the Sounder folder. Call it `Sounder.π`. Create a new source file (`Sounder.p`), and add it to `Sounder.π`. Here's the source code for `Sounder.p`:

```pascal
program Sounder;
    uses
        Sound;

    const
        BASE_RES_ID = 400;
        SYNCHRONOUS = FALSE;

        ERROR_ALERT_ID = BASE_RES_ID + 1;
        CANT_LOAD_BEEP_SND = BASE_RES_ID;
        CANT_LOAD_MONKEY_SND = BASE_RES_ID + 1;
        CANT_LOAD_KLANK_SND = BASE_RES_ID + 2;
        CANT_LOAD_BOING_SND = BASE_RES_ID + 3;

        NIL_STRING = '';
        HOPELESSLY_FATAL_ERROR = 'Game over, man!';

        BEEP_SND = 1;
        MONKEY_SND = 2;
        KLANK_SND = 3;
        BOING_SND = 4;


{---------------> ErrorHandler    <--}

    procedure ErrorHandler (stringNum: INTEGER);
        var
            errorStringH: StringHandle;
            dummy: INTEGER;
    begin
        errorStringH := GetString(stringNum);
        if errorStringH = nil then
            ParamText(HOPELESSLY_FATAL_ERROR, NIL_STRING,
            NIL_STRING, NIL_STRING)
        else
            ParamText(errorStringH^^, NIL_STRING, NIL_STRING,
            NIL_STRING);

        dummy := StopAlert(ERROR_ALERT_ID, nil);
        ExitToShell;
    end;
```

```
{----------------> MakeSound  <--}

    procedure MakeSound;
        var
            soundHandle: Handle;
            dummy: OSErr;
    begin
        soundHandle := GetResource('snd ', BEEP_SND);

        if soundHandle = nil then
            ErrorHandler(CANT_LOAD_BEEP_SND);

        dummy := SndPlay(nil, soundHandle, SYNCHRONOUS);

        soundHandle := GetResource('snd ', MONKEY_SND);

        if soundHandle = nil then
            ErrorHandler(CANT_LOAD_MONKEY_SND);

        dummy := SndPlay(nil, soundHandle, SYNCHRONOUS);

        soundHandle := GetResource('snd ', KLANK_SND);

        if soundHandle = nil then
            ErrorHandler(CANT_LOAD_KLANK_SND);

        dummy := SndPlay(nil, soundHandle, SYNCHRONOUS);

        soundHandle := GetResource('snd ', BOING_SND);

        if soundHandle = nil then
            ErrorHandler(CANT_LOAD_BOING_SND);

        dummy := SndPlay(nil, soundHandle, SYNCHRONOUS);
    end;


{---------------> Sounder <--}

begin
    MakeSound;
end.
```

Walking Through the Sounder Code

Sounder is short and sweet. These constants should be familiar to you Chapter 7 *cognoscenti*.

```
program Sounder;
    uses
        Sound;

    const
        BASE_RES_ID = 400;
        SYNCHRONOUS = FALSE;

        ERROR_ALERT_ID = BASE_RES_ID + 1;
        CANT_LOAD_BEEP_SND = BASE_RES_ID;
        CANT_LOAD_MONKEY_SND = BASE_RES_ID + 1;
        CANT_LOAD_KLANK_SND = BASE_RES_ID + 2;
        CANT_LOAD_BOING_SND = BASE_RES_ID + 3;

        NIL_STRING = '';
        HOPELESSLY_FATAL_ERROR = 'Game over, man!';

        BEEP_SND = 1;
        MONKEY_SND = 2;
        KLANK_SND = 3;
        BOING_SND = 4;
```

Sounder's main routine consists of a call to `MakeSound`.

```
{---------------> Sounder     <--}

begin
    MakeSound;
end.
```

The key to this program is the Sound Manager routine `SndPlay`. Load each of the four `'snd '` resources normally found in the system file, and play them with `SndPlay`.

Because the Mac System file didn't always use `'snd '` resources, older systems may cause an error `ALRT` to appear. Check out the Sound Manager (Chapter 27) in *Inside Macintosh, Volume V*, for more detail.

The first parameter to `SndPlay` is the `SndChannelPtr`. By passing `nil`, you've told `SndPlay` to allocate a channel for you. The second parameter is the `'snd '` handle. The third parameter tells `SndPlay` whether or not to play the sound asynchronously. When you pass `nil` as the `SndChannelPtr`, you must pass `FALSE` as the third parameter. That is, if you ask `SndPlay` to allocate a channel for you, you must play the sound synchronously. If you cannot find the `'snd '` resource, go to the beloved `ErrorHandler`.

```
{----------------> MakeSound   <--}

procedure MakeSound;
    var
        soundHandle: Handle;
        dummy: OSErr;
begin
    soundHandle := GetResource('snd ', BEEP_SND);

    if soundHandle = nil then
        ErrorHandler(CANT_LOAD_BEEP_SND);

    dummy := SndPlay(nil, soundHandle, SYNCHRONOUS);

    soundHandle := GetResource('snd ', MONKEY_SND);

    if soundHandle = nil then
        ErrorHandler(CANT_LOAD_MONKEY_SND);

    dummy := SndPlay(nil, soundHandle, SYNCHRONOUS);

    soundHandle := GetResource('snd ', KLANK_SND);

    if soundHandle = nil then
        ErrorHandler(CANT_LOAD_KLANK_SND);

    dummy := SndPlay(nil, soundHandle, SYNCHRONOUS);

    soundHandle := GetResource('snd ', BOING_SND);

    if soundHandle = nil then
        ErrorHandler(CANT_LOAD_BOING_SND);
    dummy := SndPlay(nil, soundHandle, SYNCHRONOUS);
end;
```

The error-handling routine is similar to what you've seen in the other Chapter 7 programs:

```
{---------------> ErrorHandler   <--}

procedure ErrorHandler (stringNum: INTEGER);
    var
        errorStringH: StringHandle;
        dummy: INTEGER;
begin
    errorStringH := GetString(stringNum);
    if errorStringH = nil then
        ParamText(HOPELESSLY_FATAL_ERROR, NIL_STRING,
        NIL_STRING, NIL_STRING)
    else
        ParamText(errorStringH^^, NIL_STRING, NIL_STRING,
        NIL_STRING);

    dummy := StopAlert(ERROR_ALERT_ID, nil);
    ExitToShell;
end;
```

In Review

We covered a lot of ground in this chapter. Each of the four programs we presented involved a different part of the Mac Toolbox. If you're unsure about any of the concepts discussed, take the time to read about them in their respective *Inside Macintosh* chapters. The Scrap Manager is covered in Volume I, Chapter 15. The Standard File Package is covered in Volume I, Chapter 20 and updated in Volume IV, Chapter 15. The File Manager is covered in Volume IV, Chapter 19. (*Warning:* Don't be fooled by imitations! The File Manager section in Volume II, Chapter 4, has been completely replaced by Chapter 19 of Volume IV.) The Printing Manager is covered in Volume II, Chapter 5.

The Control Manager is covered in Volume I, Chapter 10. Scroll bars make up a small part of this chapter, but the concepts implemented in Pager will carry through to other types of controls.

Finally, the Sound Manager is covered in Volume V, Chapter 27. An authoritative version of this chapter has been published by Macintosh Developer Technical Support under the title *The Sound Manager*. If you're really interested in sound on the Mac, read the "Sound Driver" chapter (Volume I, Chapter 8). This is the way sound originally worked on the Mac, and many of the basic concepts are still supported.

Chapter 8 introduces the wonderful world of ResEdit. See you there!

Using ResEdit

ResEdit provides a simple, yet powerful way to edit resources. This chapter shows you how to use this tool to create the Finder resources necessary to turn your projects into stand-alone applications.

By Now, You should have a good grip on the most important aspects of Macintosh application programming. We've described how to handle events, access files, and display pictures and text. You've worked with menus, windows, and dialogs. This chapter discusses some issues that become important after you have your basic programming problems in hand.

After you compile your debugged application, but before you announce your first stock offering, you need to take care of a few loose ends. For example, you'll want to turn your code into a stand-alone application. Then, you'll want to design your own custom icon. These finishing touches require the creation of the **Finder resources**. These resources do not affect the operation of the application; rather, they affect the way your application interfaces with the Finder. This chapter discusses how to add Finder resources to your application.

If you are here because you are unfamiliar with ResEdit, read the first section of this chapter, which deals with general ResEdit operations.

As was mentioned earlier, version 2 of ResEdit is used in this chapter; please refer to the resource manual that comes with THINK Pascal if you have an earlier version of ResEdit (typically 1.2).

You may already have used other programming utilities, such as Rez or RMaker, that create and edit resources. ResEdit is used in this book because it creates and edits resources graphically, whereas Rez and RMaker build resources by describing them textually. For example, here is a text description of a WIND resource:

```
TYPE WIND
        ,128            ;; the resource number
My Window               ;; the window title
40 40 200 472           ;; the window rect (top left
                               bottom right)
Visible GoAway          ;; resource flags
0                       ;; window definition ID
0                       ;; refcon (points to user call)
```

This is the way RMaker describes resources. (RMaker also comes with THINK Pascal.)

ResEdit's WIND editor looks like Figure 8.1. When you're creating resources for the first time, ResEdit's graphic approach has many advantages: It's more intuitive, and it gives you a chance—with many resource types—to examine the appearance of a resource without actually running your program. You can use RMaker and ResEdit interchangeably; see the appendix in THINK Pascal's *User Manual* if you're interested in using RMaker.

We'll explore ResEdit in this chapter in the following way: First, you'll create the resource file needed for the first program in Chapter 3, Hello2. Then you'll compile Hello2 into a stand-alone application. Finally, you'll use ResEdit to add the Finder resources to it.

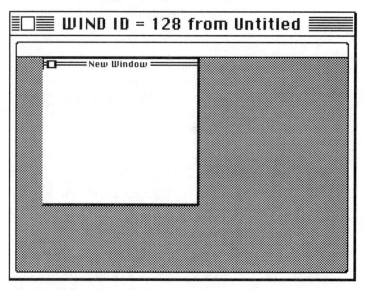

Figure 8.1   Graphic representation of WIND resource.

Notes on Using ResEdit

ResEdit works well in MultiFinder. If you plan to use MultiFinder, make sure that the application memory size used by ResEdit is at least 500K (Figure 8.2). Here are a few caveats about using ResEdit:

You can't edit resources in files that are currently in use, such as the Finder file. This is not much of a disadvantage, as editing open files is not such a hot idea anyway.

Make a copy of any file you plan to edit. It is very easy to modify resources irrevocably. Be careful. If you're planning to enter more than one or two resources in a single ResEdit session, save your file periodically.

Although ResEdit works with all resource types, it may have difficulty performing some operations on large resources, such as color icons, or sound resources ('snd') that exceed a few hundred K in size. In these cases, proceed with caution (and double ResEdit's memory allocation if you're using MultiFinder).

These guidelines are a little like the sign posted at swimming pools about waiting 30 minutes after you eat: Most of the time, they're not necessary. ResEdit is quite well mannered and will quickly become an indispensable programming tool.

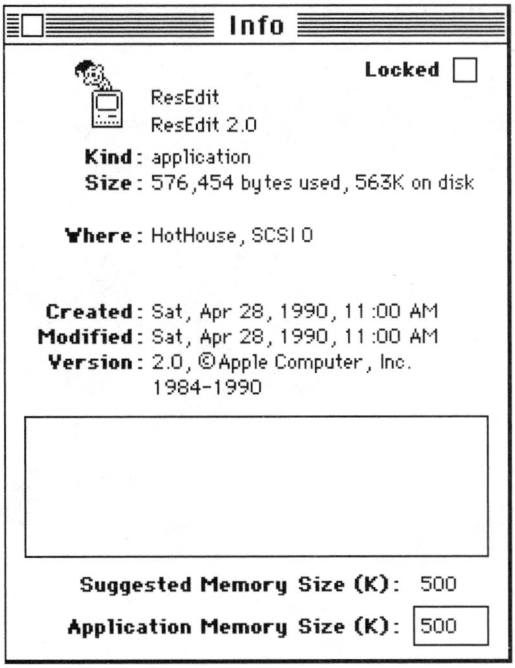

Figure 8.2 ResEdit version 2.

How ResEdit Works

Before you start using ResEdit to install the Finder resources, you should examine how ResEdit accomplishes the job of creating and editing resources in files. Let's start by building the resource file for the first program in Chapter 3: Hello2.

Double-click on ResEdit to start it up.

ResEdit will put up a dialog box asking you to select a file or to create a new one. To build a resource file for a Primer project, click on the new button and name the new resource file (in this case He l lo2.π. rsrc). ResEdit then displays Hello2's resource window, which will hold any resources that we plan to make (Figure 8.3).

ResEdit has five basic menus: **File**, **Edit**, **Resource**, **Window**, and **View**. **File** allows you to open or create resource files; **Edit** allows you to cut and paste resources between files. The **Resource** menu lists operations specific to a given resource type. **Window** lists all the currently open windows for ResEdit, so you can bring a window that is hidden by others up to the front. **View** allows you to display resources graphically (using icons) or by a regular text list. The figures in this book utilize the iconic display.

Let's build the **WIND** resource necessary to make Hello2 work. Starting from the empty resource file of Figure 8.3, choose **Create New Resource** from the **Resource** menu to add a new resource

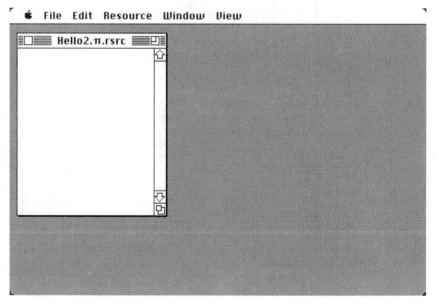

Figure 8.3   ResEdit with a new resource file.

type to the current file. The Resource Type dialog box (Figure 8.4) appears: You can either select the new resource type from the scrolling window or type in the name of the new resource type in the field provided.

Type in **WIND** or select it from the scrolling list and click on the **OK** button.

Two windows are displayed. First a **WIND** **Picker Window** is shown. This is where the list of all resources of type **WIND** is displayed. Then the **WIND** editor displays a newly created **WIND** resource, ready to be edited (Figure 8.5).

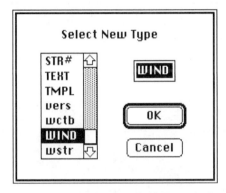

Figure 8.4   The Resource Type dialog box.

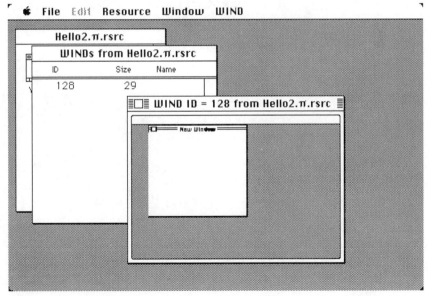

Figure 8.5   **WIND** Picker window and **WIND** Editor window (offset).

The WIND editor displays the new window in a miniaturized version of the screen. Click in the middle of the mini-window and you can drag the window around the mini-desktop. This changes its global coordinates (Figure 8.6). Click and drag on the lower right corner of the window to resize it (Figure 8.7).

Finally, select the **Display as Text** item in the **WIND** menu. This shows another way to enter the parameters for your WIND resource. If you make changes here and select **Display Graphically** from the **WIND** menu, the adjusted window will be positioned correctly on the mini-desktop.

Some information about windows can be changed only in the **Display as Text** mode. For example, Figure 8.8 shows a window whose title and procID have been changed with a new title and window type (see Chapter 3 about window types).

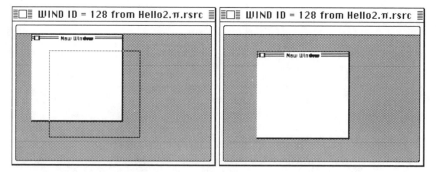

Figure 8.6 Changing WIND coordinates.

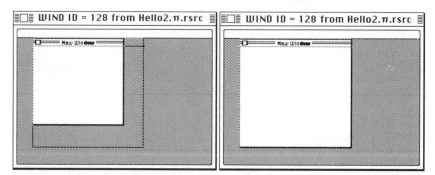

Figure 8.7 Resizing the WIND resource.

Next, select **Get Resource Info** from the **Resource** menu while the WIND editing window for WIND 128 is up. ResEdit will display information about the resource (Figure 8.9).

The only information you're concerned with is the **ID** number and the **Purgeable** flag. ResEdit defaults to a resource ID of 128 (if no other resource of that type has that ID). To finish the Hello2 resource file that you created, set the WIND's resource ID to 400 and check the **Purgeable** checkbox.

Most resources used in this book are marked **Purgeable** to conserve memory. It's not necessary, but it's a good idea (see Volume II of the *Primer* for a discussion of why that's so).

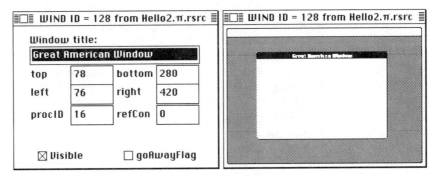

Figure 8.8   Great American WIND resource.

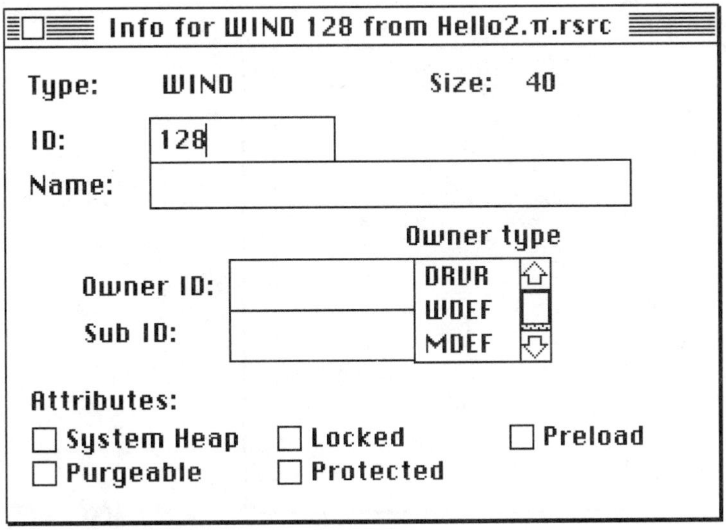

Figure 8.9   WIND resource information.

Here's a brief description of the fields and flags in the `resource info` window:

Owner Type: Special programs such as desk accessories must be handled differently. If you click on **Owner Type**, your resource ID changes. Certain programs (such as desk accessories) play by a different set of rules when it comes to resource IDs (IMI:127).

Owner ID and **Sub ID** are used when you are sharing the resource with other programs.

PreLoad resources are loaded into memory as soon as your application starts running. **Purgeable** resources are removed from memory if the Memory Manager needs to reclaim that space.

If **System Heap** is selected, the resource will be loaded into the System Heap instead of the Application Heap. If the resource is **Locked**, the Memory Manager cannot move it around when it is rearranging memory. If the resource is **Protected**, the Resource Manager can't modify it.

When you've finished with the WIND resource, choose **Save** from the **File** menu to save your changes. Your resource file now contains the information necessary for Hello2 to build a window (Figure 8.10).

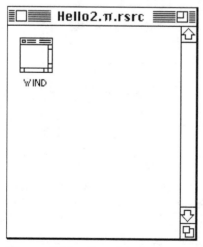

Figure 8.10   Completed resources in Hello2.π.rsrc.

Apple has authored a manual called *ResEdit Reference,* published by Addison-Wesley. Get it if you'd like more technical information about how ResEdit works. You can also procure the manual from APDA (see Chapter 9 for more information).

That's the end of the ResEdit overview. Those of you who needed to get your ResEdit feet wet should go back and finish your projects. The next step is to build an application (we'll build Hello2) and then add the **Finder** resources to it.

Everybody who wants an icon on their application, onward!

Completing a Stand-alone Application: Hello2 Revisited

The first step is to create a stand-alone application from a working project. Do this by compiling Hello2, the first program in Chapter 3. Open the Hello2 project. Select **Set Project Type...** from the **Project** menu. You should see something like Figure 8.11. There are four project options in the dialog box. Make sure the **Application** icon is selected in the dialog; click on **OK**. See THINK Pascal's *User Manual* for a description of the other three project types.

Now choose **Build Application** from the **Project** menu. If the project is up to date, it should prompt you for an application name (Figure 8.12). Call the application Hello2. (The **Smart Link** checkbox should be checked.) When you click on **Save**, THINK Pascal will build the Hello2 application. When it's completed, quit THINK Pascal and try double-clicking on the Hello2 application created in your Hello2 folder. It should display the text **Hello, World** in a window (Figure 8.13).

Now that you have a working stand-alone application, let's add the Finder resources to it. Click the mouse button to quit Hello2.

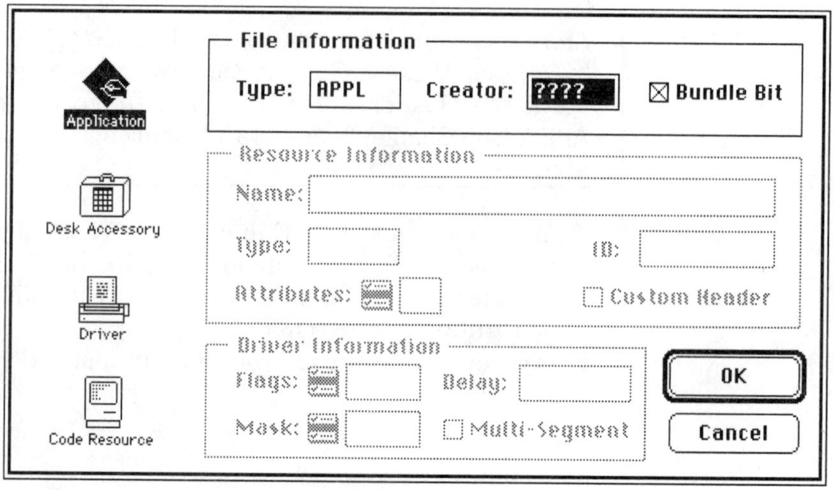

Figure 8.11   Project Type dialog box.

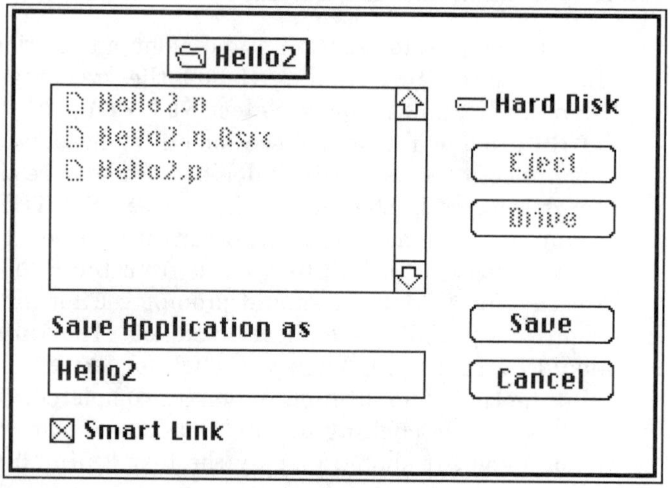

Figure 8.12   Build Application dialog box.

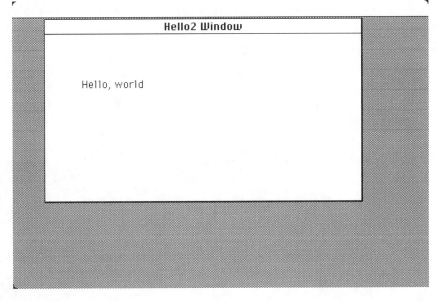

Figure 8.13 Running Hello2.

Installing the Finder Resources

Apple recommends that software developers install six special resources in their applications. Each resource plays an essential role in your application's interface to the Finder. They are grouped into three categories:

- **Application icon**: The `ICN#`, `FREF`, `BNDL`, and signature resources are used to add a unique icon to an application as it appears on the desktop.

- **Application version information:** The `vers` resource contains general information used by the Finder, including the specific version of an application, the country for which it is localized, and its creation date.

- **Application MultiFinder requirements:** The `SIZE` resource designates the recommended and minimum application memory size needed for an application; it also contains further details on the application's level of MultiFinder compatibility.

Examining the Resources of Hello2

Open up the Hello2 application you just made with ResEdit. Figure 8.14 shows the resource window for the completed Hello2. The six resources shown make up the entire Hello2 application. The compiler makes the `CODE`, `DATA`, `DREL`, `LSP`, and `ZERO` resource types; the `WIND` resource was copied from the `WIND` resource you made and put into the `Hello2.π.rsrc` file.

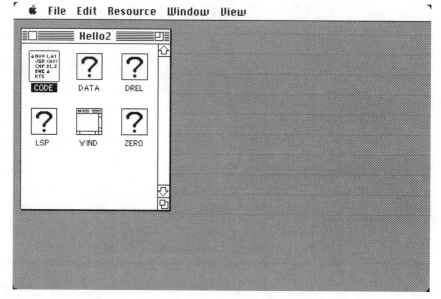

Figure 8.14   The resources of the Hello2 application.

In Figure 8.14, some resource icons in Hello2 have a question mark. This doesn't mean that there's anything wrong with these resource types. Editing information for each resource type is stored in **templates** in the ResEdit application. If there's no template for a resource type, the default question mark icon is used.

Each resource type can have a different method for editing individual resources of the type. Some resource types contain a MacPaint "fat bits" editor (ICON, ICN#). Many types simply display named fields for you to input (FREF, BNDL, MENU, MBAR). Other resource types can be resized and positioned graphically on a miniature desktop (WIND, DITL, DLOG).

If ResEdit doesn't know how to handle a certain resource type, it defaults to a hexadecimal editor.

Adding an Icon to Hello2

Four resources need to be installed in an application file to get the Finder to replace the generic application icon with a unique icon. Adding your own icon to an application used to be an involved procedure. However, with version 2 of ResEdit, the job has been simplified dramatically so that one operation automatically creates all the necessary resources for you.

Open up Hello2 with ResEdit and choose **Create New Resource** from the **Resource** menu. Either key in BNDL or select it from the scrolling list. Your screen should look something like Figure 8.15.

Type HELO in the **Signature** text field (Figure 8.16).

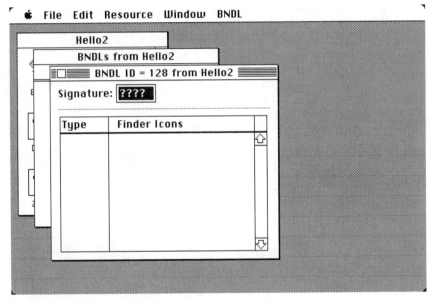

Figure 8.15   A new BNDL resource.

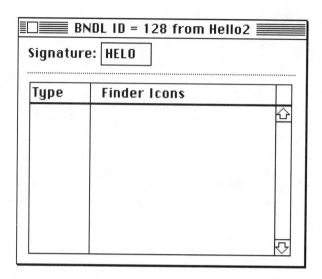

Figure 8.16   Entering the **Signature**.

Next, select **Create New File Type** from the **Resource** Menu. You should see something like Figure 8.17.

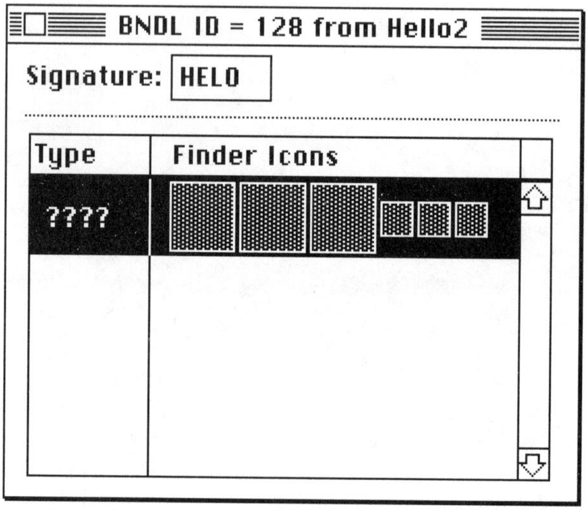

Figure 8.17   The result of **Create New File Type**.

Click on the **????** and type in **APPL**, as shown in Figure 8.18.

Now you can create the icon for Hello2. Select the boxes under the title **Finder Icons** by clicking on them. Then select the **Choose Icon...** menu item from the **BNDL** menu (Figure 8.19).

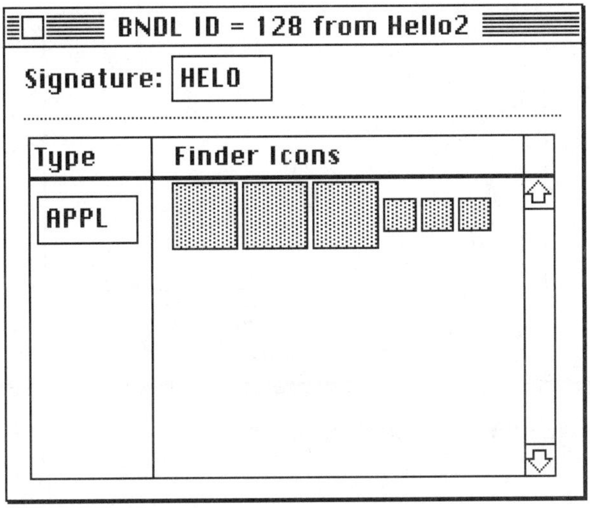

Figure 8.18   Hello2 and **APPL**.

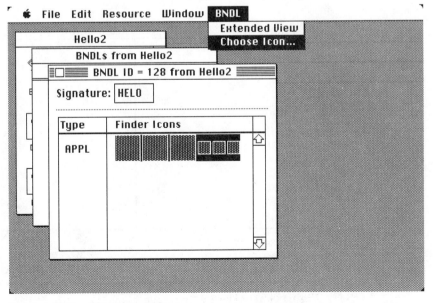

Figure 8.19   Choosing an icon . . .

The icon selection dialog box pops up (Figure 8.20). Because you don't have an icon in your resource fork yet, you'll have to make one. Click on the **New** button.

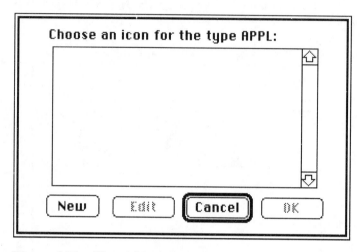

Figure 8.20   Slim pickings in the icon selection dialog box.

An **ICN#** editing window is now displayed (Figure 8.21). The special editor for **ICN#** resources allows you to build your application's icon graphically.

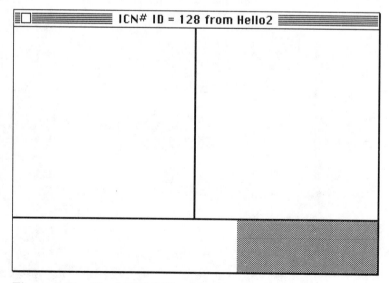

Figure 8.21   The **ICN#** Editor (blank).

The I C N # editor is like the "fat bits" mode in MacPaint. The pane on the left is the icon displayed by the application. The pane on the right is the mask, which governs the change in the application's icon when selected. Figure 8.22 shows how THINK Pascal's application icon looks in the I C N # editor.

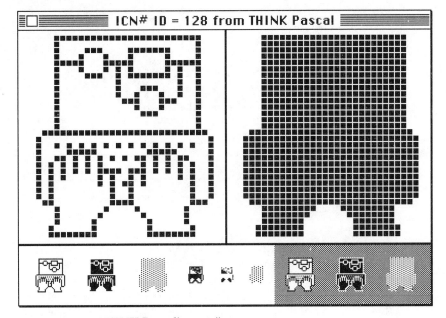

Figure 8.22   THINK Pascal's I C N #.

The I C N # Resource Editor in ResEdit allows you to preview the icon on both a light and a dark background. It also shows you what the icon will look like if the application is unavailable. (This commonly occurs if you ejected the disk with the program on it using Command E. If the application was on the desktop, it will still show up but will be dimmed, indicating that it can't be used.)

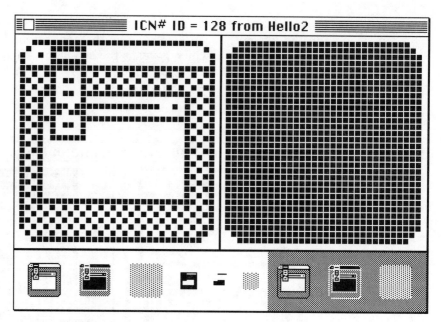

Figure 8.23   Hello2's new I C N # (with mask drawn).

Once you're comfortable drawing figures with the bit map editor, try creating an icon for your application. We'll use the icon in Figure 8.23.

When you're done with your icon, select **Data->Mask** from the **ICN#** menu. This will automatically draw a mask for your application in the right pane of the window.

A desktop icon (I C N#) actually consists of an icon and its mask. The mask is used to change the appearance of the icon to indicate a change in condition (TN:55). Resources that contain an icon without the mask are of resource type I C O N.

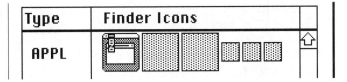

Figure 8.24 Icon attached to the BNDL.

You're almost there! Close the ICN# editor and return to the BNDL window (Figure 8.24). As you can see, the icon is now attached.

What are the other boxes, you say? The remaining five boxes are placers for icons of varying sizes and colors and are optimized for specific color display environments. These icons can be added to Hello2, but are displayed only when you are running System 7. The method used to attach these icons is similar to the method used above. See Apple's ResEdit reference manual for more information.

Now close the BNDL window.

Note that more than the BNDL resource was added (Figure 8.25).

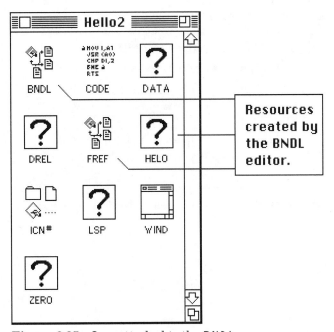

Figure 8.25 Icon attached to the BNDL.

The BNDL editor took care of the resources needed to put up an icon, which are the BNDL, ICN#, FREF, and the Signature resource (created when we put HELO in the Signature field back in Figure 8.17).

While the Hello2 resource window is still open, select **Get Info for Hello2** from the **File** menu (Figure 8.26). ResEdit doesn't always use the name **Hello2**. The name of the currently selected file resource window is placed in the menu. This dialog contains information that the system has on your new application. Files having type **APPL** are recognized as applications by the Finder.

Finish the installation of your Finder resources by changing the **Creator** from **????** to **HELO**. (Be careful: ResEdit discriminates between upper and lower case.) Now close the window by clicking in the close box, and save your changes.

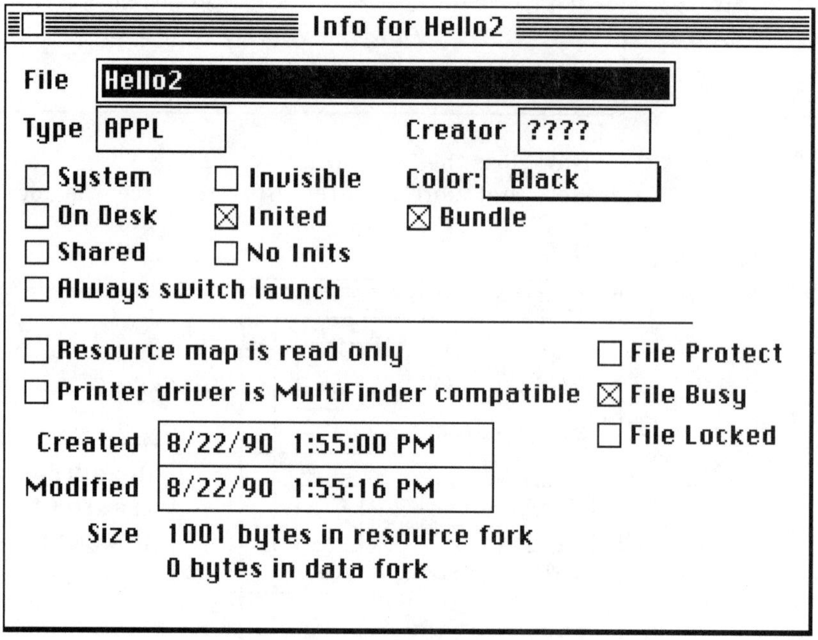

Figure 8.26 File information for the Hello2 application.

The four-character Creator name **HELO** will be used when the Finder looks for the application's icon. If, by chance, another application with a defined icon has the same Creator, the first icon the Finder finds will be used.

Be careful in your choice of Creator names. If you plan to market a Macintosh application, register the Creator name with Macintosh Developer Technical Support; they can tell you whether others have used this Creator tag. We registered **HELO**, so go ahead and use it for this Primer application.

Here is a brief description of the Finder flags found in the File Info box (see Figure 8.26).

The **System** bit indicates that the file cannot be renamed, and that a warning will be given when the file is dragged to the trash.

If the file is on the Desktop (that is, not in any folder), the **On Desk** flag is set.

If the **Shared** flag is set, the application can be opened more than once.

If the **Invisible** bit is set, the file is not displayed by the Finder. ResEdit can see it, however, as can Finder substitutes like DiskTop.

The **Inited** bit is set by the Finder when it determines the file's location and window.

The **No Inits** flag is set if an application wants to ensure that any INIT attached to the application will not be executed.

The **Color** pull-down menu shows the current color that the Finder uses to draw the file's icon.

The **Bundle** flag is set by the Finder if you have a BNDL resource in the file. We'll talk more about BNDLs later in this chapter.

The **File Protect** flag is not currently used.

If the **File Busy** bit is set, the file is open or executing.

If the **File Lock** bit is set, the file cannot be renamed (although it can be thrown away).

If the **Resource map is read only** check box is checked, the resources in the file cannot be changed.

The **Printer driver is MultiFinder compatible** flag is set only for printer drivers that work with MultiFinder.

The **File Information** dialog box also contains **created** and **modified** dates for the file.

At the bottom, the dialog box displays the size of the **resource fork** and the **data fork**. As was discussed in Chapter 2, all Macintosh applications have a resource fork and a data fork. The resource fork contains resources. The data fork may store information about user preferences or anything else you desire.

The flags displayed in the **File Information** window are information that the Finder keeps regarding your application. Normally, you should not change them.

You're done! The four required Finder resources are installed into your Hello2 application. Save your changes and quit ResEdit. You may be expecting to see something like Figure 8.27. Unfortunately, you are more likely to see Figure 8.28.

If your new icon appeared, great! If not, you'll need to rebuild your Desktop. Before you go downstairs for a hammer and nails, read the next section.

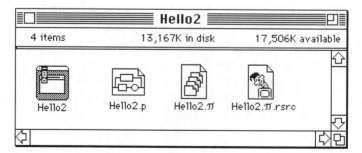

Figure 8.27   The Hello2 folder (working icon).

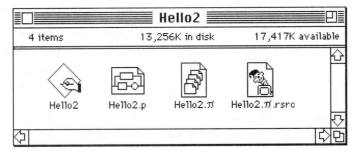

Figure 8.28   The Hello2 folder (icon out to lunch).

Rebuilding the Desktop

The icon you made failed to show up in the Finder when you quit ResEdit. The reason is that the Desktop file needs to be rebuilt after you modify the Finder resources. The Desktop file is the Finder's application database. Among other things, the Desktop file holds information about the volume's file BNDLs. So, when the Hello2 application was created, its BNDL information was noted. Unfortunately, it is hard to get the MacOS to look at a particular file whose BNDL you have modified, short of using ResEdit directly on the Desktop file (not recommended).

The way to get the icon displayed is to rebuild the Desktop file. When a volume's Desktop is rebuilt, the entire volume is searched, and the Desktop database is reconstructed.

However, rebuilding the Desktop does one irrevocable thing, so if you're not a person who likes to do seven irrevocable things before breakfast, read carefully: *It causes the loss of information that has been placed in the text box of the Get Info window for all your applications.*

Rebuilding the Desktop file is simple. First, make sure your Mac is not in MultiFinder (if you're using System 6), as you may run out of memory during the rebuilding process. Restart your Mac and keep down the **Option** and **Command** keys. Don't let them up until an alert dialog like Figure 8.29 shows up.

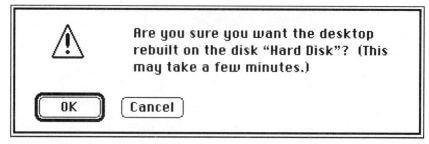

Figure 8.29   Rebuild the Desktop?

If you click on **OK**, the drive will work for a while before the Finder comes back. At this point, your icon should be proudly displayed when you open up the Hello2 folder.

Now that you understand how to install the Finder resources, add them directly to the .rsrc file of your project, instead of adding them to completed applications. That way, each time you build a stand-alone application from your project, THINK Pascal will automatically add the Finder resources to it. This normally solves the missing icon problem, as the first time that the Finder examines your application, the BNDL information is in order.

Okay! You did the icon. Now, you need to add the vers and the SIZE resources. First, let's look at the vers resource, which stores information about the current version of an application.

The vers **Resource**

Fire up ResEdit and open up the iconized Hello2. Create a new resource of type vers. Key in the fields as shown in Figure 8.30. Then close the vers edit window and change the resource ID to 1.

The information you put in tells the Finder more about your application. Most of this additional information refers to the application's version. The version is designated using Apple's intricate numbering system for program releases, which works like this: A new program has version 1.0. If there is a minor revision to the program, it is then labeled Version 1.1. If there's a **bug fix** to

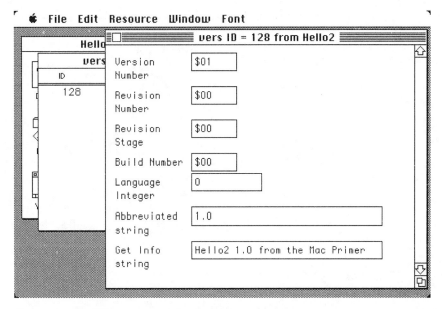

Figure 8.30   The v e r s resource.

Version 1.1, it's designated 1.1.1. So, if you have a program that just had a second bug fix to a third minor revision, it would be Version 1.3.2. If there's a **major revision** of the program, the first number is incremented. If the program has gone through a major revision, four minor revisions, and six bug fixes, the current version is 2.4.6.

There's also a **development suffix,** which is added to indicate how far along the product is. There are three different stages: The earliest is **d** for "development" (for example, 1.0d). The next level is **a** (for "alpha"—1.0a). Then, the **b** ("beta") version comes out (1.0b). Theoretically, the released version would then be 1.0. If you have a product labeled 1.3d1.2, it's the second bug fix of the first development version of the third revision of the first release of the product.

Now that we've said all that, it's unlikely that you'll need as complex a version number as that, unless you own Microsoft. This relates to the v e r s resource fields as follows:

- The **version number** is the first number—the "1" in 1.0.

- The **revision number** is the second number—the "3" in 4.3.1.

- The **revision stage** is the development level—the "b" in 1.0b2.

- The **build number** is the number following the development suffix—the "5" in 2.3a5.

- The **language integer** refers to the country to which this version of the program is headed. The United States is 0; see Figure 8.31 for a list of numbers for other countries.

- The **abbreviated string** is the whole version strung together, such as 1.2b1.1.

- The **Get Info string** is the text that is put in the Get Info box when you're in the Finder.

Test the vers resource by saving Hello2 and quitting ResEdit. Click once on the Hello2 application icon and choose **Get Info** from the **File** menu of the Finder (Figure 8.32). The dialog box should show what you put into the vers resource.

US	0
France	1
Great Britain	2
Germany	3
Italy	4
Netherlands	5
Belgium	6
Sweden	7
Spain	8
Denmark	9
Portugal	10
French Canada	11
Norway	12
Israel	13
Japan	14
Australia	15
Arabia	16
Finland	17
French Swiss	18
German Swiss	19
Greece	20
Iceland	21
Malta	22
Cyprus	23
Turkey	24
Yugoslavia	25

Figure 8.31   Country numbers.

The `vers` resource type is a relatively recent addition to the Finder resources; Apple will have plans for it in the future, so put it in your applications (TN:189).

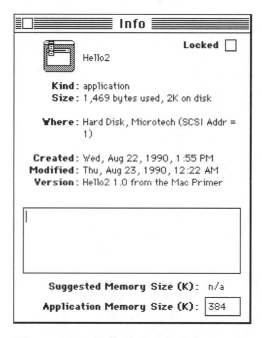

Figure 8.32 Hello2's **Get Info** box (courtesy the `vers` resource).

Some of you may have read in other places that the `signature` resource puts information into the Finder's **Get Info** box in the same way that we're saying that the `vers` resource does. You're right, and here's what happened: The `signature` resource was the old way of attaching the icon to the application and putting information in the **Get Info** box. The `vers` resource type is intended to supply the Finder with extra information, including the **Get Info** data, about your application. If there is no `vers` resource, the **Get Info** information in the `signature` resource is used. If there is a `vers` resource, the `signature` resource is ignored, and the `vers` **Get Info** field is used. In any event, don't dump the `signature` resource! It still is used to identify the desktop icon for the application. There doesn't have to be anything in it, however; version 2 of ResEdit creates a blank `signature` resource automatically when you make your `BNDL` resource.

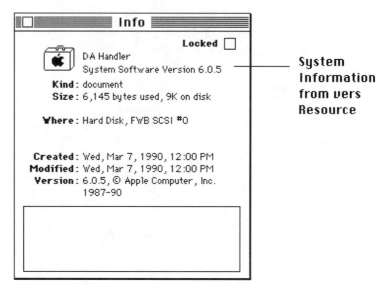

Figure 8.33   System **vers** resources.

If you have a **vers** resource with a resource ID number of **2**, it can be used to link a set of files together. Apple has used this number to identify the current system level of the files in its disks. Figure 8.33 shows how this system information is displayed.

In the bottom of the Get Info box for Hello2, there are two other fields, **Application** and **Suggested Memory Size** for the application. These fields are controlled by the **SIZE** resource, which is discussed next.

Last of the Finder Resources: The **SIZE** Resource

The last Finder resource is the **SIZE** resource, which contains MultiFinder information. Figure 8.34 (suitably elongated) shows the fields contained in a standard **SIZE** resource.

The following is a brief description of these fields:

- **Save screen (Switcher):** A flag used by the Switcher, an early version of MultiFinder.

- **Accept Suspend/Resume events:** If your application handles Suspend/Resume events, set this flag.

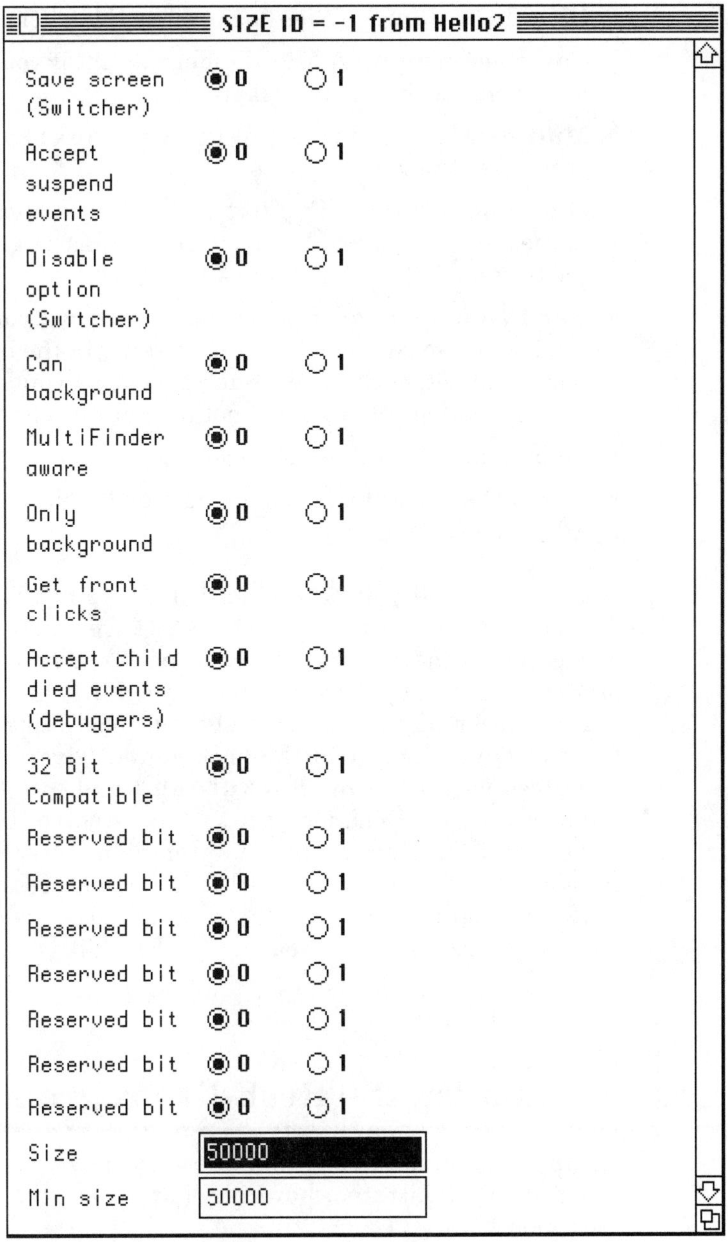

Figure 8.34 The `SIZE` resource.

- **Disable option:** Another flag used by Switcher.

- **Can Background:** A MultiFinder flag set if your application uses null events while in the background.

- **MultiFinder aware:** If you use `WaitNextEvent` in your programs, set this flag.

- **Only Background:** This flag is set if your application runs only in the background and has no user interface (e.g., Backgrounder in the System folder).

- **Get Front Clicks:** If set, this flag allows your application to receive mouse clicks even if it is working in the background. If this flag is not set, clicking on your application window will only make the application active; it will not pass on the click.

- **Accept Child died**: A debugger flag.

- **32 Bit Compatible**: Is the application 32-bit clean? (necessary for A/UX and System 7).

The rest of the bits are reserved by Apple. This is just a brief description of the flags in the `SIZE` resource. For a detailed discussion of the `SIZE` resource, read *The Programmer's Guide to MultiFinder*, available from Apple through APDA.

If you are reading this section because you'd like to make Timer or Reminder work better in the background, give your projects `SIZE` resources with the **Can Background** and **MultiFinder Aware** radio buttons set. Don't forget to set the resource ID to `-1`.

The final section of this chapter demonstrates how intrinsic resources are to the Macintosh. This section presents Minimalist, a working program that contains *nothing* except two `CODE` resources and a `WIND` resource, all created with ResEdit.

Minimalist, the ResEdit Program

Minimalist could be charitably described as a very small, useless program. It illustrates, however, how resources make Macintosh programs work.

In ResEdit, create a new file named Minimalist. Using the **Get File Info** menu item, change the file type to `APPL`. Then, create a new resource of type `CODE` (Figure 8.35). The general hexadecimal editor appears.

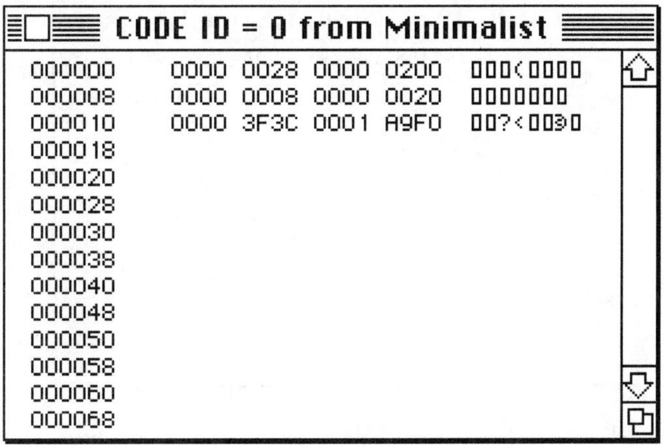

```
≣☐≣ CODE ID = 0 from Minimalist ≣
000000    0000 0028 0000 0200   000<0000    ⇧
000008    0000 0008 0000 0020   0000000
000010    0000 3F3C 0001 A9F0   00?<003▯0
000018
000020
000028
000030
000038
000040
000048
000050
000058
000060                                      ⇩
000068                                      ▯
```

Figure 8.35   A CODE resource for Minimalist.

Type in the hexadecimal code in Figure 8.35. As you're typing, alphanumeric characters will appear on the right. When you're done, click on the close box. Change the ID of the resource by choosing **Get Resource Info** from the **File** menu. Change the ID to 0.

Build the second CODE resource with the hexadecimal code in Figure 8.36.

Change the resource ID number of the second CODE resource ID to 1. Finally, build a WIND resource with a resource ID of 400. Use any size or window type that you prefer, but make sure that the **Visible** and **goAwayFlag** checkboxes are checked. Save the WIND and the two CODE resources.

You now have an application. If you double-click on Minimalist, it will display the window using the WIND specifications you entered. Clicking anywhere on the screen will return you to the Finder.

```
┌─────────────────────────────────────────────┐
│ ▤□▤  CODE ID = 1 from Minimalist ▤▤▤▤▤ │
├─────────────────────────────────────────────┤
│ 000000   0000 0001 486D FFFC  □□□□Hm□□   ⬆  │
│ 000008   A86E A8FE A912 A850  ÞnÞ□Ɑ□ƏP      │
│ 000010   594F 3F3C 0190 42A7  YO?<□èBß      │
│ 000018   2F3C FFFF FFFF A9BD  /<□□□□ƏΩ      │
│ 000020   554F A974 4A1F 67F8  UOƏtJ□g□      │
│ 000028   A9F4                  ƏП           │
│ 000030                                      │
│ 000038                                      │
│ 000040                                      │
│ 000048                                      │
│ 000050                                      │
│ 000058                                      │
│ 000060                              ⬇      │
│ 000068                              ▱      │
└─────────────────────────────────────────────┘
```

Figure 8.36   Second CODE resource for Minimalist.

To get the CODE hexadecimal, we wrote a short assembly language program that does initialization, draws a window, and quits on a mouse click. Here's the code:

```
        include 'Traps.a'
        main
        pea -4(A5)
        _InitGraf
        _InitFonts
        _InitWindows
        _InitCursor

        subq #4,sp
        move #400,-(sp)
        clr.l -(sp)
        move.l #-1,-(sp)
        _GetNewWindow

TryButton
        subq #2,sp
        _Button
        tst.b (sp)+
        beq.s TryButton
        _ExitToShell

        end
```

This strategy is not generally recommended for serious program development. Use THINK Pascal to code CODE resources.

In Review

Chapter 8 explored the use of ResEdit and discussed the steps necessary to install Finder resources into your applications. Chapter 9 discusses the issues you'll face as you start developing your own Macintosh applications. It starts by taking a look at a few Mac periodicals you may find useful. It also talks about *Inside Macintosh* and other Apple technical references. Finally, it also looks at Apple's support apparatus for Macintosh programmers and developers.

9

The Final Chapter

To successfully develop software for the Macintosh, you need current technical information. You need to know how to use the standard Macintosh references effectively. You also need to know about the different technical support programs Apple offers. In this chapter, we'll discuss these and other Macintosh development issues.

THE BASICS OF programming the Macintosh have been laid out in the eight preceding chapters. Familiarity with these basics is half the job of becoming a successful developer. The other half is understanding how the Macintosh programming world works and knowing where to get the information you, as a Macintosh software developer, will need.

To succeed in developing software for the Macintosh, you need current technical information. You need to be able to use the standard Macintosh references effectively. You also need to know about the different technical support programs Apple offers.

This chapter investigates the periodicals that are your link to the Macintosh community. It looks at *Inside Macintosh* and other Mac technical texts, as well as software tools, from compilers to debuggers. The chapter also examines Apple's support programs for Macintosh software developers.

The *Macintosh Programming Primer* is your passport to Mac application programming. When you've finished reading this book, join a local Macintosh users group, and buy a copy of the best Mac programmer's magazine, *MacTutor*. Get involved and write some code!

Macintosh Periodicals

Whether you're interested in making a commercial product or a shareware product, or whether you just want to know the inside stories of the Mac community, get the trade magazines. *MacWeek* is great, and *PCWeek* and *InfoWorld* are good, if less oriented to the Macintosh computer line. All three magazines deliver timely dollops of news: the new software packages, scoops on company goings-on, and juicy industry gossip.

The Macintosh programming journal is *MacTutor*, an invigorating monthly discourse on the art of Mac programming. Popular Mac magazines include *MacUser* and *MacWorld*. Their broad viewpoint can show you what is of interest to Macintosh users and what's available.

While you wait for the idea that will make you the seventh richest person in the world, you need to learn the Macintosh inside out. To do this, you need *Inside Macintosh*.

The *Inside Macintosh* technical reference series is written by Apple and published by Addison-Wesley. The series has seven books (Volumes I–VI and the *Inside Macintosh X-Ref*). In Chapter 1, we suggested that you could get by with Volumes I and V.

We lied. Get them all.

Volumes I, II, and III represent the Mac technical world as it was before the Mac Plus was introduced. All three volumes focus on the original 128K Mac, describing interfaces to the ROM routines, memory management, hardware specs, and more.

Volume IV was released after the Mac Plus and the Mac 512KE were introduced. Both of these new Macs sported 128K ROMs (as opposed to the 128K Macintoshes' 64K ROMs). These larger ROMs contain the routines that handle the Hierarchical File System (HFS), routines that interface to the SCSI (Small Computer System Interface) port, and updates to most of the 64K ROM routines. Volume IV covers all these changes.

Volume V was released after the introduction of the Mac SE and the Mac II. The Mac II and the SE have 256K ROMs and support features like pop-up, hierarchical, and scrolling menus; a sophisticated sound manager; new text edit routines; and more. Perhaps the biggest change was the addition of color support to the Mac II series.

Finally, Volume VI explains the enhancements provided by the long-awaited **System 7**: InterApplication Communication (IAC), virtual memory, AppleEvents, a redesigned Finder, new printing, database routines, and more!

The Typical *Inside Mac* Chapter

One of the best features of the *Inside Mac* volumes is their consistency. Each chapter starts with a table of contents, followed by the "About This Chapter" section, which gives you an overview of what the chapter covers and what you should already be familiar with before you continue.

The next section or sections give an overview of the chapter's technical premise—for example, "About the Event Manager" or "About the Window Manager." The fundamental concepts are explained in great detail. At first, you may be overwhelmed by the wealth of detail, but after a few readings (and a little experimentation), you'll warm to the concept.

Next, the chapter's data structures, constants, and essential variables are detailed. These are presented in Pascal and/or assembly language. Then come the chapter's Toolbox routines. Each routine's calling sequence is presented in Pascal, along with a detailed explanation of the uses of the routine. This section includes notes and warnings, as appropriate.

Some chapters follow the Toolbox routines section with a few additional sections. Among these extras are a description of the resources pertinent to that chapter and, perhaps, a description of extensions available to the advanced programmer.

Finally, there's a chapter summary, with unadorned lists of constants, data types, routines, and variables.

Appendixes and Special Sections

Inside Macintosh, Volume I, Chapter 1, contains a road map that gives you a feel for the basics of the Macintosh and how the *Inside Mac* volumes work. The road map suggests you read Chapters 1 through 4, then read the chapters that are relevant to your current development effort. This is sage advice. These chapters offer an excellent grounding in Mac basics (or an excellent review if you've been at it for a while).

Volume III contains three chapters, some appendixes, a glossary, and an index. Chapter 1 discusses the Finder (with an emphasis on Finder-related resources). Chapter 2 discusses the pre-Mac Plus hardware. Chapter 3 is a compendium of all the summary sections from Volumes I and II. Appendix A is a handy, if occasionally inaccurate, table of result codes from the functions defined in Volumes I and II. The rest of the appendixes in Volume III have been superseded by the appendixes in the *Inside Macintosh X-Ref.*

The *Inside Mac X-Ref* starts off with a general index covering the first five *Inside Mac* volumes, the Macintosh *Technical Notes, Programmer's Introduction to the Macintosh Family, Technical Introduction to the Macintosh Family,* and *Designing Cards and Drivers for the Macintosh II and Macintosh SE.* The general index is followed by an index of constants and field names. Appendix A of the *X-Ref* lists every Toolbox routine that may move or purge memory. A new version of the *X-Ref* should be out shortly that also includes Volume VI of *Inside Mac.*

Appendix B of *Inside Mac* consists of two lists. The first is a list of Toolbox routines presented alphabetically by name, with each name followed by the routine's **trap address**, which is the four-byte instruction the compiler generates to call the routine. The second is a list of the trap addresses, in order, with each trap address followed by the routine name. This information is extremely useful if you ever have to look at code in hexadecimal format, a likely event if you use TMON or MacsBug, two Mac debuggers.

Appendix C lists most of the operating system global variables, with their memory location and a brief description. Finally, Appendix C is followed by a glossary of terms presented in Volumes I through V.

Apple Technical References

In the first few years of the Mac era, *Inside Macintosh* was the only definitive reference on the Macintosh. Recently, however, Apple has published some additional reference texts for the Macintosh, including *Technical Introduction to the Macintosh Family*, *Programmer's Introduction to the Macintosh Family*, and *Designing Cards and Drivers for the Macintosh II and Macintosh SE*. These books are all part of Addison-Wesley's Apple Technical Library. Another excellent source of technical information is the Macintosh *Technical Notes*.

Macintosh Technical Notes

Macintosh Technical Notes are published on a regular basis by Apple and distributed to developers free of charge. The *Tech Notes* are a necessity for serious Mac developers. They contain technical information that was not yet available when the latest volume of *Inside Macintosh* went to press. For example, *Tech Note* #184 describes the Notification Manager (used in Chapter 6). Without this *Tech Note*, developers wouldn't even know the Notification Manager existed, let alone know how to use it.

A timely way to receive *Tech Notes* if you are not a developer is to become a member of APDA, the Apple Programmer's and Developer's Association (developers are automatically members of APDA). APDA charges $20.00 per year for membership, and they sell most of the technical references mentioned in this chapter. They sell the *Tech*

Notes in both hard copy and disk formats. For more information on APDA, contact:

> Apple Programmer's and Developer's Association
> Apple Computer, Inc.
> 20525 Mariani Avenue, MS: 33-G
> Cupertino, CA 95014-6299

If you're not either a developer or a member of APDA, you can still get *Tech Notes* by downloading them from Mac-oriented bulletin boards around the country.

Other Books

There are a number of excellent books on Mac programming. The classic is Scott Knaster's *How to Write Macintosh Software*. This book is little too advanced for the beginner, but it's worth the struggle to get through it. If you plan on writing a lot of Mac code, read this book.

Another popular set of books is the *Macintosh Revealed* series, written by Stephen Chernicoff.

Last but not least, you might want to try the *Macintosh Pascal Programming Primer,* Volume II. Object programming, color QuickDraw, INITs, CDEVs, and other interesting Toolbox routines are examined, with lots of examples and code walkthroughs. Be sure to get the Pascal version of Volume II. Volume II, like this volume, also comes in a C flavor.

Apple's Developer Programs

The Apple Partners program provides additional technical support from Apple. Developers accepted into the new Apple Partners program receive complete Apple technical documentation, system software updates, membership in APDA, access to training classes, and discounts on Apple hardware and software. Developers also get a year's subscription to AppleLink, Apple's electronic communication network, and access to Macintosh Developer Technical Support (see below). If you have a CD-ROM drive, you may want to take advantage of the Developer CD Series, which is a set of CD-ROMs shipped to developers every few months, containing sample code, utility programs, and *Inside Macintosh* in HyperCard!

The only disadvantage of being a developer is in parting with the check you include with your Apple Partners application (currently $600).

You don't have to be a Fortune 500 company to qualify as an Apple Partner, but Apple is looking specifically for developers of Apple hardware and software who intend to resell their products. If you are interested in developing software but don't have an immediate plan to market it, you might consider the Apple Associates Program, another support program from Apple.

The Apple Associates Program is aimed at educators, in-house developers, and shareware programmers. It provides a basic level of support, including AppleLink (one month prepaid), system software upgrades, APDA, *Tech Notes*, and access to other technical information. The Associates program currently has a yearly charge of $350.00.

If you plan on writing a product for the Mac, the information you receive in either program is invaluable. Call the Developer Programs Hotline at (408) 974–4897 and ask them to send you an application.

If you are a developer, there's nothing more satisfying than talking to people who have solved, or at least are aware of, the technical programs you encounter in writing programs. At Apple, these people come from Macintosh Developer Technical Support, or MacDTS.

Macintosh Developer Technical Support and AppleLink

Macintosh Developer Technical Support is composed of talented Mac software engineers dedicated to helping developers with their technical problems. To work with MacDTS, send them a message via MCI Mail. Or you can use AppleLink.

AppleLink is Apple's electronic communication network. It gives access to information about Apple products, prices, programs, and policy information. You can write to Developer Technical Support at MacDTS on AppleLink, and they will make every possible effort to answer your question promptly.

Both Apple Partners and Apple Associates receive subscriptions to AppleLink: Apple Partners receive a full year's subscription with the minimum monthly fees prepaid; Apple Associates receive one month of the minimum monthly fee prepaid.

Besides access to MacDTS, AppleLink gives you access to a lot of other services. You can download the new system utilities or look at the Help Wanted ads posted on the bulletin board. You can send beta versions of your products to your evangelist at Apple or to other developers. AppleLink makes you a part of the developer community.

Software Development Tools

All the applications presented in this book were written in Pascal, using the THINK Pascal development environment from Symantec. The advantages of THINK Pascal lie primarily in its ease of use and debugging facilities. Symantec also makes a powerful, yet friendly, C development environment called THINK C.

Both THINK environments are basically nonextensible. This means that you can't create shell scripts to back up your files automatically, or rebuild an older version of your project. You also can't create custom menu items that automate your development process. THINK environments handle most of the development cycle so thoroughly that you may not miss these features. If you do, you may want to take a look at the Macintosh Programmer's Workshop (MPW) from Apple.

MPW from Apple

MPW is an extremely powerful development environment that is totally extensible—so extensible, in fact, that several third parties have produced compilers that run under MPW. MPW is like a Mac-based UNIX shell. You can write shell scripts, tie them to your own menus, and create tools that have total access to the Toolbox yet run inside the Toolbox environment with access to all your data. The catch is that MPW is more complex than THINK Pascal and, therefore, more difficult to master. MPW also is not cheap, typically costing more than three times as much as THINK Pascal or C.

Both MPW and THINK have many followers and are supported by MacDTS. Whichever way you go, you'll be in good company.

Debugging with THINK Pascal, TMON, and MacsBug

Debugging on any computer can be a tedious and frustrating experience. Luckily, there are some excellent tools that you can use to fix up your code.

Normally, THINK Pascal will handle most debugging tasks quickly and efficiently. The editor automatically catches syntax errors on the fly. After your program compiles successfully, you can easily step through your code while it executes, and you can examine or change variable values as you go. THINK Pascal's **Observe** window lets you track a list of variable or expression values. The **Instant** window allows you to insert new lines of code during execution! All in all, you probably will be able to solve most problems without leaving THINK Pascal. If you need lower level support, however, two other products are available.

MacsBug is an object-level debugger developed by Motorola for the 68000 family of processors. For a long time, it was the only debugger available for the Mac.

If you need a little more horsepower than MacsBug offers, consider TMON. TMON is the pro's debugger. Instead of running as a separate program under MultiFinder, TMON takes over the processor when it runs. TMON preserves your program's run-time environment by not calling any of the Mac Toolbox routines (which might alter the state of your program). Instead, the folks at ICOM Simulations cleverly wrote their own window and menu handlers. Although TMON is somewhat difficult to learn, it's worth it. When you run into an exasperatingly unexplainable bug, pop into TMON and step through your program. You can set breakpoints, disassemble your executable image, and even make changes to your program and data. For debugging drivers, INITs, and DAs, TMON can't be beat.

To Boldly Go

The Macintosh world is accelerating.

New hardware and software products are being designed and marketed faster than ever before. Each successive system software version paves the way to wonderful things: multimedia, image processing, CD-quality sound, voice recognition. There's a feeling that everything is finally arriving. This vision may seem daunting, but remember—a few years ago, the Mac was an intriguing experiment; the people who gambled on it won big.

The changes that Apple is making are setting the stage for machines that will be as big a jump as the Macintosh was from the Apple II line. In the Mac world, you're close to the edge.

Enjoy it!

Appendix A

Glossary

access path: A description of the route that the File Manager follows to access a file; created when a file is opened.

access path buffer: Memory used by the File Manager to transfer data between an application and a file.

action procedure: A procedure, used by the Control Manager function TrackControl, that defines an action to be performed repeatedly for as long as the mouse button is held down.

activate event: An event generated by the Window Manager when a window changes from active to inactive or vice versa.

active control: A control that will respond to the user's actions with the mouse.

active end: In a selection, the location to which the insertion point moves to complete the selection.

active window: The frontmost window on the desktop.

address: A number used to identify a location in the computer's address space. Some locations are allocated to memory, others to I/O devices.

alert: A warning or report of an error, in the form of an alert box, sound from the Macintosh's speaker, or both.

alert box: A box that appears on the screen to give a warning or report an error during a Macintosh application.

alert template: A resource that contains information from which the Dialog Manager can create an alert.

alert window: The window in which an alert box is displayed.

allocate: To reserve an area of memory for use.

Source: *Inside Macintosh X-Ref* © 1988 Apple Computer, Inc. Reprinted with permission of Addison-Wesley Publishing Company.

application font: The font your application will use unless you specify otherwise—Geneva, by default.

application list: A data structure, kept in the Desktop file, for launching applications from their documents in the hierarchical file system. For each application in the list, an entry is maintained that includes the name and signature of the application, as well as the directory ID of the folder containing it.

application window: A window created as the result of something done by the application, either directly or indirectly (as through the Dialog Manager).

asynchronous execution: After calling a routine asynchronously, an application is free to perform other tasks until the routine is completed.

auto-key event: An event generated repeatedly when the user presses and holds down a character key on the keyboard or keypad.

auto-key rate: The rate at which a character key repeats after it's begun to do so.

auto-key threshold: The length of time a character key must be held down before it begins to repeat.

background activity: A program or process that runs while the user is engaged with another application.

bit image: A collection of bits in memory that have a rectilinear representation. The screen is a visible bit image.

bit map: A set of bits that represent the position and state of a corresponding set of items; in QuickDraw, a pointer to a bit image, the row width of that image, and its boundary rectangle.

boundary rectangle: A rectangle, defined as part of a QuickDraw bit map, that encloses the active area of the bit image and imposes a coordinate system on it. Its top left corner is always aligned around the first bit in the bit image.

bundle: A resource that maps local IDs of resources to their actual resource IDs; used to provide mappings for file references and icon lists needed by the Finder.

button: A standard Macintosh control that causes some immediate or continuous action when clicked or pressed with the mouse. See also **radio button**.

catalog tree file: A file that maintains the relationships between the files and directories on a hierarchical directory volume. It corresponds to the file directory on a flat directory volume.

cdev: A resource file containing device information, used by the Control Panel.

channel: A queue that's used by an application to send commands to the Sound Manager.

character code: An integer representing the character that a key or combination of keys on the keyboard or keypad stands for.

character key: A key that generates a keyboard event when pressed; any key except Shift, Caps Lock, Command, or Option.

character style: A set of stylistic variations, such as bold, italic, and underline. The empty set indicates plain text (no stylistic variations).

character width: The distance to move the pen from one character's origin to the next character's origin.

check box: A standard Macintosh control that displays a setting, either checked (on) or unchecked (off). Clicking inside a check box reverses its setting.

Chooser: A desk accessory that provides a standard interface for device drivers to solicit and accept specific choices from the user.

clipping: Limiting drawing to within the bounds of a particular area.

clipping region: Same as **clipRgn**.

clipRgn: The region to which an application limits drawing in a grafPort.

closed file: A file without an access path. Closed files cannot be read from or written to.

compaction: The process of moving allocated blocks within a heap zone in order to collect the free space into a single block.

content region: The area of a window that the application draws in.

control: An object in a window on the Macintosh screen with which the user, moving the mouse, can cause instant action with visible results or change settings to modify a future action.

Control Manager: The part of the Toolbox that provides routines for creating and manipulating controls (such as buttons, check boxes, and scroll bars).

control definition function: A function called by the Control Manager when it needs to perform type-dependent operations on a particular type of control, such as drawing the control.

control definition ID: A number passed to control-creation routines to indicate the type of control. It consists of the control definition function's resource ID and a variation code.

control list: A list of all the controls associated with a given window.

control record: The internal representation of a control, where the Control Manager stores all the information it needs for its operations on that control.

control template: A resource that contains information from which the Control Manager can create a control.

coordinate plane: A two-dimensional grid. In QuickDraw, the grid coordinates are integers ranging from -32,767 to 32,767, and all grid lines are infinitely thin.

current resource file: The last resource file opened, unless you specify otherwise with a Resource Manager routine.

cursor: A 16-by-16 bit image that appears on the screen and is controlled by the mouse; called the "pointer" in Macintosh user manuals.

cursor level: A value, initialized by InitCursor, that keeps track of the number of times the cursor has been hidden.

data fork: The part of a file that contains data accessed via the File Manager.

data mark: In a sector, information that primarily contains data from an application.

date/time record: An alternate representation of the date and time (which is stored on the clock chip in seconds since midnight, January 1, 1904).

default button: In an alert box or modal dialog, the button whose effect will occur if the user presses Return or Enter. In an alert box, it's boldly outlined; in a modal dialog, it's boldly outlined or the OK button.

default directory: A directory that will be used in File Manager routines whenever no other directory is specified. It may be the root directory, in which case the default directory is equivalent to the default volume.

default volume: A volume that will receive I/O during a File Manager routine call, whenever no other volume is specified.

dereference: To refer to a block by its master pointer instead of its handle.

Desk Manager: The part of the Toolbox that supports the use of desk accessories from an application.

desk accessory: A "mini-application," implemented as a device driver, that can be run at the same time as a Macintosh application.

desk scrap: The place where data is stored when it's cut (or copied) and pasted among applications and desk accessories.

desktop: The screen as a surface for doing work on the Macintosh.

Desktop file: A resource file in which the Finder stores the version data, bundle, icons, and file references for each application on the volume.

device driver event: An event generated by one of the Macintosh's device drivers.

device driver: A program that controls the exchange of information between an application and a device.

dial: A control with a moving indicator that displays a quantitative setting or value. Depending on the type of dial, the user may be able to change the setting by dragging the indicator with the mouse.

dialog: Same as **dialog box**.

dialog box: A box that a Macintosh application displays to request information it needs to complete a command, or to report that it's waiting for a process to complete.

Dialog Manager: The part of the Toolbox that provides routines for implementing dialogs and alerts.

dialog record: The internal representation of a dialog, where the Dialog Manager stores all the information it needs for its operations on that dialog.

dialog template: A resource that contains information from which the Dialog Manager can create a dialog.

dialog window: The window in which a dialog box is displayed.

dimmed: Drawn in gray rather than black.

directory ID: A unique number assigned to a directory, which the File Manager uses to distinguish it from other directories on the volume. (It's functionally equivalent to the file number assigned to a file; in fact, both directory IDs and file numbers are assigned from the same set of numbers.)

directory: A subdivision of a volume that can contain files as well as other directories; equivalent to a folder.

disabled: A disabled menu item or menu is one that cannot be chosen; the menu item or menu title appears dimmed. A disabled item in a dialog or alert box has no effect when clicked.

Disk Initialization Package: A Macintosh package for initializing and naming new disks; called by the Standard File Package.

disk-inserted event: An event generated when the user inserts a disk in a disk drive or takes any other action that requires a volume to be mounted.

display rectangle: A rectangle that determines where an item is displayed within a dialog or alert box.

document window: The standard Macintosh window for presenting a document.

double-click time: The greatest interval between a mouse-up and mouse-down event that would qualify two mouse clicks as a double-click.

draft printing: Printing a document immediately as it's drawn in the printing grafPort.

drag delay: A length of time that allows a user to drag diagonally across a main menu, moving from a submenu title into the submenu itself without the submenu disappearing.

drag region: A region in a window frame. Dragging inside this region moves the window to a new location and makes it the active window unless the Command key was down.

drive number: A number used to identify a disk drive. The internal drive is number 1, the external drive is number 2, and any additional drives will have larger numbers.

empty handle: A handle that points to a NIL master pointer, signifying that the underlying relocatable block has been purged.

end-of-file: See **logical end-of-file** or **physical end-of-file**.

event: A notification to an application of some occurrence that the application may want to respond to.

event code: An integer representing a particular type of event.

Event Manager: See **Toolbox Event Manager**.

event mask: A parameter passed to an Event Manager routine to specify which types of events the routine should apply to.

event message: A field of an event record containing information specific to the particular type of event.

event queue: The Operating System Event Manager's list of pending events.

event record: The internal representation of an event, through which your program learns all pertinent information about that event.

exception: An error or abnormal condition detected by the processor in the course of program execution; includes interrupts and traps.

external reference: A reference to a routine or variable defined in a separate compilation or assembly.

file: A named, ordered sequence of bytes; a principal means by which data is stored and transmitted on the Macintosh.

file catalog: A hierarchical file directory.

file control block: A fixed-length data structure, contained in the file-control-block buffer, where information about an access path is stored.

file directory: The part of a volume that contains descriptions and locations of all the files and directories on the volume. There are two types of file directories: hierarchical file directories and flat file directories.

File Manager: The part of the Operating System that supports file I/O.

file name: A sequence of up to 255 printing characters, excluding colons (:), that identifies a file.

file number: A unique number assigned to a file, which the File Manager uses to distinguish it from other files on the volume. A file number specifies the file's entry in a file directory.

file reference: A resource that provides the Finder with file and icon information about an application.

file type: A four-character sequence, specified when a file is created, that identifies the type of file.

Finder information: Information that the Finder provides to an application upon starting it up, telling it which documents to open or print.

font: A complete set of characters of one typeface, which may be restricted to a particular size and style, or may comprise multiple sizes, or multiple sizes and styles, as in the context of menus.

Font Manager: The part of the Toolbox that supports the use of various character fonts for QuickDraw when it draws text.

font number: The number by which you identify a font to QuickDraw or the Font Manager.

font size: The size of a font in points; equivalent to the distance between the ascent line of one line of text and the ascent line of the next line of single-spaced text.

fork: One of the two parts of a file; see **data fork** and **resource fork**.

free block: A memory block containing space available for allocation.

full pathname: A pathname beginning from the root directory.

global coordinate system: The coordinate system based on the top left corner of the bit image being at (0,0).

go-away region: A region in a window frame. Clicking inside this region of the active window makes the window close or disappear.

grafPort: A complete drawing environment, including such elements as a bit map, a subset of it in which to draw, a character font, patterns for drawing and erasing, and other pen characteristics.

graphics device: A video card, a printer, a display device, or an offscreen pixel map. Any of these device types may be used with Color QuickDraw.

GrayRgn: The global variable that in the multiple screen desktop describes and defines the desktop, the area on which windows can be dragged.

grow image: The image pulled around when the user drags inside the grow region; whatever is appropriate to show that the window's size will change.

grow region: A window region, usually within the content region, where dragging changes the size of an active window.

handle: A pointer to a master pointer, which designates a relocatable block in the heap by double indirection.

heap: The area of memory in which space is dynamically allocated and released on demand, using the Memory Manager.

hierarchical menu: A menu that includes, among its various menu choices, the ability to display a submenu. In most cases the submenu appears to the right of the menu item used to select it, and is marked with a filled triangle indicator.

highlight: To display an object on the screen in a distinctive visual way, such as inventing it.

hotSpot: The point in a cursor that's aligned with the mouse location.

icon: A 32-by-32 bit image that graphically represents an object, concept, or message.

icon list: A resource consisting of a list of icons.

icon number: A digit from 1 to 255 to which the Menu Manager adds 256 to get the resource ID of an icon associated with a menu item.

inactive control: A control that won't respond to the user's actions with the mouse. An inactive control is highlighted in some special way, such as dimmed.

inactive window: Any window that isn't the frontmost window on the desktop.

indicator: The moving part of a dial that displays its current setting.

interface routine: A routine called from Pascal whose purpose is to trap to a certain Toolbox or Operating System routine.

International Utilities Package: A Macintosh package that gives you access to country-dependent information such as the formats for numbers, currency, dates, and times.

invert: To highlight by changing white pixels to black and vice versa.

invisible control: A control that's not drawn in its window.

invisible window: A window that's not drawn in its plane on the desktop.

item: In dialog and alert boxes, a control, icon, picture, or piece of text, each displayed inside its own display rectangle. See also **menu item**.

item list: A list of information about all the items in a dialog or alert box.

item number: The index, starting from 1, of an item in an item list.

IWM: "Integrated Woz Machine"; the custom chip that controls the 3 1/2-inch disk drives.

job dialog: A dialog that sets information about one printing job; associated with the Print command.

jump table: A table that contains one entry for every routine in an application and is the means by which the loading and unloading of segments is implemented.

key code: An integer representing a key on the keyboard or keypad, without reference to the character that the key stands for.

key-down event: An event generated when the user presses a character key on the keyboard or keypad.

key-up event: An event generated when the user releases a character key on the keyboard or keypad.

keyboard equivalent: The combination of the Command key and another key, used to invoke a menu item from the keyboard.

keyboard event: An event generated when the user presses, releases, or holds down a character key on the keyboard or keypad; any key-down, key-up, or auto-key event.

List Manager: The part of the Operating System that provides routines for creating, displaying, and manipulating lists.

local coordinate system: The coordinate system local to a `grafPort`, imposed by the boundary rectangle defined in its bit map.

local ID: A number that refers to an icon list or file reference in an application's resource file and is mapped to an actual resource ID by a bundle.

localization: The process of adapting an application to different languages, including converting its user interface to a different script.

lock: To temporarily prevent a relocatable block from being moved during heap operation.

lock bit: A bit in the master pointer to a relocatable block that indicates whether the block is currently locked.

locked file: A file whose data cannot be changed.

locked volume: A volume whose data cannot be changed. Volumes can be locked by either a software flag or a mechanical setting.

logical end-of-file: The position of one byte past the last byte in a file; equal to the actual number of bytes in the file.

main event loop: In a standard Macintosh application program, a loop that repeatedly calls the Toolbox Event Manager to get events and then responds to them as appropriate.

main screen: On a system with multiple display devices, the screen with the menu bar is called the main screen.

main segment: The segment containing the main program.

master pointer: A single pointer to a .relocatable block, maintained by the Memory Manager and updated whenever the block is moved, purged, or reallocated. All handles to a relocatable block refer to it by double indirection through the master pointer.

Memory Manager: The part of the Operating System that dynamically allocates and releases memory space in the heap.

menu: A list of menu items that appears when the user points to a menu title in the menu bar and presses the mouse button. Dragging through the menu and releasing over an enabled menu item chooses that item.

menu bar: The horizontal strip at the top of the Macintosh screen that contains the menu titles of all menus in the menu list.

menu definition procedure: A procedure called by the Menu Manager when it needs to perform type-dependent operations on a particular type of menu, such as drawing the menu.

menu ID: A number in the menu record that identifies the menu.

menu item: A choice in a menu, usually a command to a current application.

menu list: A list containing menu handles for all menus in the menu bar, along with information on the position of each menu.

Menu Manager: The part of the Toolbox that deal with setting up menus and letting the user choose from them.

menu title: A word or phrase in the menu bar that designates one menu.

modal dialog: A dialog that requires the user to respond before doing any other work on the desktop.

modeless dialog: A dialog that allows the user to work elsewhere on the desktop before responding.

mounted volume: A volume that previously was inserted into a disk drive and had descriptive information read from it by the File Manager.

mouse-down event: An event generated when the user presses the mouse button.

mouse-up event: An event generated when the user releases the mouse button.

network event: An event generated by the AppleTalk Manager.

null event: An event reported when there are no other events to report.

offspring: For a given directory, the set of files and directories for which it is the parent.

on-line volume: A mounted volume with its volume buffer and descriptive information contained in memory.

open file: A file with an access path. Open files can be read from and written to.

open permission: Information about a file that indicates whether the file can be read from, written to, or both.

Operating System: The lowest-level software in the Macintosh. It does basic tasks such as I/O, memory management, and interrupt handling.

Operating System Utilities: Operating System routines that perform miscellaneous tasks such as getting the date and time, finding out the user's preferred speaker volume and other preferences, and doing simple string comparison.

page rectangle: The rectangle marking the boundaries of a printed page image. The boundary rectangle, portRect, and clipRgn of the printing grafPort are set to this rectangle.

panel: An area of a window that shows a different interpretation of the same part of a document.

part code: An integer between 1 and 253 that stands for a particular part of a control (possibly the entire control).

partial pathname: A pathname beginning from any directory other than the root directory.

path reference number: A number that uniquely identifies an individual access path; assigned when the access path is created.

pathname: A series of concatenated directory and file names that identifies a given file or directory. See also **partial pathname** and **full pathname**.

pattern: An 8-by-8 bit image, used to define a repeating design (such as stripes) or tone (such as gray).

physical end-of-file: The position of one byte past the last allocation block of a file; equal to 1 more than the maximum number of bytes the file can contain.

picture: A saved sequence of QuickDraw drawing commands (and, optionally, picture comments) that you can play back later with a single procedure call; also, the image resulting from these commands.

pixel: A dot on a display screen. Pixel is short for picture element.

plane: The front-to-back position of a window on the desktop.

point: The intersection of a horizontal grid line and a vertical grid line on the coordinate plane, defined by a horizontal and a vertical coordinate; also, a typographical term meaning approximately 1/72 inch.

polygon: A sequence of connected lines, defined by QuickDraw line-drawing commands.

pop-up menu: A menu not located in the menu bar, which appears when the user presses the mouse button in a particular place.

port: See **grafPort**.

portBits: The bit map of a grafPort.

portRect: A rectangle, defined as part of a grafPort, that encloses a subset of the bit map for use by the grafPort.

post: To place an event in the event queue for later processing.

print record: A record containing all the information needed by the Printing Manager to perform a particular printing job.

Printer Driver: The device driver for the currently installed printer.

printer resource file: A file containing all the resources needed to run the Printing Manager with a particular printer.

Printing Manager: The routines and data types that enable applications to communicate with the Printer Driver to print on any variety of printer via the same interface.

printing grafPort: A special grafPort customized for printing instead of drawing on the screen.

purgeable block: A relocatable block that can be purged from the heap.

queue: A list of identically structured entries linked together by pointers.

QuickDraw: The part of the Toolbox that performs all graphic operations on the Macintosh screen.

radio button: A standard Macintosh control that displays a setting, either on or off, and is part of a group in which only one button can be on at a time.

RAM: The Macintosh's random access memory, which contains exception vectors, buffers used by hardware devices, the system and application heaps, the stack, and other information used by applications.

reallocate: To allocate new space in the heap for a purged block, updating its master pointer to point to its new location.

reference number: A number greater than 0, returned by the Resource Manager when a resource file is opened, by which you can refer to that file. In Resource Manager routines that expect a reference number, 0 represents the system resource file.

region: An arbitrary area or set of areas on the QuickDraw coordinate plane. The outline of a region should be one or more closed loops.

release. To free an allocated area of memory, making it available for reuse.

relocatable block: A block that can be moved within the heap during compaction.

resource: Data or code stored in a resource file and managed by the Resource Manager.

resource attribute: One of several characteristics, specified by bits in a resource reference, that determine how the resource should be dealt with.

resource data: In a resource file, the data that comprises a resource.

resource file: The resource fork of a file.

resource fork: The part of a file that contains data used by an application (such as menus, fonts, and icons). The resource fork of an application file also contains the application code itself.

resource header: At the beginning of a resource file, data that gives the offsets to and lengths of the resource data and resource map.

resource ID: A number that, together with the resource type, identifies a resource in a resource file. Every resource has an ID number.

Resource Manager: The part of the Toolbox that reads and writes resources.

resource name: A string that, together with the resource type, identifies a resource in a resource file. A resource may or may not have a name.

resource specification: A resource type and either a resource ID or a resource name.

resource type: The type of a resource in a resource file, designated by a sequence of four characters (such as 'MENU' for a menu).

result code: An integer indicating whether a routine completed its task successfully or was prevented by some error condition (or other special condition, such as reaching the end of a file).

resume procedure: A procedure within an application that allows the application to recover from system errors.

ROM: The Macintosh's permanent Read-Only Memory, which contains the routines for the Toolbox and Operating System, and the various system traps.

root directory: The directory at the base of a file catalog.

row width: The number of bytes in each row of a bit image.

Scrap Manager: The part of the Toolbox that enables cutting and pasting between applications, desk accessories, or an application and a desk accessory.

scrap: A place where cut or copied data is stored.

scrap file: The file containing the desk scrap (usually named "Clipboard File").

SCSI: See **Small Computer Standard Interface**.

SCSI Manager: The part of the Operating System that controls the exchange of information between a Macintosh and peripheral devices connected through the Small Computer Standard Interface (SCSI).

segment: One of several parts into which the code of an application may be divided. Not all segments need to be in memory at the same time.

selection range: The series of characters (inversely highlighted), or the character position (marked with a blinking caret), at which the next editing operation will occur.

signature: A four-character sequence that uniquely identifies an application to the Finder.

Small Computer Standard Interface (SCSI): A specification of mechanical, electrical, and functional standards for connecting small computers with intelligent peripherals such as hard disks, printers, and optical disks.

solid shape: A shape that's filled in with any pattern.

Sound Driver: The device driver that controls sound generation in an application.

sound procedure: A procedure associated with an alert that will emit one of up to four sounds from the Macintosh's speaker. Its integer parameter ranges from 0 to 3 and specifies which sound.

source transfer mode: One of eight transfer modes for drawing text or transferring any bit image between two bit maps.

stack: The area of memory in which space is allocated and released in LIFO (last-in-first-out) order.

Standard File Package: A Macintosh package for presenting the standard user interface when a file is to be saved or opened.

startup screen: When the system is started up, one of the display devices is selected as the **startup screen,** the screen on which the "happy Macintosh" icon appears.

structure region: An entire window; its complete "structure."

style: See **character style**.

style dialog: A dialog that sets options affecting the page dimensions; associated with the Page Setup command.

subdirectory: Any directory other than the root directory.

submenu delay: The length of time before a submenu appears as a user drags through a hierarchical main menu; it prevents rapid flashing of submenus.

System Error Handler: The part of the Operating System that assumes control when a fatal system error occurs.

system error alert: An alert box displayed by the System Error Handler.

system error ID: An ID number that appears in a system error alert to identify the error.

system event mask: A global event mask that controls which types of events get posted into the event queue.

system font: The font that the system uses (in menus, for example). Its name is Chicago.

system font size: The size of text drawn by the system in the system font; 12 points.

system heap: The portion of the heap reserved for use by the Operating System.

system resource: A resource in the system resource file.

system resource file: A resource file containing standard resources, accessed if a requested resource wasn't found in any of the other resource files that were searched.

system window: A window in which a desk accessory is displayed.

target device: An SCSI device (typically an intelligent peripheral) that receives a request from an initiator device to perform a certain operation.

thumb: The Control Manager's term for the scroll box (the indicator of a scroll bar).

tick: A sixtieth of a second.

Toolbox: Same as **User Interface Toolbox**.

Toolbox Event Manager: The part of the Toolbox that allows your application program to monitor the user's actions with the mouse, keyboard, and keypad.

Toolbox Utilities: The part of the Toolbox that performs generally useful operations such as fixed-point arithmetic, string manipulation, and logical operations on bits.

transfer mode: A specification of which Boolean operation QuickDraw should perform when drawing or when transferring a bit image from one bit map to another.

trap dispatcher: The part of the Operating System that examines a trap word to determine what operation it stands for, looks up the address of the corresponding routine in the trap dispatch table, and jumps to the routine.

trap word: An unimplemented instruction representing a call to a Toolbox or Operating System routine.

type coercion: Many compilers feature type coercion (also known as typecasting), which allows a data structure of one type to be converted to another type. In many cases, this conversion is simply a relaxation of type-checking in the compiler, allowing the substitution of a differently typed but equivalent data structure.

unlock: To allow a relocatable block to be moved during heap compaction.

unmounted volume: A volume that hasn't been inserted into a disk drive and had descriptive information read from it, or a volume that previously was mounted and has since had the memory used by it released.

unpurgeable block: A relocatable block that can't be purged from the heap.

update event: An event generated by the Window Manager when a window's contents need to be redrawn.

update region: A window region consisting of all areas of the content region that have to be redrawn.

User Interface Toolbox: The software in the Macintosh ROM that helps you implement the standard Macintosh user interface in your application.

version data: In an application's resource file, a resource that has the application's signature as its resource type; typically a string that gives the name, version number, and date of the application.

vertical blanking interval: The time between the display of the last pixel on the bottom line of the screen and the first one on the top line.

virtual key codes: The key codes that appear in keyboard events.

visible control: A control that's drawn in its window (but may be completely overlapped by another window or other object on the screen).

visible window: A window that's drawn in its plane on the desktop (but may be completely overlapped by another window or object on the screen).

visRgn: The region of the grafPort, manipulated by the Window Manager, that's actually visible on the screen.

volume: A piece of storage medium formatted to contain files; usually a disk or part of a disk. A 3.5-inch Macintosh disk is one volume.

volume attributes: Information contained on volumes and in memory indicating whether the volume is locked, whether it's busy (in memory only), and whether the volume control block matches the volume information (in memory only).

volume name: A sequence of up to 27 printing characters that identifies a volume; followed by a colon (:) in File Manager routine calls, to distinguish it from a file name.

window: An object on the desktop that presents information, such as a document or a message.

window class: In a window record, an indication of whether a window is a system window, a dialog or alert window, or a window created directly by the application.

window definition function: A function called by the Window Manager when it needs to perform certain type-dependent operations on a particular type of window, such as drawing the window frame.

window definition ID: A number passed to window-creation routines to indicate the type of window. It consists of the window definition function's resource ID and a variation code.

window frame: The structure region of a window minus its content region.

window list: A list of all windows ordered by their front-to-back positions on the desktop.

Window Manager: The part of the Toolbox that provides routines for creating and manipulating windows.

Window Manager port: A grafPort that has the entire screen as its portRect and is used by the Window Manager to draw window frames.

window record: The internal representation of a window, where the Window Manager stores all the information it needs for its operations on that window.

window template: A resource from which the Window Manager can create a window.

word wraparound: Keeping words from being split between lines when text is drawn.

working directory: An alternative way of referring to a directory. When opened as a working directory, a directory is given a working directory reference number that's used to refer to it in File Manager calls.

working directory control block: A data structure that contains the directory ID of a working directory, as well as the volume reference number of the volume on which the directory is located.

working directory reference number: A temporary reference number used to identify a working directory. It can be used in place of the volume reference number in all File Manager calls; the File Manager uses it to get the directory ID and volume reference number from the working directory control block.

Appendix B

Code Listings

The following pages contain complete listings of all the source code presented in Chapters 1–9. The listings are presented in order by chapter. Remember, you can send in the coupon in the back of the book for a disk containing the complete set of Macintosh Pascal Primer applications.

Chapter2: Hello.p

```
program Hello;
begin
    ShowText;
    writeln('Hello, world!');
end.
```

Chapter 3: Hello2.p

```
program Hello2;
    const
        BASE_RES_ID = 400;
        HORIZONTAL_PIXEL = 30;
        VERTICAL_PIXEL = 50;


{- ------------> WindowInit <--}

    procedure WindowInit;
        var
            helloWindow: WindowPtr;
    begin
        helloWindow := GetNewWindow(BASE_RES_ID, nil,
                                    WindowPtr(-1));
        ShowWindow(helloWindow);
        SetPort(helloWindow);
        MoveTo(HORIZONTAL_PIXEL, VERTICAL_PIXEL);
        DrawString('Hello, world!');
    end;


{----------------> Hello2 <--}

begin
    WindowInit;
    while (not Button) do
        begin
        end;
end.
```

Chapter 3: Mondrian.p

```pascal
program Mondrian;
    const
        BASE_RES_ID = 400;

    var
        gDrawWindow: WindowPtr;
        gFillColor: LONGINT;


{----------------->   Randomize   <--}

    function Randomize (range: INTEGER): INTEGER;
        var
            rawResult: LONGINT;
    begin
        rawResult := Random;
        rawResult := abs(rawResult);

        Randomize := (rawResult * range) div 32768;
    end;


{----------------->   RandomRect   <--}

    procedure RandomRect (var myRect: Rect; boundingWindow:
                    WindowPtr);
    begin
        myRect.left := Randomize(boundingWindow^.portRect.right -
                    boundingWindow^.portRect.left);
        myRect.right := Randomize(boundingWindow^.portRect.right -
                    boundingWindow^.portRect.left);
        myRect.top := Randomize(boundingWindow^.portRect.bottom -
                    boundingWindow^.portRect.top);
        myRect.bottom := Randomize(boundingWindow^.
                    portRect.bottom -
                    boundingWindow^.
                    portRect.top);
    end;


{----------------->   DrawRandomRect   <--}

    procedure DrawRandomRect;
        var
            myRect: Rect;
    begin
        RandomRect(myRect, gDrawWindow);
        ForeColor(gFillColor);
        PaintOval(myRect);
    end;
```

```
{---------------->  MainLoop  <--}

    procedure MainLoop;
    begin
        GetDateTime(randSeed);
        gFillColor := blackColor;

        while (not Button) do
            begin
                DrawRandomRect;
                if (gFillColor = blackColor) then
                    gFillColor := whiteColor
                else
                    gFillColor := blackColor
            end;
    end;


{---------------->  WindowInit  <--}

    procedure WindowInit;
    begin
        gDrawWindow := GetNewWindow(BASE_RES_ID, nil,
                                    WindowPtr(-1));
        ShowWindow(gDrawWindow);
        SetPort(gDrawWindow);
    end;


{---------------->  Mondrian  <--}

begin
    WindowInit;
    MainLoop;
end.
```

Chapter 3: ShowPICT.p

```
program ShowPICT;
    const
        BASE_RES_ID = 400;

    var
        gPictureWindow: WindowPtr;
```

```
{----------------> CenterPict <--}

    procedure CenterPict (thePicture: PicHandle; var myRect:
                          Rect);
        var
            windRect, pictureRect: Rect;
    begin
        windRect := myRect;
        pictureRect := thePicture^^.picFrame;
        myRect.top := (windRect.bottom - windRect.top -
                      (pictureRect.bottom - pictureRect.top))
                      div 2 + windRect.top;
        myRect.bottom := myRect.top + (pictureRect.bottom -
                                      pictureRect.top);
        myRect.left := (windRect.right - windRect.left -
                       (pictureRect.right - pictureRect.left))
                       div 2 + windRect.left;
        myRect.right := myRect.left + (pictureRect.right -
                                      pictureRect.left);
    end;


{----------------> DrawMyPicture <--}

    procedure DrawMyPicture (pictureWindow: WindowPtr);
        var
            myRect: Rect;
            thePicture: PicHandle;
    begin
        myRect := pictureWindow^.portRect;

        thePicture := GetPicture(BASE_RES_ID);

        CenterPict(thePicture, myRect);
        DrawPicture(thePicture, myRect);
    end;


{----------------> WindowInit <--}

    procedure WindowInit;
    begin
        gPictureWindow := GetNewWindow(BASE_RES_ID, nil,
                                       WindowPtr(-1));
        ShowWindow(gPictureWindow);
        SetPort(gPictureWindow);
    end;
```

```
{---------------->   ShowPICT   <--}

begin
    WindowInit;
    DrawMyPicture(gPictureWindow);

    while (not Button) do
        begin
        end;
end.
```

Chapter 3: Flying Line.p

```
program FlyingLine;
    const
        NUM_LINES = 50;
        NIL_STRING = '';
        NIL_TITLE = '';
        VISIBLE = TRUE;
        NO_GO_AWAY = FALSE;
        NIL_REF_CON = 0;

    type
        IntPtr = ^INTEGER;

    var
        gLineWindow: WindowPtr;
        gLines: array[1..NUM_LINES] of Rect;
        gDeltaTop, gDeltaBottom: INTEGER;
        gDeltaLeft, gDeltaRight: INTEGER;
        gOldMBarHeight: INTEGER;
        gMBarHeightPtr: IntPtr;


{---------------->   DrawLine   <--}

    procedure DrawLine (i: INTEGER);
    begin
        MoveTo(gLines[i].left, gLines[i].top);
        LineTo(gLines[i].right, gLines[i].bottom);
    end;


{---------------->   RecalcLine   <--}

    procedure RecalcLine (i: INTEGER);
    begin
        gLines[i].top := gLines[i].top + gDeltaTop;
```

```
        if ((gLines[i].top < gLineWindow^.portRect.top) |
            (gLines[i].top > gLineWindow^.portRect.bottom)) then
            gDeltaTop := gDeltaTop * (-1);
        gLines[i].top := gLines[i].top + 2 * gDeltaTop;

        gLines[i].bottom := gLines[i].bottom + gDeltaBottom;
        if ((gLines[i].bottom < gLineWindow^.portRect.top) |
            (gLines[i].bottom > gLineWindow^.portRect.bottom))
            then gDeltaBottom := gDeltaBottom * (-1);
        gLines[i].bottom := gLines[i].bottom + 2 * gDeltaBottom;

        gLines[i].left := gLines[i].left + gDeltaLeft;
        if ((gLines[i].left < gLineWindow^.portRect.left) |
            (gLines[i].left > gLineWindow^.portRect.right)) then
            gDeltaLeft := gDeltaLeft * (-1);
        gLines[i].left := gLines[i].left + 2 * gDeltaLeft;

        gLines[i].right := gLines[i].right + gDeltaRight;
        if ((gLines[i].right < gLineWindow^.portRect.left) |
            (gLines[i].right > gLineWindow^.portRect.right))
            then gDeltaRight := gDeltaRight * (-1);
        gLines[i].right := gLines[i].right + 2 * gDeltaRight;
    end;


{---------------->   MainLoop   <--}

    procedure MainLoop;
        var
            i: INTEGER;

    begin
        while (not Button) do
            begin
                DrawLine(NUM_LINES);
                for i := NUM_LINES downto 2 do
                    gLines[i] := gLines[i - 1];
                RecalcLine(1);
                DrawLine(1);
                gMBarHeightPtr^ := gOldMBarHeight;
            end;
    end;


{---------------->   Randomize   <--}

    function Randomize (range: INTEGER): INTEGER;
        var
            rawResult: LONGINT;

    begin
```

```
        rawResult := Random;
        rawResult := abs(rawResult);

        Randomize := (rawResult * range) div 32768;
    end;


{----------------> RandomRect <--}

    procedure RandomRect (var myRect: Rect;
                          boundingWindow: WindowPtr);
    begin
        myRect.left := Randomize(boundingWindow^.portRect.right -
                            boundingWindow^.portRect.left);
        myRect.right := Randomize(boundingWindow^.portRect.right -
                            boundingWindow^.portRect.left);
        myRect.top := Randomize(boundingWindow^.portRect.bottom -
                            boundingWindow^.portRect.top);
        myRect.bottom := Randomize(boundingWindow^.portRect.bottom
                            - boundingWindow^.portRect.top);
    end;


{----------------> LinesInit <--}

    procedure LinesInit;
        var
            i: INTEGER;

    begin
        gDeltaTop := 3;
        gDeltaBottom := 3;
        gDeltaLeft := 2;
        gDeltaRight := 6;

        HideCursor;
        GetDateTime(randSeed);
        RandomRect(gLines[1], gLineWindow);
        DrawLine(1);

        for i := 2 to NUM_LINES do
            begin
                gLines[i] := gLines[i - 1];
                RecalcLine(i);
                DrawLine(i);
            end;
    end;
```

```
{----------------->   WindowInit   <--}

    procedure WindowInit;
        var
            totalRect, mBarRect: Rect;
            mBarRgn: RgnHandle;

    begin
        gMBarHeightPtr := IntPtr($baa);
        gOldMBarHeight := gMBarHeightPtr^;
        gMBarHeightPtr^ := 0;
        gLineWindow := NewWindow(nil, screenBits.bounds,
                                 NIL_TITLE, VISIBLE, plainDBox,
                                 WindowPtr(-1), NO_GO_AWAY,
                                 NIL_REF_CON);
        SetRect(mBarRect, screenBits.bounds.left,
                screenBits.bounds.top, screenBits.bounds.right,
                screenBits.bounds.top + gOldMBarHeight);
        mBarRgn := NewRgn;
        RectRgn(mBarRgn, mBarRect);
        UnionRgn(gLineWindow^.visRgn, mBarRgn,
                 gLineWindow^.visRgn);
        DisposeRgn(mBarRgn);
        SetPort(gLineWindow);
        FillRect(gLineWindow^.portRect, black);
                { Change black to ltGray, }
        PenMode(patXor);        {   <-- and comment out this line  }
    end;


{----------------->   FlyingLine   <--}

begin
    WindowInit;
    LinesInit;
    MainLoop;
end.
```

Chapter 4: EventTutor.p

```
program EventTutor;
    const
        BASE_RES_ID = 400;
        LEAVE_WHERE_IT_IS = FALSE;
        NORMAL_UPDATES = TRUE;
        SLEEP = 60;
        WNE_TRAP_NUM = $60;
        UNIMPL_TRAP_NUM = $9F;
```

```
            SUSPEND_RESUME_BIT = $0001;
            ACTIVATING = 1;
            RESUMING = 1;
            TEXT_FONT_SIZE = 12;
            DRAG_THRESHOLD = 30;
            MIN_WINDOW_HEIGHT = 50;
            MIN_WINDOW_WIDTH = 50;
            SCROLL_BAR_PIXELS = 15;
            ROWHEIGHT = 15;
            LEFTMARGIN = 10;
            STARTROW = 0;
            HORIZONTAL_OFFSET = 0;

        var
            gPictWindow, gEventWindow: WindowPtr;
            gDone, gWNEImplemented: BOOLEAN;
            gTheEvent: EventRecord;
            gCurRow, gMaxRow: INTEGER;
            gSizeRect: Rect;


{---------------->   CenterPict   <--}

    procedure CenterPict (thePicture: PicHandle; var myRect:
                            Rect);
        var
            windRect, pictureRect: Rect;

    begin
        windRect := myRect;
        pictureRect := thePicture^^.picFrame;
        myRect.top := (windRect.bottom - windRect.top -
                        (pictureRect.bottom - pictureRect.top))
                        div 2 + windRect.top;
        myRect.bottom := myRect.top + (pictureRect.bottom -
                                        pictureRect.top);
        myRect.left := (windRect.right - windRect.left -
                        (pictureRect.right - pictureRect.left))
                        div 2 + windRect.left;
        myRect.right := myRect.left + (pictureRect.right -
                                        pictureRect.left);
    end;


{---------------->   DrawMyPicture   <--}

    procedure DrawMyPicture (drawingWindow: WindowPtr);
        var
            drawingClipRect, myRect: Rect;
            oldPort: GrafPtr;
            tempRgn: RgnHandle;
```

```
        thePicture: PicHandle;
    begin
        GetPort(oldPort);
        SetPort(drawingWindow);
        tempRgn := NewRgn;
        GetClip(tempRgn);
        EraseRect(drawingWindow^.portRect);
        DrawGrowIcon(drawingWindow);

        drawingClipRect := drawingWindow^.portRect;
        drawingClipRect.right := drawingClipRect.right -
            SCROLL_BAR_PIXELS;
        drawingClipRect.bottom := drawingClipRect.bottom -
            SCROLL_BAR_PIXELS;
        myRect := drawingWindow^.portRect;

        thePicture := GetPicture(BASE_RES_ID);
        CenterPict(thePicture, myRect);
        ClipRect(drawingClipRect);
        DrawPicture(thePicture, myRect);

        SetClip(tempRgn);
        DisposeRgn(tempRgn);
        SetPort(oldPort);
    end;



{----------------->   HandleMouseDown   <--}

    procedure HandleMouseDown;
        var
            whichWindow: WindowPtr;
            thePart: INTEGER;
            windSize: LONGINT;
            oldPort: GrafPtr;
    begin
        thePart := FindWindow(gTheEvent.where, whichWindow);
        case thePart of
            inSysWindow:
                SystemClick(gTheEvent, whichWindow);
            inDrag:
                DragWindow(whichWindow, gTheEvent.where,
                        screenBits.bounds);
            inContent:
                if whichWindow <> FrontWindow then
                    SelectWindow(whichWindow);
            inGrow:
                begin
                    windSize := GrowWindow(whichWindow,
                                    gTheEvent.where,
                                    gSizeRect);
```

```
                    if (windSize <> 0) then
                        begin
                            GetPort(oldPort);
                            SetPort(whichWindow);
                            EraseRect(whichWindow^.portRect);
                            SizeWindow(whichWindow,
                                    LoWord(windSize),
                                    HiWord(windSize),
                                    NORMAL_UPDATES);
                            InvalRect(whichWindow^.portRect);
                            SetPort(oldPort);
                        end;
                end;
            inGoAway:
                gDone := TRUE;
            inZoomIn, inZoomOut:
                if TrackBox(whichWindow, gTheEvent.where, thePart)
                        then
                    begin
                        GetPort(oldPort);
                        SetPort(whichWindow);
                        EraseRect(whichWindow^.portRect);
                        ZoomWindow(whichWindow, thePart,
                                LEAVE_WHERE_IT_IS);
                        InvalRect(whichWindow^.portRect);
                        SetPort(oldPort);
                    end;
        end;
    end;
end;


{----------------->  ScrollWindow  <--}

procedure ScrollWindow;
    var
        tempRgn: RgnHandle;
    begin
        tempRgn := NewRgn;
        ScrollRect(gEventWindow^.portRect, HORIZONTAL_OFFSET, -
                ROWHEIGHT, tempRgn);
        DisposeRgn(tempRgn);
    end;


{----------------->  DrawEventString  <--}

procedure DrawEventString (s: Str255);
    begin
        if (gCurRow > gMaxRow) then
            ScrollWindow
```

```
            else
                gCurRow := gCurRow + ROWHEIGHT;

            MoveTo(LEFTMARGIN, gCurRow);
            DrawString(s);
        end;


{--------------->   HandleEvent   <--}

    procedure HandleEvent;
        var
            gotOne: BOOLEAN;
    begin
        if gWNEImplemented then
            gotOne := WaitNextEvent(everyEvent, gTheEvent,
                            SLEEP, nil)
        else
            begin
                SystemTask;
                gotOne := GetNextEvent(everyEvent, gTheEvent);
            end;

        if gotOne then
            case gTheEvent.what of
                nullEvent:
                    begin
        {   DrawEventString('nullEvent');                )
        {   Uncomment the previous line for a burst of flavor!}
                    end;
                mouseDown:
                    begin
                        DrawEventString('mouseDown');
                        HandleMouseDown;
                    end;
                mouseUp:
                    DrawEventString('mouseUp');
                keyDown:
                    DrawEventString('keyDown');
                keyUp:
                    DrawEventString('keyUp');
                autoKey:
                    DrawEventString('autoKey');
                updateEvt:
                    if (WindowPtr(gTheEvent.message) =
                        gPictWindow) then begin
                            DrawEventString('updateEvt: gPictWindow');
```

```
                    BeginUpdate(WindowPtr(gTheEvent.message));
                    DrawMyPicture(WindowPtr(gTheEvent.message));
                    EndUpdate(WindowPtr(gTheEvent.message));
              end
          else
              begin
                  DrawEventString('updateEvt: gEventWindow');
                  BeginUpdate(WindowPtr
                              (gTheEvent.message));
{   We won't handle updates to gEventWindow,      }
{   but we still need to empty the gEventWindow    }
{   Update Region so the Window Manager will stop  }
{   queing UpdateEvts.  We do this with calls to   }
{   BeginUpdate and EndUpdate.                      }
                  EndUpdate(WindowPtr(gTheEvent.message));
              end;
diskEvt:
      DrawEventString('diskEvt');
activateEvt:
      if (WindowPtr(gTheEvent.message) = gPictWindow)
          then begin
                  DrawGrowIcon(WindowPtr(gTheEvent.message));
                  if (BitAnd(gTheEvent.modifiers,
                      activeFlag) = ACTIVATING) then
                      DrawEventString
                          ('activateEvt: activating gPictWindow')
                  else
                      DrawEventString
                          ('activateEvt: deactivating gPictWindow');
              end
          else
              begin
                  if (BitAnd(gTheEvent.modifiers,
                      activeFlag) = ACTIVATING) then
                      DrawEventString
                          ('activateEvt: activating gEventWindow')
                  else
                      DrawEventString
                          ('activateEvt:  deactivating gEventWindow');
              end;
networkEvt:
      DrawEventString('networkEvt');
driverEvt:
      DrawEventString('driverEvt');
```

```
                    app1Evt:
                        DrawEventString('app1Evt');
                    app2Evt:
                        DrawEventString('app2Evt');
                    app3Evt:
                        DrawEventString('app3Evt');
                    app4Evt:
                        if (BitAnd(gTheEvent.message,
                            SUSPEND_RESUME_BIT) = RESUMING) then
                            DrawEventString('Resume event')
                        else
                            DrawEventString('Suspend event');
                end;
        end;


{---------------->   MainLoop   <--}

    procedure MainLoop;
    begin
        gDone := FALSE;
        gWNEImplemented := (NGetTrapAddress(WNE_TRAP_NUM,
                            ToolTrap) <>
                            NGetTrapAddress(UNIMPL_TRAP_NUM,
                            ToolTrap));

        while gDone = FALSE do
            HandleEvent;
    end;


{---------------->   SetUpSizeRect   <--}

    procedure SetUpSizeRect;
    begin
        gSizeRect.top := MIN_WINDOW_HEIGHT;
        gSizeRect.left := MIN_WINDOW_WIDTH;

        gSizeRect.bottom := 32767;
        gSizeRect.right := 32767;
    end;


{---------------->   SetupEventWindow   <--}

    procedure SetupEventWindow;
        var
            eventRect: Rect;
            fontNum: INTEGER;
    begin
```

```
        eventRect := gEventWindow^.portRect;
        gMaxRow := eventRect.bottom - eventRect.top - ROWHEIGHT;
        gCurRow := STARTROW;

        SetPort(gEventWindow);
        GetFNum('monaco', fontNum);
        TextFont(fontNum);
        TextSize(TEXT_FONT_SIZE);
    end;


{----------------->   WindowInit   <--}

    procedure WindowInit;
    begin
        gPictWindow := GetNewWindow(BASE_RES_ID, nil,
                            WindowPtr(-1));
        gEventWindow := GetNewWindow(BASE_RES_ID + 1, nil,
                            WindowPtr(-1));

        SetupEventWindow;

        ShowWindow(gEventWindow);
        ShowWindow(gPictWindow);
    end;


{----------------->   EventTutor   <--}

begin
    WindowInit;
    SetUpSizeRect;

    MainLoop;
end.
```

Chapter 5: Timer.p

```
program Timer;
    const
        BASE_RES_ID = 400;

        PLAIN = [];
        PLAIN_ITEM = 1;
        BOLD_ITEM = 2;
        ITALIC_ITEM = 3;
        UNDERLINE_ITEM = 4;
        OUTLINE_ITEM = 5;
```

```
            SHADOW_ITEM = 6;

            INCLUDE_SECONDS = TRUE;

            ADD_CHECK_MARK = TRUE;
            REMOVE_CHECK_MARK = FALSE;

            SLEEP = 60;
            WNE_TRAP_NUM = $60;
            UNIMPL_TRAP_NUM = $9F;

            QUIT_ITEM = 1;
            ABOUT_ITEM = 1;

            NOT_A_NORMAL_MENU = -1;
            APPLE_MENU_ID = BASE_RES_ID;
            FILE_MENU_ID = BASE_RES_ID + 1;
            FONT_MENU_ID = 100;
            STYLE_MENU_ID = 101;

            CLOCK_LEFT = 12;
            CLOCK_TOP = 25;
            CLOCK_SIZE = 24;

            ABOUT_ALERT = 400;

      var
            gClockWindow: WindowPtr;
            gDone, gWNEImplemented: BOOLEAN;
            gCurrentTime, gOldTime: LONGINT;
            gTheEvent: EventRecord;
            gLastFont: INTEGER;
            gCurrentStyle: Style;


{---------------->   HandleStyleChoice   <--}

   procedure CheckStyles;
      var
            styleMenu: MenuHandle;
   begin
      styleMenu := GetMHandle(STYLE_MENU_ID);
      CheckItem(styleMenu, PLAIN_ITEM, (gCurrentStyle =
                PLAIN));
      CheckItem(styleMenu, BOLD_ITEM, (bold in gCurrentStyle));
      CheckItem(styleMenu, ITALIC_ITEM, (italic in
                gCurrentStyle));
      CheckItem(styleMenu, UNDERLINE_ITEM, (underline in
                gCurrentStyle));
      CheckItem(styleMenu, OUTLINE_ITEM, (outline in
                gCurrentStyle));
```

```
                CheckItem(styleMenu, SHADOW_ITEM, (shadow in
                        gCurrentStyle));
        end;


{----------------->  HandleStyleChoice  <--}

    procedure HandleStyleChoice (theItem: INTEGER);
    begin
        case theItem of
            PLAIN_ITEM:
                gCurrentStyle := PLAIN;
            BOLD_ITEM:
                if bold in gCurrentStyle then
                    gCurrentStyle := gCurrentStyle - [bold]
                else
                    gCurrentStyle := gCurrentStyle + [bold];
            ITALIC_ITEM:
                if italic in gCurrentStyle then
                    gCurrentStyle := gCurrentStyle - [italic]
                else
                    gCurrentStyle := gCurrentStyle + [italic];
            UNDERLINE_ITEM:
                if underline in gCurrentStyle then
                    gCurrentStyle := gCurrentStyle - [underline]
                else
                    gCurrentStyle := gCurrentStyle + [underline];
            OUTLINE_ITEM:
                if outline in gCurrentStyle then
                    gCurrentStyle := gCurrentStyle - [outline]
                else
                    gCurrentStyle := gCurrentStyle + [outline];
            SHADOW_ITEM:
                if shadow in gCurrentStyle then
                    gCurrentStyle := gCurrentStyle - [shadow]
                else
                    gCurrentStyle := gCurrentStyle + [shadow];
        end;
        CheckStyles;
        TextFace(gCurrentStyle);
    end;


{----------------->  HandleFontChoice  <--}

    procedure HandleFontChoice (theItem: INTEGER);
        var
            fontNumber: INTEGER;
            fontName: Str255;
            fontMenu: MenuHandle;
```

```
    begin
        fontMenu := GetMHandle(FONT_MENU_ID);
        CheckItem(fontMenu, gLastFont, REMOVE_CHECK_MARK);
        CheckItem(fontMenu, theItem, ADD_CHECK_MARK);
        gLastFont := theItem;
        GetItem(fontMenu, theItem, fontName);
        GetFNum(fontName, fontNumber);
        TextFont(fontNumber);
    end;


{---------------->   HandleFileChoice   <--}

    procedure HandleFileChoice (theItem: INTEGER);
    begin
        case theItem of
            QUIT_ITEM:
                gDone := TRUE;
        end;
    end;


{---------------->   HandleAppleChoice   <--}

    procedure HandleAppleChoice (theItem: INTEGER);
        var
            accName: Str255;
            accNumber, itemNumber, dummy: INTEGER;
            appleMenu: MenuHandle;
    begin
        case theItem of
            ABOUT_ITEM:
                dummy := NoteAlert(ABOUT_ALERT, nil);
            otherwise
                begin
                    appleMenu := GetMHandle(APPLE_MENU_ID);
                    GetItem(appleMenu, theItem, accName);
                    accNumber := OpenDeskAcc(accName);
                end;
        end;
    end;


{---------------->   HandleMenuChoice   <--}

    procedure HandleMenuChoice (menuChoice: LONGINT);
        var
            theMenu, theItem: INTEGER;
    begin
        if menuChoice <> 0 then
            begin
```

```
                theMenu := HiWord(menuChoice);
                theItem := LoWord(menuChoice);

                case theMenu of
                    APPLE_MENU_ID:
                        HandleAppleChoice(theItem);
                    FILE_MENU_ID:
                        HandleFileChoice(theItem);
                    FONT_MENU_ID:
                        HandleFontChoice(theItem);
                    STYLE_MENU_ID:
                        HandleStyleChoice(theItem);
                end;

                HiliteMenu(0);
            end;
    end;


{----------------> HandleMouseDown <--}

    procedure HandleMouseDown;
        var
            whichWindow: WindowPtr;
            thePart: INTEGER;
            menuChoice, windSize: LONGINT;
    begin
        thePart := FindWindow(gTheEvent.where, whichWindow);
        case thePart of
            inMenuBar:
                begin
                    menuChoice := MenuSelect(gTheEvent.where);
                    HandleMenuChoice(menuChoice);
                end;
            inSysWindow:
                SystemClick(gTheEvent, whichWindow);
            inDrag:
                DragWindow(whichWindow, gTheEvent.where,
                            screenBits.bounds);
            inGoAway:
                gDone := TRUE;
        end;
    end;


{----------------> DrawClock <--}

    procedure DrawClock (theWindow: WindowPtr);
        var
            myTimeString: Str255;
    begin
```

```
              IUTimeString(gCurrentTime, INCLUDE_SECONDS,
                         myTimeString);
              EraseRect(theWindow^.portRect);
              MoveTo(CLOCK_LEFT, CLOCK_TOP);
              DrawString(myTimeString);
              gOldTime := gCurrentTime;
       end;


{----------------->  HandleNull  <--}

       procedure HandleNull;
       begin
              GetDateTime(gCurrentTime);
              if gCurrentTime <> gOldTime then
                     DrawClock(gClockWindow);
       end;


{----------------->  HandleEvent  <--}

       procedure HandleEvent;
           var
                  theChar: CHAR;
                  dummy: BOOLEAN;
       begin
              if gWNEImplemented then
                  dummy := WaitNextEvent(everyEvent, gTheEvent,
                                         SLEEP, nil)
              else
                  begin
                     SystemTask;
                     dummy := GetNextEvent(everyEvent, gTheEvent);
                  end;

              case gTheEvent.what of
                  nullEvent:
                     HandleNull;
                  mouseDown:
                     HandleMouseDown;
                  keyDown, autoKey:
                     begin
                         theChar := CHR(BitAnd(gTheEvent.message,
                                       charCodeMask));
                         if (BitAnd(gTheEvent.modifiers, cmdKey) <> 0)
                             then
                                HandleMenuChoice(MenuKey(theChar));
                     end;
                  updateEvt:
                     begin
```

```
                        BeginUpdate(WindowPtr(gTheEvent.message));
                        EndUpdate(WindowPtr(gTheEvent.message));
                end;
        end;
    end;


{---------------->   MainLoop   <--}

    procedure MainLoop;
    begin
        gDone := FALSE;
        gWNEImplemented := (NGetTrapAddress(WNE_TRAP_NUM,
                            ToolTrap) <>
                            NGetTrapAddress(UNIMPL_TRAP_NUM,
                            ToolTrap));
        while (gDone = FALSE) do
            HandleEvent;
    end;


{---------------->   MenuBarInit   <--}

    procedure MenuBarInit;
        var
            myMenuBar: Handle;
            aMenu: MenuHandle;
    begin
        myMenuBar := GetNewMBar(BASE_RES_ID);
        SetMenuBar(myMenuBar);
        DisposHandle(myMenuBar);

        aMenu := GetMHandle(APPLE_MENU_ID);
        AddResMenu(aMenu, 'DRVR');

        aMenu := GetMenu(FONT_MENU_ID);
        InsertMenu(aMenu, NOT_A_NORMAL_MENU);
        AddResMenu(aMenu, 'FONT');

        aMenu := GetMenu(STYLE_MENU_ID);
        InsertMenu(aMenu, NOT_A_NORMAL_MENU);
        CheckItem(aMenu, PLAIN_ITEM, TRUE);

        DrawMenuBar;
        gLastFont := 1;
        gCurrentStyle := PLAIN;
        HandleFontChoice(gLastFont);
    end;
```

```
{----------------->  WindowInit  <--}

    procedure WindowInit;
    begin
        gClockWindow := GetNewWindow(BASE_RES_ID, nil,
                                     WindowPtr(-1));
        SetPort(gClockWindow);
        ShowWindow(gClockWindow);

        TextSize(CLOCK_SIZE);
    end;


{----------------->  Timer  <--}

begin
    WindowInit;
    MenuBarInit;

    MainLoop;
end.
```

Chapter 5: Zinger.p

```
program Zinger;
    const
        BASE_RES_ID = 400;
        SLEEP = 60;
        DRAG_THRESHOLD = 30;
        WNE_TRAP_NUM = $60;
        UNIMPL_TRAP_NUM = $9F;
        POPUP_MENU_ID = BASE_RES_ID;
        NOT_A_NORMAL_MENU = -1;
        POPUP_LEFT = 100;
        POPUP_TOP = 35;
        POPUP_RIGHT = 125;
        POPUP_BOTTOM = 52;
        SHADOW_PIXELS = 1;
        RIGHT_MARGIN = 5;
        BOTTOM_MARGIN = 4;
        LEFT_MARGIN = 5;
        PIXEL_FOR_TOP_LINE = 1;

    var
        gDone, gWNEImplemented: BOOLEAN;
        gPopUpItem, gPopUpLabelWidth: INTEGER;
        gPopUpMenu: MenuHandle;
        gTheEvent: EventRecord;
```

```
        gPopUpRect, gLabelRect, gDragRect: Rect;
        gPopUpLabelH: StringHandle;


{----------------->   DrawPopUpNumber   <--}

    procedure DrawPopUpNumber;
        var
            menuItem: Str255;
            itemLeftMargin: INTEGER;
    begin
        GetItem(gPopUpMenu, gPopUpItem, menuItem);
        itemLeftMargin := (gPopUpRect.right - gPopUpRect.left -
                            StringWidth(menuItem)) div 2;
        MoveTo(gPopUpRect.left + itemLeftMargin,
                gPopUpRect.bottom - BOTTOM_MARGIN);
        DrawString(menuItem);
    end;


{----------------->   DrawPopUp   <--}

    procedure DrawPopUp;
    begin
        SetRect(gPopUpRect, POPUP_LEFT, POPUP_TOP, POPUP_RIGHT,
                POPUP_BOTTOM);
        FrameRect(gPopUpRect);

        MoveTo(gPopUpRect.left + SHADOW_PIXELS,
                gPopUpRect.bottom);
        LineTo(gPopUpRect.right, gPopUpRect.bottom);
        LineTo(gPopUpRect.right, gPopUpRect.top + SHADOW_PIXELS);

        MoveTo(gPopUpRect.left - gPopUpLabelWidth - RIGHT_MARGIN,
            gPopUpRect.bottom - BOTTOM_MARGIN);
        HLock(Handle(gPopUpLabelH));
        DrawString(gPopUpLabelH^^);
        HUnlock(Handle(gPopUpLabelH));

        gLabelRect.top := gPopUpRect.top + PIXEL_FOR_TOP_LINE;
        gLabelRect.left := gPopUpRect.left - gPopUpLabelWidth -
            LEFT_MARGIN - RIGHT_MARGIN;
        gLabelRect.right := gPopUpRect.left;
        gLabelRect.bottom := gPopUpRect.bottom;

        DrawPopUpNumber;
    end;
```

```
{----------------->   HandleMouseDown   <--}

    procedure HandleMouseDown;
        var
            whichWindow: WindowPtr;
            thePart, i: INTEGER;
            theChoice: LONGINT;
            myPoint, popUpUpperLeft: Point;
    begin
        thePart := FindWindow(gTheEvent.where, whichWindow);
        case thePart of
            inContent:
                begin
                    myPoint := gTheEvent.where;
                    GlobalToLocal(myPoint);
                    if PtInRect(myPoint, gPopUpRect) then
                        begin
                            InvertRect(gLabelRect);
                            popUpUpperLeft.v := gPopUpRect.top +
                                PIXEL_FOR_TOP_LINE;
                            popUpUpperLeft.h := gPopUpRect.left;
                            LocalToGlobal(popUpUpperLeft);
                            theChoice := PopUpMenuSelect
                                (gPopUpMenu,
                                popUpUpperLeft.v, popUpUpperLeft.h,
                                gPopUpItem);
                            InvertRect(gLabelRect);
                            if LoWord(theChoice) > 0 then
                                begin
                                    gPopUpItem := LoWord(theChoice);
                                    DrawPopUpNumber;
                                    for i := 0 to gPopUpItem - 1 do
                                        SysBeep(20);
                                end;
                        end;
                end;
            inSysWindow:
                SystemClick(gTheEvent, whichWindow);
            inDrag:
                DragWindow(whichWindow, gTheEvent.where,
                        screenBits.bounds);
            inGoAway:
                gDone := TRUE;
        end;
    end;
```

```
{--------------->    HandleEvent    <--}

    procedure HandleEvent;
        var
            dummy: BOOLEAN;
    begin
        if gWNEImplemented then
            dummy := WaitNextEvent(everyEvent, gTheEvent,
                                SLEEP, nil)
        else
            begin
                SystemTask;
                dummy := GetNextEvent(everyEvent, gTheEvent);
            end;

        case gTheEvent.what of
            mouseDown:
                HandleMouseDown;
            updateEvt:
                begin
                    BeginUpdate(WindowPtr(gTheEvent.message));
                    DrawPopUp;
                    EndUpdate(WindowPtr(gTheEvent.message));
                end;
        end;
    end;


{--------------->    MainLoop    <--}

    procedure MainLoop;
    begin
        gDone := FALSE;
        gWNEImplemented := (NGetTrapAddress(WNE_TRAP_NUM,
                            ToolTrap) <>
                            NGetTrapAddress(UNIMPL_TRAP_NUM,
                            ToolTrap));
        while gDone = FALSE do
            HandleEvent;
    end;


{--------------->    MenuBarInit    <--}

    procedure MenuBarInit;
    begin
        gPopUpMenu := GetMenu(POPUP_MENU_ID);
        InsertMenu(gPopUpMenu, NOT_A_NORMAL_MENU);
        gPopUpLabelH := GetString(BASE_RES_ID);
        HLock(Handle(gPopUpLabelH));
        gPopUpLabelWidth := StringWidth(gPopUpLabelH^^);
```

```
            HUnlock(Handle(gPopUpLabelH));
            gPopUpItem := 1;
        end;


{---------------->   WindowInit   <--}

    procedure WindowInit;
        var
            popUpWindow: WindowPtr;
    begin
        popUpWindow := GetNewWindow(BASE_RES_ID, nil, WindowPtr
                                    (-1));
        SetPort(popUpWindow);
        ShowWindow(popUpWindow);

        TextFont(systemFont);
        TextMode(srcCopy);
    end;


{---------------->   Zinger   <--}

begin
    WindowInit;
    MenuBarInit;
    DrawPopUp;

    MainLoop;
end.
```

Chapter 6: Reminder.p

```
program Reminder;
    uses
        Notification;

    const
        BASE_RES_ID = 400;
        ABOUT_ALERT = 401;
        BAD_SYS_ALERT = 402;

        SLEEP = 60;

        SAVE_BUTTON = 1;
        CANCEL_BUTTON = 2;
        TIME_FIELD = 4;
        S_OR_M_FIELD = 5;
```

```
            SOUND_ON_BOX = 6;
            ICON_ON_BOX = 7;
            ALERT_ON_BOX = 8;
            SECS_RADIO = 10;
            MINS_RADIO = 11;

            DEFAULT_SECS_ID = 401;
            DEFAULT_MINS_ID = 402;

            ON = 1;
            OFF = 0;

            SECONDS_PER_MINUTE = 60;

            TOP = 25;
            LEFT = 12;

            MARK_APPLICATION = 1;

            APPLE_MENU_ID = BASE_RES_ID;
            FILE_MENU_ID = BASE_RES_ID + 1;
            ABOUT_ITEM = 1;

            CHANGE_ITEM = 1;
            START_STOP_ITEM = 2;
            KILL_ITEM = 3;
            QUIT_ITEM = 4;

            SYS_VERSION = 2;

    type
        settings = record
                timeString: Str255;
                sound, icon, alert, secsRadio, minsRadio:
INTEGER;
            end;

    var
        gSettingsDialog: DialogPtr;
        gDone, gCounting, gNotify_set: BOOLEAN;
        gSeconds_or_minutes: (seconds, minutes);
        gNotifyStrH, gDefaultSecsH, gDefaultMinsH: StringHandle;
        gMyNMRec: NMRec;
        gTheEvent: EventRecord;
        savedSettings: settings;


    procedure HandleEvent;
    forward;
```

```
{----------------> SetNotification <--}

procedure SetNotification;
    var
        itemType: INTEGER;
        itemRect: Rect;
        itemHandle: Handle;
        dummy: OSErr;
        fileMenu: MenuHandle;
begin
    if gNotify_set then
        begin
            dummy := NMRemove(QElemPtr(@gMyNMRec));
            HUnlock(Handle(gNotifyStrH));
        end;

    GetDItem(gSettingsDialog, ICON_ON_BOX, itemType,
            itemHandle, itemRect);
    if GetCtlValue(ControlHandle(itemHandle)) = ON then
        gMyNMRec.nmSIcon := GetResource('SICN',
                                        BASE_RES_ID)
    else
        gMyNMRec.nmSIcon := nil;

    GetDItem(gSettingsDialog, SOUND_ON_BOX, itemType,
            itemHandle, itemRect);
    if GetCtlValue(ControlHandle(itemHandle)) = ON then
        gMyNMRec.nmSound := GetResource('snd ',
                                        BASE_RES_ID)
    else
        gMyNMRec.nmSound := nil;

    GetDItem(gSettingsDialog, ALERT_ON_BOX, itemType,
            itemHandle, itemRect);
    if GetCtlValue(ControlHandle(itemHandle)) = ON then
        begin
            MoveHHi(Handle(gNotifyStrH));
            HLock(Handle(gNotifyStrH));
            gMyNMRec.nmStr := gNotifyStrH^;
        end
    else
        gMyNMRec.nmStr := nil;

    dummy := NMInstall(QElemPtr(@gMyNMRec));
    fileMenu := GetMHandle(FILE_MENU_ID);
    EnableItem(fileMenu, KILL_ITEM);
    gNotify_set := TRUE;
end;
```

```
{---------------->   CountDown   <--}

    procedure CountDown (numSecs: LONGINT);
        var
            myTime, oldTime, difTime: LONGINT;
            myTimeString: Str255;
            countDownWindow: WindowPtr;
    begin
        countDownWindow := GetNewWindow(BASE_RES_ID, nil,
                                        WindowPtr(-1));
        SetPort(countDownWindow);
        ShowWindow(countDownWindow);
        TextFace([bold]);
        TextSize(24);

        GetDateTime(myTime);
        oldTime := myTime;

        if gSeconds_or_minutes = minutes then
            numSecs := numSecs * SECONDS_PER_MINUTE;

        gCounting := TRUE;

        while (numSecs > 0) and gCounting do
            begin
                HandleEvent;
                if gCounting then
                    begin
                        MoveTo(LEFT, TOP);
                        GetDateTime(myTime);
                        if myTime <> oldTime then
                            begin
                                difTime := myTime - oldTime;
                                numSecs := numSecs - difTime;
                                oldTime := myTime;
                                NumToString(numSecs,
                                        myTimeString);
                                EraseRect(countDownWindow^.
                                        portRect);
                                DrawString(myTimeString);
                            end;
                    end;
            end;

        if gCounting then
            SetNotification;

        gCounting := FALSE;

        DisposeWindow(countDownWindow);
    end;
```

```
{----------------->   RestoreSettings   <--}

    procedure RestoreSettings;
        var
            itemType: INTEGER;
            itemRect: Rect;
            itemHandle: Handle;
    begin
        GetDItem(gSettingsDialog, TIME_FIELD, itemType,
                itemHandle, itemRect);
        SetIText(itemHandle, savedSettings.timeString);
        GetDItem(gSettingsDialog, SOUND_ON_BOX, itemType,
                itemHandle, itemRect);
        SetCtlValue(ControlHandle(itemHandle),
                savedSettings.sound);
        GetDItem(gSettingsDialog, ICON_ON_BOX, itemType,
                itemHandle, itemRect);
        SetCtlValue(ControlHandle(itemHandle),
                savedSettings.icon);
        GetDItem(gSettingsDialog, ALERT_ON_BOX, itemType,
                itemHandle, itemRect);
        SetCtlValue(ControlHandle(itemHandle),
                savedSettings.alert);
        GetDItem(gSettingsDialog, SECS_RADIO, itemType,
                itemHandle, itemRect);
        SetCtlValue(ControlHandle(itemHandle),
                savedSettings.secsRadio);
        GetDItem(gSettingsDialog, MINS_RADIO, itemType,
                itemHandle, itemRect);
        SetCtlValue(ControlHandle(itemHandle),
                savedSettings.minsRadio);

        if savedSettings.secsRadio = ON then
            begin
                GetDItem(gSettingsDialog, S_OR_M_FIELD, itemType,
                        itemHandle, itemRect);
                SetIText(itemHandle, 'seconds');
            end
        else
            begin
                GetDItem(gSettingsDialog, S_OR_M_FIELD, itemType,
                        itemHandle, itemRect);
                SetIText(itemHandle, 'minutes');
            end;
    end;


{----------------->   SaveSettings   <--}

    procedure SaveSettings;
        var
            itemType: INTEGER;
```

```
            itemRect: Rect;
            itemHandle: Handle;
    begin
        GetDItem(gSettingsDialog, TIME_FIELD, itemType,
                itemHandle, itemRect);
        GetIText(itemHandle, savedSettings.timeString);
        GetDItem(gSettingsDialog, SOUND_ON_BOX, itemType,
                itemHandle, itemRect);
        savedSettings.sound :=
            GetCtlValue(ControlHandle(itemHandle));
        GetDItem(gSettingsDialog, ICON_ON_BOX, itemType,
                itemHandle, itemRect);
        savedSettings.icon :=
            GetCtlValue(ControlHandle(itemHandle));
        GetDItem(gSettingsDialog, ALERT_ON_BOX, itemType,
                itemHandle, itemRect);
        savedSettings.alert :=
            GetCtlValue(ControlHandle(itemHandle));
        GetDItem(gSettingsDialog, SECS_RADIO, itemType,
                itemHandle, itemRect);
        savedSettings.secsRadio :=
            GetCtlValue(ControlHandle(itemHandle));
        GetDItem(gSettingsDialog, MINS_RADIO, itemType,
                itemHandle, itemRect);
        savedSettings.minsRadio :=
            GetCtlValue(ControlHandle(itemHandle));
    end;


{----------------->   HandleDialog   <--}

    procedure HandleDialog;
        var
            dialogDone: BOOLEAN;
            itemHit, itemType: INTEGER;
            alarmDelay: LONGINT;
            delayString: Str255;
            itemRect: Rect;
            itemHandle: Handle;
    begin
        ShowWindow(gSettingsDialog);
        SaveSettings;

        dialogDone := FALSE;
        while dialogDone = FALSE do
            begin
                ModalDialog(nil, itemHit);
                case itemHit of
                    SAVE_BUTTON:
                        begin
                            HideWindow(gSettingsDialog);
                            dialogDone := TRUE;
```

```
                            end;
                    CANCEL_BUTTON:
                        begin
                            HideWindow(gSettingsDialog);
                            RestoreSettings;
                            dialogDone := TRUE;
                        end;
                    SOUND_ON_BOX:
                        begin
                            GetDItem(gSettingsDialog,
                                    SOUND_ON_BOX, itemType,
                                    itemHandle, itemRect);
                            if GetCtlValue(ControlHandle
                                        (itemHandle)) = ON then
                                SetCtlValue(ControlHandle
                                            (itemHandle), OFF)
                            else
                                SetCtlValue(ControlHandle
                                            (itemHandle), ON);
                        end;
                    ICON_ON_BOX:
                        begin
                            GetDItem(gSettingsDialog,
                                    ICON_ON_BOX, itemType,
                                    itemHandle, itemRect);
                            if GetCtlValue(ControlHandle
                                        (itemHandle)) = ON then
                                SetCtlValue(ControlHandle
                                            (itemHandle), OFF)
                            else
                                SetCtlValue(ControlHandle
                                            (itemHandle), ON);
                        end;
                    ALERT_ON_BOX:
                        begin
                            GetDItem(gSettingsDialog,
                                    ALERT_ON_BOX, itemType,
                                    itemHandle, itemRect);
                            if GetCtlValue(ControlHandle
                                        (itemHandle)) = ON then
                                SetCtlValue(ControlHandle
                                            (itemHandle), OFF)
                            else
                                SetCtlValue(ControlHandle
                                            (itemHandle), ON);
                        end;
                    SECS_RADIO:
                        begin
                            gSeconds_or_minutes := seconds;
                            GetDItem(gSettingsDialog,
                                    MINS_RADIO, itemType,
                                    itemHandle, itemRect);
```

```
                                    SetCtlValue(ControlHandle
                                            (itemHandle), OFF);
                                    GetDItem(gSettingsDialog,
                                            SECS_RADIO, itemType,
                                            itemHandle, itemRect);
                                    SetCtlValue(ControlHandle
                                            (itemHandle), ON);
                                    GetDItem(gSettingsDialog,
                                            S_OR_M_FIELD, itemType,
                                            itemHandle, itemRect);
                                    SetIText(itemHandle, 'seconds');
                                    GetDItem(gSettingsDialog,
                                            TIME_FIELD, itemType,
                                            itemHandle, itemRect);
                                    SetIText(itemHandle, gDefaultSecsH^^);
                                end;
                        MINS_RADIO:
                                begin
                                    gSeconds_or_minutes := minutes;
                                    GetDItem(gSettingsDialog,
                                            SECS_RADIO, itemType,
                                            itemHandle, itemRect);
                                    SetCtlValue(ControlHandle
                                            (itemHandle), OFF);
                                    GetDItem(gSettingsDialog,
                                            MINS_RADIO, itemType,
                                            itemHandle, itemRect);
                                    SetCtlValue(ControlHandle
                                            (itemHandle), ON);
                                    GetDItem(gSettingsDialog,
                                            S_OR_M_FIELD, itemType,
                                            itemHandle, itemRect);
                                    SetIText(itemHandle, 'minutes');
                                    GetDItem(gSettingsDialog,
                                            TIME_FIELD, itemType,
                                            itemHandle, itemRect);
                                    SetIText(itemHandle, gDefaultMinsH^^);
                                end;
                    end;
                end;
        end;


{----------------->   HandleFileChoice   <--}

    procedure HandleFileChoice (theItem: INTEGER);
        var
            timeString: Str255;
            countDownTime: LONGINT;
            itemType: INTEGER;
            itemRect: Rect;
```

```
            itemHandle: Handle;
            dummy: OSErr;
            fileMenu: MenuHandle;
    begin
        fileMenu := GetMHandle(FILE_MENU_ID);
        case theItem of
            CHANGE_ITEM:
                HandleDialog;
            START_STOP_ITEM:
                if gCounting then
                    begin
                        gCounting := FALSE;
                        SetItem(fileMenu, theItem, 'Start
                                Countdown');
                    end
                else
                    begin
                        HiliteMenu(0);
                        GetDItem(gSettingsDialog, TIME_FIELD,
                                itemType, itemHandle, itemRect);
                        GetIText(itemHandle, timeString);
                        StringToNum(timeString, countDownTime);

                        DisableItem(fileMenu, CHANGE_ITEM);
                        SetItem(fileMenu, theItem, 'Stop
                                Countdown');
                        CountDown(countDownTime);
                        EnableItem(fileMenu, CHANGE_ITEM);
                        SetItem(fileMenu, theItem, 'Start
                                Countdown');
                    end;
            KILL_ITEM:
                begin
                    dummy := NMRemove(QElemPtr(@gMyNMRec));
                    HUnlock(Handle(gNotifyStrH));
                    DisableItem(fileMenu, KILL_ITEM);
                    gNotify_set := FALSE;
                end;
            QUIT_ITEM:
                begin
                    gCounting := FALSE;
                    gDone := TRUE;
                end;
        end;
    end;


{--------------->  HandleAppleChoice  <--}

    procedure HandleAppleChoice (theItem: INTEGER);
        var
            accName: Str255;
            accNumber, itemNumber, dummy: INTEGER;
```

```
                  appleMenu: MenuHandle;
        begin
            case theItem of
                ABOUT_ITEM:
                    dummy := NoteAlert(ABOUT_ALERT, nil);
                otherwise
                    begin
                        appleMenu := GetMHandle(APPLE_MENU_ID);
                        GetItem(appleMenu, theItem, accName);
                        accNumber := OpenDeskAcc(accName);
                    end;
            end;
        end;


{----------------->   HandleMenuChoice   <--}

    procedure HandleMenuChoice (menuChoice: LONGINT);
        var
            theMenu, theItem: INTEGER;
        begin
            if menuChoice <> 0 then
                begin
                    theMenu := HiWord(menuChoice);
                    theItem := LoWord(menuChoice);

                    case theMenu of
                        APPLE_MENU_ID:
                            HandleAppleChoice(theItem);
                        FILE_MENU_ID:
                            HandleFileChoice(theItem);
                    end;

                    HiliteMenu(0);
                end;
        end;


{----------------->   HandleMouseDown   <--}

    procedure HandleMouseDown;
        var
            whichWindow: WindowPtr;
            thePart: INTEGER;
            menuChoice, windSize: LONGINT;
        begin
            thePart := FindWindow(gTheEvent.where, whichWindow);
            case thePart of
                inMenuBar:
                    begin
                        menuChoice := MenuSelect(gTheEvent.where);
```

```
                            HandleMenuChoice(menuChoice);
                    end;
                inSysWindow:
                    SystemClick(gTheEvent, whichWindow);
                inDrag:
                    DragWindow(whichWindow, gTheEvent.where,
                                screenBits.bounds);
                inGoAway:
                    gDone := TRUE;
            end;
        end;


{---------------->   HandleEvent   <--}

    procedure HandleEvent;
        var
            theChar: CHAR;
            dummy: BOOLEAN;
    begin
        dummy := WaitNextEvent(everyEvent, gTheEvent, SLEEP, nil);

        case gTheEvent.what of
            mouseDown:
                HandleMouseDown;
            keyDown, autoKey:
                begin
                    theChar := CHR(BitAnd(gTheEvent.message,
                                    charCodeMask));
                    if (BitAnd(gTheEvent.modifiers, cmdKey) <> 0)
                        then
                            HandleMenuChoice(MenuKey(theChar));
                end;
        end;
    end;


{---------------->   MainLoop   <--}

    procedure MainLoop;
    begin
        gDone := FALSE;
        gCounting := FALSE;
        gNotify_set := FALSE;

        while gDone = FALSE do
            HandleEvent;
    end;
```

```
{---------------->    NotifyInit   <--}

    procedure NotifyInit;
    begin
        gNotifyStrH := GetString(BASE_RES_ID);
        gMyNMRec.qType := nmType;
        gMyNMRec.nmMark := MARK_APPLICATION;
        gMyNMRec.nmResp := nil;
    end;


{---------------->    MenuBarInit   <--}

    procedure MenuBarInit;
        var
            myMenuBar: Handle;
            aMenu: MenuHandle;
    begin
        myMenuBar := GetNewMBar(BASE_RES_ID);
        SetMenuBar(myMenuBar);
        DisposHandle(myMenuBar);

        aMenu := GetMHandle(APPLE_MENU_ID);
        AddResMenu(aMenu, 'DRVR');

        DrawMenuBar;
    end;


{---------------->    DialogInit   <--}

    procedure DialogInit;
        var
            itemType: INTEGER;
            itemRect: Rect;
            itemHandle: Handle;
    begin
        gDefaultSecsH := GetString(DEFAULT_SECS_ID);
        gDefaultMinsH := GetString(DEFAULT_MINS_ID);

        gSettingsDialog := GetNewDialog(BASE_RES_ID, nil,
                                        WindowPtr(-1));
        GetDItem(gSettingsDialog, SECS_RADIO, itemType,
                 itemHandle, itemRect);
        SetCtlValue(ControlHandle(itemHandle), ON);
        GetDItem(gSettingsDialog, SOUND_ON_BOX, itemType,
                 itemHandle, itemRect);
        SetCtlValue(ControlHandle(itemHandle), ON);
        GetDItem(gSettingsDialog, ICON_ON_BOX, itemType,
                 itemHandle, itemRect);
        SetCtlValue(ControlHandle(itemHandle), ON);
```

```
        GetDItem(gSettingsDialog, ALERT_ON_BOX, itemType,
            itemHandle, itemRect);
        SetCtlValue(ControlHandle(itemHandle), ON);

        gSeconds_or_minutes := seconds;
    end;


{---------------->  Sys6OrLater  <--}

    function Sys6OrLater: BOOLEAN;
        var
            status: OSErr;
            SysEnvData: SysEnvRec;
            dummy: INTEGER;
    begin
        status := SysEnvirons(SYS_VERSION, SysEnvData);
        if (status <> noErr) or (SysEnvData.systemVersion
            < $0600) then
            begin
                dummy := StopAlert(BAD_SYS_ALERT, nil);
                Sys6OrLater := FALSE;
            end
        else
            Sys6OrLater := TRUE;
    end;


{---------------->  Reminder  <--}

begin
    if Sys6OrLater then
        begin
            DialogInit;
            MenuBarInit;
            NotifyInit;

            MainLoop;
        end;
end.
```

Chapter 7: WindowMaker.p

```
program WindowMaker;
    const
        BASE_RES_ID = 400;

        APPLE_MENU_ID = 400;
```

```
          FILE_MENU_ID = 401;
          EDIT_MENU_ID = 402;

          ABOUT_ITEM = 1;
          ABOUT_ALERT = 400;
          ERROR_ALERT_ID = 401;

          NO_MBAR = BASE_RES_ID;
          NO_MENU = BASE_RES_ID + 1;
          NO_PICTURE = BASE_RES_ID + 2;
          NO_WIND = BASE_RES_ID + 3;

          NEW_ITEM = 1;
          CLOSE_ITEM = 2;
          QUIT_ITEM = 3;

          UNDO_ITEM = 1;
          CUT_ITEM = 3;
          COPY_ITEM = 4;
          PASTE_ITEM = 5;
          CLEAR_ITEM = 6;

          EDGE_THRESHOLD = 30;

          WINDOW_HOME_LEFT = 5;
          WINDOW_HOME_TOP = 45;
          NEW_WINDOW_OFFSET = 20;

          MIN_SLEEP = 60;

          LEAVE_WHERE_IT_IS = FALSE;

          WNE_TRAP_NUM = $60;
          UNIMPL_TRAP_NUM = $9F;

          NIL_STRING = '';
          HOPELESSLY_FATAL_ERROR = 'Game over, man!';

     var
          gDone, gWNEImplemented: Boolean;
          gTheEvent: EventRecord;
          gNewWindowLeft, gNewWindowTop: INTEGER;


{--------------->  ErrorHandler  <--}

     procedure ErrorHandler (stringNum: INTEGER);
          var
              errorStringH: StringHandle;
              dummy: INTEGER;
     begin
```

```
        errorStringH := GetString(stringNum);
        if errorStringH = nil then
            ParamText(HOPELESSLY_FATAL_ERROR, NIL_STRING,
                    NIL_STRING, NIL_STRING)
        else
            ParamText(errorStringH^^, NIL_STRING, NIL_STRING,
                    NIL_STRING);

        dummy := StopAlert(ERROR_ALERT_ID, nil);
        ExitToShell;
    end;


{----------------->   CenterPict   <--}

    procedure CenterPict (thePicture: PicHandle; var myRect:
                        Rect);
        var
            windRect, pictureRect: Rect;
    begin
        windRect := myRect;
        pictureRect := thePicture^^.picFrame;
        myRect.top := (windRect.bottom - windRect.top -
                    (pictureRect.bottom - pictureRect.top)) div
                    2 + windRect.top;
        myRect.bottom := myRect.top + (pictureRect.bottom -
                                    pictureRect.top);
        myRect.left := (windRect.right - windRect.left -
                    (pictureRect.right - pictureRect.left))
                    div 2 + windRect.left;
        myRect.right := myRect.left + (pictureRect.right -
                                    pictureRect.left);
    end;


{----------------->   DrawMyPicture   <--}

    procedure DrawMyPicture (pictureWindow: WindowPtr);
        var
            myRect: Rect;
            thePicture: PicHandle;
    begin
        myRect := pictureWindow^.portRect;

        thePicture := GetPicture(BASE_RES_ID);
        if thePicture = nil then
            ErrorHandler(NO_PICTURE);

        CenterPict(thePicture, myRect);
        SetPort(pictureWindow);
        DrawPicture(thePicture, myRect);
    end;
```

```
{----------------->   CreateWindow   <--}

    procedure CreateWindow;
        var
            theNewestWindow: WindowPtr;
    begin
        theNewestWindow := GetNewWindow(BASE_RES_ID, nil,
                                    WindowPtr(-1));
        if theNewestWindow = nil then
            ErrorHandler(NO_WIND);

        if ((screenBits.bounds.right - gNewWindowLeft) <
            EDGE_THRESHOLD) or ((screenBits.bounds.bottom -
            gNewWindowTop) < EDGE_THRESHOLD) then
            begin
                gNewWindowLeft := WINDOW_HOME_LEFT;
                gNewWindowTop := WINDOW_HOME_TOP;
            end;

        MoveWindow(theNewestWindow, gNewWindowLeft, gNewWindowTop,
                LEAVE_WHERE_IT_IS);
        gNewWindowLeft := gNewWindowLeft + NEW_WINDOW_OFFSET;
        gNewWindowTop := gNewWindowTop + NEW_WINDOW_OFFSET;
        ShowWindow(theNewestWindow);
    end;


{----------------->   HandleEditChoice   <--}

    procedure HandleEditChoice (theItem: INTEGER);
        var
            dummy: Boolean;
    begin
        dummy := SystemEdit(theItem - 1);
    end;


{----------------->   HandleFileChoice   <--}

    procedure HandleFileChoice (theItem: INTEGER);
        var
            whichWindow: WindowPtr;
    begin
        case theItem of
            NEW_ITEM:
                CreateWindow;
            CLOSE_ITEM:
                begin
                    whichWindow := FrontWindow;
                    if whichWindow <> nil then
                        DisposeWindow(whichWindow);
```

```
                        end;
            QUIT_ITEM:
                gDone := TRUE;
        end;
    end;


{---------------->   HandleAppleChoice  <--}

    procedure HandleAppleChoice (theItem: INTEGER);
        var
            accName: Str255;
            accNumber, itemNumber, dummy: INTEGER;
            aMenu: MenuHandle;
    begin
        case theItem of
            ABOUT_ITEM:
                dummy := NoteAlert(ABOUT_ALERT, nil);
            otherwise
                begin
                    aMenu := GetMHandle(APPLE_MENU_ID);
                    GetItem(aMenu, theItem, accName);
                    accNumber := OpenDeskAcc(accName);
                end;
        end;
    end;


{---------------->   HandleMenuChoice  <--}

    procedure HandleMenuChoice (menuChoice: LONGINT);
        var
            theMenu, theItem: INTEGER;
    begin
        if menuChoice <> 0 then
            begin
                theMenu := HiWord(menuChoice);
                theItem := LoWord(menuChoice);

                case theMenu of
                    APPLE_MENU_ID:
                        HandleAppleChoice(theItem);
                    FILE_MENU_ID:
                        HandleFileChoice(theItem);
                    EDIT_MENU_ID:
                        HandleEditChoice(theItem);
                end;

                HiliteMenu(0);
            end;
    end;
```

```
{---------------->   IsDAWindow   <--}

    function IsDAWindow (whichWindow: WindowPtr): BOOLEAN;
    begin
        if whichWindow = nil then
            IsDAWindow := FALSE
        else
            IsDAWindow := (WindowPeek(whichWindow)^.windowKind < 0);
    end;


{---------------->   AdjustMenus   <--}

    procedure AdjustMenus;
        var
            aMenu: MenuHandle;
    begin
        aMenu := GetMHandle(FILE_MENU_ID);
        if FrontWindow = nil then
            DisableItem(aMenu, CLOSE_ITEM)
        else
            EnableItem(aMenu, CLOSE_ITEM);

        aMenu := GetMHandle(EDIT_MENU_ID);
        if IsDAWindow(FrontWindow) then
            begin
                EnableItem(aMenu, UNDO_ITEM);
                EnableItem(aMenu, CUT_ITEM);
                EnableItem(aMenu, COPY_ITEM);
                EnableItem(aMenu, PASTE_ITEM);
                EnableItem(aMenu, CLEAR_ITEM);
            end
        else
            begin
                DisableItem(aMenu, UNDO_ITEM);
                DisableItem(aMenu, CUT_ITEM);
                DisableItem(aMenu, COPY_ITEM);
                DisableItem(aMenu, PASTE_ITEM);
                DisableItem(aMenu, CLEAR_ITEM);
            end;
    end;


{---------------->   HandleMouseDown   <--}

    procedure HandleMouseDown;
        var
            whichWindow: WindowPtr;
            thePart: INTEGER;
            menuChoice, windSize: LONGINT;
    begin
```

```
            thePart := FindWindow(gTheEvent.where, whichWindow);
            case thePart of
                inMenuBar:
                    begin
                        AdjustMenus;
                        menuChoice := MenuSelect(gTheEvent.where);
                        HandleMenuChoice(menuChoice);
                    end;
                inSysWindow:
                    SystemClick(gTheEvent, whichWindow);
                inDrag:
                    DragWindow(whichWindow, gTheEvent.where,
                                screenBits.bounds);
                inGoAway:
                    DisposeWindow(whichWindow);
                inContent:
                    SelectWindow(whichWindow);
            end;
        end;


{--------------->   HandleEvent   <--}

    procedure HandleEvent;
        var
            theChar: CHAR;
            dummy: BOOLEAN;
            oldPort: GrafPtr;
    begin
        if gWNEImplemented then
            dummy := WaitNextEvent(everyEvent, gTheEvent,
                                MIN_SLEEP, nil)
        else
            begin
                SystemTask;
                dummy := GetNextEvent(everyEvent, gTheEvent);
            end;

        case gTheEvent.what of
            mouseDown:
                HandleMouseDown;
            keyDown, autoKey:
                begin
                    theChar := CHR(BitAnd(gTheEvent.message,
                                    charCodeMask));
                    if (BitAnd(gTheEvent.modifiers, cmdKey) <> 0)
                        then
                        begin
                            AdjustMenus;
                            HandleMenuChoice(MenuKey(theChar));
                        end;
```

```
                        end;
                updateEvt:
                    if not IsDAWindow(WindowPtr(gTheEvent.message))
                                    then
                        begin
                            GetPort(oldPort);
                            SetPort(WindowPtr(gTheEvent.message));
                            BeginUpdate(WindowPtr(gTheEvent.message));
                            DrawMyPicture(WindowPtr(gTheEvent.message));
                            EndUpdate(WindowPtr(gTheEvent.message));
                            SetPort(oldPort);
                        end;
            end;
        end;


{----------------->  MainLoop  <--}

    procedure MainLoop;
    begin
        gDone := FALSE;
        gNewWindowLeft := WINDOW_HOME_LEFT;
        gNewWindowTop := WINDOW_HOME_TOP;

        gWNEImplemented := (NGetTrapAddress(WNE_TRAP_NUM,
                            ToolTrap) <> NGetTrapAddress
                            (UNIMPL_TRAP_NUM, ToolTrap));
        while (gDone = FALSE) do
            HandleEvent;
    end;


{----------------->  MenuBarInit  <--}

    procedure MenuBarInit;
        var
            myMenuBar: Handle;
            aMenu: MenuHandle;
    begin
        myMenuBar := GetNewMBar(BASE_RES_ID);
        if myMenuBar = nil then
            ErrorHandler(NO_MBAR);
        SetMenuBar(myMenuBar);

        aMenu := GetMHandle(APPLE_MENU_ID);
        if aMenu = nil then
            ErrorHandler(NO_MENU);

        AddResMenu(aMenu, 'DRVR');

        aMenu := GetMHandle(EDIT_MENU_ID);
```

```
        if aMenu = nil then
            ErrorHandler(NO_MENU);

        aMenu := GetMHandle(FILE_MENU_ID);
        if aMenu = nil then
            ErrorHandler(NO_MENU);

        DrawMenuBar;
    end;


{--------------->   WindowMaker   <--}

begin
    MenuBarInit;

    MainLoop;
end.
```

Chapter 7: ShowClip.p

```
program ShowClip;
    const
        BASE_RES_ID = 400;
        ERROR_ALERT_ID = BASE_RES_ID + 1;
        NO_WIND = BASE_RES_ID;
        EMPTY_SCRAP = BASE_RES_ID + 1;

        NIL_STRING = '';
        HOPELESSLY_FATAL_ERROR = 'Game over, man!';

    var
        gClipWindow: WindowPtr;


{--------------->   ErrorHandler   <--}

    procedure ErrorHandler (stringNum: INTEGER);
        var
            errorStringH: StringHandle;
            dummy: INTEGER;
    begin
        errorStringH := GetString(stringNum);
        if errorStringH = nil then
            ParamText(HOPELESSLY_FATAL_ERROR, NIL_STRING,
                    NIL_STRING, NIL_STRING)
        else
```

```
                ParamText(errorStringH^^, NIL_STRING, NIL_STRING,
                          NIL_STRING);

          dummy := StopAlert(ERROR_ALERT_ID, nil);
          ExitToShell;
       end;


{----------------->   CenterPict   <--}

    procedure CenterPict (thePicture: PicHandle; var myRect:
                          Rect);
        var
            windRect, pictureRect: Rect;
    begin
        windRect := myRect;
        pictureRect := thePicture^^.picFrame;
        myRect.top := (windRect.bottom - windRect.top -
                       (pictureRect.bottom - pictureRect.top))
                       div 2 + windRect.top;
        myRect.bottom := myRect.top + (pictureRect.bottom -
                                        pictureRect.top);
        myRect.left := (windRect.right - windRect.left -
                        (pictureRect.right - pictureRect.left))
                        div 2 + windRect.left;
        myRect.right := myRect.left + (pictureRect.right -
                                       pictureRect.left);
       end;


{----------------->   MainLoop   <--}

    procedure MainLoop;
        var
            myRect: Rect;
            clipHandle: Handle;
            length, offset: LONGINT;
    begin
        clipHandle := NewHandle(0);
        length := GetScrap(clipHandle, 'TEXT', offset);
        if length < 0 then
            begin
                length := GetScrap(clipHandle, 'PICT', offset);
                if length < 0 then
                    ErrorHandler(EMPTY_SCRAP)
                else
                    begin
                        myRect := gClipWindow^.portRect;
                        CenterPict(PicHandle(clipHandle),
                                   myRect);
```

```
                            DrawPicture(PicHandle(clipHandle), myRect);
                        end;
                end
            else
                begin
                    HLock(clipHandle);
                    TextBox(Ptr(clipHandle^), length,
                            thePort^.portRect, teJustLeft);
                    HUnlock(clipHandle);
                end;

        while not Button do
                begin
                end;
        end;


{---------------->   WindowInit   <--}

    procedure WindowInit;
    begin
        gClipWindow := GetNewWindow(BASE_RES_ID, nil,
                                    WindowPtr (-1));

        if gClipWindow = nil then
            ErrorHandler(NO_WIND);

        ShowWindow(gClipWindow);
        SetPort(gClipWindow);
    end;


{---------------->   ShowClip   <--}

begin
    WindowInit;
    MainLoop;
end.
```

Chapter 7: PrintPICT.p

```
program PrintPICT;
    uses
        Printing;

    const
        HEADER_SIZE = 512;
        BASE_RES_ID = 400;
```

```
            ERROR_ALERT_ID = BASE_RES_ID;
            CANT_OPEN_FILE = BASE_RES_ID;
            GET_EOF_ERROR = BASE_RES_ID + 1;
            HEADER_TOO_SMALL = BASE_RES_ID + 2;
            OUT_OF_MEMORY = BASE_RES_ID + 3;
            CANT_READ_HEADER = BASE_RES_ID + 4;
            CANT_READ_PICT = BASE_RES_ID + 5;

            NIL_STRING = '';
            IGNORED_STRING = NIL_STRING;
            HOPELESSLY_FATAL_ERROR = 'Game over, man!';

    var
        gPrintRecordH: THPrint;
        gReply: SFReply;


{----------------->   ErrorHandler   <--}

    procedure ErrorHandler (stringNum: INTEGER);
        var
            errorStringH: StringHandle;
            dummy: INTEGER;
    begin
        errorStringH := GetString(stringNum);
        if errorStringH = nil then
            ParamText(HOPELESSLY_FATAL_ERROR, NIL_STRING,
                    NIL_STRING, NIL_STRING)
        else
            ParamText(errorStringH^^, NIL_STRING, NIL_STRING,
                    NIL_STRING);

        dummy := StopAlert(ERROR_ALERT_ID, nil);
        ExitToShell;
    end;


{----------------->   PrintPictFile   <--}

    procedure PrintPictFile (reply: SFReply);
        var
            srcFile: INTEGER;
            printPort: TPPrPort;
            printStatus: TPrStatus;
            thePict: PicHandle;
            pictHeader: packed array[0..HEADER_SIZE] of CHAR;
            pictSize, headerSize: LONGINT;
            dummy: OSErr;
    begin
        if (FSOpen(reply.fName, reply.vRefNum, srcFile)
                <> noErr) then
            ErrorHandler(CANT_OPEN_FILE);
```

```
    if (GetEOF(srcFile, pictSize) <> noErr) then
        ErrorHandler(GET_EOF_ERROR);

    headerSize := HEADER_SIZE;
    if (FSRead(srcFile, headerSize, @pictHeader) <> noErr)
        then ErrorHandler(CANT_READ_HEADER);

    pictSize := pictSize - HEADER_SIZE;
    if pictSize <= 0 then
        ErrorHandler(HEADER_TOO_SMALL);

    thePict := PicHandle(NewHandle(pictSize));
    if thePict = nil then
        ErrorHandler(OUT_OF_MEMORY);

    HLock(Handle(thePict));

    if FSRead(srcFile, pictSize, Ptr(thePict^)) <> noErr then
        ErrorHandler(CANT_READ_PICT);

    dummy := FSClose(srcFile);

    printPort := PrOpenDoc(gPrintRecordH, nil, nil);
    PrOpenPage(printPort, nil);
    DrawPicture(thePict, thePict^^.picFrame);
    PrClosePage(printPort);
    PrCloseDoc(printPort);

    PrPicFile(gPrintRecordH, nil, nil, nil, printStatus);

    HUnlock(Handle(thePict));
end;


{---------------->   DoDialogs   <--}

function DoDialogs: BOOLEAN;
    var
        keepGoing: BOOLEAN;
begin
    keepGoing := PrStlDialog(gPrintRecordH);

    if keepGoing then
        DoDialogs := PrJobDialog(gPrintRecordH)
    else
        DoDialogs := FALSE;
end;
```

```
{--------------->   GetFileName   <--}

    procedure GetFileName (var replyPtr: SFReply);
        var
            myPoint: Point;
            typeList: SFTypeList;
            numTypes: INTEGER;
    begin
        myPoint.h := 100;
        myPoint.v := 100;
        typeList[0] := 'PICT';
        numTypes := 1;
        SFGetFile(myPoint, IGNORED_STRING, nil, numTypes,
                typeList, nil, replyPtr);
    end;


{--------------->   PrintInit   <--}

    procedure PrintInit;
    begin
        gPrintRecordH := THPrint(NewHandle(sizeof(TPrint)));
        PrOpen;
        PrintDefault(gPrintRecordH);
    end;


{--------------->   PrintPICT   <--}

begin
    PrintInit;
    GetFileName(gReply);
    if gReply.good then
        begin
            if DoDialogs then
                PrintPictFile(gReply);
        end;
end.
```

Chapter 7: Pager.p

```
program Pager;
    const
        BASE_RES_ID = 400;

        SCROLL_BAR_PIXELS = 16;

        MIN_SLEEP = 0;
        NIL_REF_CON = 0;
```

```
        WNE_TRAP_NUM = $60;
        UNIMPL_TRAP_NUM = $9F;

        ERROR_ALERT_ID = BASE_RES_ID + 1;
        NO_WIND = BASE_RES_ID;
        NO_PICTS = BASE_RES_ID + 1;
        CANT_LOAD_PICT = BASE_RES_ID + 2;

        NIL_STRING = '';
        NIL_TITLE = NIL_STRING;
        VISIBLE = TRUE;
        START_VALUE = 1;
        MIN_VALUE = 1;
        HOPELESSLY_FATAL_ERROR = 'Game over, man!';

    var
        gPictWindow: WindowPtr;
        gScrollBarHandle: ControlHandle;
        gDone, gWNEImplemented: BOOLEAN;
        gTheEvent: EventRecord;


{---------------->   ErrorHandler   <--}

    procedure ErrorHandler (stringNum: INTEGER);
        var
            errorStringH: StringHandle;
            dummy: INTEGER;
    begin
        errorStringH := GetString(stringNum);
        if errorStringH = nil then
            ParamText(HOPELESSLY_FATAL_ERROR, NIL_STRING,
                    NIL_STRING, NIL_STRING)
        else
            ParamText(errorStringH^^, NIL_STRING, NIL_STRING,
                    NIL_STRING);

        dummy := StopAlert(ERROR_ALERT_ID, nil);
        ExitToShell;
    end;


{---------------->   CenterPict   <--}

    procedure CenterPict (thePicture: PicHandle; var myRect:
                        Rect);
        var
            windRect, pictureRect: Rect;
    begin
        windRect := myRect;
        pictureRect := thePicture^^.picFrame;
```

```
        myRect.top := (windRect.bottom - windRect.top -
                         (pictureRect.bottom - pictureRect.top))
                      div 2 + windRect.top;
        myRect.bottom := myRect.top + (pictureRect.bottom -
                                        pictureRect.top);
        myRect.left := (windRect.right - windRect.left -
                         (pictureRect.right - pictureRect.left))
                      div 2 + windRect.left;
        myRect.right := myRect.left + (pictureRect.right -
                                        pictureRect.left);
    end;


{---------------->   UpdateMyWindow   <--}

    procedure UpdateMyWindow (drawingWindow: WindowPtr);
        var
            currentPicture: PicHandle;
            drawingClipRect, myRect: Rect;
            tempRgn: RgnHandle;
    begin
        tempRgn := NewRgn;
        GetClip(tempRgn);

        myRect := drawingWindow^.portRect;
        myRect.right := myRect.right - SCROLL_BAR_PIXELS;
        EraseRect(myRect);

        currentPicture := PicHandle(GetIndResource('PICT',
                                        GetCtlValue
                                        (gScrollBarHandle)));

        if currentPicture = nil then
            ErrorHandler(CANT_LOAD_PICT);

        CenterPict(currentPicture, myRect);

        drawingClipRect := drawingWindow^.portRect;
        drawingClipRect.right := drawingClipRect.right -
            SCROLL_BAR_PIXELS;
        ClipRect(drawingClipRect);

        DrawPicture(currentPicture, myRect);

        SetClip(tempRgn);
        DisposeRgn(tempRgn);
    end;
```

```
{--------------->  ScrollProc  <--}

    procedure ScrollProc (theControl: ControlHandle; theCode:
                          INTEGER);
        var
            curControlValue, maxControlValue, minControlValue:
                INTEGER;
    begin
        maxControlValue := GetCtlMax(theControl);
        curControlValue := GetCtlValue(theControl);
        minControlValue := GetCtlMin(theControl);

        case theCode of
            inPageDown, inDownButton:
                if curControlValue < maxControlValue then
                    curControlValue := curControlValue + 1;
            inPageUp, inUpButton:
                if curControlValue > minControlValue then
                    curControlValue := curControlValue - 1;
        end;
        SetCtlValue(theControl, curControlValue);
    end;


{--------------->  SetUpScrollBar  <--}

    procedure SetUpScrollBar;
        var
            vScrollRect: Rect;
            numPictures: INTEGER;
    begin
        numPictures := CountResources('PICT');
        if numPictures <= 0 then
            ErrorHandler(NO_PICTS);
        vScrollRect := gPictWindow^.portRect;
        vScrollRect.top := vScrollRect.top - 1;
        vScrollRect.bottom := vScrollRect.bottom + 1;
        vScrollRect.left := vScrollRect.right -
            SCROLL_BAR_PIXELS + 1;
        vScrollRect.right := vScrollRect.right + 1;
        gScrollBarHandle := NewControl(gPictWindow,
                                vScrollRect, NIL_TITLE,
                                VISIBLE,  START_VALUE,
                                MIN_VALUE, numPictures,
                                scrollBarProc,
                                NIL_REF_CON);
    end;
```

```
{--------------->    HandleMouseDown   <--}

    procedure HandleMouseDown;
        var
            whichWindow: WindowPtr;
            thePart: INTEGER;
            thePoint: Point;
            theControl: ControlHandle;
    begin
        thePart := FindWindow(gTheEvent.where, whichWindow);
        case thePart of
            inSysWindow:
                SystemClick(gTheEvent, whichWindow);
            inDrag:
                DragWindow(whichWindow, gTheEvent.where,
                        screenBits.bounds);
            inContent:
                begin
                    thePoint := gTheEvent.where;
                    GlobalToLocal(thePoint);
                    thePart := FindControl(thePoint, whichWindow,
                                        theControl);
                    if theControl = gScrollBarHandle then
                        begin
                            if thePart = inThumb then
                                begin
                                    thePart := TrackControl
                                        (theControl, thePoint,
                                        nil);
                                    UpdateMyWindow(whichWindow);
                                end
                            else
                                begin
                                    thePart := TrackControl
                                        (theControl, thePoint,
                                        @ScrollProc);
                                    UpdateMyWindow(whichWindow);
                                end;
                        end;
                end;
            inGoAway:
                gDone := TRUE;
        end;
    end;
```

```
{----------------->   HandleEvent   <--}

    procedure HandleEvent;
        var
            dummy: BOOLEAN;
    begin
        if gWNEImplemented then
            dummy := WaitNextEvent(everyEvent, gTheEvent,
                                   MIN_SLEEP, nil)
        else
            begin
                SystemTask;
                dummy := GetNextEvent(everyEvent, gTheEvent);
            end;

        case gTheEvent.what of
            mouseDown:
                HandleMouseDown;
            updateEvt:
                begin
                    BeginUpdate(WindowPtr(gTheEvent.message));
                    DrawControls(WindowPtr(gTheEvent.message));
                    UpdateMyWindow(WindowPtr(gTheEvent.message));
                    EndUpdate(WindowPtr(gTheEvent.message));
                end;
        end;
    end;


{----------------->   MainLoop   <--}

    procedure MainLoop;
    begin
        gDone := FALSE;

        gWNEImplemented := (NGetTrapAddress(WNE_TRAP_NUM,
                            ToolTrap) <> NGetTrapAddress
                            (UNIMPL_TRAP_NUM, ToolTrap));
        while (gDone = FALSE) do
            HandleEvent;
    end;


{----------------->   WindowInit   <--}

    procedure WindowInit;
    begin
        gPictWindow := GetNewWindow(BASE_RES_ID, nil,
                                    WindowPtr(- 1));
```

```
        if gPictWindow = nil then
            ErrorHandler(NO_WIND);

        SelectWindow(gPictWindow);
        ShowWindow(gPictWindow);
        SetPort(gPictWindow);
    end;


{----------------->  Pager  <--}

begin
    WindowInit;
    SetUpScrollBar;

    MainLoop;
end.
```

Chapter 7: Sounder.p

```
program Sounder;
    uses
        Sound;

    const
        BASE_RES_ID = 400;
        SYNCHRONOUS = FALSE;

        ERROR_ALERT_ID = BASE_RES_ID + 1;
        CANT_LOAD_BEEP_SND = BASE_RES_ID;
        CANT_LOAD_MONKEY_SND = BASE_RES_ID + 1;
        CANT_LOAD_KLANK_SND = BASE_RES_ID + 2;
        CANT_LOAD_BOING_SND = BASE_RES_ID + 3;

        NIL_STRING = '';
        HOPELESSLY_FATAL_ERROR = 'Game over, man!';

        BEEP_SND = 1;
        MONKEY_SND = 2;
        KLANK_SND = 3;
        BOING_SND = 4;
```

```
{---------------->  ErrorHandler  <--}

    procedure ErrorHandler (stringNum: INTEGER);
        var
            errorStringH: StringHandle;
            dummy: INTEGER;
    begin
        errorStringH := GetString(stringNum);
        if errorStringH = nil then
            ParamText(HOPELESSLY_FATAL_ERROR, NIL_STRING,
                    NIL_STRING, NIL_STRING)
        else
            ParamText(errorStringH^^, NIL_STRING, NIL_STRING,
                    NIL_STRING);

        dummy := StopAlert(ERROR_ALERT_ID, nil);
        ExitToShell;
    end;


{---------------->  MakeSound  <--}

    procedure MakeSound;
        var
            soundHandle: Handle;
            dummy: OSErr;
    begin
        soundHandle := GetResource('snd ', BEEP_SND);

        if soundHandle = nil then
            ErrorHandler(CANT_LOAD_BEEP_SND);

        dummy := SndPlay(nil, soundHandle, SYNCHRONOUS);

        soundHandle := GetResource('snd ', MONKEY_SND);

        if soundHandle = nil then
            ErrorHandler(CANT_LOAD_MONKEY_SND);

        dummy := SndPlay(nil, soundHandle, SYNCHRONOUS);

        soundHandle := GetResource('snd ', KLANK_SND);

        if soundHandle = nil then
            ErrorHandler(CANT_LOAD_KLANK_SND);

        dummy := SndPlay(nil, soundHandle, SYNCHRONOUS);

        soundHandle := GetResource('snd ', BOING_SND);
```

```
        if soundHandle = nil then
            ErrorHandler(CANT_LOAD_BOING_SND);

        dummy := SndPlay(nil, soundHandle, SYNCHRONOUS);
    end;


{---------------->   Sounder   <--}

begin
    MakeSound;
end.
```

Appendix C

Debugging Techniques

One of the most frustrating experiences in programming is running up against a really tough bug. In this appendix, we'll discuss some techniques for hunting down bugs, and some others for avoiding them in the first place.

Compilation Errors

The First Bugs you're likely to encounter will pop up during compilation, when you've typed in your code and selected **Go** from the **Project** menu. When THINK Pascal asks you if you'd like to rebuild your project, click **Yes**.

THINK Pascal will attempt to compile your program. More often than not, it will not be able to complete its job. Let's look at some of the basic errors that occur.

Typing Mistakes

Because THINK Pascal has a "smart" editor, many typing mistakes are found immediately, such as the space typed in between Show and Window in Figure C.1.

Mistakes in typing that the editor doesn't find are usually caught by the compiler, which will display a bug alert. The one in Figure C.2 is straightforward, unlike others that may occur.

```
procedure WindowInit;
begin
  gClockWindow := GetNewWindow(BASE_RES_ID, nil, WindowPtr(-1));
  SetPort(gClockWindow);
  Show Window ( gClockWindow );

  TextSize(CLOCK_SIZE);
end;
```

Figure C.1   THINK Pascal editor highlights typing mistakes.

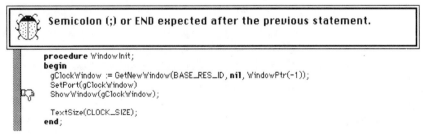

Figure C.2   Missing semicolon.

Syntax errors are usually indicative of a misspelled keyword or bad programming grammar. For example, if you misspell **const** or type something like:

```
program Hello2;
    const
        VERTICAL_PIXEL := 50;
```

instead of

```
program Hello2;
    const
        VERTICAL_PIXEL = 50;
```

you'll end up with a syntax error. This happens frequently. Carefully review the line of code with the "thumbs down" in the left-hand column. If you still can't find the bug, check the previous line. Is there a semicolon at the end of the line? Is there supposed to be one?

Another popular error message is the **xxx has not been declared** alert. Sometimes this is the result of a missing declaration, but often it's the result of a misspelled variable name.

Indirect Compiler Errors

An example of a indirect compiler error is one caused by a missing library file. For example, the printing program presented in Chapter 7 depended on the library file `PrintCalls.lib`. This file is not one of the two standard libraries automatically included by THINK Pascal. If you leave out this file, you get a **Link Failed** alert with a list of the procedures and functions that were undefined:

```
undefined: "PrJobDialog"
undefined: "PrintDefault"
undefined: "PrOpen"
undefined: "PrPicFile"
undefined: "PrStlDialog"
undefined: "PrOpenPage"
undefined: "PrClosePage"
undefined: "PrOpenDoc"
undefined: "PrCloseDoc"
```

The real trick is to figure out which file to add to your project. Chapter 7 lists all the library files not automatically included by THINK Pascal. You'll find these files in the `Libraries` folder on one of your THINK Pascal disks. The files are well named, so picking a likely candidate shouldn't be too hard. Use the THINK Pascal Find facility to search for the missing type or global variable.

Linker Errors

If you call a procedure or function in your program that was never declared, you'll get a **Not Declared** alert with the "thumbs down" displayed at the line containing the procedure or function that the linker couldn't locate. This error is often the result of a misspelled procedure name, such as the following:

```
sysBeeep( 20 );
```

The compiler will accept this line because it will assume that you've written a routine called `sysBeeep` that will be provided at link time.

Improving Your Debugging Technique

Once your program compiles, your next step is to get the bugs out. One of the best ways to debug a Mac program is to use the debugging utilities in THINK Pascal or the TMON debugger from ICOM Simulations. Debuggers are real life-savers.

No matter which debugging tool you use, there are some things you can do to improve your debugging technique.

Being a Good Detective

When your program crashes or exhibits some unusual behavior, you have to be a detective. Did the system error occur just before your dialog box was scheduled to appear? Did those wavy lines start appearing immediately after you clicked on the OK button?

The key to being a good detective is having a good surveillance technique. Try to establish a definite pattern in your program's misbehavior. Can you pinpoint exactly where in your code things started to go awry? These clues will help you home in on the offending code.

If you can't tell by observation exactly when things went sour, don't give up. You can always use the binary method of bug control.

The Binary Method

The key to the binary method lies in establishing good boundary conditions for the bug. First, you'll need to establish a **lower limit**, a place in your code at which you feel fairly certain the bug has not yet occurred. You'd like the lower limit to be as close to the actual bug as possible, but make sure the bug has not yet happened.

Next, establish an **upper limit** in your code, a point by which you're certain the bug has occurred (because the system has crashed, or the screen has turned green, or whatever).

To use the binary method, split the difference between the upper and lower limits. If the bug still has not occurred, split the difference again. Now, if the bug has occurred, you have a new upper limit. By repeating this procedure, you'll eventually locate the exact line of source code in which the bug occurs.

There are several different ways to split the difference between two lines of source code. If you're using a debugger, you can set a breakpoint halfway between the lines of code representing the upper and lower limits. Did you hit the breakpoint without encountering the bug? If so, set a new breakpoint, halfway between this one and the upper limit.

If you don't have a debugger, use a ROM call like `SysBeep` to give you a clue. Did you hear the beep before the bug occurred? If so, put a new `SysBeep` halfway between the old one and the upper limit. The nice thing about using `SysBeep` is that it is reasonably nonintrusive, unlike putting up a new window and drawing some debugging information in it, which tends to interfere with your program's basic algorithm.

Recommended Reading

In closing, we'd like to recommend some good reading material: your THINK Pascal *User Manual!* The *User Manual* is a treasure trove of valuable tips for writing and debugging Mac programs. The more you know about the Macintosh and the THINK Pascal development environment, the better you'll be at debugging your programs.

Appendix D

Building Hypercard XCMDs

The introduction of HyperCard in August 1987 caused quite a stir in the Macintosh world. A complete programming environment in its own right, HyperCard became even richer with the addition of XCMDs and XFCNs. Now you can access the raw power of THINK Pascal from inside HyperCard.

HYPERCARD COMES WITH its own powerful programming language: **HyperTalk**. The designers of HyperTalk thoughtfully provided a mechanism for adding extensions to the HyperTalk command set. These extensions are code resources of type **XCMD** and **XFCN**.

XCMDs (X-Commands) take a pointer to a record as input from HyperCard, perform some calculations, put the results back into the record, and return to the calling script. XFCNs (X-functions) take a pointer to the same record as input, perform the same types of calculations, but return the results as a Pascal function would.

We've written an XCMD (called XChooser) that puts the Chooser name in the record and returns to HyperCard. A typical call of XChooser looks like this:

```
XChooser
Put the result into card field 1
```

We also created an XFCN (called FChooser) that performs the same service. A typical call of FChooser looks like this:

```
Put FChooser() into card field 1
```

The source code for FChooser and XChooser is identical. Although this appendix presents the steps necessary to build an XCMD, you can use the same project to build an XFCN by selecting **Set Project Type...** from the **Project** menu and changing the resource type from XCMD to XFCN. We've included the source code (as well as a HyperCard test stack and a resource mover stack) on the *Mac Primer* source code disk (use the coupon on the last page).

The XChooser XCMD

Create a new folder in your development folder called XChooser. Create a new project in the XChooser folder called XChooser.π. Select **Set Project Type...** from the **Project** menu and click the Code Resource icon on the left side of the dialog box. Next, fill in the dialog according to the specifications in Figure D.1. Click **OK** to save your changes.

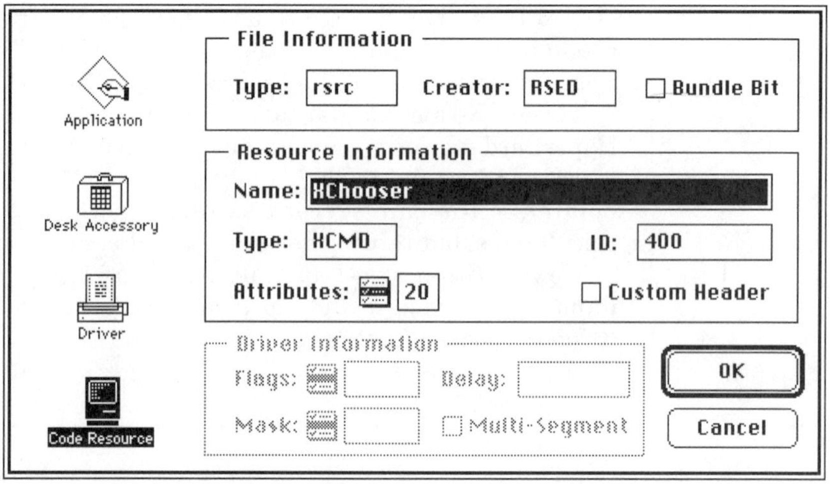

Figure D.1 **Set Project Type...** dialog box.

Next, you'll need to add some files to the project that are necessary for creating stand-alone code resources that work with HyperCard. First, you'll replace the file `Runtime.lib` with its code resource counterpart, `DRVRRuntime.lib`. Click on the file `Runtime.lib` in the project window. Remove it from the project by selecting **Remove** from the **Project** menu. The file `Runtime.lib` should disappear from the project window.

Select **Add File...** from the **Project** menu and add the files `DRVRRuntime.lib`, `HyperXLib.lib`, and `HyperXCmd.p` to the project. All three files can be found within the `THINK Pascal` folder. `DRVRRuntime.lib` and `HyperXLib.lib` are in the `Libraries` subfolder. `HyperXCmd.p` is in the `Interfaces` subfolder.

Next, create a new source code file and type in the following code:

```
unit DummyUnit;

interface
    uses
        HyperXCmd;

    procedure Main (paramPtr: XCmdPtr);

implementation
```

```
procedure Main (paramPtr: XCmdPtr);
    var
        chooserStr255H: StringHandle;
begin
    chooserStr255H := GetString(-16096);
    HLock(Handle(chooserStr255H));
    paramPtr^.returnValue :=
PasToZero(paramPtr, Str255(chooserStr255H^^));
    HUnlock(Handle(chooserStr255H));
    end;
end.
```

Save the file as XChooser.p and add the file to the project. Next, rearrange the order of the project files, using the hand cursor that appears when the mouse is inside the project window. Drag the files up or down until the order matches that of Figure D.2. Now you're ready to build the code resource.

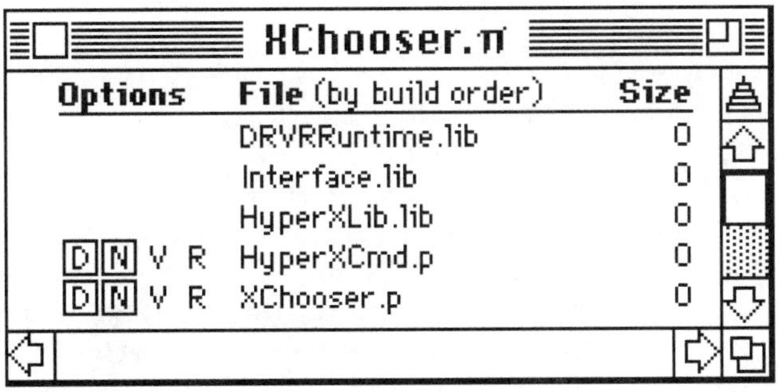

Options	File (by build order)	Size	
	DRVRRuntime.lib	0	
	Interface.lib	0	
	HyperXLib.lib	0	
D N V R	HyperXCmd.p	0	
D N V R	XChooser.p	0	

Figure D.2   XChooser's project window.

Building the XChooser Code Resource

Select **Build Code Resource...** from the **Project** menu. You'll be prompted for a file name. Save the XCMD as XChooser Resource. To add the XCMD to your HyperCard stack, use ResEdit to copy the XCMD resource in the file XChooser Resource into the resource fork of your stack. This will automatically make the XCMD available to your stack. If you copy the resource directly into the HyperCard application itself, the XCMD will be available to all of your stacks. Several different resource mover stacks are also available that allow you to copy resources directly within HyperCard. One of these has been included on the *Mac Primer* source code disk.

The release of HyperCard 2.0 opened up a world of possibilities for XCMD programmers. One key feature of HyperCard 2.0 is the addition of external windows, windows that are created and controlled by your XCMD. When HyperCard receives an event associated with an external window, it passes the event on to the XCMD. Here's how this works.

As was described earlier, each XCMD receives a pointer to a record as its sole parameter. The pointer and record are declared as follows:

```
XCmdPtr = ^XCmdBlock;
XCmdBlock = RECORD
    paramCount: INTEGER;
    params: ARRAY [1..16] OF Handle;
    returnValue: Handle;
    passFlag: BOOLEAN;
    entryPoint: ProcPtr; {to call back to HyperCard}
    request: INTEGER;
    result: INTEGER;
    inArgs: ARRAY [1..8] OF LONGINT;
    outArgs: ARRAY [1..4] OF LONGINT;
    END;
```

The first time your XCMD is called, it can create a new window by calling either NewXWindow or GetNewXWindow. NewXWindow takes the same parameters as NewWindow, and GetNewXWindow takes the same parameters as GetNewWindow. Because THINK Pascal 3.0 was released long before HyperCard 2.0, support for the two external window routines was not built into THINK Pascal 3.0. Check with Symantec technical support for information about the THINK Pascal HyperCard 2.0 interface library.

Once your XCMD has created an external window, return control to HyperCard. HyperCard will call the XCMD again as soon as an event has occurred that concerns your XCMD's window. HyperCard sets the paramCount field to −1, telling your XCMD not to create a new window, just to handle an event associated with an existing window. If the paramCount field is set to −1, params[1] will be a handle to an event data structure, XWEventInfo:

```
XWEventInfoPtr = ^XWEventInfo;
XWEventInfo = RECORD
    event:        EventRecord;
    eventWindow:  WindowPtr;
    eventParams:  ARRAY[ 1..9 ] OF Longint;
    eventResult:  Handle;
    END;
```

The event field behaves in much the same way as a standard toolbox EventRecord.

Getting More Specific

There's a lot more to HyperCard 2.0 XCMDs than we could cover in this appendix. Several excellent texts on HyperCard 2.0 have been published, and several more are in the works. Apple has published a treatise entitled *HyperCard: The Extended XCMD Interface*. Get a copy wherever you get your technical documentation.

Appendix E

Bibliography

Apple Computer. *Inside Macintosh,* Volume I. Reading, MA: Addison-Wesley, 1985. $24.95.

Apple Computer. *Inside Macintosh,* Volume II. Reading, MA: Addison-Wesley, 1985. $24.95.

Apple Computer. *Inside Macintosh,* Volume III. Reading, MA: Addison-Wesley, 1985. $19.95.

Apple Computer. *Inside Macintosh,* Volume IV. Reading, MA: Addison-Wesley, 1986. $24.95.

Apple Computer. *Inside Macintosh,* Volume V. Reading, MA: Addison-Wesley, 1988. $26.95.

Apple Computer. *Inside Macintosh X-Ref.* Reading, MA: Addison-Wesley, 1988. $9.95.

Apple Computer. *Programmer's Introduction to the Macintosh Family.* Reading, MA: Addison-Wesley, 1988. $22.95 (HC).

Apple Computer. *Technical Introduction to the Macintosh Family.* Reading, MA: Addison-Wesley, 1987. $19.95.

Chernicoff, Stephen. *Macintosh Revealed, Volume One: Unlocking the Toolbox,* 2nd edition. Indianapolis, IN: Hayden, 1987. $26.95.

Chernicoff, Stephen. *Macintosh Revealed, Volume Two: Programming with the Toolbox,* 2nd edition. Indianapolis, IN: Hayden, 1987. $26.95.

Chernicoff, Stephen, *Macintosh Revealed, Volume Three: Mastering the Toolbox.* Indianapolis, IN: Hayden, 1989. $26.95.

Goodman, Paul. *Advanced Macintosh Pascal.* Indianapolis, IN: Hayden, 1986. $19.95.

Knaster, Scott. *How to Write Macintosh Software.* Indianapolis, IN: Hayden, 1988. $28.95.

Knaster, Scott. *Macintosh Programming Secrets.* Reading, MA: Addison-Wesley, 1988. $24.95.

Smith, David E., ed. *The Best of MacTutor, The Macintosh Programming Journal,* Volume 1. Placentia, CA. 1985. $24.95.

Smith, David E., ed. *The Complete MacTutor, The Macintosh Programming Journal,* Volume 2. Placentia, CA. 1986. $24.95.

West, Joel. *Programming with Macintosh Programmer's Workshop.* New York: Bantam, 1987. $29.95.

A good Pascal language reference is:

Cooper, Doug, and Michael Clancy. *Oh! Pascal,* 2nd edition. New York: W.W. Norton, 1982. $29.95.

Index

511

Macintosh® Pascal
Programming Primer, Volume I:
The Disk!

If you'd like to receive a complete set of source code, projects, and resources from Volume I of the Mac Pascal Primer:

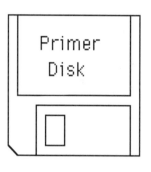

1) Fill out the coupon. Print clearly.

2) Attach a check for $30. Make the check out to **M/MAC**. Make sure that the check is in **U.S. dollars**, drawn on a U.S. or Canadian bank. If you'd like the disk shipped outside the United States, please add $5.

3) Send the check and the coupon to:

   Pascal Primer Disk, Volume I
   2534 North Jefferson Street
   Arlington, Virginia 22207

Here's my $30!
Send me the Pascal Primer Disk I,
quick!!! Mail the disk to:

Name _____

Company _____

Address _____

City _____ State ____ Zip _____

No Credit Cards, Please!